THE ELGAR COMPANION TO REGULATING PLATFORM WORK

The Elgar Companion to Regulating Platform Work

Insights from the Food Delivery Sector

Edited by

Kurt Vandaele

Senior Researcher, European Trade Union Institute (ETUI), Brussels, Belgium

Silvia Rainone

Senior Researcher, European Trade Union Institute (ETUI), Brussels, Belgium

Edward Elgar PUBLISHING

Cheltenham, UK • Northampton, MA, USA

Published by
Edward Elgar Publishing Limited
The Lypiatts
15 Lansdown Road
Cheltenham
Glos GL50 2JA
UK

Edward Elgar Publishing, Inc.
William Pratt House
9 Dewey Court
Northampton
Massachusetts 01060
USA

Authorised representative in the EU for GPSR queries only: Easy Access System Europe – Mustamäe tee 50, 10621 Tallinn, Estonia, gpsr.requests@easproject.com

A catalogue record for this book
is available from the British Library

Library of Congress Control Number: 2024952810

This book is available electronically in the **Elgar**online
Sociology, Social Policy and Education subject collection
https://doi.org/10.4337/9781035321148

MIX
Paper | Supporting responsible forestry
FSC® C013604

ISBN 978 1 0353 2113 1 (cased)
ISBN 978 1 0353 2114 8 (eBook)

Printed and bound by CPI Group (UK) Ltd, Croydon, CR0 4YY

Contents

PART III OUTCOMES AND REGULATION

Figures

Tables

Contributors

Antonio Aloisi is an associate professor of European and comparative labour law at IE University Law School in Madrid, where he leads the 'Lawtomation' Jean Monnet Centre. He is a former Marie Skłodowska-Curie fellow and the co-author of *Your Boss is an Algorithm. Artificial Intelligence, Platform Work and Labour* (with Valerio De Stefano, Hart Publishing, 2022). Favourite cuisine: parmigiana lover.

Ioulia Bessa is Associate Professor, based in the Centre for Employment Relations Innovation and Change (CERIC) at the University of Leeds. Her research looks at non-standard forms of employment and working conditions linked to precarity and underemployment/unemployment, typically utilising a range of secondary datasets (national and international). She has published in outlets such as the *British Journal of Industrial Relations* and *Human Resource Management*. Favourite cuisine: Indian and Thai, especially in Leeds.

Lorenzo Cini is a lecturer in employment relations and HRM at Cork University Business School, Ireland. His research interests are labour conflicts in the platform economy and the precarious world of work, publishing on these topics in leading international journals. He sits on the editorial board of *Work, Employment and Society* and is an associate editor of *Frontiers in Sociology*. Lorenzo loves pizza and ice-cream, in that order.

María Figueroa is Director of Labor Policy at the SUNY Rockefeller Institute of Government. She has more than 30 years' experience in labour research, having worked as Director of Labor Policy Research at Cornell's ILR School, Dean of Labor Studies at SUNY Empire State University, and as a researcher for US labour unions. She has a doctorate in law and policy from Northeastern University, a master's in public administration from New York University, and a BA from the New School for Social Research. Favourite cuisine: Italian.

Despoina Georgiou is a legal expert specialising in the areas of EU labour and competition law. She holds a PhD (Cantab), an LLM (UCL) and an LLB (DUTH), and is a member of the Athens Bar Association. She has been Affiliated Lecturer at the University of Cambridge and a visiting researcher at Harvard Law School, publishing articles in esteemed peer-reviewed journals and participating in many international conferences, in some of which she has won 'best paper' awards (Marco Biagi Award of the International Association of Labour Law Journals, Yale European Studies Graduate Fellows Conference Award, CERIC award). She has also received multiple prestigious scholarships for her work on various areas of EU labour law (Onassis Foundation Scholarship, Cambridge Arts and Humanities Council DTP Studentship, Cambridge European Scholarship, Pilkington Prize). Finally, she has served as Editor-in-Chief of the *Cambridge Law Review* and has acted as a peer reviewer for the *Industrial Law Journal* and the *Cambridge International Law Journal*. Favourite cuisine: Japanese.

Damian Grimshaw is Professor of Employment Studies and Associate Dean for Research Impact at King's College, London. His published work covers international comparisons of low-wage labour markets, outsourcing, precarious work and gender inequality. He currently leads ESRC research projects on digitalisation, skills and innovation strategies, alongside undertaking advisory work for the ILO.

Anke Hassel is Professor of Public Policy at the Hertie School. She specializes in the labour market, social partnership, codetermination and the comparative political economy of developed industrial nations. In 2021, she co-edited with Bruno Palier Growth and Welfare in Advanced Capitalist Economies, Oxford University Press and in 2022 published How to do Public Policy. Oxford University Press with Kai Wegrich. She has many favourite cuisines including Thai, Japanese, Indian and Middle Eastern.

Heiner Heiland is postdoctoral researcher at the University of Göttingen. His research interests include the digitalisation of labour, workers' agency, labour and space, algorithmic management and corporate public spheres. His work has appeared in *Human Relations*, *Theory, Culture & Society*, *New Technology, Work and Employment* and many others. Heiner enjoys the variety of Mediterranean cuisine, but has also recently discovered some eastern European dishes.

Christina Hiessl is Professor of Labour Law at KU Leuven (Belgium), Invited Professor of Social Welfare at Yonsei University (Seoul) and Consulting Expert of the European Commission's Centre of Expertise in the Field of Labour Law (ECE). She has worked and/or studied in eight countries, focusing on comparative social law and policy research. She is a board member of *European Labour Law Journal*, scientific advisory board member of *Frankfurt Law Review*, European correspondent of 국제사회보장리뷰 (*International Social Security Review*) and managing board member of the honours programme 'KU Leuven Engage'. As part of a project commissioned by DG EMPL to inform EU-level policymaking, she keeps track of and analyses case law developments related to platform work across Europe. Favourite cuisine: Korean.

Kristin Jesnes is a researcher at Fafo Institute for Labour and Social Research in Norway, where her main areas of research are non-standard forms of work (including platform work) and industrial relations. She is also a doctoral research fellow at the University of Gothenburg in Sweden. In her PhD work, she is exploring how institutional conditions and actors shape platform work. Favourite cuisine: Italian.

Simon Joyce is Research Fellow at the Digital Futures at Work (Digit) Research Centre at Leeds University Business School. His main research interests are worker responses to changing management methods, work organisation and technology. He has been researching platform work since 2016 and has published in journals such as *Capital & Class* and *New Technology, Work and Employment*. Favourite cuisine: home-grown and home-cooked.

Denise Kasparian is a researcher for the National Scientific and Technical Research Council and an assistant professor in the Faculty of Social Sciences at the University of Buenos Aires. Previously, she was a research fellow at the Institute for the Cooperative Digital Economy (The New School) and a fellow at the Institute for the Study of Employee Ownership and Profit Sharing (Rutgers University). In 2022 she published the book *Co-operative Struggles* (Brill). Favourite cuisine: Armenian.

Vincenzo Maccarrone is a Marie Skłodowska-Curie postdoctoral fellow at the Scuola Normale Superiore, Florence. His research interests include employment relations, political economy and the sociology of work. Some of his recent research works have been published in the *ILR Review*; *Work, Employment and Society* and *British Journal of Industrial Relations*. His favourite cuisine is, stereotypically, pasta.

Denis Neumann is a doctoral researcher at the Digital Futures at Work (Digit) Research Centre at Leeds University Business School. His research interests are power relations in platform work and young precarious workers' relationships with trade unions. Favourite cuisine: Thai.

Jörg Nowak is an assistant professor in international political economy at the Institute of International Relations at University of Brasilia, Brazil. His most recent publications are *Labour Conflicts in the Global South* (edited with Andreas Bieler, Routledge, 2023) and *Mass Strikes and Social Movements in Brazil and India* (Springer, 2019). His areas of research are the digitalisation of transport, labour and social movements, and racial capitalism. Favourite cuisine: steak and fries.

Agnieszka Piasna is Senior Researcher at the European Trade Union Institute (ETUI) in Brussels and Associate Researcher at KU Leuven. Her research focuses on job quality, working time (reduction), digitalisation, algorithmic management and gender equality. She is an advocate of putting decent work on the menu.

Cosmin Popan is a sociologist at Grenoble Alpes University, where he leads the project 'Hopes, movement, labour. Irregular migration imaginaries' (MOBILISE). Cosmin holds a doctorate from Lancaster University (2018) and has previously worked at Manchester Metropolitan University. His areas of interest are mobilities, migration, labour, future studies and creative methods. He is the author of *Bicycle Utopias* (Routledge, 2019). Favourite cuisine: kebab on Curry Mile, Manchester.

Nastazja Potocka-Sionek is a postdoctoral researcher at the University of Luxembourg. Her PhD is from the European University Institute in Florence (2023). She has been a postdoctoral researcher at Ca' Foscari University in Venice and a visiting scholar at Ewha Womans University and Sogang University in Seoul. Favourite cuisine: tiramisu.

Valeria Pulignano is Professor of Sociology of Work and Industrial Relations, CESO – KU Leuven, Francqui Research Professor and Principal Investigator on an ERC Advanced Grant ResPecTMe project. Her research includes comparative industrial (employment) relations, precarious work, inequality and voice at work, while recent books are *Shifting Solidarities* (edited with Ine Van Hoyweghen and Gert Meyers, Springer, 2020) and *Labour Unions, Precarious Work, and the Politics of Institutional Change in Europe* (edited with Virginia Doellgast and Nathan Lillie, OUP, 2018). Favourite cuisine: Italian.

Silvia Rainone is a labour lawyer and Senior Researcher at the European Trade Union Institute (Brussels) covering developments in EU labour and social policy with a predominant focus on the future of work, platform work and European socioeconomic governance. Silvia is also an affiliated member of the Institute for Labour Law (KU Leuven) and Lecturer at Université Libre de Bruxelles (ULB). Favourite dish: Tortellini al ragù.

María Eugenia Rodríguez is an international consultant on labour and social policies and disasters in Latin America, collaborating with organisations like ECLAC, UNDP and IDB. She holds a BA in economics from Universidad Central de Venezuela, a masters in public policy from Universidad de Chile and a masters in industrial and labour relations from Cornell University. Favourite cuisine: Japanese.

Carl Fredrik Söderqvist (PhD, industrial economics) is an economist at the Swedish LO. His research focuses on the dynamics of bargaining power and structural change in workplaces and the labour market at large. Favourite cuisine: broccoli and bulgur.

Mark Stuart is Montague Burton Professor of Human Resource Management and Employment Relations at the University of Leeds, and Co-Director of the ESRC Digital Futures at Work Research Centre. His current research focuses on technological change, the future of work and worker voice. Mark is ex-Editor-in-Chief of *Work, Employment and Society* and a fellow of the Academy of Social Sciences and British Universities Industrial Relations Association. Favourite cuisine: Indian.

Arianna Tassinari is Assistant Professor at the Department of Social and Political Sciences of the University of Bologna. She is a comparative political economist specialised in the politics of work, labour relations and growth models. She completed her PhD at the University of Warwick in 2019 and has subsequently held positions at the European University Institute and the Max Planck Institute for the Study of Societies. Arianna loves noodles in all their forms – from Italian spaghetti to udon to pad thai.

Vera Trappmann is Professor of Comparative Employment Relations at Leeds University Business School and Associate Member of the Digital Futures at Work (Digit) Research Centre. Her research focuses on the response of workers and trade unions towards the precarisation of work, organisational restructuring and climate change. She is the author of *Fallen Heroes in Global Capitalism: Workers and the Restructuring of the Polish Steel Industry* (Palgrave Macmillan, 2013). Favourite cuisine: Italian.

Charles Umney is Professor of International Work and Employment at Leeds University Business School. His main research interests include digitalisation and the future of work, with a particular focus on warehousing; more broadly, the relationship between the dynamics of market competition and those of workplace power. He is the author of *Class Matters* (Pluto Press, 2018) and co-author of Marketization (with Ian Greer, Bloomsbury, 2022). Favourite cuisine: Lebanese.

Kurt Vandaele is a political scientist and Senior Researcher at the European Trade Union Institute (ETUI) in Brussels. His areas of activity include the history and sociology of the trade union movement in Europe; the collective action repertoire of workers; the platform economy and labour; and the political economy of Belgium and the Netherlands. Favourite cuisine: Italian.

Wouter Zwysen is a quantitative social scientist and Senior Researcher at the European Trade Union Institute (ETUI) in Brussels. He works primarily on labour market trends and inequalities with a focus on precarious work and wages. Favourite cuisines: Belgian and Thai.

Acknowledgements

This book analyses food delivery platform companies before there was certainty about agreement on the Platform Work Directive of the European Union in early February 2024.

Now that the ink has dried on this Directive, we hope that this book will inform national debates between social partners, policymakers and platforms as to how the Directive should be implemented in the member states. We also hope that the book will further stimulate the European Trade Union Confederation and its affiliates in their never-ending endeavour to improve the pay and terms and conditions of employment for couriers and other 'atypical' workers in and outside the platform economy.

As editors, we have explicitly strived to find gender balance among the authors (at different career stages). Women are lead authors in 8 of the 15 chapters. We are thankful to the authors for their engagement and involvement in the book process.

We are grateful to our employer, the European Trade Union Institute (ETUI), based in Brussels, for creating a pleasant and stimulating intellectual environment for discussing themes and issues related to the platform economy. We are thankful to Nicola Countouris and Bart Vanhercke, former and current Directors of the ETUI's Research Department, for respectively encouraging us to initiate and finalise this book project. Our colleague Torsten Müller kindly responded to a late request of ours.

We would like to thank our colleague Angélique Vanhoutte in particular for organising the authors' event in June 2023 and for handling administrative matters in such an efficient manner. We express our gratitude as well to our colleague and documentalist Jacqueline Rotty, who patiently checked the references, and we wish documentalist Giovanna Corda a happy retirement. Furthermore, with eyes on the detail but never losing sight of the overall message, we are undoubtedly deeply indebted to Calvin Allen for his – as always – excellent language editing work and feedback. Finally, we are grateful to Daniel Mather for offering us the opportunity to publish with Edward Elgar.

Brussels, 15 July 2024
Kurt Vandaele and Silvia Rainone

1. Regulating platform work: insights from the food delivery sector in Europe and beyond

Kurt Vandaele and Silvia Rainone

APP-BASED FOOD DELIVERY – THE EPICENTRE OF A CHANGING WORLD OF WORK

The delivery of cooked meals is nothing new. Changes in lifestyle and customers willing to pay for this personal service, the increased variation of food offered, and telephone ordering all paved the way for in-house home delivery in the twentieth century (Alvarez-Palau et al. 2022; Lord et al. 2023). The advent of the internet offered a place to advertise menus online and, later on, for online ordering, with takeaway restaurants themselves still providing the food to customers' doorsteps. Relying on internet and satellite communications technology as a precondition for their development, app-based food delivery platform companies have standardised, facilitated and outsourced the way that delivery service operates today.

A wider range of foods, how these are marketed by the platforms, and shifts in consumer behaviour have further driven the demand for online ordering. Subsequently, the delivery of meals has been strengthened in urban areas, enabling local restaurants to open new consumer markets beyond their physical premises. The Covid-19 pandemic undoubtedly further boosted these dynamics. As such, like other platform companies, app-based food delivery has been ingrained in the urban life of especially higher-income households (Graham 2020). Platforms are geographically restructuring the economies of urban areas by, for instance, setting up 'ghost kitchens' as virtual restaurants. However, given that they are location-based, they are simultaneously bounded by local labour and product market regulations (Ametowobla and Kirchner 2023; Muszyński et al. 2022; Chapter 2 of this volume), while they could also be confronted by urban traditions in political and militant action, in particular the existing informal networks of activists present at this spatial level (Cini et al. 2022).

Together with platform-based ride-hailing, app-based food delivery is one of the most visible forms of platform work in the urban context. Couriers are easily identifiable on city streets and in restaurant areas by their branded backpacks and uniforms – at least if they are delivering by bike or scooter. Their number in Europe in 2021 has been estimated at 2.2 million (Piasna et al. 2022). Moreover, food delivery couriers were even promoted as 'essential workers' for isolating households in locked-down cities during the Covid-19 pandemic.

Other dynamics have also given prominence to food delivery as an especially interesting sector within the wider platform economy. With Europe as its epicentre, followed by Asia and Latin America, collective resistance in the platform economy has predominantly surfaced in food delivery (Bessa et al, 2022; Stuart et al, 2023; Umney et al. 2024). This has attracted considerable press and media coverage at times, at least in liberal democracies, denoting the ideational power of couriers. Furthermore, it is in food delivery that collective bargaining agreements in the platform economy have mostly been concluded (Kilhoffer et al. 2020; Lamannis 2023), while litigation actions seeking to change the employment (mis)classification of platform workers predominantly concern food delivery couriers (Hiessl 2022; see Chapter 10 of this volume). In addition, regulatory efforts for embedding the platform economy into labour law frameworks are often oriented towards food delivery. This is particularly evident in Spain and Italy, where ad hoc norms have been adopted (Aloisi 2022). Even in broader attempts to regulate platform work at large, the chosen normative paradigm and wording often indirectly reflect the food delivery employment model. This is the case when legal provisions refers to platform policies on clothing and appearance and on geolocalisation among the relevant criteria for determining the existence of an employment relationship. Examples can be found in the European Commission's proposal for a Platform Work Directive, which subsequently inspired reforms in Belgium and Portugal (Chapter 11).

Its prominence in street protests, in courts and in platform regulation makes food delivery, together with ride-hailing, almost symbolic of platform work as a whole. This is a charm that is appealing yet partly misleading. As an offline, location-based type of on-demand platform work, developments and outcomes in food delivery are sometimes hard to generalise to other types of platform work, marked by different forms and locations. Nevertheless, studying sectoral platforms like those active in food delivery might offer a valuable lens for understanding the characteristics and features of the platform economy as a whole and its possible interaction with the conventional economy. It is therefore no coincidence that scholarship on food delivery is extant within the platform economy in Europe and across the globe. App-based food delivery is a well-researched sector across various disciplines in social science, including anthropology, business studies and economics, communications and media studies, employment relations and industrial relations, labour geography, labour sociology; and in legal disciplines such as competition and internal market law, data protection law and labour law.

Empirical studies on food delivery in the platform economy predominantly focus on unpacking algorithmic management and its data utilisation, applied by the platforms for monitoring and controlling labour, often in relation to the practical experiences of couriers or its impact on working conditions (for instance, Griesbach et al. 2019; Huang 2023; Veen et al. 2020; Woodcock 2020; van Doorn and Chen 2021). Scholars have also investigated forms of individual or collective resistance by couriers (Cant 2020), in which resistance or lack of has mainly been explained via labour process theory (Cini et al. 2022; Tassinari and Maccarrone 2020). Additionally, research has explored and categorised emerging forms of collective representation and (informal) organisation (Alberti and Joyce 2023; Atzeni and Cini 2023; Cini et al. 2022; Vandaele 2021), including the roles of labour market intermediaries (Charles et al. 2020) and the revival of the 'old' cooperative model in a new platform coat (Christiaens 2024; Davis and Shibulal 2018; see Chapter 13 of this volume).

Food delivery has, furthermore, attracted considerable attention from legal scholars, as platform companies have the capacity to circumvent existing labour norms and tend to bypass collective bargaining practices (Aloisi and Gramano 2019). The legal literature typically seeks to situate platform work within existing labour law paradigms, predominantly within the bounds of the employment relationship (De Stefano et al. 2022; Gruber-Risak 2022; Gyulavári 2020). To this aim, the analysis of judicial strategies and their normative implications has unveiled interesting dynamics and trends (Hiessl 2022; Menegatti 2022). The policymaking momentum that was reached in Europe with the elaboration and adoption of the Platform Work Directive and the European Commission's Guidelines on collective bargaining and solo self-employed individuals has further spurred reflections on the need to reform existing regulatory frameworks (Aloisi et al. 2023; see also Chapter 11). Juridical discussions have thus focused on legislative approaches to the best design of the presumption of employment envisaged by the European Commission (Kullmann 2022) and the extension of collective labour rights to self-employed platform workers (Daskalova 2022; Rainone and Countouris 2021; Stylogiannis 2023). Furthermore, more holistic and 'global' studies have emerged in reaction to the decision of the governing body of the International Labour Organization (ILO), in 2022, to place on the agenda of the 2025 International Labour Conference a standard-setting discussion possibly leading to the adoption of an ILO convention on decent work in the platform economy (Rani 2023).

Some issues remain rather unexplored, however. By integrating insights from various research branches and disciplines, this book seeks to contribute to the already rich body of research by addressing some remaining gaps in the literature from a multidisciplinary perspective and by exploring dynamics and trends in app-based food delivery in order to enhance the understanding necessary for the effective regulatory embeddedness of this sector and the platform economy in general. As such, the objective of this volume is to propose and advance avenues for improving working conditions for platform workers, both in the food delivery sector and beyond.

FROM INNOVATORS TO GIANTS WITH FEET OF CLAY: ARGUMENTS

Many policymakers initially heralded digital labour platforms with enthusiasm and praise, as the growing investments in digital architecture and skills testified (Drahokoupil and Vandaele 2021; ILO 2021; Schor 2020). Platforms' flattering halo of technological innovation, their supposed environmental friendliness and the offer of new employment opportunities all contributed to the warm welcome of what was then commonly known as the 'sharing economy'. Today's platform economy and internationally operating food delivery platform companies illustrate that this narrative is simply outdated, if, indeed, it was ever accurate in the first place. Several developments demonstrate the undercutting of this initial flattering picture.

First, app-based food delivery appears to be one of the most conflict-ridden industries in the platform economy (Bessa et al. 2022; see Chapter 6 of this volume), with couriers challenging uncontrolled technological change and putting pressure on platform companies to adhere to (emerging) regulation (Vandaele 2023).

Second, while couriers in food delivery have never only used bicycles,[1] some have quickly come to rely on polluting mopeds or cars to increase their productivity in a piece-rate pay model (Cant 2020). Together with short-term rental platforms, food delivery platforms have also further boosted the touristification of cities, putting pressure on the urban environment (Marrone and Peterlongo 2020; see Chapter 2 of this volume).

Third, while platform work, with its low entry barriers, is expected to be a stepping stone to traditional jobs in the labour market, especially for workers with a migrant background (see Chapter 5), some platform workers are more likely to be caught in the trap of continuing precarious, non-standard work arrangements (Adermon and Hensvik 2022; van Doorn 2021). The platform economy simply aggravates the existing vulnerabilities to which today's workers are subject: motives for engaging in platform work are associated with specific dynamics in local labour markets, with relatively poor offline working conditions and fewer employment opportunities steering workers to juggle these with work on digital labour platforms (Zwysen and Piasna 2024). Moreover, the food delivery job, marked by unpaid work (see Chapter 8), comes not without its own health and safety risks (Cefaliello and Inversi 2022; Chapter 7 of this volume). The Californian dream of platform business owners has turned into a nightmare for some food delivery couriers, their friends and families as deadly traffic accidents across the globe have made their vulnerability as road users agonisingly clear (Gregory 2020; ILO 2021).

Apart from debunking the idea that food delivery platforms are heralds of the future of work, this book broadly develops five other arguments. While these are not necessarily new, having been highlighted by earlier research, the studies presented in this volume contribute to the creation of a holistic picture of the food delivery sector. This comprehensive approach facilitates the emergence of connections and complementarities between seemingly unrelated dynamics and trends.

First, in terms of the scale of the analysis and methodological framework, the urban context is pivotal in comprehending and shaping app-based food delivery. As the last-mile logistics for the immediate delivery of food or groceries are an urban phenomenon, the city becomes the focal hub as well as a geographical battleground for a bottom-up revitalisation of existing trade unions and for the newly established associational forms set up by the couriers themselves.[2] Concurrently, the local urban context intertwines with the global level, as the major food delivery platforms operate internationally and are intricately linked to global streams of venture capital (Herr et al. 2021).

Second, while the food delivery workforce shares a condition of precarity and vulnerability vis-à-vis the dominant bargaining power of platforms, its composition is rather volatile. Often reflecting a self-employment model and characterised by informality, fully gauging its complexity proves challenging. Studies indicate that, as a cohort, couriers are generally younger and less feminised,[3] exhibit higher levels of educational attainment, and demonstrate a higher proportion of foreign-born individuals compared to other platform workers and the general population (see Chapter 7). Notably, the migrant background of many couriers opens opportunities for platforms to install and exploit labour market segmentation, hindering workers' integration into more standard forms of employment. Thus, where food delivery platforms perch in local economic geographies, they wield the power to make, unmake and remake the courier workforce (Schmalz et al. 2023).

In response to the disruptions caused by the platforms, different forms of associational power – associations of couriers, cooperatives and mutuals, grassroots unions and mainstream unions – are today (again) either opportunistically or dedicatedly experimenting with models of work reregulation and the establishment of employment rules (Murray et al. 2020). 'Platform unionism' in food delivery has not crystallised in a dominant associational form so far, as this is rather developing as a patchwork of forms incorporating digital technologies. While there is a certain unmet demand for collective representation among couriers (Martindale et al. 2024; Vandaele et al. 2024), this is likely to be voiced more loudly among those who are more economically dependent on their delivery income (Bonifacio and Marcolin, 2024).

Third, food delivery platforms are economic giants with feet of clay. Their business model, based on regulatory arbitrage and network effects, looks fragile; the former being sustained by exploiting regulatory loopholes and by their financial and organisational ability to influence the policymaking process, the latter via 'platform sabotage' – that is, applying tactics for 'establishing and exercising… discretionary power' to turn people's resources 'into revenue-generating assets and just as easily deactivate that revenue-generating capacity' (Shapiro

2023: 209). Furthermore, they are hinged on fractures or openings within traditional welfare-state systems as these shift to workfare regimes, under which the platforms could therefore be considered 'parasitic' (Schor et al. 2020).

Fourth, food delivery platforms adapt to regulatory and institutional local and national contexts while simultaneously shaping them. Acting as 'institutional chameleons' (Vallas and Schor 2020: 281), platforms exploit regulatory gaps and the inherent idiosyncrasies arising from the application of pre-digital labour law frameworks to technology-shaped and enabled work environments (Rainone 2023). The role of the judiciary is crucial in this respect. Judges are at the forefront of responding to platform workers' demands for legal protection and may need to resort to creative interpretations to avoid frustrating the effectiveness of existing legal frameworks. This, in turn, creates fertile ground for normative innovation and developments that may further pave the way for regulatory reforms.

Fifth, closely intertwined with the previous argument, the disruptive implications of the platform economy are beginning to breed efforts by policymakers towards regulation. As a fairly new sector, food delivery in the platform economy has been subject to various parallel and, at times, complementary regulatory initiatives. It is therefore possible to identify a slow and uneven, yet steady, progression towards regulatory embeddedness in Europe, driven by pressures from couriers and their associations, trade unions, a growing body of case law and (left of centre) political parties. In this regard, the app-based food delivery sector is not only an incubator of 'disruptive' business practices but also of constructive and innovative regulatory approaches that can potentially be transposed to other sectors within the platform economy.

This book embarks on a multidimensional exploration of these emerging characteristics, which, stemming from the food delivery sector, are gradually extending into the broader platform economy and, to some extent, even to the conventional economy (see Chapter 14). In this respect, the Platform Work Directive adopted by the European Union in November 2024 is illustrative as it marks a significant milestone, to be followed by a two-year transposition period for implementation into national legal systems.

THE EU PLATFORM WORK DIRECTIVE: A STEP INTO THE DOORWAY?

The legislative journey of the Platform Work Directive began in 2021 with a social dialogue consultation by the European Commission, in which the European Trade Union Confederation and business organisations were both able to provide input on how to regulate the evolving complexity of the platform economy. In December 2021, the Commission presented a legislative proposal mainly aiming to address two key issues: the widespread misclassification of platform workers as self-employed, depriving them of key labour standards, and the extensive reliance on automated systems and digital ecosystems for the management of workers, posing new risks of bias, lack of transparency and reduced worker agency while masking the expansion of managerial prerogative (Kelly-Lyth and Adams-Prassl 2021).

The Commission's proposal produced mixed reactions. Trade union organisations and labour advocates, including the European Parliament's rapporteur Elisabetta Gualmini, welcomed it as a step towards better protection for platform workers. Conversely, employer groups and digital platforms expressed concerns about the potential impact on flexibility and innovation. These differing views set the stage for 16 months of complex negotiations between the European Parliament and the Council of the European Union, culminating in agreement on the final compromise text in March 2024.

The Directive introduces several innovative provisions in three main areas: employment status, algorithmic management and data rights, and enforcement mechanisms.

First of all, the introduction of a rebuttable presumption of employment is a key feature. This means that individuals working on platforms will be presumed to be employees unless the platform can prove otherwise. This shift places the burden of proof on platforms, making it easier for workers to claim employment status and access associated rights. This presumption aims to simplify the process of determining who qualifies as an employee, thereby ensuring that more of those working in the platform economy are covered by labour protections. Recognising the widespread use of subcontracting arrangements, whereby digital labour platforms outsource the recruitment and management of workers to third parties, the Directive extends the applicability of the presumption to contractual relationships with these intermediaries.

Yet, despite its broad scope, the effectiveness of this presumption may be limited by several factors (Aloisi et al. 2023). It only applies to platforms that organise work and show signs of the control and direction of workers – criteria that already suggest the existence of an employment relationship. In addition, EU member states have the discretion to add further specifications in the form of additional criteria, as is already the case in Belgium and Portugal, which could hamper the smooth and uniform application of this simplification. Finally, the presumption does not apply to tax, criminal or social security matters unless member states decide otherwise during their transposition processes.

Second, besides addressing the employment status of platform workers, the Directive makes significant progress in addressing the challenges posed by algorithmic management and decision-making systems, overcoming most of the shortcomings highlighted by the application of the EU General Data Protection Regulation in the context of work (Rainone and Aloisi 2024). These systems are widely used by platforms to monitor, manage and evaluate workers, raising concerns about transparency, accountability and fairness. Importantly, most of the rights and prohibitions introduced by the Directive in this context also apply to self-employed platform workers. This extension of labour rights beyond the employment relationship is particularly significant as it represents a partial departure from traditional paradigms and a step towards a more universalistic approach to labour rights.

Key provisions include bans on the processing of sensitive personal data, such as emotional state or private conversations, and for predictive purposes, including for inferring trade union activity. In addition, the Directive prohibits fully automated decisions that affect the contractual relationship, demanding human oversight of critical decisions such as hiring and firing (Adams-Prassl et al. 2023). It also requires transparency around the use of algorithmic systems. Transparency standards are essential in providing workers with access to an informed understanding of how their data is being used, including for challenging unfair practices and informing litigation strategies in employment status reclassification proceedings. Platforms must provide detailed information on the data they collect, the parameters they use and their relative importance, while workers are guaranteed the right to an explanation of the decisions made or supported by these systems and are empowered to seek accountability and redress. Finally, the Directive integrates the provisions on algorithmic management with a significant collective rights dimension. Workers' representatives and, in a number of cases, representatives of self-employed workers are granted information and consultation rights, giving them a key role in ensuring uniform application and compliance with the rights and obligations that have been laid down (Otto 2022).

Third, the Directive also contains robust enforcement provisions, again with an enhanced role for the social partners and channels for collective voice. It is significant, for example, that the Directive devotes one of its final provisions to the promotion of collective bargaining, explicitly encouraging the adoption by the social partners of 'measures to ascertain the correct employment status of platform workers and to facilitate the exercise of their rights related to algorithmic management'. In addition, it gives workers' representatives the right to participate in judicial or administrative proceedings in support of or on behalf of platform workers. The presence of a collective dimension in the enforcement structure established by the Directive harnesses the support and resources of workers' representatives and valorises systems of collective representation as a potential means of improving compliance.

Overall, the Directive looks to represent a significant step forward in the regulation of platform work, addressing some of the most pressing challenges. Its innovative provisions on employment status, algorithmic management and enforcement mechanisms promise to improve working conditions for platform workers. Several areas, however, require close attention during the implementation phase and beyond.

The wide discretion granted to member states will, in all probability, lead to fragmented and inconsistent implementation, potentially undermining the effectiveness of the Directive, particularly in relation to the presumption of employment. While the Directive sets a minimum threshold of rights, the different legal and regulatory contexts across the EU could result in significant differences in how these rights are applied and enforced. This variability underlines the importance of harmonised implementation and the active involvement of trade unions and labour advocates to prevent the dilution or fragmentation of the provisions.

Furthermore, the exclusion of the presumption from tax, criminal and social security matters also reduces its potential impact. These areas are key to ensuring comprehensive labour protection and to addressing the wider socio-economic impact of platform work; so, by excluding them, the Directive leaves significant gaps that could undermine its overall effectiveness. There is scope, however, to fill these loopholes during the transposition period. In addition, the ability of platforms to adapt quickly to new regulatory frameworks and conceal key aspects of their operations poses a constant challenge to adequate enforcement. It is, therefore, regrettable that the Directive does not include provisions for much-needed support for technical expertise and capacity building for workers' representatives, trade unions and national authorities.

Whether the implementation of the Directive lives up to the expectations of the actors who have sought to promote better working conditions in the platform economy will also serve as a lesson for succeeding political efforts to embed the digital transformation of work fully in the regulatory framework. Given the richness of knowledge contributed by existing studies, the time is ripe to provide a 'testimony' of the state-of-the-art in research on app-based food delivery in Europe prior to the transposition and implementation of the Directive in the member states.

A MULTIDISCIPLINARY AND COMPARATIVE APPROACH

This volume reflects the efforts of researchers from various disciplines. The involvement of economists, industrial relations experts, labour market sociologists and legal scholars testifies to its multidisciplinary character. Accordingly, the researchers draw on insights from a diverse set of conceptual and theoretical frameworks, such as labour geography, labour process theory, migration studies, the power resource approach, protest event analysis and strategic corporate research. This multidisciplinary approach is also translated into the use of quantitative and qualitative methods, such as ethnographic fieldwork and participant observation, narrative and semi-structured interviews and working diaries, primary document analysis, secondary research and statistical techniques including inferential statistics and regression analysis based on administrative data, self-compiled data or survey data.

Almost all the chapters take a comparative approach, with the units of comparison being either the platforms themselves or geographical areas, whether cities or countries. The focus is mainly on Europe, partly due to the initial concept of the book and partly due to the background of the editors. The regulatory analysis and qualitative case studies cover: Austria, Belgium, France, Germany, Greece, Hungary, Italy, Ireland, the Netherlands, Norway, Portugal, Romania, Spain, Sweden and the United Kingdom. The overarching and borderless nature of the challenges posed by platform work in food delivery prompts a broad perspective. Analyses of regulatory developments regarding platform work at EU level are therefore included, as well as case studies of countries in the Americas: Argentina, Brazil, Canada, Chile, Mexico and the United States.

The study of app-based food delivery also requires an exploration of societal dynamics that goes beyond pure labour issues. Key to understanding the disruptive impact of this form of work are contextual factors – migration being one of them. The precarious residence status of migrants makes them particularly vulnerable to forms of exploitation, a risk exacerbated by platforms (see Chapter 5). At the same time, migrant workers have emerged as key actors in the analysed forms of resistance to the platform business model. The Covid-19 pandemic also emerges as another relevant contextual factor. The pandemic boosted the revenues of food delivery platform companies while bringing new, urgent courier demands to the fore, with the platforms taking on some responsibility as employers for mitigating health risks and perhaps stimulating in the long term a collective consciousness among some of the courier workforce.

Finally, several chapters approach food delivery as an accessible entry point to draw a larger picture of possible regulatory (dis)embeddedness and its implications for platform work in general, as well as for digital work in the conventional economy. These reflections are based on the conviction that dynamics and trends have a wider significance beyond the sector, and therefore the exploration of existing challenges and constructive approaches should be placed in a broader scenario. The possible influence of dynamics and trends in the conventional economy upon food delivery in the platform economy is not explored, however.

Turning to the structure of the book, the contributions are divided into four parts. Part I focuses on the actors in food delivery in the platform economy. The mobilisation of food delivery couriers, their issues and grievances and their working conditions are the focus of Part II; then Part III examines the outcomes of courier mobilisation and the emerging regulation of food delivery. Finally, Part IV extends the analysis. Geographically, the focus shifts from Europe to the Americas in two chapters. Thematically, alternatives to corporate platforms are explored, regulation is assessed in terms of the implications of algorithmic management in the workplace in general, and concluding thoughts are formulated beyond the food delivery sector in the platform economy.

ACTORS IN APP-BASED FOOD DELIVERY: CHAPTERS 2 TO 5

Part I sets out some of the actors central to food delivery. Chapter 2, written by Heiner Heiland, starts off with the observation that food delivery platform companies have become a visible part of the urban infrastructure. Food delivery is essentially a spatially fixed service locally tethered to the urban context: only here are restaurants, couriers and customers found in sufficiently dense quantities for building the network effects on which platforms' business model strongly depends. The urban infrastructure is, simultaneously, increasingly reliant on food platforms and other platform-mediated services. Heiland insightfully develops the argument that platforms physically influence and transform existing urban spaces, while this very urban context simultaneously shapes their business strategies.

Food delivery platforms give rise to newly located restaurants, grocery hubs and their virtual 'dark' equivalents. Equally, they might stimulate the fall of established restaurants, while local retail outlets might suffer from mounting competitive pressures due to platforms' spatial urban restructuring. Altered customer habits and practices, and new social inequalities, follow from this. Yet, as evidenced, for instance in their customised interfaces for restaurants, couriers and customers, food delivery platforms are also spatially bounded by the local regulations which shape their variegated practices. Spatial and related social realities are also of importance in local labour and product markets: for example, these influence courier supply and its composition, while customer bases align demand within delivery zones. To conclude: food delivery platforms render socio-spatial dynamics in the urban context both proactively and reactively.

Chapter 3, by Kurt Vandaele, provides a detailed analysis of the operational dynamics and challenges faced by three main food delivery platforms in Europe: Deliveroo, Delivery Hero SE and Just Eat Takeaway. The chapter draws a parallel between the high-flying promises of these platforms and their failure to deliver so far in terms of economic profit. Food delivery platforms are confronted with labour unrest, while public opinion and attempts at regulation put further pressure on them. Using a comparative qualitative multi-case design, based on insights from strategic corporate research and the power resource approach, Vandaele's analysis puts forward an understanding of power relations and corporate structures within food delivery platforms, as well as their business models and operational workings, in order to distil potential strategies for couriers to challenge their dominance. What emerges is a weaker-than-they-appear scenario in terms of the profitability and resilience of digital labour platforms in food delivery since the all-important network effects might vanish into thin air, reliant as they are on the oversupply of the courier workforce, restaurant chains willing to pay commission fees, and consumer behaviour.

The issue of couriers developing associational power is further developed by Vincenzo Maccarrone, Lorenzo Cini, Jörg Nowak and Arianna Tassinari in Chapter 4. Couriers exercise this power resource through heterogeneous organisational forms. This might – though not necessarily – raise tensions where two or more forms are present in competition for organising the courier workforce (Stuart and Joyce 2021). Organisational forms of associational power include autonomous, self-organised courier associations, grassroots unions and established or mainstream ones; and they vary between countries in Europe. The question is, then, why do couriers have different preferences in their expressions of associational power despite a very similar labour process? Based on a comparison of Germany, Italy, Ireland and the UK, the authors thoughtfully identify the contextual and agential factors relevant for explaining the heterogeneous outcomes in organisational form.

First, context-specific labour market institutions and regulations might shape the action repertoire of couriers and their aims and whether they turn to mainstream unions for achieving them. Second, existing political traditions within supportive communities and groups might influence couriers' ideological orientations and their attitudes; these might equally provide them with resources and skills in their mobilisation efforts. Third, as an agential factor, the strategic capabilities of the unions involved in courier mobilisation are considered key. In particular, trade unions with experience and expertise in organising a dispersed, precarious workforce outside the platform economy are seen as relevant.

These three factors explain why couriers have either stayed self-organised, as in Ireland, especially along ethnic lines, and in Italy; become active in grassroots unions, as in Germany and the UK; or gained the support of mainstream unions catching up with the platform economy, in Germany and Italy and, more recently, the UK. The framework developed by the authors is an open invitation for bringing in other case studies from other cities and countries to test its validity.

While Chapters 3 and 4 have a more hopeful tone about couriers building associational power in food delivery, such optimism is less shared by Cosmin Popan and Kristin Jesnes. Chapter 5 sheds light on the dynamics of the socio-demographic (re)composition of the courier workforce over time. The authors carefully put forward a periodisation involving a gradual shift from relatively few local students to migrant workers to undocumented migrants. Migrants are indeed over-represented in today's courier workforce with respect to native-born couriers in Europe (Zwysen and Piasna 2024), although those racialised dynamics are contingent on the urban context. In explaining the latter, Popan and Jesnes incorporate the concept of 'migration regimes' in their case studies, illustrating a mediating effect on the workplace regime installed by the food delivery platforms in Cluj, Lyon, Manchester and Oslo.

Accordingly, the interplay between the formal and informal rules governing international migration movements and platforms' strategies regarding their workforce results in relatively variable degrees and types of migrant labour in each of the cities studied (see also Orth 2024). In particular, cities in countries with a colonial past and geographical proximity to migration routes are marked by undocumented workers. Their vulnerability and their exploitability by platforms might be thought to have a negative impact on courier mobilisation and organisation in trade unions or other associational forms. While the financial dependence of couriers on platforms has been highlighted (Schor et al. 2020), this dependency intersects with migrant status and racialised dynamics. Consequently, the reclassification of couriers as employees is only a part of the puzzle as it does not address migrant status (van Doorn et al. 2023). All of this should not necessarily be interpreted deterministically, however. The chapter shows that migrant workers and undocumented workers, with the support of community organisations, are able to mobilise (see also, for example, Connolly and Contrepois 2018; Jiang and Korczynski 2024; Schaupp 2022).

MOBILISATION AND ISSUES: CHAPTERS 6 TO 8

Part II provides more detail on the mobilisation of couriers in Europe, as well as the issues and grievances that are indisputably linked to their overall low and erratic incomes and precarious working conditions.

The 'Leeds team', of Mark Stuart, Vera Trappmann, Denis Neumann, Simon Joyce, Ioulia Bessa and Charles Umney, quantitatively addresses labour unrest in app-based food delivery in the platform economy in Chapter 6. The team compellingly discerns the following findings based on a sample of 430 protest events across 23 European countries during 2017 to 2023. First, protest is typically brief, small and 'spontaneous' in food delivery. Second, pay is the most common reason for labour unrest. This corresponds to wage demands being the predominant issue behind strikes in the conventional economy as they, 'unlike aspirations for workers' control, are culturally defined as legitimate' (Hyman 1989: 129). Third, labour unrest in food delivery manifests itself mostly through strikes and public demonstrations followed by legal action. Fourth, various organisational forms of associational power are involved in protests, with informal groups of couriers being the most prominent. Often, however, mixtures of forms – informal groups of couriers, grassroots unions and mainstream unions – are responsible for staging the protests.

Moreover, a more nuanced picture emerges when the data is grouped and analysed along the lines of industrial relations regimes across Europe. These regimes show distinctive patterns, especially regarding the organisational form involved and the action repertoire. For instance, those based on liberal pluralism, such as the UK, see a greater role for grassroots unions in strikes; mainstream unions prevail in social partnership countries like Germany, oriented towards demonstrations and institutionalisation via, for instance, works councils; and polarised state-centred regimes like Italy allow more scope for courier collectives in strikes and see more litigation. As such, patterns of labour unrest in food delivery seem to be affected by industrial relations regimes and these are, of course, country-specific.

Chapter 7 addresses the job quality of app-based food delivery couriers, enabling an identification of their possible grievances and issues. Agnieszka Piasna and Wouter Zwysen take inspiration from the concept of job quality in the conventional economy and model and update its dimensions by integrating empirical findings on outcomes in food delivery and the platform economy in general. The authors helpfully deduce four dimensions for measuring and studying job quality in courier work: flexibility, fragmentation, economic insecurity and the shifting of costs and risks to couriers. All of these influence the power balance between courier and platform, with the former suffering from the latter's lack of transparency in its algorithms, causing information asymmetries.

'Flexibility' denotes the trade-off between platform-led and courier-led flexibility. 'Fragmentation' is conceived in terms of the intermittent nature of courier work, resulting in unpaid labour, and how work is often combined with other sources of income, either from jobs in the conventional economy or from welfare state benefits, leading to fragmented employment patterns. 'Economic insecurity' is related to the organisational work model provoking low and variable earnings, although this is mediated by the degree of dependence on courier work for general income, while the 'shifting of cost and risk' dimension relates to the self-contracted employment status of couriers.

Emphasising their mutual dependence and interactions, the four dimensions of the conceptual framework are operationalised and empirically tested on the basis of a non-probability survey undertaken among a large sample of platform workers, including food delivery couriers, across 14 European countries. The results demonstrate that couriers in the platform economy experience stronger job insecurity overall compared to platform workers in other sectors and to similar workers in the conventional economy, alluding to their lack of social protection and the significant power imbalance between them and the food delivery platforms.

While in Chapter 2 Heiland speaks to socio-spatial relations in app-based food delivery, Chapter 8 ensures that time is put at the centre of the analysis. Valeria Pulignano and Damian Grimshaw further develop the theme of precariousness among the courier workforce by focusing on unpaid labour. The authors sagaciously advance the argument that the extent and form of unpaid labour across various platforms and countries are explained by the presence of 'open' and 'closed' socio-technical regimes for worker autonomy and the interaction between these and couriers' employment status, with couriers either being self-employed (open) or employees (closed).

Open regimes allow for relatively high access to platform jobs as well as to paid tasks once on the platform, and relatively high control over work activities such as working time, whereas closed regimes are exactly the opposite. Open regimes combined with (bogus) self-employment, for example in Deliveroo, go hand in hand, however, with low and unpredictable income and unpaid work. The latter results, for instance, from waiting to access a task, search time in case of errors and delays at restaurants or from addressing conflicts. Unpaid waiting time is strongly reduced in a 'closed' regime where couriers have employee status, although not completely. Unpaid breaks and unpaid time still occur when shifts assigned to couriers are reduced due to, for example, a lack of demand. Consequently, the authors conclude that addressing employment status would only be a part of the answer for improving couriers' pay and employment terms and conditions.

OUTCOMES AND REGULATION: CHAPTERS 9 TO 11

Part III shifts the focus to wage outcomes and (legal) regulation in the food delivery sector.

In Chapter 9, Carl Fredrik Söderqvist empirically observes a doubling of (food delivery) couriers in and outside the platform economy in Sweden in the period 2014 to 2020, when year-on-year wages and earnings were relatively stagnant or declining. While the data used only allow for including couriers for whom food delivery work is the main source of income and cannot exclude non-food courier work, the socio-demographic profile sounds familiar. The courier workforce is male-dominated and has a relatively young age profile, while a gradual shift towards more couriers with a migrant background – often students – has occurred over time. The workforce is also marked by relatively large turnover. Couriers are trapped in their platform delivery job because outside, alternative options are even worse in terms of wages, while, for about half, the courier job also implies becoming worse off over time, although those coming out of unemployment do increase their earnings.

The arrival of food delivery platform companies in Sweden has reduced employer concentration in the courier sector, yet their significant wage-setting power has led to worsening income for couriers and fewer couriers being in full-time jobs. Consequently, couriers' individual bargaining power has decreased. Neoclassical economic theory would predict otherwise, however: it is expected that the arrival of food delivery platforms should provide couriers with stronger leverage vis-à-vis the platforms as they have more outside occupational opportunities, increasing the competition for labour. Yet, instead, competition in food delivery is reduced. To explain this phenomenon, Söderqvist points to the domestic outsourcing behaviour of the food delivery platforms, which tend to subcontract their couriers via staffing agencies and umbrella companies where wages are lower. The result is that, while actual employer concentration is lower compared to direct employment by the platforms, platforms remain the dominant market players with high wage-setting power. Their strong economic position overshadows the bargaining agency of subcontractors and self-employed workers. A disruptive picture emerges: if the market dominance of companies often facilitates concessions towards trade unions in the conventional economy – big business, big unions –, then monopolisation, going hand in hand with the fissuring processes in food delivery in the platform economy, runs in the other direction.

In Chapter 10, Silvia Rainone and Christina Hiessl qualitatively and quantitatively analyse the case law of national courts in Europe with regards to the employment status misclassification of platform workers, with a focus on food delivery couriers in particular. The authors put forward the argument that the dominant normative models in labour law, based on subordination, control and direction to determine access to labour protection, require reconsideration for fully cushioning the vulnerabilities associated with platform work. In particular, those models require a broadening of their scope and more judicial creativity.

The argument is analytically developed in three ways. First, relying on the normative model of subordination for determining the employment status of platform workers and for making platforms accountable as employers is considered inadequate for addressing the regulatory gaps in the platform economy. Second, based on a database of national jurisprudence on platform work, consisting of 531 judgments from 17 European countries, the judicial approaches and outcomes of national judges are mapped, revealing that, while the vast majority of judgments directly concern issues of reclassification or third-category worker status, there is a non-negligible number of judgments addressing other crucial issues in addition. An interesting development concerns proceedings relating to the allocation of employer accountabilities in cases where the platform has externalised the hiring of workers to intermediaries. Third, focusing on reclassification cases, it is empirically found that creative and flexible legal judicial argumentation beyond the strict notion of subordination models has, in general, a high(er) success rate across countries and this especially holds true for issues of reclassification in food delivery. Rainone and Hiessl therefore call for judicial and regulatory innovation beyond subordination models to guarantee and strengthen inclusiveness in social protection, of which case law in food delivery seems to take a precursive role.

In Chapter 11, Despoina Georgiou deals with developments in the legal classification of food delivery couriers in the platform economy. Georgiou scrutinises recent regulatory initiatives by legislators in several EU member states for increasing couriers' labour rights and offering them better social protection, while also reporting on the steps taken at the European level prior to agreement being reached between member states on the Platform Work Directive. Georgiou shows that the various national initiatives in countries like Belgium, France, Greece, Italy, Portugal and Spain suggest gradual progress for couriers – to different degrees – but these are not without their shortcomings. Certain categories of platform worker remain outside the coverage, or a de facto intermediate category is being installed. In particular, national initiatives as well as the Directive are basically aimed at preventing the misclassification of couriers as self-employed contractors by introducing procedural facilitations (a presumption of employment) that are grounded on the traditional paradigm of subordination. However, the centrality of this classical legal notion does not sit well with the emergence of new dimensions of vulnerability in the platform economy that transcend the degree of autonomy that workers can enjoy in the performance of their tasks. To extend the level of labour protection, Georgiou therefore explores four creative, alternative paradigms in labour law beyond the subordination model and its troublesome classification issue.

BEYOND EUROPE AND APP-BASED FOOD DELIVERY: CHAPTERS 12 TO 15

The research lens in the final part of this volume – Part IV – moves away from Europe, and extends the scope of analysis beyond food delivery.

Approaches for fair pay and decent employment terms and conditions for couriers are examined in four countries in the Americas – Argentina, Chile, Mexico, and the cities of Seattle and New York in the US – by María Figueroa and María Eugenia Rodríguez in Chapter 12. Rich in detail, their chapter stresses the influence of the Covid-19 pandemic (in terms of changing consumer preferences) and migration as exogenous factors that have escalated the demand for food delivery and boosted the supply of couriers. In particular, platform work represents the primary source of income for many (undocumented) migrants and has further contributed to the growth of informal and precarious work, especially in Latin American countries. In addition, the argument is made that the specific composition of the courier workforce and independent contractor status shape associational power and regulatory dynamics, the latter being oriented towards legal enactment (due to the lack of collective bargaining rights), across the countries studied.

In the US, with the ride-hailing sector often prevalent and setting the example for other on-location platform sectors, the legal enactment of social and employment protection for independent contractors is taking place, especially at local or municipal levels, as long as state or federal laws do not pre-empt this. As such, minimum pay rates for food delivery couriers were set in New York City in 2021 and Seattle in 2022, despite fierce platform opposition via litigation or otherwise. Minimum rates and other protections, such as data transparency, have resulted from rallies and demonstrations during and after the pandemic – supported by grassroots worker organisations – as well as from the influence of powerful mainstream trade unions and responsive progressive local governments. The predominance of immigrants in the platform courier workforce has facilitated their associational power via self-organisation, but immigration status has also necessitated rather non-traditional solutions, thereby leaving the question of their status untouched.

Equally, legal and judicial battles about the employment status of couriers have dominated the platform economy more than collective bargaining initiatives in Argentina, Chile and Mexico, with Chile as a rather positive case of the extension of labour rights. However, based as it is along ethnic lines, other than in Mexico, the associational power of couriers seems more fragmented and less dominated by mainstream unions, which are not as resourceful and are certainly less active in the informal economy. Often reflecting different constituencies, organisational forms in the urban context include mutualism, courier-led collectives and grassroots organisations, with 'spontaneous' institutionalisation preceding the Covid-19 pandemic but sometimes then being accelerated by it as a result of its exposure of couriers' vulnerabilities.

In Chapter 13, Denise Kasparian analyses platform cooperatives in food delivery and beyond that are emerging and developing in a diverse set of countries. Four worker cooperatives and two multi-stakeholder cooperatives are considered from western Europe and the Americas. In terms of the economic challenges and sustainability, their foundation proves the significance of the presence of a benevolent institutional-regulatory context. Network effects are equally key, and some strategies resemble those of corporate platforms, including service diversification and the targeting of chain restaurants. Yet the co-ops studied are hesitant to scale-up beyond their local communities as this might endanger political aims such as democratic participation.

Kasparian meaningfully proposes a framework based on the social empowerment of platform workers and couriers in evaluating platform cooperatives. Indeed, instead of focusing solely on whether tech-driven co-ops could be an economic alternative to venture-injected corporate platforms, it looks more fruitful to widen the perspective and bring in other dimensions highlighting specific identities centred on fairness and equity. As such, a hundred co-ops seem to bloom, all aiming to contribute in different ways to the social empowerment of workers or stakeholders, in either the economic or political realm, or both. Improving couriers' pay and terms and conditions of employment, and thereby helping to end their precarity, is just one of these aims. Others in the economic realm could comprise the cooperative-based provision of open-source software and the offer of training; whereas digital democracy and governance are important aims in the political realm. None is without challenges (see Bunders et al. 2022), but they do set a different benchmark for assessing the platform economy.

Given the laboratory function of app-based food delivery for algorithmic management, Nastazja Potocka-Sionek and Antonio Aloisi take this sector in Chapter 14 as a starting point to assess its spillover impact on jobs in conventional workplaces and labour markets from a legal perspective (see also Krzywdzinski et al. 2024). This impact is considered in three ways: factual, jurisprudential and legislative. First, while forms of algorithmic management are already present in the conventional economy, the widespread diffusion of digital labour platforms has foreboded their organisational embeddedness, combined with bogus self-employment, piece-rate pay and gamification across economic activities and sectors. In addition, the rise of remote work due to the pandemic has accelerated organisational work arrangements involving algorithmic management. Second, the authors note that the focus of jurisprudence on algorithmic management in EU member states has shifted from employment reclassification in the platform economy to broader concerns such as data protection, non-discrimination and the employment conditions of workers in general. Finally, legislative initiatives at national and European levels have been rather narrowly defined so far, either by considering algorithmic management in the platform economy or by regulating certain aspects in the conventional one.

Stressing the gaps and risks connected with these fragmented frameworks, the authors make a normative plea for a holistic, cohesive approach. They argue that greater effectiveness and enforceability will come from regulating algorithmic management in an encompassing way – that is, across the entire labour market, including both the platform economy and conventional settings – that takes into account its ubiquity and interconnectedness with existing legal frameworks.

Finally, the concluding chapter by Anke Hassel (Chapter 15) draws on the insights from the volume, highlighting the distinctive nature of food delivery platform work as a niche market with disruptive implications. Hassel underscores the dual challenges of low profitability and the complexity of regulating a diverse workforce, while also pointing to the ongoing mobilisation efforts by couriers and the implications of the EU Platform Work Directive for improving labour conditions. Whether policymakers should still be so benevolent to platform companies in food delivery and beyond is an open question. Given labour shortages in several economic sectors and the associated demographic challenges, part of the workforce in the platform economy could instead be trained and oriented towards sectors with higher economic and societal value.

CONCLUSIONS

Today's context is marked by a new epoch in capitalist development, with disruptive technologies challenging the existing regulation of work and employment (Murray et al. 2020). However, from a historical, longitudinal perspective, this new epoch looks more like the return of nineteenth-century 'merchant capital', characterised by the financialisation of the economy, powerful platform corporations and a putting-out system (van der Linden 2023). The key question is whether this will lead to a new, long cycle of workers once again influencing the course of capitalism, especially in the Global North, as they did in the first cycle that ran from around the mid-eighteenth century to the 1980s (Silver 2003). A relatively new sector such as app-based food delivery demonstrates that, even in the age of the platform economy with its exploitative dynamics and aggravated vulnerabilities, the generally successful attempts by corporate actors to claim impunity are being met with resistance from couriers and their associations, grassroots and mainstream trade unions, and from regulatory attempts by labour advocates and (left-of-centre) policymakers.

The fight for social justice and for decent working conditions is an uphill one, however. Collective labour faces organisational difficulties in mobilising and organising a heterogeneously racial courier workforce amid legislators' unresponsiveness, while labour advocates are struggling with largely outdated normative frameworks.

Yet, the overall picture arising from this collection is one of multidimensional, progressive and promising moves towards taming and embedding the disruptive spirit of digital labour platforms such as those in food delivery. The empirical analyses and normative approaches that characterise this book are thus geared towards drawing up constructive and innovative proposals for the role of regulatory actors in evolving a more comprehensive coverage for labour protection mechanisms in the increasingly digital and fissuring future of work. In this way, the book aims not only to contribute to the academic debate but also to inform and inspire practitioners such as trade unions and policymakers in Europe and beyond.

NOTES

1. This is particularly the case in bad weather conditions or bike-unfriendly cities.
2. At the same time, some couriers have to travel to the delivery job because they cannot afford housing in urban areas.
3. Gender might, therefore, be a rather underexplored subject in this volume.

REFERENCES

Adams-Prassl J., Abraha H., Kelly-Lyth A., Silberman M.S. and Rakshita S. (2023) Regulating algorithmic management: a blueprint, *European Labour Law Journal*, 14 (2), 124–151.

Adermon A. and Hensvik L. (2022) Gig-jobs: stepping stones or dead ends?, *Labour Economics*, 76. https://doi.org/10.1016/j.labeco.2022.102171

Alberti G. and Joyce S. (2023) Mutualism, class composition, and the reshaping of worker organisation in platform work and the gig economy, *Global Labour Journal*, 14 (3), 220–235.

Aloisi A. (2022) Platform work in Europe: lessons learned, legal developments and challenges ahead, *European Labour Law Journal*, 13 (1), 4–29.

Aloisi A. and Gramano E. (2019) Workers without workplaces and unions without unity: non-standard forms of employment, platform work and collective bargaining, in Pulignano V. and Hendrickx F. (eds.) *Employment relations in the 21st century: challenges for theory and research in a changing world of work*, Kluwer Law International.

Aloisi A., Rainone S. and Countouris N. (2023) An unfinished task? Matching the Platform Work Directive with the EU and international 'social acquis', Working Paper 101, ILO.

Alvarez-Palau E.J. et al. (2022) Economic profitability of last-mile food delivery services: lessons from Barcelona, *Research in Transportation Business & Management*, 45 Part A. https://doi.org/10.1016/j.rtbm.2021.100659

Ametowobla D. and Kirchner S. (2023) Varieties of platform capitalism? How competition and regimes relate to the diversity of food delivery platforms across Europe and North America, Working Paper 'Fachgebiet Digitalisierung der Arbeitswelt' 07, Technische Universität Berlin.

Atzeni M. and Cini L. (2023) New theories and politics for working class organizing in the gig and precarious world of work, *Economic and Industrial Democracy*, 45 (3). https://doi.org/10.1177/0143831X231201009

Bessa I., Joyce S., Neumann D., Stuart M., Trappmann V. and Umney C. (2022) A global analysis of worker protest in digital labour platforms, Working Paper 70, ILO. https://www.ilo.org/wcmsp5/groups/public/---dgreports/---inst/documents/publication/wcms_849215.pdf

Bonifacio F. and Marcolin A. (2024) Unpacking the role of workers' heterogeneity in the representation and regulation of platform work. A focus of the case of the Just Eat Takeaway agreement in Italy, *Cuadernos de relaciones laborales*, 42 (1), 125–141.

Bunders D.J., Arets M., Frenken K. and De Moor T. (2022) The feasibility of platform cooperatives in the gig economy, *Journal of Co-operative Organization and Management*, 10 (1). https://doi.org/10.1016/j.jcom.2022.100167

Cant C. (2020) *Riding for Deliveroo: resistance in the new economy*, Polity Press.

Cefaliello A. and Inversi C. (2022) The impact of the gig-economy on occupational health and safety: just an occupational hazard?, in De Stefano V., Durri I., Stylogiannis C. and Wouters M. (eds.) *A research agenda for the gig economy and society*, Edward Elgar Publishing, 33–52.

Charles J., Ferreras I. and Lamine A. (2020) A freelancers' cooperative as a case of democratic institutional experimentation for better work: a case study of SMart-Belgium, *Transfer*, 26 (2), 157–174.

Christiaens T. (2024) Platform cooperativism and freedom as non-domination in the gig economy, *European Journal of Political Theory*. https://doi.org/10.1177/14748851241227121

Cini L., Maccarrone V. and Tassinari A. (2022) With or without U(nions)? Understanding the diversity of gig workers' organizing practices in Italy and the UK, *European Journal of Industrial Relations*, 28 (3), 1–22.

Connolly H. and Contrepois S. (2018) From social movement to labour protest: the case of the sans papiers in France, in Fishwick A. and Connolly H. (eds.) *Austerity and working-class resistance: survival, disruption and creation in hard times*, Rowman & Littlefield, 109–128.

Daskalova V. (2022) Rethinking collective bargaining for the self-employed: European Commission publishes Guidelines on exemption and non-enforcement, Kluwer Competition Law Blog, 7 October. https://competitionlawblog.kluwercompetitionlaw.com/2022/10/07/rethinking-collective-bargaining-for-the-self-employed-european-commission-publishes-guidelines-on-exemption-and-non-enforcement

Davis G.F. and Shibulal S.D. (2018) Taming platform capitalism to meet human needs, in Rangan S. (ed.) *Capitalism beyond mutuality? Perspectives integrating philosophy and social science*, Oxford University Press, 207–226.
De Stefano V., Durri I., Stylogiannis C. and Wouters M. (2022) Exclusion by default: platform workers' quest for labour protections, in De Stefano V., Durri I., Stylogiannis C. and Wouters M. (eds.) *A research agenda for the gig economy and society*, Edward Elgar Publishing, 13–31.
Drahokoupil J. and Vandaele K. (eds.) (2021) *A modern guide to labour and the platform economy*, Edward Elgar Publishing.
Graham M. (2020) Regulate, replicate, and resist: the conjunctural geographies of platform urbanism, *Urban Geography*, 41 (3), 453–457.
Gregory K. (2020) 'My life is more valuable than this': understanding risk among on-demand food couriers in Edinburgh, *Work, Employment and Society*, 35 (2), 316–331.
Griesbach K., Reich A., Elliott-Negri L. and Milkman R. (2019) Algorithmic control in platform food delivery work, *Socius*, 5. https://doi.org/10.1177/2378023119870041
Gruber-Risak M. (2022) Classification of platform workers: a scholarly perspective, in Gyulavári T. and Menegatti E. (eds.) *Decent work in the digital age: European and comparative perspectives*, Hart Publishing, 85–105.
Gyulavári T. (2020) Collective rights of platform workers: the role of EU law, *Maastricht Journal of European and Comparative Law*, 27 (4), 406–424.
Herr B., Schörpf P. and Flecker J. (2021) How place and space matter for union organizing in the platform economy, in Drahokoupil J. and Vandaele K. (eds.) *A modern guide to labour and the platform economy*, Edward Elgar Publishing, 112–127.
Hiessl C. (2022) Case law on the classification of platform workers: cross-European comparative analysis and tentative conclusions, *Comparative Labour Law & Policy Journal*. http://dx.doi.org/10.2139/ssrn.3839603
Huang H. (2023) Algorithmic management in food-delivery platform economy in China, *New Technology, Work and Employment*, 38 (2), 185–205.
Hyman R. (1989) *Strikes*, 4th edn, Macmillan.
ILO (2021) *World employment and social outlook: the role of digital labour platforms in transforming the world of work*, ILO.
Jiang J. and Korczynski M. (2024) The role of community organisations in the collective mobilisation of migrant workers: the importance of a 'community'-oriented perspective, *Work, Employment and Society*, 38 (2), 339–357.
Kelly-Lyth A. and Adams-Prassl J. (2021) The EU's proposed Platform Work Directive, Verfassungsblog, 14 December. https://verfassungsblog.de/work-directive
Kilhoffer Z. et al. (2020) *Study to gather evidence on the working conditions of platform workers: final report*, European Commission Publications Office.
Krzywdzinski M., Schneiß D. and Sperling A. (2024) Between control and participation: the politics of algorithmic management, *New Technology, Work and Employment*. https://doi.org/10.1111/ntwe.12293
Kullmann M. (2022) 'Platformisation' of work: an EU perspective on introducing a legal presumption, *European Labour Law Journal*, 13 (1), 66–80.
Lamannis M. (2023) *Collective bargaining in the platform economy: a mapping exercise of existing initiatives*, Report 2023.02, ETUI.
Lord C. et al. (2023) The sustainability of the gig economy food delivery system (Deliveroo, UberEATS and Just-Eat): histories and futures of rebound, lock-in and path dependency, *International Journal of Sustainable Transportation*, 17 (5), 490–502.
Marrone M. and Peterlongo G. (2020) Where platforms meet infrastructures: digital platforms, urban resistance and the ambivalence of the city in the Italian case of Bologna, *Work Organisation, Labour & Globalisation*, 14 (1), 119–135. https://doi.org/10.13169/workorgalaboglob.14.1.0119
Martindale N., Wood A.J. and Burchell B.J. (2024) What do platform workers in the UK gig economy want?, *British Journal of Industrial Relations*, 62 (3). https://doi.org/10.1111/bjir.12797
Menegatti E. (2022) The classification of platform workers through the lens of judiciaries: a comparative analysis, in Gyulavári T. and Menegatti E. (eds.) *Decent work in the digital age: European and comparative perspectives*, Hart Publishing.

Murray G., Lévesque C., Morgan G. and Roby N. (2020) Disruption and re-regulation in work and employment: from organisational to institutional experimentation, *Transfer*, 26 (2), 135–156.
Muszyński K., Pulignano V. and Marà C. (2022) Product markets and working conditions on international and regional food delivery platforms: a study in Poland and Italy, *European Journal of Industrial Relations*, 28 (3), 295–316.
Orth B. (2024) Stratified pathways into platform work: migration trajectories and skills in Berlin's gig economy, *Environment and Planning A: Economy and Space*, 56 (2), 476–490.
Otto M. (2022) A step towards digital self- & co-determination in the context of algorithmic management systems, *Italian Labour Law e-Journal*, 15 (1), 51–64.
Piasna A., Zwysen W. and Drahokoupil J. (2022) The platform economy in Europe: results from the second ETUI Internet and Platform Work Survey (IPWS), Working Paper 2022.05, ETUI.
Rainone S. (2023) Digital and remote work: pushing EU labour law beyond its limits, in Countouris N., De Stefano V., Piasna A. and Rainone S. (eds.) *The future of remote work*, ETUI, 163–183.
Rainone S. and Aloisi A. (2024) The EU Platform Directive. What's new, what's missing, what's next? ETUI Policy Brief 2024.06.
Rainone S. and Countouris N. (2021) Collective bargaining and self-employed workers: the need for a paradigm shift, Policy Brief 2021.11, ETUI.
Rani U. (2023) Remote platform work and the flexible workforce: what global dynamics can we see?, in Countouris N., De Stefano V., Piasna A. and Rainone S. (eds.) *The future of remote work*, ETUI, 29–43.
Schaupp S. (2022) Algorithmic integration and precarious (dis)obedience: on the co-constitution of migration regime and workplace regime in digitalised manufacturing and logistics, *Work, Employment and Society*, 36 (2), 310–327.
Schmalz S. et al. (2023) Varieties of platform unionism: a view from the Global South on workers' power in the digital economy, *Work in the Global Economy*, 3 (2), 201–224.
Schor J.B. (2020) *After the gig: how the sharing economy got hijacked and how to win it back*, University of California Press.
Schor J.B. et al. (2020) Dependence and precarity in the platform economy, *Theory and Society*, 49, 833–861.
Shapiro A. (2023) Platform sabotage, *Journal of Cultural Economy*, 16 (2), 203–220.
Silver B.J. (2003) *Forces of labor: workers' movements and globalization since 1870*, Cambridge University Press.
Stuart M. and Joyce S. (2021) Trade union responses to platform work: an evolving tension between mainstream and grassroots approaches, in Drahokoupil J. and Vandaele K. (eds.) *A modern guide to labour and the platform economy*, Edward Elgar Publishing, 177–192.
Stuart M. et al. (2023) Labor unrest and the future of work: global struggles against food delivery platforms, *Labor Studies Journal*, 48 (3), 287–297.
Stylogiannis C. (2023) Freedom of association and collective bargaining in the platform economy: a human rights-based approach and an ever-increasing mobilization of workers, *International Labour Review*, 162 (1), 123–145.
Tassinari A. and Maccarrone V. (2020) Riders on the storm: workplace solidarity among gig economy couriers in Italy and the UK, *Work, Employment and Society*, 34 (1), 35–54.
Umney C., Stuart M., Bessa I., Joyce S., Neumann D. and Trappmann V. (2024) Platform labour unrest in a global perspective: how, where and why do platform workers protest?, *Work, Employment and Society*, 38 (1), 3–26.
Vallas S. and Schor J.B. (2020) What do platforms do? Understanding the gig economy, *Annual Review of Sociology*, 46, 273–294.
Vandaele K. (2021) Collective resistance and organizational creativity amongst Europe's platform workers: a new power in the labour movement?, in Haidar J. and Keune M. (eds.) Work and labour relations in global platform capitalism, Edward Elgar Publishing, 205–234.
Vandaele K. (2023) Vulnerable food delivery platforms under pressure: protesting couriers seeking 'algorithmic justice' and alternatives, in Ness I. (ed.) *Routledge handbook of the gig economy*, Routledge, 205–219.
Vandaele K., Piasna A. and Zwysen W. (2024) Are platform workers willing to unionize? Exploring survey evidence from 14 European countries, Working Paper 106, ILO.

van der Linden M. (2023) *The world wide web of work: a history in the making*, UCL Press.
van Doorn N. (2021) Stepping stone or dead end? The ambiguities of platform-mediated domestic work under conditions of austerity. Comparative landscapes of austerity and the gig economy: New York and Berlin, in Baines D. and Cunningham I. (eds.) *Working in the context of austerity: challenges and struggles*, Bristol University Press, 49–69.
van Doorn N. and Chen J.Y. (2021) Odds stacked against workers: datafied gamification on Chinese and American food delivery platforms, *Socio-Economic Review*, 19 (4), 1345–1367.
van Doorn N., Ferrari F. and Graham M. (2023) Migration and migrant labour in the gig economy: an intervention, *Work, Employment and Society*, 37 (4), 1099–1111.
Veen A., Barratt T. and Goods C. (2020) Platform-capital's 'app-etite' for control: a labour process analysis of food-delivery work in Australia, *Work, Employment and Society*, 34 (3), 388–406.
Woodcock J. (2020) The algorithmic panopticon at Deliveroo: measurement, precarity, and the illusion of control, *Ephemera: theory & politics in organizations*, 20 (3), 67–95.
Zwysen W. and Piasna A. (2024) Digital labour platforms and migrant workers: analysing migrants' working conditions and (over)representation in platform work in Europe, Working Paper 2024.06, ETUI.

PART I

ACTORS

2. Shaping space and being shaped by it: analysing the socio-spatial dialectic of food delivery platforms

Heiner Heiland

INTRODUCTION

Capitalism and space have always been intertwined, as can be seen in Karl Marx's description of the primitive accumulation of capital which transformed both economic and social structures, radically altering the shape and division of space by means of enclosures and clearances. The capitalist production of space is particularly evident in urban centres. In the Baroque city, the role of the ruling aristocracy was reflected in the structure and design of streets, squares and houses. The axial orientation towards the royal palace determined the representative visibility of the aristocratic nobility. With the rise of the capitalist economy, production and distribution have come to determine the constitution of space, its centres shifting to other places primarily determined by the circulation of goods and people, such as railway stations (Mumford 2009). Moreover, space has become primarily an in-between realm, an obstacle to be bridged as quickly as possible.

As capitalism develops, new spaces are constantly being produced. These have a formative influence on the conditions of the people who live and work in them. Cities remain the points of culmination where spaces are destroyed and produced in a particularly dynamic way, in that they are particularly located in the contestation of existing structures and orders ranging from protests to labour disputes: 'The metropolis is to the multitude what the factory was to the industrial working class' (Hardt and Negri 2011: 250).

At the centre of the latest chapter of this development are platforms that have 'penetrated the heart of societies' (van Dijck et al. 2018: 2). They no longer merely shape virtual space but increasingly penetrate material reality. With them, consumption practices are changing, new forms and contexts of work are emerging, and logistical processes are gaining in importance. Platforms – both on site and distance-based – are located in space, are influenced by it and restructure it (Heiland 2021; Herr et al. 2021). The result is a contested 'platform metropolis' that is a 'site of confrontation between high-tech corporations and subaltern subjectivities reclaiming their role in the redistribution of socially produced wealth' (Rossi 2019: 1429; see also Turner and Cornfield 2007).

Food delivery platforms are emblematic of the role of platforms in urban space and its (re) production. The focus of this chapter is on the socio-spatial dialectic of these platforms, as there is a mutual constitutive interplay between social and spatial relations that also affects platforms. On the one hand, they produce specific spaces and transform existing urban structures; on the other, space itself determines and influences the platforms. Accordingly, the chapter develops a twofold argument. After setting the context of the relationship between platforms and cities and the increasing relevance of last-mile logistics, the effects of platforms on urban space and, conversely, the effects of space on platforms are analysed.

PLATFORM URBANISM

Platforms are an urban phenomenon, especially on-location platforms that deliver goods such as food and groceries and services such as private ride-hailing and domestic care: 'the population density of cities has created particularly fertile ground' (World Economic Forum 2017: 6). Only here do demand and supply for the platforms' services exist in such a dense space that they can mediate between them efficiently and effectively. And only here is there sufficient infrastructure and labour.

Regarding the analysis of platforms and their influence, '[u]rban studies scholars have been rather late to the discussion' (Stabrowski 2017: 328). However, there has been a shift in recent years, with the existence of platform urbanism being acknowledged and explicitly examined (Barns 2020; Hodson et al. 2020). This adds to the portfolio of design and analysis of the urban space. To date, the influence and opportunities of digital technologies on the design of urban spaces have primarily been discussed in the context of smart city debates. Their aim is to 'connect the physical, IT, social and business infrastructure to harness the collective intelligence of the city' (Harrison et al. 2010: 2). In the first place, smart city initiatives were launched by city administrations, think tanks and states to achieve an efficient organisation of urban space through the integration of information technologies and the collection and use of data. While this remains an aspiration, particularly in the Global South, smart cities are now primarily pursued by private companies (Marvin et al. 2015). The emergence of platforms is further driving this development:

> Smart urbanism is primarily about optimizing oversight of city systems through state procured, corporate provided 'solutions', whereas platform urbanism aims to transform and/or take over the operations of city services that tend to be more market or consumer oriented. These two models don't necessarily supersede or even compete with each other, but rather work simultaneously in different spaces. (Sadowski 2020: 449)

Platforms are thus less concerned with complementing the public provision of goods and services, but rather act from a market-driven interest, seeking to identify market gaps and fill them with new or, in most cases, reorganised services, such as arranging accommodation through Airbnb or passenger transport through Uber. As a result, a large number of platforms now offer a differentiated portfolio of services in urban centres. In many places, this has made platforms key actors in the urban economy so that local infrastructures are significantly influenced and produced by them. Infrastructures refer to 'built networks that facilitate the flow of goods, people or ideas and allow their exchange over space' (Larkin 2013: 328). While at the beginning of the debates, the public sector was concerned with making digital technologies usable for the entire urban infrastructure, this is now mainly done by platforms that organise only the potentially profitable parts. And, because they rely on self-reinforcing network effects, they have an inherent tendency to create monopoly or oligopoly-like structures that reinforce their central position (Evans 2011).

Thus, platforms increasingly determine access to labour markets, services and goods. For example, the provision of private cleaning services, transport services or food deliveries tends to be 'monopolised' by a few platforms in a number of cities. Often, when the same platform-mediated services exist alongside traditionally organised services, terms and conditions in the latter change significantly. It is likely that, in the future, it will be difficult for customers and workers to access these services and labour markets without going through the platforms, making them key elements of urban infrastructures.

As a result, 'a platformisation of infrastructure and an infrastructuralisation of platforms' is reported (Plantin et al. 2018: 3), such that platforms are described 'per se as a new form of urban infrastructure' (Moore and Rodgers 2018). The influence of platforms that mediate goods and services 'now far exceeds that of the social web' (Barns 2020: 2) and 'cities and their information infrastructure [are] now increasingly framed as dense landscapes of platform intermediation' (Barns 2020: 18). It should be emphasised, however, that on-location platforms are almost exclusively an urban phenomenon, especially large cities, leaving rural populations and economies largely unaffected.

In general, and particularly in the Global North, this development often goes hand in hand with the formalisation and monopolisation of informal urban economies. Above all, however, a 'platformisation of urban space' can be observed with regard to the so-called 'logistical-urban frontier' (Shapiro 2023: 170). It is the delivery platforms that organise those logistical processes that have an impact on urban space. The last mile of deliveries is both a novelty and a driver of spatial change and, at the same time, is influenced by the spatial conditions.

LAST-MILE LOGISTICS AS 'ANNIHILATION OF SPACE'

Work, life and consumption are becoming increasingly location-independent. This development has been reinforced in particular by the proliferation of digital technologies and, more recently, by the Covid-19 pandemic. More and more people work from home or flexibly from other locations and have goods for their daily needs delivered to them on the spur of the moment. Cities in particular have become 'factories without walls' (Allen 1997). However, the loss of relevance of spatial ties applies primarily to white-collar workers. Moreover, spatial and temporal flexibility in the consumption of goods and services is provided by others, for example by delivery workers who bring orders to specific places at specific times. This is particularly true in the last mile of the logistics process. While earlier in the process orders can be aggregated and transported to hubs, the last few kilometres are a laborious task for individual workers delivering to individual addresses. This last mile is the least efficient and most complicated part of logistics, typically accounting for around 28 per cent (Ranieri et al. 2018) to 41 per cent of total delivery costs in the Global North (Capgemini 2018). And it is precisely this part that has experienced rapid growth in recent years.

This development is the result of supply chain capitalism in which companies 'compete on the basis of the distribution of goods and services, rather than merely the products themselves' (Chua et al. 2018: 619). In this, products only become fully fledged commodities when they are transported, so transport technologies and arrangements are closely linked to capitalist commodity production. This is also the result of saturated markets in the Global North, where attempts are made to initiate consumption that would otherwise not materialise by means of immediate delivery to the doorstep. Moreover, with often similar or even identical products, companies are striving for 'lean consumption' – trying 'to meet customer needs without squandering their own - or the consumer's - time, effort, and resource' (Womack and Jones

2005: 59). As a result, consumer decisions are not based just on the usual factors of price and quality but, above all, on the expectation of immediate delivery. The result is an ever faster and more flexible 'annihilation of space' (Marx 1953: 423), reducing transport costs to such an extent that different spaces lose their differences. It (almost) no longer matters where a desired good is located, whether it is in the shop around the corner or in the warehouse at the other end of town. It is delivered to the doorstep as soon as it is needed. With the Covid-19 pandemic, this expansion of delivery services has intensified and, with that, the challenges for bricks-and-mortar retail and thus for urban space (Beckers et al. 2021).

Marx already pointed to the importance of logistics when he described how it changed the 'local existence' of goods and thus increased their value (Marx 1962: 387). According to this, the spatial distance between goods and their destination is a means of production and the raw material of the transport industry (Smith 2011: 71). While Heinrich Heine (2014: 65), a German writer and poet and a contemporary of Marx with whom he corresponded, complained about the expansion of the railway that it would kill space and leave only time, this is precisely the purpose and selling point of last-mile logistics. The destruction of space is offset by the gain of time. Delivery services offer the transport of ordered goods but, in reality, the customer buys time and flexibility by not having to prepare, organise, buy or fetch a meal. The result is a real-time city (Kitchin 2014) in which consumers' desires do not have to be postponed but can be satisfied at any time. This is accompanied by a shift in power from the producers and suppliers of goods to the organisers of logistics (Alimahomed-Wilson and Ness 2018). Given the wide range of goods on offer, the (platform-based) organisers of logistics differ from each other only to a limited extent, and thus immediate delivery to the doorstep becomes a crucial factor. This is exemplified by the range of products offered by food delivery services, which is significantly smaller than that offered by traditional supermarkets. Moreover, these last-mile logistics reproduce and reinforce social inequalities when necessary reproductive activities such as shopping and food preparation can be outsourced to often lower-class workers (Heiland 2019), with the latter forced to align their working and living hours with those of their often higher-class customers (Heiland 2022b).

Regarding the last mile, the focus is on the urban scale. It is here that 'the centralization of capital finds its most accomplished geographical expression' (Smith 1984: 136). While there are close links to other scales, such as the global financial markets, which are crucial for the venture capital-led funding of platforms (Zwick 2022; also Chapter 3 of this volume), or the national scale, which determines the overall regulatory framework and possible regulations (Thelen 2018), the urban is the central 'scale of experience' (Taylor 1982). It is here that the effects of logistical change are immediately felt and seen, as more delivery vehicles and bicycle couriers are visible on the streets and neighbourhoods change as a result.

This logistics revolution (Allen 1997) has opened a market gap for the last mile of the transport process, which is increasingly being filled by on-location digital platforms (Altenried 2019). Such platform-mediated services have emerged only in the last decade, related to both the new relevance of this part of logistics and the corresponding funding opportunities due to the financial and economic crisis in 2007 and its effects in the following years. As a result of the Covid-19 pandemic, last-mile logistics, and platform-mediated logistics in particular, have experienced a further growth spurt (Curry 2023). On the supply side, however, the technical capabilities of platforms in terms of efficient algorithms and so on are not new. What is new on the demand side is the widespread adoption of smartphones and the mobile internet, which makes these app-based technologies available to the masses (Valenduc 2021). This has made it possible to coordinate and control, in real time and in an automated way, the logistical processes as well as the small-scale and fluid labour processes of couriers. As a result, platform-mediated last-mile logistics go hand in hand with particularly precarious and intensively monitored work (Altenried 2019).

Another specific feature of platform-mediated last-mile logistics is its spatial fixity. In contrast to the usual situation, it is not only labour that is tied to locations and capital that is free and less fixed. Relocations are not possible when space itself is the key component of the product. Moreover, such platforms and their services are not tied only to space as such, but above all to urban contexts. Only here is the necessary density of customers, workers and, for example, restaurants, between which efficient spatial mediation can take place. The result is an augmented interdependency between the labour process of food delivery platforms and urban space.

THE URBAN GEOGRAPHIES OF FOOD DELIVERY PLATFORMS

Capital is spatially flexible. However, the actual process of production must take place in specific locations 'since there is no ethereal way of accumulating' (Herod et al. 2010: 7). For the accumulation process to be successful, specific conditions are needed that differ from place to place, for example available labour or logistical connections. Capital thus requires a specific spatial arrangement that leads to its fixation (Harvey 1982). However, this arrangement and its fit are not accidental but actively produced, as David Harvey writes (1982: 416–517): 'the territorial and regional coherence that... is at least partially discernible within capitalism is actively produced rather than passively received as a concession to "nature" or "history"'. Capital thus creates the space it needs – 'a physical landscape created in its own image' (Harvey 1978: 124) – or it moves to places with better conditions for efficient accumulation (Silver 2003).

Space is not only voluntarily shaped by capital. It also affects capital. The result is a 'socio-spatial dialectic' (Soja 2009) according to which there is a mutual constitutive interplay between social and spatial relations. For instance, corporations can only supposedly decide where they prefer to produce. In reality, their decisions are influenced by workers and their unions, by labour markets and the local environment. Labour cannot produce space unilaterally either; it is part of this process of making space (Herod 1997). Space thus produces social relations and, conversely, social relations produce space. In other words, in the context of labour processes, labour has an impact on space and thus on capital. It is true that 'labour-power has to go home every night' (Harvey 1989: 19) and is therefore 'stubbornly local' (Coe et al.: 506), but, at the same time, workers also have geographical agency and their own spatial fix (Herod 1997). In other words, they can and do influence space and its making. As a result, urban space is always 'the product of conflict' (Massey 2005: 135). Capital and labour thus struggle over its constitution – from its place of production to its design and use.

For delivery platforms in particular, space is more than just 'background scenery' (Herod et al. 2003: 176) as they are, by definition, particularly constrained by their spatial fixity. Space, or rather its destruction, is their central resource, which would lose its importance through relocation to a non-urban area. Only urban centres offer the densities of supply, demand and labour that make efficient delivery possible. Freshly prepared meals lose their quality as soon as they are cooked, and ordered food is expected immediately. As a result, restaurants and warehouses need to be close to customers. Gevaers and colleagues (2014: 410) estimate that the cost difference for last-mile logistics between densely populated urban areas and rural areas is €5 (€2.75 versus €7.75). Additionally, a large local labour force is needed to make the labour process reliable and efficient. The result is the specific socio-spatial dialectic of food delivery platforms.

SHAPING: FOOD DELIVERY PLATFORMS AND URBAN SPACE

Looking at the impact of food delivery platforms on urban space, the first thing that stands out is the increase in traffic and the change in the urban landscape. Due to the increase in last-mile logistics, the presence of delivery vehicles and thus the volume of traffic in cities have increased significantly, which is also reflected in the exacerbation of parking problems in densely populated areas (Dablanc et al. 2017). In addition, food delivery platforms have a direct and lasting impact on urban spaces when numerous warehouses emerge as hubs for the rapid delivery of food orders or when restaurants close and new 'ghost kitchens' emerge. These are restaurants without physical shopfronts that are solely responsible for serving online orders (Choudhary 2019). On the one hand, platforms exploit the 'infrastructural surplus', referring to 'the excess of value derived from collective resources embedded in the urbanised landscape' (Shapiro 2021: 103). In addition, platforms restructure existing spatial patterns with regard to local retail and restaurant structures, the labour process of couriers and the reproduction and widening of social inequalities.

In general, a change in the intra-urban retail hierarchy can be observed (Jones 2021). This is partly the result of a decline in the frequency of daily trips by shoppers to city centres as the possibility of home delivery of all kinds of products reduces the need for analogue shopping (Arranz-López et al. 2023; Dolega et al. 2021; Nahiduzzaman et al. 2019). In the urban landscape, this translates into a decline in large shopping malls and an increase in vacant commercial spaces in city centres, as evidenced in different urban settings (Delage et al. 2020; Guimarães 2019; Hallsworth and Coca-Stefaniak 2018; Lee et al. 2017). On the one hand, this can lead to a self-reinforcing effect: according to the efficiency hypothesis, people with reduced access to local shops tend to purchase more items online where they have a wider choice of goods without having to travel (Farag et al. 2006). On the other hand, it has been shown that larger retailers sometimes move closer to city centres and residential areas in response to changing consumption habits (Jones and Livingstone 2018).

Food delivery platforms are part of this trend. They have a direct impact on restaurants. Relying on visibility, accessibility and sufficient pedestrian traffic, urban geography has always been crucial for the location of restaurants (Jung and Jang 2019; Pillsbury 1987). Restaurants are therefore sensitive to changes in the spaces surrounding them, as well as to the consumption habits of potential customers. This makes them a seismograph for changes in urban space, reflecting, for example, processes of gentrification (Bourlessas et al. 2022).

Platforms create intermediaries that both compete with bricks-and-mortar restaurants and enable them to reach new customers. Often, there is a limited economic case for restaurants to participate in platform-mediated delivery services (Chen et al. 2022): the expected increase in orders is offset by the commission paid to the platforms. In addition, restaurants are often required to give preference to platform orders, so the more profitable in-store orders are disadvantaged when demand is high. Many established restaurants participate primarily out of perceived competitive pressure. The shift towards ordering prepared meals via platforms often leads to less in-house dining. It reduces the effect of a central and visible location of restaurants in the city, which is usually associated with high rents. Through the platforms, locally (more) distant restaurants can enter into increased competition with centrally located ones. Accordingly, Talamini and colleagues (2022) show that the historically common centralisation of different restaurants has been reduced with the appearance of platforms as they have become more spatially dispersed.

Platforms also produce specific spaces for the efficient organisation of the labour process (Heiland 2021; Newlands 2021). Typically, platforms assign specific zones to customers, couriers and restaurants within which they may operate. However, as Heiland (2021) shows, platforms continuously reorganise these zones according to demand and order volume. For example, when demand is high, the zones are reduced in size to allow for more efficient working and faster order processing, or, sometimes, the zones are substantially reorganised. The composition of the zones and their changes are known only to the platforms; and the other players involved cannot deviate from them. Couriers are monitored by geo-fencing and their GPS signals, and leaving their assigned delivery zones is penalised. By creating specific spaces, the platforms significantly restrict the agency of customers, restaurants and, above all, couriers. Moreover, these practices have been shown to affect workers' mental maps of urban spaces and their subjective perceptions of space so that they see neigbourhood boundaries differently (Heiland 2021).

In addition to ready-to-eat meals, the provision of groceries is progressively gaining significance (Statista 2023). This business model is based less on the intermediation of third-party products (such as restaurants) and rather on the self-organised sale and delivery of groceries. Crucial to this approach is a closely interconnected network of warehouses that enables order processing and delivery in dense urban areas within a few minutes. Here too it is evident that e-grocery is affecting consumption practices in urban contexts, leading to changes in urban space. For instance, those who opt for grocery deliveries tend to visit supermarkets less frequently (Bjørgen et al. 2021). Grocery sales are commonly characterised by razor-thin profit margins; therefore, reduced sales following e-grocery offers can cause shop closures, potentially increasing the usage of e-grocery and leading to self-reinforcing developments and raised platformisation. As a result, platforms are becoming increasingly centralised and critical components of urban infrastructure. This has led Qiu and colleagues (2021: 304) to argue that platforms, especially those for food delivery, are 'digital utilities' whose processes and effects are of public interest. This phenomenon was especially noticeable during the Covid-19 pandemic as segments of urban communities transferred their personal infection risk to the couriers who guaranteed their food supply. Within metropolises under stringent lockdowns, couriers constituted one of the rare categories with unrestricted movement rights in public spaces.

Platforms continue the trend observed in large cities in which 'massive investments directed to expand the infrastructure of production rather than that for social reproduction' have been made (Sassen 2010: 332). Reproduction as the care of oneself and others in the form of, for example, the provision of food, and leisure activities is thus made more difficult in cities. Such trends could result in the exclusion of non-platform users and a shift in public space as warehouses replace supermarkets. Furthermore, the high investment costs and economies of scale required for this type of distribution make the platform business model accessible mostly to larger organisations, leading to a monopolistic trend. While there were usually numerous different food delivery platforms in the early days, only a few could survive the cut-throat competition, leaving a handful or even single platforms operating in most cities today. Moreover, the platformisation of the grocery market, typically dominated by a small number of providers, exacerbates the marginalisation of smaller individual suppliers, as reflected in the urban image through the further reduction of such supermarkets and traditional markets.

Common across the food delivery industry, be it for groceries or prepared meals, is the trend of 'going dark'. This pertains to kitchens (ghost kitchens) and warehouses ('dark stores') situated in the vicinity of customers but not accessible for on-location consumption. They serve as strictly functional physical presences in the urban space that can only be utilised online via the platforms. Ordered meals and groceries are exclusively available for delivery and cannot be accessed by walk-in customers. Couriers are therefore the only ones who can enter them.

Dark stores are a crucial aspect of e-grocery business models, and they are becoming increasingly pertinent for prepared meal delivery platforms (Shapiro 2023). Food delivery platforms continuously collect data on their customers' preferences and consumption habits to create individualised advertisements and offers. Furthermore, this knowledge is leveraged to create customised and new meals, prepared in ghost kitchens. These establishments usually offer not just one type of cuisine and virtual restaurant but a range of different options under one roof and in the same kitchen, such as Thai, Indian and Italian. Each option is presented as an individual entity on the platform, allowing for the easy scaling and optimisation of standard food preparation processes that utilise large quantities of prepared ingredients. The primary focus is on efficiently processing orders to establish streamlined labour processes.

Ghost kitchens permit platforms to expand their product range and increase their market share. They can also lead to vertical integration of platform services, as they are frequently managed by the platforms themselves or subcontracted to third parties affiliated with the platforms. Ghost kitchens and dark stores are often located in unoccupied buildings or even containers in remote urban areas. In some cases, they may displace local residents. Recently, platforms, as well as some other companies, have purchased numerous urban properties specifically for ghost kitchen operations (Snyder 2020) while e-grocery platforms are also constantly looking for new locations for warehouses.

The strained situation of local retail as a result of competing online structures, especially during and after the pandemic, benefits the platforms so that, in many places, a substitution of reproductive structures by platforms can be observed. Thus, the platform economy becomes reflexive in the sense that it benefits from and reinforces the effects that it initiates. This process triggers an urban centre's restructuring. The spaces occupied by the platforms become useful to their neighbours and inhabitants only through the platform. The conversion from traditional bricks-and-mortar shopping options to virtual alternatives allows for material space to be effectively utilised and understood only when viewed through a digital lens, which is controlled by the platforms. Everyday online consumption results in a detachment from the experience and awareness of the geography of its fulfilment (Hill 2020). This leads to the development of 'logistical fetishism' (Shapiro 2023: 172).

Usually, entering and using a space implies an implicit or explicit agreement with the local order. Behaviour differs between the church and the street, while companies must follow national and regional laws as well as adapt to the local structures and traditions of industrial relations. However, platforms attempt to avoid local responsibility for their new spatial and working arrangements, and often succeed in doing so, creating 'conjunctural geographies' which allow them to be 'simultaneously embedded in and disembedded from the space-times they mediate' (Graham 2020: 2). These platforms operate on a local level where they generate new spaces, yet retreat to the virtual level in terms of accountability, which is strategic for escaping local regulation.

Meanwhile, the reach, and therefore the impact, of the platforms is constantly expanding. Not only do they provide additional luxury services, such as the delivery of prepared meals, they are also expanding their services in order to become key players and contributors to the local infrastructure, providing the population with essential goods. However, this is accompanied by social inequalities in accessing food and even being excluded from infrastructure (Deener 2017; Shapiro 2023). If access to food is increasingly facilitated by platforms, meeting care obligations may become more challenging for people who cannot afford or manage a platform account, or whose physical location falls outside delivery zones. The inclusion of such marginalised areas tends to be possible at a higher fee, though this approach results in further exclusion and inequality. This is apparent from the growing discrepancies in food accessibility between rural and urban regions, which are already significant but are compounded by food delivery platforms (Newing et al. 2022). This can lead to food swamps with a large and wide selection of food, and food deserts with little, one-sided or no offer at all, with a potential impact on the dietary practices of local residents and implications for health disparities (Story et al. 2008).

BEING SHAPED: URBAN SPACE AND PLATFORMS

'Everything we study is emplaced; it happens somewhere and involves material stuff' (Gieryn 2000: 466). This is particularly true of delivery platforms: they restructure space and their spatial and organisational arrangements are influenced by urban space, resulting in a 'socio-spatial dialectic'. Labour geography has highlighted the spatial impact of workers, revealing that labour has an impact on capital. Thus, geographies of labour 'are formed at this intersection where flows of capital accumulation collide with structures of community' (Peck 1996: 16).

In general, platforms are subject to the local regulation of labour (Thelen 2018), leading to varieties of platform capitalism. Additionally, the spatial aspects of these platforms are evident in their apps. Platforms do not present themselves uniformly to users. Instead, various platform instances cater to different user groups, resulting in personalised feeds on social media platforms (Nieborg and Helmond 2019). Similarly, food delivery platforms offer customised interfaces for customers, restaurants and couriers. Although these platforms typically use a single piece of software, they occasionally modify it to suit local environments. For instance, when couriers receive an order from a platform, they may be presented via the app with the option of declining it. Nevertheless, this option is often displayed without functionality for many couriers and is actually available only in countries where, for example, it is a legal requirement for self-employed workers to have the option to refuse an order. Similarly, the functionality of an 'order acceptance rate' is exhibited within the app, but gathered and utilised only in particular countries (Heiland 2022a).

Platforms also need to address spatial and related social realities. During the early stages of Deliveroo's expansion, the management established new delivery zones in Berlin. The platform focused on the local population's purchasing power, thus identifying one middle-class suburb as a promising area but disregarding the lack of restaurants and couriers residing in the area. As a result, there was demand but insufficient supply and labour, leading to the quick closure of those delivery zones.

Additionally, differing delivery zones represent varying customer bases. In accordance with my own research, couriers often exchange information about the characteristics of certain neighbourhoods and emphasise the different demands of the respective customers, some of whom, according to the couriers, are more inclined to complain. As a consequence, couriers adapt their emotional work towards customers and feel the need to be more polite and courteous in some areas.

Couriers do resist, on an individual level, the generation and control of space by online platforms. For instance, some disable their GPS signal to avoid receiving orders in specific areas or at undesirable times, while others use fake GPS apps that allow them to send the platforms a 'fake' location (Heiland 2021). Thus, they can shape the labour process by, for instance, providing inaccurate signals from the periphery of the zone, resulting in decreased order volume, or using GPS to relocate themselves to the delivery zone centre, when situated in an outer district, to receive orders from restaurants more quickly – depending on whether they are employed or self-employed. Gregory and Maldonado (2020: 1198) also show that couriers actively influence where they work, and resist the spatial demands of the platforms, based on a preference to work in familiar or safe neighbourhoods.

Local labour markets are also significant. Labour is 'idiosyncratic and spatially differentiated' (Storper and Walker 1983: 4), so capital has to act accordingly, as is evident in food delivery platforms. This is apparent in the case of remuneration. While delivery costs for customers are identical regardless of the city, platforms differentiate wages: in cities with higher local wage standards, increased payment per delivery or hour is often the norm. Otherwise, recruiting enough couriers can, with management's experience and concerns in view, be challenging, particularly during winter months.

A significant factor in the success of food delivery platforms is the availability of a sufficiently large pool of potential workers; an industrial reserve army. This is especially the case given platforms' steady growth and the very high turnover of couriers. Platform-mediated food delivery has a low barrier to entry: few specific skills are needed and the apps provide a choice of language. Often, the only necessary requirement for applicants is a work permit. Consequently, migrants who have limited job alternatives and have to accept precarious forms of employment often carry out delivery work (see Chapter 5). A (migrant) reserve army can be found especially in large cities, as one manager for a platform confirms: 'You only need to place small advertisements in Berlin and you have a thousand people on your doorstep' (Heiland 2022b: 1838). Accordingly, there is also a close correlation between the existence of this reserve army – an oversupply of labour – and the level of wages. If the labour pool is limited, the platforms try to expand it by offering better pay.

Spatial variation is also evident with regard to the working time regimes of platforms. Couriers are frequently pitted against each other in these arrangements. Priority in shift selection is given to those with good and reliable performance. However, a sufficient number of couriers vying for work is a prerequisite for such competition. This system is ineffective in smaller cities where a reduced reserve army cannot exert a disciplining effect (Heiland 2022b). Foodora's workers in Cologne, who established a works council, have been able to resist the implementation of performance-based shift systems.

This highlights another spatial difference regarding workers' agency and its impact on the platforms. Although platform labour shows a significant fragmentation of workers in general

(Heiland 2022c), food delivery couriers in particular have been able to demonstrate remarkable resistance, resulting in various protests by this specific group (Bessa et al. 2022; Heiland 2020; Vandaele 2021; see also Chapter 6 of this volume). It is worth noting that couriers often utilise the spaces developed by platforms to ensure efficient labour processes as a means of organising and mobilising their colleagues. Thus, courier personnel are able to contact others stationed in central delivery zones. In order to begin their shift, couriers can only log in at these locations, although some platforms have responded to this restriction by widening the log-in radius, as noted by Heiland (2021: 12). Furthermore, couriers who deliver groceries use various warehouses to approach colleagues, identifying them as choke points to block the labour process (Ewen et al. 2022).

However, the distribution of these protests is not consistent across different countries and cities, often being concentrated in larger urban areas due to the advantage of higher population density. Additionally, protest tactics vary depending on the local political structures and norms of each city and country, as highlighted by Cini et al. (2021; see also Chapter 4 of this volume). For instance, in Germany (Heiland 2023), courier protests were first and most pronounced in Berlin where creative demonstration strategies were implemented, resulting in high visibility. However, the movement was primarily propelled by alt-labour and anarcho-syndicalist factions that maintained tight links with Berlin's left-wing political tradition and communities. As a result, the main trade union objective of establishing works councils was not explicitly pursued for a long time, with the first such election only occurring in 2022. In contrast, demonstrations in Cologne were initially arranged independently by the couriers, but, soon enough, the established trade unions also became involved (see Chapter 4). Given the lack of comparable alternative communities and structures, the election of works councils was a crucial objective for couriers in Cologne right from the start. This turned out to have a significant impact on platform arrangements, resulting in the rejection of the performance-based shift system.

CONCLUSIONS

App-based food delivery work is particularly tied to the specific local space in which it operates and on which it relies for resources and structures. Urban areas, where there are adequate concentrations of customers, restaurants and staff, are particularly important for facilitating efficient delivery. As space is the primary component of delivery services' labour processes, viewed as a product, relocation is not an option. This indicates that platforms do not act independently of space but are reliant on it and its features.

Consequently, the chapter demonstrates the existence of a socio-spatial dialectic. Food delivery platforms restructure and produce urban space; they are not just virtual arrangements that mediate previously existing services in a different way. First, they actively intervene in a city's physical infrastructure by occupying retail and urban spaces that, in the case of ghost kitchens and dark warehouses, can only become intelligible and usable to residents through the platforms' virtual portals. Second, they significantly reorganise and reterritorialise existing economic and thus spatial structures by changing consumption habits and practices, creating new and often asymmetrical competition. As a consequence, the distribution and accessibility of food change to the point of reproducing and reinforcing social inequalities, with food deserts on the one hand and food swamps on the other, including the associated inequalities in diet and health within the population.

At the same time, the idea of a socio-spatial dialectic points to the existence of an antithesis. According to this, platforms are also influenced by space; they are not only proactive actors but also react to their environment. Platforms tailor their services and labour processes to local spaces that are not equally suited to their business models. For instance, they have responded to local social structures by creating delivery zones. They must consider the composition of regional labour markets, which dictates labour costs and availability. Beyond that, they also react to the activities of restaurants, customers and, above all, couriers. The latter are proving to be particularly resistant in the field of food delivery and frequently engage in individual resistance and collective protests, including the formation of works councils.

How the socio-spatial dialectic ultimately plays out, what effects it has on the platforms, urban space and the actors involved, and what synthesis results from it, are unknown. While the initial trends and the potential future of urban space have been presented here, it is important to note that platform-mediated work and its analyses have yet to become the dominant model of food distribution, even in Western metropolises. Especially with regard to platforms and internet-based economies, expectations have often been disappointed, bubbles have burst and business models have proven to be unsustainable. It is also possible that this is the case for food delivery platforms. However, the initial impacts of this sector are already apparent. With their new forms of work organisation and the circumvention of established regulatory dispositives, their influence extends beyond their respective domain. Although food delivery may not achieve wide market penetration and widespread adoption in the future, its effects on the socio-spatial dynamics of urban areas will endure.

REFERENCES

Alimahomed-Wilson J. and Ness I. (2018) *Choke points: logistics workers disrupting the global supply chain*, Pluto Press.

Allen W.B. (1997) The logistics revolution and transportation, *The Annals of the American Academy of Political and Social Science*, 553 (1), 106–116.

Altenried M. (2019) On the last mile: logistical urbanism and the transformation of labour, *Work Organisation, Labour & Globalisation*, 13 (1), 114–129.

Arranz-López A., Blitz A. and Lanzendorf M. (2023) Exploring the associations between e-shopping and the share of shopping trip frequency and travelled time over total daily travel demand, *Travel Behaviour and Society*, 31, 202–208.

Barns S. (2020) *Platform urbanism: negotiating platform ecosystems in connected cities*, Palgrave Macmillan.

Beckers J., Weekx J., Beutels P. and Verhetsel A. (2021) COVID-19 and retail: the catalyst for e-commerce in Belgium?, *Journal of Retailing and Consumer Services*, 62, 102645.

Bessa I. et al. (2022) *A global analysis of worker protest in digital labour platforms*, ILO.

Bjørgen A., Bjerkan K.Y. and Hjelkrem O.A. (2021) E-groceries: sustainable last mile distribution in city planning, *Research in Transportation Economics*, 87, 100805.

Bourlessas P., Cenere S. and Vanolo A. (2022) The work of foodification: an analysis of food gentrification in Turin, Italy, *Urban Geography*, 43 (9), 1328–1349.

Capgemini (2018) *The last-mile delivery challenge*, Capgemini Research Institute.

Chen M., Hu M. and Wang J. (2022) Food delivery service and restaurant: friend or foe?, *Management Science*, 68 (9), 6355–7064.

Choudhary N. (2019) Strategic analysis of cloud kitchen: a case study, *Management Today*, 9 (3), 184–190.

Chua C., Danyluk M., Cowen D. and Khalili, L. (2018) Introduction: Turbulent circulation: building a critical engagement with logistics, *Environment and Planning D: Society and Space*, 36 (4), 617–629.
Cini L., Maccarrone V. and Tassinari A. (2021) With or without u(nions)? Understanding the diversity of gig workers' organizing practices in Italy and the UK, *European Journal of Industrial Relations*, 28 (3), 341–362.
Coe N.M., Johns J. and Ward K. (2007) Mapping the globalization of the temporary staffing industry, *Professional Geographer* 59 (4), 503–520.
Curry D. (2023) *Food delivery app revenue and usage statistics*. www.businessofapps.com/data/food-delivery-app-market
Dablanc L. et al. (2017) The rise of on-demand 'instant deliveries' in European cities, *Supply Chain Forum: An International Journal*, 18 (4), 203–217.
Deener A. (2017) The origins of the food desert: urban inequality as infrastructural exclusion, *Social Forces*, 95 (3), 1285–1309.
Delage M. et al. (2020) Retail decline in France's small and medium-sized cities over four decades: evidences from a multi-level analysis, *Cities*, 104, 102790.
Dolega L., Reynolds J., Singleton A. and Pavlis M. (2021) Beyond retail: new ways of classifying UK shopping and consumption spaces, *Environment and Planning B: Urban Analytics and City Science*, 48 (1), 132–150.
Evans D. (ed.) (2011) *Platform economics: essays on multi-sided businesses*, Competition Policy International.
Ewen J., Heiland H. and Seeliger M. (2022) Dynamiken autonomer Arbeitskonflikte im digitalen Kapitalismus: der Fall 'Gorillas', in Ewen J., Nies S. and Seeliger M. (eds.) *Sozialpartnerschaft im digitalisierten Kapitalismus: hat der institutionalisierte Klassenkompromiss eine Zukunft?*, Beltz Juventa, 234–258.
Farag S. et al. (2006) E-shopping in the Netherlands: does geography matter?, *Environment and Planning B: Planning and Design*, 33 (1), 59–74.
Gevaers R., Van de Voorde E. and Vanelslander T. (2014) Cost modelling and simulation of last-mile characteristics in an innovative B2C supply chain environment with implications on urban areas and cities, *Procedia, Social and Behavioral Sciences*, 125, 398–411.
Gieryn T.F. (2000) A space for place in sociology, *Annual Review of Sociology*, 26 (1), 463–496.
Graham M. (2020) Regulate, replicate, and resist: the conjunctural geographies of platform urbanism, *Urban Geography*, 41 (3), 453–457.
Gregory K. and Maldonado M.P. (2020) Delivering Edinburgh: uncovering the digital geography of platform labour in the city, Information, *Communication & Society*, 23 (8), 1187–1202.
Guimarães P. (2019) Shopping centres in decline: analysis of demalling in Lisbon, *Cities*, 87, 21–29.
Hallsworth A. and Coca-Stefaniak A. (2018) National high street retail and town centre policy at a cross roads in England and Wales, *Cities*, 79, 134–140.
Hardt M. and Negri A. (2011) *Commonwealth*, Harvard University Press.
Harrison C. et al. (2010) Foundations for smarter cities, *IBM Journal of Research and Development*, 54 (4), 1–16.
Harvey D. (1978) The urban process under capitalism: a framework for analysis, *International Journal of Urban and Regional Research*, 2 (1–3), 101–131.
Harvey D. (1982) *The limits to capital*, Blackwell.
Harvey D. (1989) *The condition of postmodernity: an enquiry into the origins of cultural change*, Blackwell.
Heiland H. (2019) The reproduction and restructuring of inequality through platforms, in *Proceedings of the Weizenbaum Conference 2019 'Challenges of Digital Inequality – Digital Education, Digital Work, Digital Life'*. https://doi.org/10.34669/wi.cp/2.1
Heiland H. (2020) Workers' voice in platform labour: an overview, WSI Study 21, Hans-Böckler-Stiftung.
Heiland H. (2021) Controlling space, controlling labour? Contested space in food delivery gig work, *New Technology, Work and Employment*, 36 (1), 1–16.
Heiland H. (2022a) Black box power: zones of uncertainty in algorithmic management, in Armano E., Briziarelli M. and Risi E. (eds.) *Digital platforms and algorithmic subjectivities*, Westminster University Press, 75–86.

Heiland H. (2022b) Neither timeless, nor placeless: control of food delivery gig work via place-based working time regimes, *Human Relations*, 75 (9), 1824–1848.

Heiland H. (2022c) New forms of agency or atomization? Gig workers' power resources and fragmentation, in Ness I. (ed.) *Platform labour and global logistics: a research companion*, Routledge.

Heiland H. (2023) A tale of two cities: the intrinsic spatial logic of courier protests, *Economic and Labour Relations Review*, 34 (4), 707–719 https://doi.org/10.1017/elr.2023.47

Heine H. (2014) *Lutetia: Berichte über Politik, Kunst und Volksleben*, Contumax Hofenberg.

Herod A. (1997) From a geography of labor to a labor geography: labor's spatial fix and the geography of capitalism, *Antipode*, 29 (1), 1–31.

Herod A., McGrath-Champ S. and Rainnie A. (2010) Foundations, in McGrath-Champ S., Herod A. and Rainnie A. (eds.) *Handbook of employment and society: working space*, Edward Elgar Publishing.

Herod A., Peck J. and Wills J. (2003) Geography and industrial relations, in Ackers P. and Wilkinson A. (eds.) *Understanding work and employment: industrial relations in transition*, Oxford University Press, 175–194.

Herr B., Schörpf P. and Flecker J. (2021) How place and space matter to union organizing in the platform economy, in Drahokoupil J. and Vandaele K. (eds.) *A modern guide to labour and the platform economy*, Elgar Publishing, 112–128.

Hill D.W. (2020) The injuries of platform logistics, *Media, Culture & Society*, 42 (4), 521–536.

Hodson M. et al. (2020) *Urban platforms and the future city: transformations in infrastructure, governance, knowledge and everyday life*, Routledge.

Jones C. (2021) Reframing the intra-urban retail hierarchy, *Cities*, 109, 103037.

Jones C. and Livingstone N. (2018) The 'online high street' or the high street online? The implications for the urban retail hierarchy, *International Review of Retail, Distribution and Consumer Research*, 28 (1), 47–63.

Jung S. and Jang S. (2019) To cluster or not to cluster? Understanding geographic clustering by restaurant segment, *International Journal of Hospitality Management*, 77, 448–457.

Kitchin R. (2014) The real-time city? Big data and smart urbanism, *GeoJournal*, 79 (1), 1–14.

Larkin B. (2013) The politics and poetics of infrastructure, *Annual Review of Anthropology*, 42 (1), 327–343.

Lee R., Sener I., Mokhtarian P. and Handy S. (2017) Relationships between the online and in-store shopping frequency of Davis, California residents, *Transportation Research Part A: Policy and Practice*, 100, 40–52.

Marvin S., Luque-Ayala A. and McFarlane C. (2015) *Smart urbanism: utopian vision or false dawn?*, Routledge.

Marx K. (1953) *Grundrisse der Kritik der Politischen Ökonomie (Rohentwurf) 1857–1858*, Dietz.

Marx K. (1962) Theorien über den Mehrwert, in Marx K. and Engels F., *Werke*, Dietz.

Massey D. (2005) *For space*, Sage.

Moore S. and Rodgers S. (2018) Platform urbanism: an introduction, *Mediapolis, A Journal of Cities and Culture*, 3 (4).

Mumford L. (2009) *The city in history: its origins, its transformations, and its prospects*, Harcourt.

Nahiduzzaman K., Aldosary A. and Mohammed I. (2019) Framework analysis of e-commerce induced shift in the spatial structure of a city, *Journal of Urban Planning and Development*, 145 (3), 1–11.

Newing A., Hood N., Videira F. and Lewis J. (2022) 'Sorry we do not deliver to your area': geographical inequalities in online groceries provision, *International Review of Retail, Distribution and Consumer Research*, 32 (1), 80–99.

Newlands G. (2021) Algorithmic surveillance in the gig economy: the organization of work through Lefebvrian conceived space, *Organization Studies*, 42 (5), 719–737.

Nieborg D.B. and Helmond A. (2019) The political economy of Facebook's platformization in the mobile ecosystem: Facebook Messenger as a platform instance, *Media, Culture & Society*, 41 (2), 196–218.

Peck J. (1996) *Work-place: the social regulation of labor markets*, The Guilford Press.

Pillsbury R. (1987) From hamburger alley to hedgerose heights: towards a model or restaurant location dynamics, *The Professional Geographer*, 39 (3), 326–344.

Plantin J.-C., Lagoze C., Edwards P.N. and Sandvig C. (2018) Infrastructure studies meet platform studies in the age of Google and Facebook, *New Media & Society*, 20 (1), 293–310.

Qiu J.L., Sun P. and Chen Y. (2021) Labour management and resistance among platform-based food delivery couriers in Beijing, in Drahokoupil J. and Vandaele K. (eds.) *A modern guide to labour and the platform economy*, Edward Elgar Publishing, 290–307.

Ranieri L. et al. (2018) A review of last mile logistics innovations in an externalities cost reduction vision, *Sustainability*, 10 (3), 782.

Rossi U. (2019) The common-seekers: capturing and reclaiming value in the platform metropolis, *Environment and Planning C: Politics and Space*, 37 (8), 1418–1433.

Sadowski J. (2020) Cyberspace and cityscapes: on the emergence of platform urbanism, *Urban Geography*, 41 (3), 448–452.

Sassen S. (2010) *Globalization and its discontents: essays on the new mobility of people and money*, The New Press.

Shapiro A. (2021) Platform urbanism and infrastructural surplus, in Meijerink J., Jansen G. and Daskalova V. (eds.) *Platform economy puzzles: a multidisciplinary perspective on gig work*, Edward Elgar Publishing, 101–121.

Shapiro A. (2023) Platform urbanism in a pandemic: dark stores, ghost kitchens, and the logistical-urban frontier, *Journal of Consumer Culture*, 23 (1), 168–187.

Silver B. (2003) *Forces of labor: workers' movements and globalization since 1870*, Cambridge University Press.

Smith N. (1984) *Uneven development: nature, capital, and the production of space*, Blackwell.

Smith N. (2011) Die Produktion des Raums, in Belina B. and Boris M. (eds.) *Raumproduktionen: Beiträge der Radical Geography. Eine Zwischenbilanz*, Westfälisches Dampfboot, 61–76.

Snyder G. (2020) Rise of the ghost kitchens: how virtual restaurants are reshaping L.A.'s dining economy, *Los Angeles Times*, 24 September. www.latimes.com/food/story/2020–09–24/rise-of-the-ghost-kitchens

Soja E.W. (2009) *Postmodern geographies: the reassertion of space in critical social theory*, Verso.

Stabrowski F. (2017) 'People as businesses': Airbnb and urban micro-entrepreneurialism in New York City, *Cambridge Journal of Regions, Economy and Society*, 10 (2), 327–347.

Statista (2023) *Online Food Delivery: market data & analysis.*

Storper M. and Walker R. (1983) The theory of labour and the theory of location, *International Journal of Urban and Regional Research*, 7(1), 1–43.

Story M., Kaphingst K., Robinson-O'Brien R. and Glanz K. (2008) Creating healthy food and eating environments: policy and environmental approaches, *Annual Review of Public Health*, 29, 253–272.

Talamini G., Li W. and Li X. (2022) From brick-and-mortar to location-less restaurant: the spatial fixing of on-demand food delivery platformization, *Cities*, 128, 103820.

Taylor P.J. (1982) A materialist framework for political geography, *Transactions of the Institute of British Geographers*, 7 (1), 15–34.

Thelen K. (2018) Regulating Uber: the politics of the platform economy in Europe and the United States, *Perspectives on Politics*, 16 (4), 938–953.

Turner L. and Cornfield D. (2007) *Labor in the new urban battlegrounds: local solidarity in a global economy*, ILR Press.

Valenduc G. (2021) A historical perspective on the drivers of digital labour platforms, in Drahokoupil J. and Vandaele K. (eds.) *A modern guide to labour and the platform economy*, Edward Elgar Publishing, 96–111.

Vandaele K. (2021) Collective resistance and organizational creativity amongst Europe's platform workers: a new power in the labour movement?, in Haidar J. and Keune M. (eds.) *Work and labour relations in global platform capitalism*, Edward Elgar Publishing, 206–235.

van Dijck J., Poell T. and de Waal M. (2018) *The platform society: public values in a connective world*, Oxford University Press.

Womack J. and Jones D. (2005) Lean consumption, *Harvard Business Review*, 83 (3), 58–68.

World Economic Forum (2017) *Collaboration in cities: from sharing to 'sharing economy'*. www3.weforum.org/docs/White_Paper_Collaboration_in_Cities_report_2017.pdf

Zwick A. (2022) Entrepreneurial finance capital and the gig economy, in Ness I. (ed.) *The Routledge handbook of the gig economy*, Routledge, 46–63.

All links were checked on 30 November 2023.

3. Icarus in a coma: mapping food delivery platform companies in Europe

Kurt Vandaele

INTRODUCTION

App-based food delivery platforms bear a resemblance to Icarus. Like the character in Greek mythology, they risk hubris in setting out high-flying promises on environmental sustainability, social emancipation and their business prospects. However, labour unrest, attempts at stronger regulatory embeddedness and the search for alternatives to corporate platforms all raise the pressure (Vandaele 2023). The Covid-19 pandemic boosted food delivery, but today's unlocked cities are less in need of deliveries, which may question continued growth. In addition, restaurants are faced with food price inflation, high energy costs and increasing rents, making them reluctant to pay the platforms' commissions. Couriers on motorised vehicles have been confronted with rising fuel prices since summer 2022, which, in turn, drives anger about low or declining earnings. As delivery work is often a side job, increased wages in low-income sectors in the conventional economy might move couriers away from the platform economy on the supply side, while the cost of living crisis might shrink the budgets of urban households for convenient food delivery on the demand side. Above all, food delivery platforms encounter difficulties in achieving profitability, although venture capital investors are so far continuing to throw them a lifeline. Financially speaking, the beleaguered platforms thus resemble Icarus in a coma – yet, is it really serious?

Based on a comparative, qualitative multi-case design, this largely descriptive chapter principally explores food delivery platforms as companies – a conceptual focus allowing for a comprehensive understanding of the actors involved in platform work and their power relations. Although smaller platforms operating in local and regional markets can be analytically interesting too, as they might diverge from dominant business models, three internationally operating ones are selected here: Deliveroo; Delivery Hero SE (DH), which is the parent company of Foodora and Glovo, among others; and Just Eat Takeaway (JET). Platforms such as DoorDash and Uber Eats, both based in the US, are also important as they are competitors of these platforms in several European markets, although the analysis is restricted to European platforms for manageability reasons and for those of space. Deliveroo, DH and JET are listed companies nowadays, so business reports are publicly available. Applying secondary research, a total of 29 annual reports, including accounting data, and other corporate material have been examined in conjunction with the financial press and academic studies. Utilising the latter sources facilitates, in terms of methodology, a highlighting of the non-explicitly articulated practices of the business model in its wider context (Howcroft and Leaver 2024; Shapiro 2023). The period 2013–23 can, in terms of data, be almost fully covered.

The analysis is grounded in the field of employment relations research and, as such, is undertaken in relation to the possible strategies through which couriers may challenge food delivery platforms to improve their working conditions. The chapter develops the argument that centre-staging corporate structure enables the identification of how to build countervailing power as well as an assessment of its possibilities. To underpin this argument, the platforms are mapped and diagnosed through the lens of strategic corporate research combined with insights from the power-resource approach, putting couriers at the heart.

THE BUSINESS MODEL OF FOOD DELIVERY PLATFORMS

Before swooping into the platforms themselves, this section analyses the business model as a means of better understanding their operational and financial performance. Platforms offered a destination for surplus capital hoarded after the financial crisis of 2007–08, linking them with the financialisation of the economy (Srnicek 2017). Close relationships between investors, start-up leaders and management typify the platform economy (Zwick 2023). Venture capital is identified as the main financial source for food delivery platforms, backing their business model's logic of capital accumulation and value capture (Ametowobla and Kirchner 2023). Venture capital can be considered 'patient capital' (Rahman and Thelen 2019), with investors tolerant of losses in the short to medium term with the prospect or promise of monopolising rents in the long run through network effects, implying that the greater the number of buyers, sellers or users, the greater the value created by the offering (Langley and Leyshon 2017). Such 'patient' investor relations in the platform economy resemble those of industrial companies in the mid-twentieth century, although those relations were then motivated by the prospect of stable long-term productivity growth instead of prioritising market expansion through network effects (Rahman and Thelen 2019).

Regional food delivery platforms active in niche markets might operate differently (Muszyński et al. 2022), but the business model of the internationally operating platforms is essentially built on rents coming from digitally matching customers and restaurants and from practices of regulatory arbitrage.

The matching function involves charging a (distance-based) delivery fee to food-ordering customers and a commission to restaurants for each completed order. The latter is particularly significant in achieving economic profitability, which explains why platforms aim to build exclusive and long-standing relations with restaurants (Alvarez-Palau et al. 2022).[1] Rents in food delivery seem feasible, especially due to the first-mover advantages deriving from positive feedback loops, enabling platforms to achieve strong market dominance in the localities in which they arrive first (Drahokoupil 2021). Investments in incentives such as 'predatory pricing' (below-cost pricing) for boosting network dynamics are therefore crucial (Shapiro 2023) in attracting and retaining restaurants and customers, especially as markets are highly competitive due to low entry barriers.

A critical mass of users, in turn related to city size, is required to guarantee a minimum volume of deliveries. Moreover, the value of the delivery service increases with stronger network density (Drahokoupil 2021). Restaurants and customers are dependent on the numbers in the just-in-time workforce as the presence of more couriers reduces waiting times for both; equally, the more restaurants and customers and thus orders, the lower the idle time for couriers. The influence of such network effects on delivery capacity explains why platforms try to discourage multi-apping where couriers work for two or more competing platforms. Network effects facilitate more effective demand coordination and offer possibilities of organic growth, but they are limited for food delivery platforms, having to be developed and sustained in every new urban context as scaling-up is impossible beyond the local scale: delivery services are, quite simply, place-based.

Making profit is also contingent on an organisational model fostering regulatory arbitrage for lowering labour costs. This implies that (international) food delivery platforms prefer contractual arrangements with couriers over a genuine employment relationship associated with making social security contributions. Although employment status variation exists within a platform and between markets or platforms, contractual arrangements are dominant in food delivery (Ametowobla and Kirchner 2023). Couriers have thus come to resemble the fissured workforce on steroids; yet fissuring itself is not new. Companies in the conventional economy have been franchising, outsourcing and streamlining activities to subsidiaries and subcontractors since the end of the twentieth century, with the aim of reducing labour costs as direct employment by a parent company is associated with more favourable pay and working conditions (Weil 2014). There is a difference, however: while workforce fissuring by conventional companies is motivated by shareholder interests oriented to short-term profit, this contrasts with the 'patient' business model in the platform economy (Rahman and Thelen 2019).

The predominant model of self-employment allows for an asset-light approach. Fixed capital for platforms is thus minimised as couriers mostly bring their own smartphones and vehicles. Hinting at the Californian ideology of Silicon Valley, this is discursively obfuscated by reference to 'micro-entrepreneurship' (Srnicek 2017), which might influence the mindset of couriers, possibly leading to self-exploitative behaviour (Vieira 2023) and undermining collective resistance (Barratt et al. 2020; Galière 2020; Schor et al. 2023). Contractual arrangements break delivery work into discrete tasks, colloquially known as 'gigs', as delivery services are concerted around culturally defined mealtimes. Although idle time is lessened, unpaid labour is nevertheless in abundance due to 'algorithmic performance pressures' (see Chapter 8 this volume). Labour costs are further reduced as the self-employment model is synonymised with piece-rate pay and minimal social protection – all of which are reminiscent of older work arrangements associated with precarious employment (Stanford 2017).

As sectoral platforms, food delivery is specialised in last-mile logistic services, part of the expansion and transformation of business logistics since the 1960s (Danyluk 2018). This 'logistics revolution' in capitalism implies an acceleration in the time-space compression of commodity flows due to technological and other advances. From this perspective, they are logistic platforms coordinating demand and lowering transaction costs for restaurants and customers. Algorithmic management optimises those transactions and is useful for monitoring and steering couriers and customers based on extracting and processing digital data, ensuring platform dependency (Franke and Pulignano 2023; van Doorn and Badger 2020). Moreover, algorithmic attempts aim at disciplinary control and productivity gains via gamification and performance-based scheduling, produce hierarchies among the just-in-time workforce (Griesbach et al. 2019; Heiland 2022).

Algorithmic management, with its essentially automated decision-making, also makes the building of relationships among couriers seemingly futile. Yet, the algorithms betray the presence of a labour-capital relationship since managerial authority and control, and information asymmetry, are built in (Gandini 2019). Food delivery platforms as neutral, digital intermediaries or 'tech solutions' is a mere fable (Frenken and Fuenfschilling 2020). Bringing in a wider scope on corporate structure, therefore, beyond faceless management, can enable the identification of alternative points of leverage for couriers in their collective effort.

A HEURISTIC FRAMEWORK: COMBINING SCR WITH PRA

This section lays out a heuristic framework for studying the corporate structure of platform companies, relying on strategic corporate research (SCR) and the power-research approach (PRA). As a method for practitioners preparing union campaigns, looking for vulnerabilities and potential points of leverage in the broad corporate structure, SCR offers a comprehensive understanding of the targeted company and the industry in which it is situated (Juravich 2011). Modern SCR has been developed in the context of the hostile US union environment for analysing ever-changing corporate structures and for supporting trade unions in launching comprehensive strategic campaigns in organising or collective bargaining. This marks SCR as relevant for studying food delivery platforms, given that they equally foster union avoidance strategies.

Platforms do call for an industry-wide approach: multi-apping, for example, stands largely in contrast to workers in conventional companies. SCR can, nevertheless, still be vital for selecting and targeting specific platforms for the improvement of employment terms and conditions in the whole sector. The SCR model itself discerns three levels of analysis for studying corporate structure: 'command and control', the 'operational level' and 'outside stakeholders', the latter especially allowing for a less workplace-based focus. Each level consists of a number of areas, 24 in total, relating to what is either inside or outside the company. Those areas enable a delineation of the three levels and provide guidance to practitioners in their search for corporate information and data gathering.[2] For each area, a number of checklist questions could be asked.

A dialogue between SCR and PRA is pursued here. Such a dialogue is largely missing in research as PRA tends to conceive power in a rather non-relational way, thereby losing sight of interactions with employer resources and the shifting nature of corporate structures. Whereas SCR puts the emphasis on corporate structure, PRA takes workers' structural position in capitalism as the point of departure for identifying the different power resources of the working class (Wright 2000). Bringing the PRA palette into SCR enables the deductive assignation and mapping of the possible power resources of food delivery couriers to the three levels of analysis in the SCR model. This should not be considered a prescriptive exercise; in practice, the dynamics and interactions between resources will be significant in understanding power strategies. Moreover, specific (organisational) capabilities are needed to mobilise those resources collectively (Lévesque and Murray 2010).

Structural leverage is fundamental in PRA: a power resource inherently contingent on workers' (un)lucky material circumstances within capitalist employment relationships and labour markets. However, it is a latent power resource: structural leverage only manifests itself and gains momentum when workers collectively activate it through associational power in, for instance, trade unions (Rhomberg and Lopez 2021). Associational power, therefore, looks especially pertinent at the operational level as this is where possible structural leverage via workplace or marketplace bargaining power is rooted. Both influence couriers' disruptive capacity via a withdrawal of labour or other manifestations of collective resistance.

The self-employment status of food delivery couriers might affect associational power negatively, since not all trade unions tend to be open to this status (for diverse reasons). In fact, couriers exercise associational power through non-union forms such as self-organised, collective associations, which either stay autonomous or seek cooperation with grassroots or mainstream unions (Chapter 4 of this volume; Vandaele 2021). Unions are thus not the only organisational form of associational power. Yet, both PRA and SCR suffer from the same flaw: although SCR could be conducted irrespective of organisational form, unions have been the dominant point of reference, while associational power and other power resources have often been shifted in recent PRA in a 'reifying way' towards unions instead of workers.

Associational power might also play a role concerning the outside stakeholders of food delivery platforms: couriers can lobby labour-friendly political parties to influence law-making processes. The enactment, enforcement or expansion of labour rights can all contribute to couriers' institutional power (Joyce et al. 2023), with labour market institutions making decommodification possible, conceived of in PRA as the (robust) residue of workers' past achievements (Korpi 1983). Besides external stakeholders, institutional power also looks relevant at the command-and-control level in structures like works councils or co-determination, which could theoretically assist in the search for stronger socio-economic security. Where such institutional structures are present, they might thus add leverage to local unions in the home country of the company or beyond.

At the command-and-control level, trade unions together with NGOs could gain access to shareholder meetings if they buy shares. Equally, crafting alliances with other actors such as restaurants is possible at the operational level, while such coalitional power can be equally pertinent with outside stakeholders. Similarly, ideational power is relevant at all levels given its transcending character, with food delivery platforms likely to be sensitive to local communities and public opinion.

Not all SCR areas can be covered by the following analysis. Primary research and other research methods and techniques are more suitable for collecting information in some areas, including those covering corporate decision-making and key relationships, whereas others are less relevant for analysing platforms. In addition, while international food delivery platforms adapt to the regulatory and institutional environment (Ametowobla and Kirchner 2023; Muszyński et al. 2022), this interaction will not be studied here as it ideally implies an analysis of each and every labour and product market in which they are active. The same reasoning applies to exploring the competitors of the selected platforms across urban economies. Instead, an overall picture through some telling snapshots will be sketched; it is acknowledged that contextual and temporal contingencies should be brought into SCR when preparing actual campaigns.

COMMAND-AND-CONTROL STRUCTURE: ASSESSING PLATFORMS' 'COMA STATUS'

This section offers some basic information about Deliveroo, DH, and JET, to set the scene, partly with reference to their main competitors in Europe, and to identify formal sources of couriers' potential workplace-based institutional power. This section thus basically concerns areas at the command-and-control level.

Deliveroo was established in 2013 with its headquarters in London, today being active in ten countries with five of them outside Europe. Its European market presence was larger before: activities have ceased in Germany (2019), Spain (2021), and the Netherlands (2022) as those markets were seen as detrimental to its business model. Deliveroo's flotation in 2021 was depicted as the 'worst Initial Public Offering (IPO) in London's history', losing more than 25 per cent of its £7.6 billion valuation on the opening day of trading,[3] which could be linked to courier protests exposing morally and socially disputed practices like regulatory arbitrage. Workplace-based institutional power for couriers is practically absent, however; only Deliveroo's Rider Forums, unilaterally set up in some markets, enable them to share ideas and feedback informally.

Amazon is Deliveroo's major shareholder, holding a 14.5 per cent stake; an investment that was finally cleared by the UK's competition watchdog, the Competition and Markets Authority (CMA), in 2020. One of the founders, Shu, is still chief executive officer (CEO); his control over the platform is guaranteed via 'class B' shares that provide additional voting power. This dual-class share structure expired in April 2024, feeding speculation over a possible takeover, although the CMA might be a burden to it. DH, its rival, sold its 4.5 per cent stake in Deliveroo for £77 million at the beginning of 2024, less than one-third of the initial purchase price, triggering a fall in the shares of both platforms. Talks with DoorDash, based in San Francisco and founded in 2013, over acquiring Deliveroo stalled in June 2024 due to differences about the company's valuation.

Berlin-based holding company Delivery Hero launched in 2011; its co-founder Östberg remains CEO. The group has been listed on the Frankfurt Stock Exchange since 2017, with technology investor group Prosus, a division of South African holding company Naspers, being the largest stakeholder with a share of some 25–30 per cent. Using various brand names, DH is active in more than 70 countries across the Americas, Asia, Europe (with a discontinuation of the foodpanda brand in Germany in 2022) and the Middle East and North Africa. A partial sale of the loss-making foodpanda brand in south-east Asia failed in early 2024, although California-based Uber reached a deal with DH in May 2024 to acquire foodpanda in Taiwan for $950 million; and, equally important, Uber committed to buying $300 million of newly issued DH shares.

A non-organic growth strategy partly marks DH. One year after its launch, the original Munich-based Foodora became a subsidiary in 2015, active in seven European countries today after announcing it would end activities in Denmark in May 2024. In 2022, DH acquired the Catalan-based operator Glovo, founded in 2015, which operates across 26 markets in Africa, Asia and Europe. Spanish social security authorities investigated Glovo's classification of couriers both before and after the 2021 'Riders' Law' that presumes their employment status. If a back payment of social security charges and penalties materialises, Glovo will require additional financing from its parent company – DH has only guaranteed such support until May 2025.[4] Glovo and DH were raided in 2022–23 by EU anti-trust regulators investigating alleged market allocations, hiring practices and information sharing. DH warned investors in July 2014 that it might face an anti-trust fine up to €400 million.

DH has been a Societas Europaea (SE) since 2018 – a public company in accordance with EU corporate law. The platform states that this expresses its 'self-image as an internationally oriented company with European roots', but its motives are probably less poetic in practice: SE status is often sought by German companies to circumvent stricter national rules on board-level employee representation (Keller and Rosenbohm 2024). This might be only half successful: in early 2024, DH employees started a procedure for establishing a works council in Germany – a far more vigorous type of employee representation compared to the required transnational SE works council currently in place – which turned out to be successful in the first round.[5] If further successes are forthcoming, a works council could provide more tangible institutional leverage to tech workers vis-à-vis management in the home country. In addition, works councils are already present in some DH subsidiaries, such as in Foodora in Austria since 2017 (Geyer et al. 2023) and in Glovo since 2022, the latter in response to the platform's attempt to circumvent the 'Riders' Law' (Arasanz Díaz and Sanz de Miguel 2023).

Dutch-based JET is the result of a merger of two platforms in 2020: Amsterdam-based Takeaway.com, founded by Groen in 2000, which went public at Euronext Amsterdam in 2016, and London-based Just Eat, established in Denmark in 2001, with an IPO at the London Stock Exchange in 2014. Both were originally online food marketplaces, not delivery platforms, and they continue to operate here alongside delivery work. Groen remains JET's largest shareholder with about 7 per cent of the shares. The platform operates under diverse brand names in 20 countries in the Americas, Asia, Europe[6] and Oceania, for instance as Lieferando in Germany, where, not without difficulties, works councils have been set up since 2017 (see Chapter 4). A works council has also been present in JET's home country, the Netherlands, since 2017. Moreover, a special negotiating body was initiated in 2023 to discuss the establishment of a European Works Council.

Both DH and Uber showed interest in Chicago-based Grubhub, founded in 2004, but it was JET that bought this food delivery platform for $7.3 billion in 2021, providing JET with a base in the US. However, one of its largest shareholders was sceptical about the acquisition from the start. Concerns were also raised when DoorDash entered European markets in 2022 through the $8.1 billion acquisition of Wolt, a Finnish platform founded in 2014 operating in 27 countries, most in Europe. Grubhub reached a settlement of a purported $42 million in 2023 with a stakeholder who had accused the platform of withholding data about financial performance. JET has been eyeing a (partial) sale of Grubhub since April 2022.

Compared to private ride-hailing platforms, food delivery sees a lower level of competition with established sectors in the conventional economy, although competition is fierce in food delivery as funding is more equally distributed compared to private ride-hailing (ILO 2021). Panels A–C in Figure 3.1 demonstrate how share values peaked during the pandemic, though at different times, but have languished afterwards. Deliveroo's share price stands at about one-third of its maximum value, but DH and JET are performing even worse. Market capitalisation stands at £2.11 billion, €8.44 billion and €3.08 billion, respectively. To guarantee continued investor support, via improving future earnings per share, both Deliveroo (£304 million) and JET (€300 million) engaged in share buyback programmes or similar in 2023–24.

Panel D indicates to what extent the platforms are financed by shareholders as opposed to debt. All have been reliant on 'patient' funding from shareholder equity, other than Deliveroo (before its IPO) and DH (in the last couple of years). DH is more leveraged compared to the conservative way that Deliveroo and JET fund their asset requirements. The latter two platforms, nevertheless, note in their post-2021 annual reports how the context of low interest rates has altered: shareholders' patience has been challenged as 'investor appetite to finance growth companies decreased because interest rates rapidly increased', resulting in a shift from 'a growth-first mentality to focusing on improving profitability' and 'a de-rating especially for currently non-profitable technology companies'.

Assessing platforms' reliance on debt, the debt-to-equity ratios in panel E confirm that DH substantially uses debt financing instead of its own resources for its operations; existing credit lines were extended and amended in 2023. The platform, nevertheless, looks fragile and relatively unattractive to shareholders. The agreement with Uber in May 2024, under which Uber will buy new shares, brings some relief to DH.

Finally, Figure 3.2 maps the geographical penetration of the selected platforms with regard to their international competitors in Europe at country level. Thus, a a standalone app, Uber

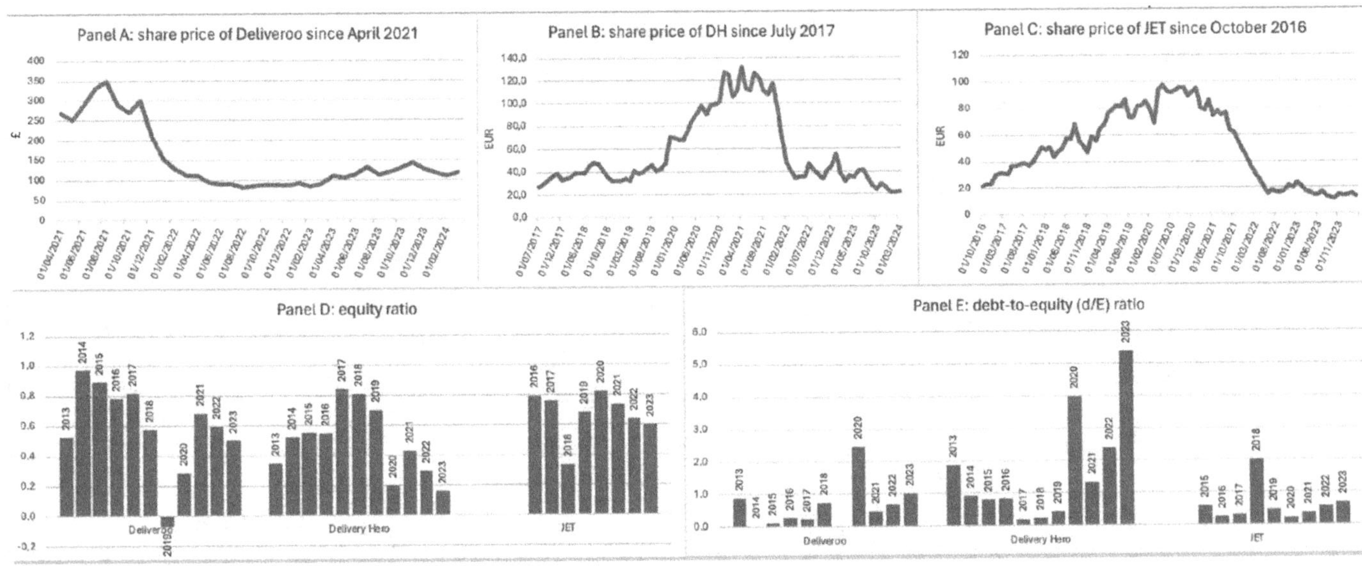

Note: Excluded debt-to-equity ratio of –15.3 for Deliveroo in 2019.
Source: Panels A–C – Yahoo Finance, 6 March 2024; panels D–E – author's calculation based on annual reports.

Figure 3.1 *Monthly share price, equity ratio and debt-to-equity ratio of Deliveroo, Delivery Hero and Just Eat Takeaway*

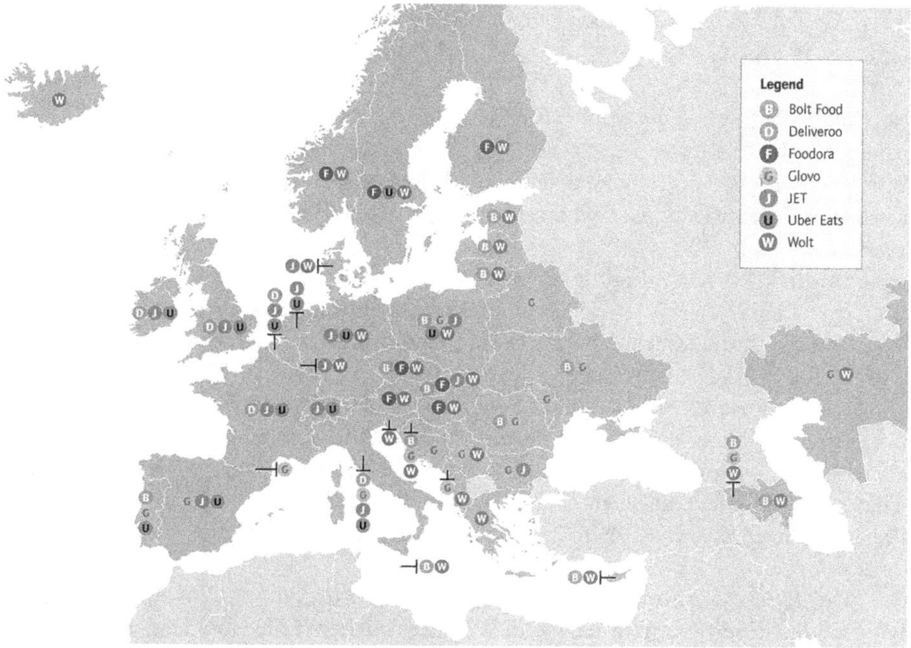

Source: Author's elaboration based on corporate websites with design assistance from Aymone Lamborelle.

Figure 3.2 *Geographical spread of major food delivery platforms in Europe (early 2024)*

Eats was launched in 2016 by Uber and operates in 29 countries, of which 12 are European. Like Uber Eats, JET predominantly operates in western European markets. These two platforms, together with Deliveroo, are also active in Ireland and the UK. Large markets in southern Europe look equally strongly divided. Bolt Food (present in 16 countries and established by the Estonian mobility company Bolt in 2019) and Wolt are both available in central and eastern Europe and Eurasia. Foodora and Wolt prevail in Nordic Europe. A duopoly of international platforms in these three regions seems typical, but markets are more crowded in, for instance, Poland and Slovakia.

This overview gives an indication of the degree of competitiveness between internationally operating food delivery platforms in national markets. It provides information on the extent to which network effects could be exploited, as couriers pitting platforms against each other is assumed to be an effective tactic for improving working conditions in a given urban area, given that network effects in the labour market are crucial to platforms' business models (Maffie and Gough 2023). While ideational power becomes more relevant in the case of a powerful monopolist platform, where multi-apping would not be an option, couriers guaranteeing to work exclusively for a single platform plausibly augment their associational power in competitive markets.

HIGH-FLYING AMBITIONS DRAGGED DOWN AT OPERATIONAL LEVEL

This section turns to a comparative multi-year analysis of platforms' operating and financial performance, which relates to some areas at the operational level within the SCR method. While linkage with PRA cannot be directly made in this section, focusing on product markets enables a loose identification of where couriers' distributive justice campaigns might reap dividends.

The platforms themselves highlight some indicators regarding their operating results; that is, the metrics considered as part of their 'investor-focused narrative' as they emphasise the 'ability to scale at speed and the prospects for capital growth (rather than profit)' (Howcroft and Leaver 2024: 11–12). The three indicators selected are the total number of restaurants (including grocery stores for Deliveroo), with an impact on network effects; the number of active customers, reflecting market position and penetration; and gross transaction value (GTV), including customer delivery fees, or gross merchandise value (GMV) in the case of DH. These provide information about the combined value of overall orders, which influences gross revenue development as platforms are highly dependent on the commission charged to restaurants.

Panel A in Figure 3.3 shows an overall expansion in restaurants for both Deliveroo and JET but growth slowdowns in 2023. Panel B depicts customer development. After significant progress in 2021, this has declined for Deliveroo, which the platform attributes to 'inflationary pressures' in 2023. JET has seen a fall in customers since 2022 as not all pandemic-gained customers have remained, especially in North America. The average monthly order frequency in 2023 reached 3.4 for Deliveroo and 2.8 for JET.

Panel C demonstrates that DH is the largest platform in terms of overall transaction value, followed by JET and then, at a distance, Deliveroo. Pre-pandemic order value has continuously increased, with Covid-19 measures contributing to changed consumer behaviour. Deliveroo, however, attained a lower order value in 2023. Its main market is the 'UK and Ireland' geographical segment, with an order value of about £4.2 billion, increasing from 47 per cent of GTV in 2019 to 59 per cent in 2023. DH and JET have also propelled order value through non-organic growth. For instance, DH's progress since 2021 can be ascribed to the acquisition of the South Korean subsidiary Woowa, and Glovo, contributing to the rise in GMV in 2022–23. Markets in Asia are especially important for DH (though declining); order value there stood at €25 billion (56 per cent of GMV) in 2023, whereas European markets were €7.5 billion (16.6 per cent). JET's merger helps to explain its growth in order value in 2021. Slowdown and decline, in contrast, describe its post-pandemic development, although order value is still significantly above pre-pandemic levels, reaching €16.5 billion (62.5 per cent of GTV) in 'Europe'. Its main markets in 2023 were the US, UK and Germany; southern Europe seems of lesser importance.

Other revenue streams may include service fees for processing online payments, advertising (based on data extraction from consumers) and subscription-based models aiming to lock consumers into platforms' ecosystems. Furthermore, platforms have diversified their product offerings beyond fast-food delivery through quick commerce (q-commerce) via their own on-demand services or in-store picks of groceries or other consumer goods (retail). Q-commerce in Deliveroo rose from 6 per cent in the second half of 2020 to 13 per cent, in terms of total GTV, in the last half of 2023, but commission rates are reported to be lower compared to

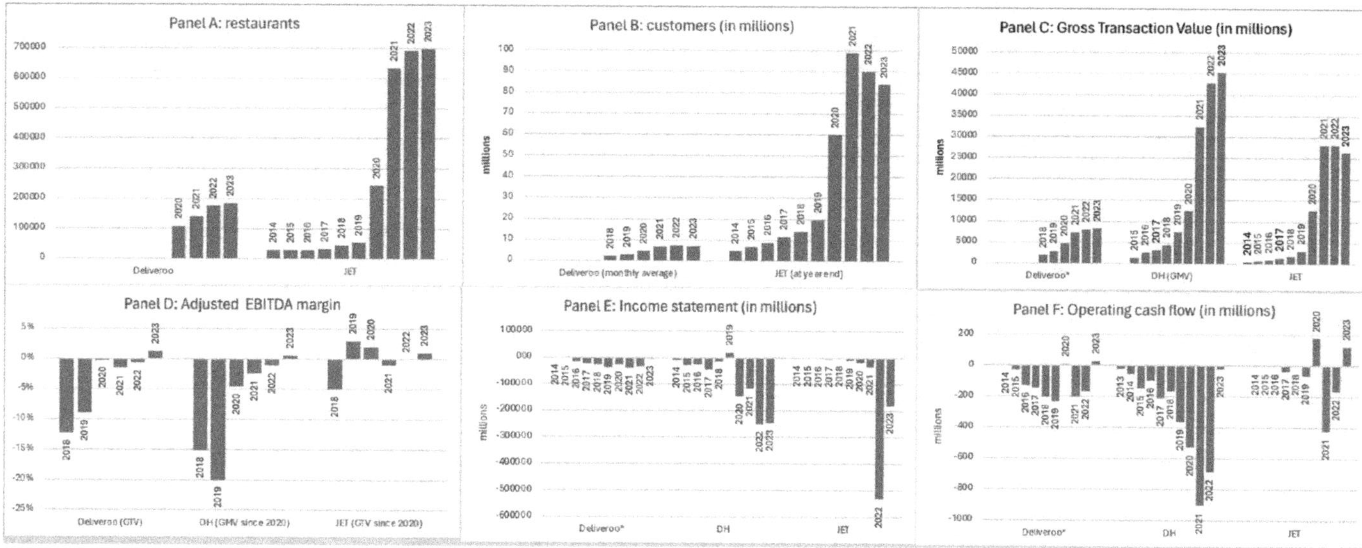

Note: *Exchange rate: £1 to €1.17.
Source: Company annual reports.

Figure 3.3 *Selected performance indicators for Deliveroo, Delivery Hero and Just Eat Takeaway, 2014–23*

restaurants. DH has begun q-commerce, including via its small warehouses called Dmarts, mainly consisting of its own warehouse operations for selling on-demand groceries: revenue increased between 2020 and 2023 from 7.3 per cent to 19.7 per cent. JET piloted q-commerce in the Netherlands in 2022 and has been scaling-up this business ever since.

Panel D of Figure 3.3 depicts the adjusted EBIDTA margin.[7] Margins are negative overall, but have improved over time for all platforms, a result largely of increased network effects and order value. All three platforms sketch a picture that is overly rosy, however, as that adjustment to the margin is achieved via the exclusion of one-off, non-operating expenses. Differences between markets are apparent, implying that profitability can, nevertheless, be a battlefield for couriers. Deliveroo had a positive EBIDTA margin in 2023 (due to cost reductions), with the margin especially higher in the UK and Ireland segment. DH's negative margin persists in its European segment because of 'marketing investment in connection with rebranding our Foodora business'. The measure was slightly positive for JET in 2020 and 2023, with the EBITDA margin being negative in the last year for southern Europe and Australia and New Zealand. JET claims that it has been profitable since its inception in its home market, the Netherlands.

The income statements in Panel E show how overall negative or low EBIDTA margins translate into non-profitability. Negative income in Deliveroo has reached over €200 million or even €300 million since 2017, except for 2023, when the loss was €32 million. Apart from 2019, DH equally marks 'profitless growth'. JET has been confronted with escalating losses since 2021 due to the 'impairment of goodwill and acquired other intangible assets', which should be read as far fewer Grubhub orders than expected due to competitiveness pressures arising from DoorDash and Uber Eats in the US.

Finally, turning to Panel F, operating cash flow measures how much money the platforms have generated from normal, daily business operations. This indicator is negative for Deliveroo except for 2020 and 2023. DH has failed to generate a positive operating cash flow in any year. This is also the case for JET, other than in 2018, 2020 and 2023.

In conclusion, additional external financing is required to keep Icarus alive; that is, to maintain and advance operations.

POSSIBLE ACTORS AT OPERATIONAL LEVEL FOR BUILDING POWER

This section contrasts platforms' financial reporting with a presentation of research accounting for the various actors in the quadrangular relationship that applies in food delivery: their directly employed workers, the couriers, restaurants and customers.

First, all three platforms evidently do employ workers in their own operations. Panel A in Figure 3.4 outlines the actual size of the employed workforce in each organisation, with different growth rates reflecting variety in business expansion. Workforce growth came to a halt in 2023 when they all laid off workers, on a particularly pronounced basis in JET, given the slowdown in orders after the pandemic-induced takeaway bubble. A 'redundancy process' affected 9 per cent of the Deliveroo workforce, mostly in the UK. Subsequently, Deliveroo attributed this process to the 2023 decline in its score in the regular employee engagement surveys measuring loyalty and job satisfaction. Furthermore, a 6.5 per cent workforce reduction was mainly felt in Glovo's Barcelona offices, with foodpanda already having conducted

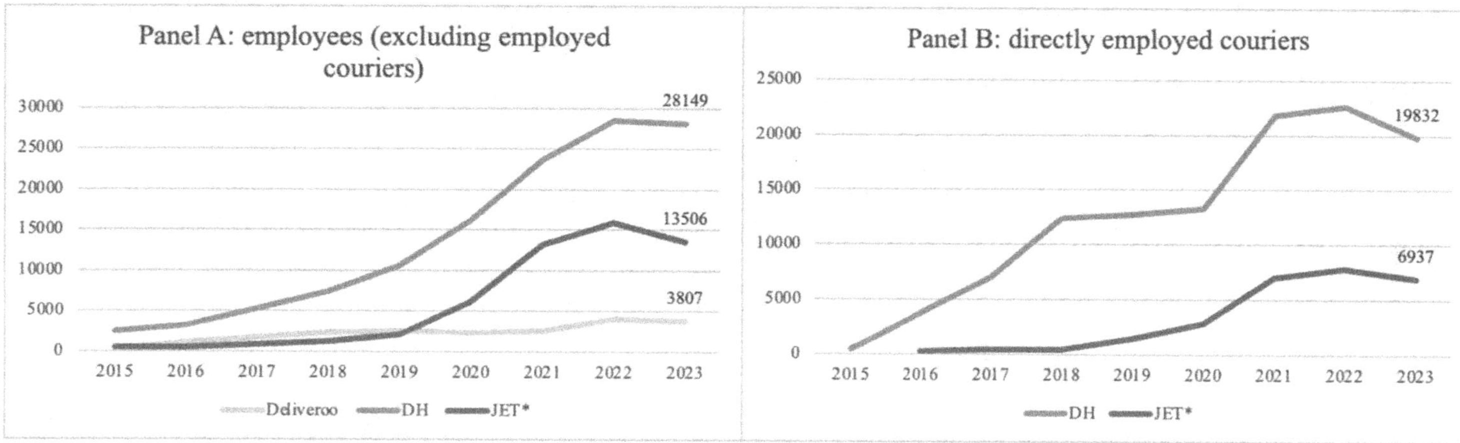

Note: *Full-time equivalents; annual averages except year-end data for JET until 2017.
Source: Company annual reports.

Figure 3.4 *Workforce in Deliveroo, Delivery Hero and Just Eat Takeaway, 2015–23*

layoffs in 2022. JET introduced a temporary 'hiring pause' that year, also sacking 170 head-office staff in Just Eat in the UK and cutting 400 jobs in Grubhub in 2023. DH claims that the 2022 scores in its employee engagement surveys were on a par with the industry benchmark but, one year later, these were not contextualised. JET saw its scores as above average in 2023, despite 'restructuring activities'.

Providing a more detailed comparative picture of the non-courier workforce is not possible as departments are defined differently. Those associated with research and development have nevertheless been growing in recent years, suggesting that 'computational data expropriation' has gained more significance (Shapiro 2023; van Doorn and Badger 2020). Deliveroo's workforce employed in 'sales, marketing and operations' has decreased over time, from 82 per cent in 2015 to 59 per cent in 2023, while the share of employees in 'technology' has risen from 10 to 28 per cent. An engineering centre in Hyderabad, India, employing about 200 technology staff, was set up in 2022, but was then closed, together with a Taiwanese hub, just one year later. Furthermore, most of the DH and JET non-courier workforce belongs to 'sales' or 'customer service/logistics' – both at 42 per cent in 2023 – while 'product development' and 'product and technology' increased their shares between 2017 and 2023 (respectively from 11 per cent to 21 per cent; and from 13 per cent to 23 per cent). DH's largest 'tech team' works at the Berlin headquarters, although it was hit by staff reductions in 2023, while tech hubs in Taiwan and Türkiye are earmarked for closure.

Developments hint at a stronger focus on process optimisation and innovation in platforms' technological architecture with the integration of artificial intelligence, especially in tailoring consumer preferences. The tech workforce's partial outsourcing offshore, alongside that of other departments, undermines workers' structural power, however, and adds to the complications in building their associational power, which thus requires a cross-border approach. Moreover, a prerequisite for confronting the platforms as employers is that tech employees self-identify as workers alongside their prevailing identity of cherishing entrepreneurial values (Rothstein 2022). Yet, coalitional power between these workers and low-paid couriers cannot be excluded: a shared migrant background, for example, might be helpful in the local context in overcoming possible differences in terms of loyalties towards the platforms, and interests and attitudes towards collective representation (Niebler 2023). Moreover, although management-controlled online systems are challenging for building associational power, they may still act as an entry point for organising the high-paid tech workforce (Vandaele and Piasna 2023).

Turning to couriers, Deliveroo does not employ them directly, although an estimate of their total number is available. That has fallen from around 180,000 (2021) to 150,000 (2022) and to 135,000 (2023) because of declining order value and the 'optimisation' of network dynamics. A very small percentage of the global courier workforce of DH and JET are genuine direct employees – see panel B in Figure 3.4. For DH, it can be calculated that employed couriers accounted for less than 1 per cent in 2023.[8] In addition, their distribution is highly concentrated: 60 per cent of JET's employed couriers are in Nordic Europe; the rest are in southern Europe. Where couriers are employed, minimum legal standards apply and collective agreements might then have to be negotiated, advancing couriers' institutional power (Geyer et al. 2023). Recent market dynamics have put more pressure on the courier employment model: both DH and JET moved to third-party models in some markets, causing a more than 10 per cent drop in employed couriers in 2023.

Deliveroo has built relationships with the GMB, an affiliate of the Trades Union Congress, in its home market of the UK since 2022, signing a voluntary partnership agreement.[9] The agreement implies that Deliveroo will consult with the union on issues including benefits, health and safety and diversity and inclusion. In turn, the GMB is able to represent and support members in resolving certain issues directly with the platform – some progress has recently been made by setting a minimum pay floor. The agreement recognises the employment status of platform couriers in the UK as 'self-employed'. The Supreme Court confirmed this status in 2023, implying that Deliveroo is not required to engage in collective bargaining, to the disappointment of the Independent Workers' Union of Great Britain, the grassroots union which brought the case. Deliveroo considers the agreement with the GMB as 'a blueprint to support positive engagement with unions in other markets'. Apart from a disputed collective agreement with the Italian corporatist Unione Generale del Lavoro (General Labour Union), signed in 2020, and having entered into social dialogue in France in 2022, Deliveroo's engagement with couriers is otherwise restricted to surveys, an in-app feedback tool and focus groups. More than four in five couriers are '(very) satisfied' according to the monthly surveys run by the platform. A critical mass of couriers looks not entirely satisfied, however: strike-banned migrant Deliveroo couriers even dared to take industrial action against pay cuts and long working hours in the United Arab Emirates in 2023.

There is, indeed, no lack of evidence of couriers' social protests across Europe and beyond (see Chapter 6), more than likely driven predominantly by those who 'are significantly more (or even completely) dependent on their gig earnings' (Schor et al. 2023: 14). How digital online communities can form breeding grounds for couriers' associational power and collective resistance is well-documented (Tassinari and Maccarrone 2020; Hau and Savage 2023; Kougiannou and Mendonça 2021). This must be offset against rather weak marketplace bargaining power, but, being attached to transportation, couriers possess some noteworthy workplace bargaining power compared to most other types of platform work (Vandaele 2021). Indeed, they hold a strategic position in the supply chain: couriers are the rope stretched between customers and the 'uber'-platforms, delivering food ordered from restaurants at the arranged time. Attempts at utilising their disruptive capacity typically tend to be local and short-lived, as well as being well-timed in high-demand hours for maximising disruption. Deliveroo's disastrous IPO has demonstrated that strikes feed into ideational power. Equally, DH, in its 2022 risk report, considered strikes to have 'negative effects' on 'delivery services and associated gross profit losses as well as [causing] reputational damage'.

Restaurants in the product market are also of interest at the operational level. They might offer courier associations opportunities for coalition-building intended to build pressure towards the enforcement of existing regulations, or for new, better versions. Differentiation can be made between types of restaurants. First, individual restaurant owners might be inclined to support protesting couriers as they could suffer from high commission charges despite benefiting from a broader customer base through the food delivery platforms (ILO 2021). Deliveroo's revenue take rate in 2023 stood at 28.7 per cent, while commission fees represent 41.2 per cent of DH's revenue (no recent public information is available for JET). Second, targeting restaurant chains seems fruitful for two reasons. They strongly guarantee network effects as platforms have often built long-standing relations with them. In addition, comprehensive campaigning can enable food delivery couriers to connect with (equally) low-paid hospitality workers in the conventional economy, as the 2018 fast-food shutdown in the UK evidenced (Cant and Woodcock 2020). Third, targeting delivery-only kitchens has a very direct impact on platforms' revenues as they go together with purchases or leases and depreciation costs. 'Editions' – dark kitchens; that is, 'restaurants' selling meals only through delivery – grew from about 200 for Deliveroo in 2019 to over 380 in 2022, but their roll-out is now decelerating.[10] They accounted for 10–15 per cent of total orders in certain zones in 2022, according to the platform.

Finally, building alliances with customers to improve couriers' working conditions seems more ambiguous. Ordering food and tipping entail 'at least passive endorsement' (Healy and Pekarek 2023: 249) of the platforms' business model, while this same model cannot avoid abusive customer behaviour (Schor et al. 2023). Furthermore, consumers who evaluate the delivery service via rating systems are contributing to feeding the algorithms that surveil the couriers. Also, importantly, platform owners or investors aim to forge alliances with their consumer base (Culpepper and Thelen 2020; Rahman and Thelen 2019). They do so as a means of influencing the political field for legitimising and securing their business model, especially its reliance on regulatory arbitrage, achieved through rhetorically invoking the flexibility of contracted couriers alongside consumer interest in low prices and convenience, and, if needed, mobilising the consumer base. This investor-consumer alliance thus questions whether consumers could ever be an ally to couriers.

Alternatively, there might be growing consumer awareness about couriers' working conditions such that consumer choices could shift, while consumer activism is possible as well (Goods et al. 2024). One way to pursue such activism is via the promotion of courier-led platform cooperatives as local alternatives (Christiaens 2024), but their charm seems limited – so far. They are predominantly active in niche product markets, while platform cooperatives especially seem to appeal only to those consumers who are morally inclined to pay more for better working conditions or who attach strong importance to environmentally friendly production or distribution (Muszyński et al. 2022; Smith et al. 2021). Stimulating consumer activism as such appears to be a more fruitful route, one example being the social media campaign #cancel_efood in Greece in 2021, proving that consumer activism can support couriers in their resistance. After the unilateral decision of efood, a food delivery platform acquired by DH in 2015, to alter couriers' contractual terms, consumers, anticipating the further flexibilisation of labour law, supported the protesting couriers, discrediting the platform and putting the blame via social media on the government (Vrikki and Lekakis 2023). Apart from reputational damage, at least equally important, consumers negatively rated or deleted the efood app so that network effects weakened, resulting in efood reverting its decision.

OUTSIDE STAKEHOLDERS: ACTION-REACTION IN THE REGULATORY FIELD

This section highlights how platforms' corporate practices affect the external stakeholders who may challenge their legitimacy, particularly regarding the regulatory/legal field in which they operate.[11]

Business model framing has been vital for food delivery platforms, enabling them to gain organisational legitimacy, especially as they are start-up companies with no history of economic performance (Howcroft and Leaver 2024; Shapiro 2023). Portraying themselves as intermediaries or tech companies has also allowed them to circumvent stricter regulations and not assume full responsibility as an employer vis-à-vis couriers. It looks increasingly difficult to hold on to such legitimacy-building narratives, however, as recent policies towards couriers are blurring independent contractor status. For instance, Deliveroo's UK couriers have been provided with accident and injury cover and third-party liability insurance since 2018, and earnings support for those couriers working regularly with the platform since 2021; they are also entitled to a one-off lump-sum payment following the birth or adoption of a child. Platforms like Deliveroo thus lean towards self-regulation, undermining states' post-1945 welfare functions.

Codes of conduct in DH and JET 'respect' the rights to freedom of association and to engage in collective bargaining. A 'fair pay initiative' since 2021 in DH should guarantee that couriers are 'compensated fairly', while the platform aims to reduce the accident rate per delivery. JET has, since that same year, launched a survey among its employed couriers for improving employment policies. All the platforms have modern slavery statements in place condemning forms of exploitation and discrimination such as forced labour, child labour and human trafficking. Media reports have revealed, however, the existence of a digital shadow market for account sharing with underage teenagers or undocumented migrants ('despite' facial recognition technology). Equally, occupational health and safety risks, including (fatal) injuries due to traffic accidents, are being widely reported (Gregory 2020). Furthermore, data protection authorities and courts across Europe have contested platforms' algorithmic management as infringing data protection rights and violating non-discrimination laws (see Chapter 14 of this volume). Above all, it is the employment status of couriers that has increasingly provoked controversy over time. The question of this status largely influences their institutional power – a power resource that can be Janus-faced. For instance, independent contractor status implies that they are mostly, but not always, stripped of individual and collective labour rights; yet this means, equally, that (strict) regulation on industrial action is not likely to apply to them.

Changes to independent contractor status are considered a principal risk by Deliveroo, about which it confesses its 'low risk appetite' (sic). The platform assures that it 'will be involved in regulatory investigations, audits, claims, court cases and appeals, as well as individual and collective legal claims in any market'. Similarly, contractors' employment status is evaluated as high risk by DH; JET also has 'minimal appetite' for 'restrictive (or changing) laws and regulations'. DH applies a 'chameleon-like' style (Ilsøe and Larsen 2023; Jesnes 2024); its subsidiaries simply adjust to the varying regulatory contexts regarding employment status. JET's CEO follows a publicly understanding tone which is supportive of the EU Platform Work Directive (Groen 2021). Yet, as mentioned before, most JET couriers are externally employed, either via third-party providers, which was reduced in 2023, or as independent contractors. Moreover, the direct employment model introduced for Just Eat UK couriers in 2020 shifted back to a self-employed contractor model three years later, with impacts on 1,700 couriers across six cities. JET had already moved to a similar model in most of France in 2022 and plans to do so in Paris during 2024 (with an impact on about 100 jobs). Protection of this regulatory arbitrage-based business model via lobbying in the political field is secured both financially and organisationally.

Financially, this requires the hoarding of reserves for legal rulings and regulatory and contractual matters. Legal provisions in 2023 amounted to £113.9 million in Deliveroo; €111 million in DH; and €78 million in JET. With some notable exceptions, such as France and the UK, platforms' 'war chests' have not been able to overcome the reclassification of couriers' employment status. Couriers are considered genuine employees in several European countries either via tailor-made legislation, as in Spain, or through court decisions as a result of litigation actions by trade unions or otherwise (Hiessl 2022). Even so, regular retightening is not always effective given the 'recoding capacity' of platforms via modifications in their algorithms or contracts (Frenken and Fuenfschilling 2020: 107).

Organisationally, platforms have established their own employer associations at European level, mainly to enhance their lobbying power, and some are members of traditional associations at national level – platforms active in Italy established AssoDelivery, their own association, in 2020 (Vandaele 2023). Deliveroo proactively 'engage[s] with regulators', especially at EU level, 'to discuss proposals or consultations' or 'to explain the importance of flexibility' for couriers. Similarly, DH is 'continuously seeking alignment with local authorities on disputed freelance rider models' and the platform adds that operations might discontinue in markets where reclassifications ensue; JET 'intends to continue to defend itself vigorously' in matters of 'alleged misclassifications of independent contractors'. The adaptation of the EU Platform Work Directive in early 2024, when it was still a draft, denotes that its transposition and implementation in member states will equally become the object of platform lobbying.

CONCLUSIONS

This explorative chapter comparatively studies selected aspects of the corporate structures of Deliveroo, DH and JET and their operational and financial performance in relation to the possible power resources of food delivery couriers. Fusing insights from strategic corporate research and the power-resources approach, it explicitly refers to platforms for what they genuinely are: companies with employer accountability and responsibilities to build relationships with courier associations or trade unions.

The analysis presents three key findings. First, food delivery in the platform economy is still a relatively young sector, and all platforms are still founder-led. They have also kept privately owned status for a relatively long time, allegedly to escape stock market pressure to become profitable (Howcroft and Leaver 2024). The platform landscape is still in flux in Europe (and beyond), moving towards consolidation in the battle for market dominance. While regional patterns of alternating duopolies in Europe more often than not prevail between Deliveroo, DH and JET and their main competitors, competition seems especially fierce in some larger markets. Overall, in terms of revenue, DH is the largest platform, followed by JET and the much smaller Deliveroo. Acquisitions or mergers characterise DH and JET, boosting geographic expansion and revenue development. Deliveroo is focused on organic business growth, but might itself be a future takeover target. Deliveroo shows relatively strong financial viability compared to DH, which looks riskier; JET is struggling with its takeover of Grubhub.

Second, regulatory arbitrage, together with the harnessing of network effects, underpins the platforms' business model, but those effects are also their Achilles' heel since they open up possibilities for couriers, especially in those markets where sustainable profitability has been achieved. This requires an industry-wide focus where two or more platforms are active in the urban context. Combining power resources and the interaction between them suggest at least three possibilities here: through leveraging structural power, courier associations and trade unions could pit platforms against each other; likewise, they could target dark kitchens and restaurant chains in campaigns as these, in all likelihood, guarantee the network effects; lastly, fostering coalitional power together with building ideational power with consumers for making threats on social media to delete delivery apps, equally targets the network effects.

Couriers' coalitional power can be developed with platforms' tech workforces, especially where the latter have emerging workplace-based institutional power. While rights derived from workplace-based institutional power at European level are in general weaker than those at lower levels, they denote, nevertheless, the importance of a multi-scalar approach to organising couriers in their location-based delivery job. These are early days, however, since those institutions at workplace level are still weakly developed or only in the making. Furthermore, platforms have not entirely abdicated their role as employers: the tech workforce inserts them in the conventional economy, but the post-pandemic era has induced them to take cost-cutting measures, including reducing their workforce. Similar to courier protests, these measures could further undermine platforms' reputations.

Third, the operational and financial picture is nuanced for each platform. The Covid-19 pandemic largely contributed to more customers and greater order value for all platforms, but the post-pandemic era shows a decline in customers and a slowdown or even decline (in the case of JET) in terms of order value, even though this remains well above pre-pandemic levels. In addition, product differentiation via q-commerce has emerged over the last couple of years. This looks relatively more developed in Deliveroo and especially DH; it is in its infancy in JET. Performance indicators show more or less positive dynamics over time, but it is still 'cold pizza' that is being delivered in terms of profitability. All three platforms continue to be loss-making: the accumulated deficits stand at about £1.8 billion for Deliveroo (2014–23), €8.6 billion for DH (2013–23) and €7.9 billion for JET (2014–23). Put differently, and putting aside the issue of regulatory arbitrage, food delivery platforms are, hitherto, viscous, financialised cash-burning juggernauts. As a corollary, 'platform companies leverage their valuations to access cheap capital, acquire competitors, access new markets, and then repeat – even if the increased market share never yields expected profits' (Shapiro 2023: 206–207). Deliveroo and JET are trying to placate shareholders with share buyback programmes or otherwise aiming to increase future earnings per share; DH has managed to extend and amend its lines of credit. Cash generation from operating activities is either negative or low, and this equally applies to profit margins, although the latter are improving over time, somehow justifying 'patient' investor relations.

Overall, therefore, the platforms studied here may remain a lingering, comatose Icarus. At the same time, however, they may yet progressively show some small signs of a Lazarus-like tendency.

NOTES

1. Restaurants could, in theory, circumvent commission via their own (online) advertising and delivery service.
2. For details, see https://strategiccorporateresearch.org
3. *Financial Times*, 31 March 2021.
4. Similarly, a possible reclassification of couriers to employee status in Portugal might result in payments ranging from €1.2 million to €9 million.
5. See www.workerheroes.com
6. The platform ended loss-making activities in Norway, Portugal and Romania in 2022.
7. Earnings before interest, taxes, depreciation and amortisation – a measure of operational efficiency.

8. The number of non-employed couriers has increased: from 700,000 in DH (2020) to over 1,400,000 (2021) and 1,700,000 (2022), to 3,000,000 (2023); the last, remarkable, rise remains unexplained. More than 800,000 DH couriers made at least one delivery in 2023. There are no data available for JET.
9. See www.gmb.org.uk/private-sector/logistics/deliveroo-hub
10. The number of Glovo dark kitchens is unknown.
11. Actions undertaken to support local communities via charity partnerships and to increase sustainability by reducing food waste, plastic waste and carbon emissions and other greenhouse gases are not reported here.

REFERENCES

Alvarez-Palau E.J. et al. (2022) Economic profitability of last-mile food delivery services: lessons from Barcelona, *Research in Transportation Business & Management*, 45 (Part A). https://doi.org/10.1016/j.rtbm.2021.100659

Ametowobla D. and Kirchner S. (2023) Varieties of platform capitalism? How competition and regimes relate to the diversity of food delivery platforms across Europe and North America, Working Paper 'Fachgebiet Digitalisierung der Arbeitswelt' 05, Technische Universität Berlin.

Arasanz Díaz J. and Sanz de Miguel P. (2023) Union strategies for the representation of platform delivery workers in Spain Journal of Labor and Society, 26 (4), 510–532.

Arnholtz J. and Refslund B. (eds.) (2024) *Workers, power and society: power resource theory in contemporary capitalism*, Routledge.

Barratt T., Goods C. and Veen A. (2020) 'I'm my own boss...': active intermediation and 'entrepreneurial' worker agency in the Australian gig-economy, *Environment and Planning A: Economy and Space*, 52 (8), 1643–1661.

Cant C. and Woodcock J. (2020) Fast food shutdown: from disorganisation to action in the service sector, *Capital & Class*, 44 (4), 513–521.

Christiaens T. (2024). Platform cooperativism and freedom as non-domination in the gig economy, *European Journal of Political Theory*. https://doi.org/10.1177/14748851241227121

Culpepper P.D. and Thelen K. (2020) Are we all Amazon primed? Consumers and the politics of platform power, *Comparative Political Studies*, 53 (2), 288–318.

Danyluk M. (2018) Capital's logistical fix: accumulation, globalization, and the survival of capitalism, *Environment and Planning D: Society and Space*, 36 (4), 630–647.

Drahokoupil J. (2021) The business model of labour platforms: creating an uncertain feature, in Drahokoupil J. and Vandaele K. (eds.) *A modern guide to labour and the platform economy*, Edward Elgar Publishing, 33–48.

Franke M. and Pulignano V. (2023) Connecting at the edge: cycles of commodification and labour control within food delivery platform work in Belgium, *New Technology, Work and Employment*, 38 (2), 371–390.

Frenken K. and Fuenfschilling L. (2020) The rise of online platforms and the triumph of the corporation, *Sociologica*, 14 (3), 101–113.

Galière S. (2020) When food delivery platform workers consent to algorithmic management: a Foucauldian perspective, *New Technology, Work and Employment*, 35 (3), 357–370.

Gandini A. (2019) Labour process theory and the gig economy, *Human Relations*, 72 (6), 1039–1056.

Geyer L., Vandaele K. and Prinz N. (2023) Riding together? Why app-mediated food delivery couriers join trade unions in Austria, *Economic and Industrial Democracy*, 45 (3). https://doi.org/10.1177/0143831X231195151

Goods C., Veen A., Barratt T. and Smith B. (2024) Power resources for disempowered workers? Re-conceptualizing the power and potential of consumers in app-based food delivery, *Industrial Relations*, 63 (2), 107–131.

Gregory K. (2020) 'My life is more valuable than this': understanding risk among on-demand food couriers in Edinburgh, *Work, Employment and Society*, 35 (2), 316–331.

Griesbach K., Reich A., Elliott-Negri L. and Milkman R. (2019) Algorithmic control in platform food delivery work, *Socius*, 5. https://doi.org/10.1177/2378023119870041

Groen J. (2021) The tide is turning for Europe's gig workers, *Financial Times*, 22 February.

Hau M.F. and Savage O.G. (2023) Building coalitions on Facebook: 'social media unionism' among Danish bike couriers, *New Technology, Work and Employment*, 38 (3), 529–547.

Healy J. and Pekarek A. (2023) Consumers in the gig economy: resisting or reinforcing precarious work?, in Ness I. (ed.) *Routledge handbook of the gig economy*, Routledge, 246–257.

Heiland H. (2022) Neither timeless, nor placeless: control of food delivery gig work via place-based working time regimes, *Human Relations*, 75 (9), 1824–1848.

Hiessl C. (2022) Case law on the classification of platform workers: cross-European comparative analysis and tentative conclusions, *Comparative Labour Law & Policy Journal*. http://dx.doi.org/10.2139/ssrn.3839603

Howcroft D. and Leaver A. (2024) Unstable platforms: Uber's business model and the challenge of organisational legitimacy, *Accounting Forum*, 1–26. https://doi.prg/10.1080/01559982.2024.2309018

ILO (2021) *World employment and social outlook: the role of digital labour platforms in transforming the world of work*, ILO.

Ilsøe A. and Larsen T.P. (2023) Why do labour platforms negotiate? Platform strategies in tax-based welfare states, *Economic and Industrial Democracy*, 44 (1), 6–24.

Jesnes K. (2024) Shifting gears: how platform companies maintain power in app-based food delivery in Norway, *Transfer*, 29 (4). https://doi.org/10.1177/10242589241228199

Joyce S., Stuart M. and Forde C. (2023) Theorising labour unrest and trade unionism in the platform economy, *New Technology, Work and Employment*, 38 (1), 21–40.

Juravich T. (2011) Beating global capital: a framework and method for union strategic corporate research and campaigns, in Bronfenbrenner K. (ed.) *Global unions: challenging transnational capital through cross-border campaigns*, Cornell University Press, 16–39.

Keller B. and Rosenbohm S. (2024) The European Company: milestone or small step towards transnational employment relations in the European Union?, *European Journal of Industrial Relations*, 30 (3). https://doi.org/10.1177/09596801241227354

Korpi W. (1983) *The democratic class struggle*, Routledge and Kegan Paul.

Kougiannou N.K. and Mendonça P. (2021) Breaking the managerial silencing of worker voice in platform capitalism: the rise of a food courier network, *British Journal of Management*, 32 (3), 744–759.

Langley P. and Leyshon A. (2017) Platform capitalism: the intermediation and capitalisation of digital economic circulation, *Finance & Society*, 3(1), 11–31.

Lévesque C. and Murray G. (2010) Understanding union power: resources and capabilities for renewing union capacity, *Transfer*, 16 (3), 333–350.

Maffie M. and Gough M.D. (2023) Bargaining against the machine: a theory of bargaining power in the gig economy, in Lewin D. and Gollan P.J. (eds.) *Advances in industrial and labor relations, 27*, Emerald Publishing, 83–99.

Muszyński K., Pulignano V. and Marà C. (2022) Product markets and working conditions on international and regional food delivery platforms: a study in Poland and Italy, *European Journal of Industrial Relations*, 28 (3), 295–316.

Niebler V. (2023) Coalitional power in the digital economy: alliances of gig and tech workers, in FES *Trajectories of platform capitalism and platform work*, Friedrich-Ebert-Stiftung, 9–13.

Rahman K.S. and Thelen K. (2019) The rise of the platform business model and the transformation of twenty-first-century capitalism, *Politics & Society*, 47 (2), 177–204.

Rhomberg C. and Lopez S. (2021) Understanding strikes in the 21st century: perspective from the United States, in Leitz L. (ed.) *Power and protest: how marginalized groups oppose the state and other institutions*, Emerald Publishing, 37–62.

Rothstein S. (2022) *Recoding power: tactics for mobilizing tech workers*, Oxford University Press.

Schor J.B., Tirrell C. and Vallas S.P. (2023) Consent and contestation. How platform workers reckon with the risks of gig labor, *Work, Employment and Society*, 38 (5). https://doi.org/10.1177/09500170231199404

Shapiro A. (2023) Platform sabotage, *Journal of Cultural Economy*, 16 (2), 203–220.

Smith B.W., Goods C., Barratt T. and Veen A. (2021) Consumer 'app-etite' for workers' rights in the Australian 'gig' economy, *Journal of Choice Modelling*, 38. https://doi.org/10.1016/j.jocm.2020.100254.

Srnicek N. (2017) *Platform capitalism*, John Wiley & Sons.

Stanford J. (2017) The resurgence of gig work: historical and theoretical perspectives, *The Economic and Labour Relations Review*, 28 (3), 382–401.

Tassinari A. and Maccarrone V. (2020) Riders on the storm: workplace solidarity among gig economy couriers in Italy and the UK, *Work, Employment and Society*, 34 (1), 35–54.

Vandaele K. (2021) Collective resistance and organizational creativity amongst Europe's platform workers: a new power in the labour movement?, in Haidar J. and Keune M. (eds.) *Work and labour relations in global platform capitalism*, Edward Elgar Publishing, 205–234.

Vandaele K. (2023) Vulnerable food delivery platforms under pressure: protesting couriers seeking 'algorithmic justice' and alternatives, in Ness I. (ed.) *Routledge handbook of the gig economy*, Routledge, 205–219.

Vandaele K. and Piasna A. (2023) Sowing the seeds of unionisation? Exploring remote work and work-based online communities in Europe during the Covid-19 pandemic, in Countouris N., De Stefano V., Piasna A. and Rainone S. (eds.) *The future of remote work*, ETUI, 103–126.

van Doorn N. and Badger A. (2020) Platform capitalism's hidden abode: producing data assets in the gig economy, *Antipode*, 52 (5), 1475–1495.

Vieira T. (2023) Platform couriers' self-exploitation: the case study of Glovo, *New Technology, Work and Employment*, 38 (3), 493–512.

Vrikki P. and Lekakis E. (2023) Digital consumers and platform workers unite and fight? The platformisation of consumer activism in the case of #cancel_efood in Greece, *Marketing Theory*, 24 (1). https://doi.org/10.1177/14705931231195191

Weil D. (2014) *The fissured workplace: why work became so bad for so many and what can be done to improve it*, Harvard University Press.

Wright E.O. (2000) Working-class power, capitalist-class interests, and class compromise, *American Journal of Sociology*, 105 (4), 957–1002.

Zwick A. (2023) Entrepreneurial finance capital and the gig economy, in Ness I. (ed.) *Routledge handbook of the gig economy*, Routledge, 46–63.

All links were checked on 12 April 2024.

4. E pluribus union(s)? Assessing the diversity of organisation among food delivery couriers across Europe

Vincenzo Maccarrone, Lorenzo Cini, Jörg Nowak and Arianna Tassinari

INTRODUCTION

Food delivery couriers have been at the forefront of labour protests within the platform economy (Vandaele 2021). This has been the case across Europe, where couriers have staged protests in almost every country, as highlighted by the Leeds Index of Platform Labour Protest (see Chapter 6 of this volume). The triggers of protests have often been similar – issues usually related to pay, working conditions, employment status or health and safety (Bessa et al. 2022) – but the organisational practices chosen by food delivery workers have been heterogeneous. Workers have not only been organising through established trade unions, they have also mobilised with grassroots and community unions, or they have chosen to self-represent through worker-led collectives. Although in Europe the role of mainstream unions has been more relevant than on other continents (Bessa et al. 2022) – arguably because of the relatively more institutionalised industrial relations framework – other labour actors and organising forms have also emerged and played a critical role.

This has been the case in countries characterised by weakened industrial relations institutions, such as in the United Kingdom, where rank-and-file unions have been the main driver of couriers' struggles until recently (Tassinari and Maccarrone 2020), as well as in countries with a stronger industrial relations framework, such as Germany. In Italy, worker self-organisation typified the first instances of couriers' mobilisations in Turin, Bologna and Milan in the autumn of 2016. Similarly, in France, couriers in Paris initially organised under the banner of Collectif Livreurs Autonomes de Paris (Borghi et al. 2021), and in Spain with the network Riders X Derechos. That said, mainstream trade unions have started to catch up and organise platform workers, including food delivery couriers (Vandaele 2021). In some countries, such as Ireland, however, food couriers remain as yet unorganised. Moreover, spontaneous worker organisation remains the dominant catalyst of labour unrest across Europe (Bessa et al. 2022).

This chapter aims to explain what lies behind the differences in workers' organisational practices within digital food delivery platforms in Europe; that is, why they opted for self-organisation or organisation through rank-and-file unions or mainstream trade unions. To do so, we compare mobilisations and organisational practices in four countries: Germany, Italy, Ireland and the UK. We chose these countries as 'vantage points' (Bieler 2021) to observe the different unfolding of couriers' organisational practices in Europe. We chose countries of which we know well the industrial relations context and of which we speak the language (Almond and Connolly 2020). For Ireland, Italy and the UK, we rely on information on food delivery workers' organising collected through different fieldwork periods conducted by two of the authors between 2016 and 2017, and then by one author between 2022 and 2023. For Germany, we rely on a systematic review of the burgeoning literature on food delivery and labour organising, as well as on media reports. We also conducted expert interviews throughout 2023 to update and validate our knowledge of the cases.

The variation observed among cases helps us in the task of explaining the diverse organisational practices chosen by food delivery workers. Germany and Italy still have relatively organised industrial relations institutions compared to other member states of the European Union – notwithstanding their ongoing neoliberalisation (Baccaro and Howell 2017) – while Ireland and the UK have a rather disorganised industrial relations system with few binding commitments. The countries have also seen different patterns of workers' organising in food delivery platforms. Germany has seen the intervention of the anarcho-syndicalist rank-and-file union Freie ArbeiterInnen Union (FAU; Free Workers Union), especially in the first years of protest, and increasing attempts at organising by Gewerkschaft Nahrung-Genuss-Gaststätten (NGG; Trade Union for Food, Entertainment and Restaurants), an affiliate of Deutscher Gewerkschaftsbund (DGB; German Trade Union Confederation) (Neumann 2023). Ireland has seen sporadic spontaneous labour protests, and workers have remained essentially unorganised. In Italy, the first wave of protest in the autumn of 2016 was driven by worker-led collectives. Subsequently, both mainstream and rank-and-file unions have intervened in the sector. In the UK, rank-and-file unions led attempts at organising until recently. In 2022, however, the general union GMB signed a recognition agreement with Deliveroo.

We argue that these trends in couriers' organisational practices can be explained by looking at agential aspects – labour actors' capabilities – and contextual features – institutional aspects of national industrial relations frameworks favouring or obstructing labour organising, and the presence or absence of supportive communities in which workers are embedded.

ANALYTICAL FRAMEWORK

The labour process is remarkably similar across the food delivery platforms that operate within the four cases and is characterised by the decentralisation of the point of production (Gandini 2019) and by the individualisation of work relations. Platforms are able to maintain a high degree of control over their workforce due to algorithmic management practices and gamification techniques (Gandini 2019). That said, the structured antagonism between capital and labour, and the ensuing contradictions within the platform labour process, can be a powerful spark for collective action (Tassinari and Maccarrone 2020). We take these similarities as given and focus on factors external to the labour process to make sense of the different patterns of organising. Notably, we identify two main sets of factors which can explain such patterns: agential and contextual aspects.

As *agential* aspects, we highlight labour actors' capabilities; that is, the 'sets of aptitudes, competencies, abilities, social skills or know-how that can be developed, transmitted and learned' (Lévesque and Murray 2010: 336) and which allow these actors to exercise power and act effectively in specific contexts. Capabilities allow labour actors to interpret the specificities of platform work and deploy strategies of organising suitable to the context of different labour platforms; understand the specific characteristics – in composition, vulnerabilities and attitudes – of the workforce and deploy demands and strategies reflective of, or responsive to, them; and build relationships of trust and confidence with the constituencies of platform workers. For instance, one capability identified by Cini et al. (2022) is the prior expertise of labour actors in organising precarious workers in similar contexts to that of the platform economy, either in terms of location (such as urban service work) or in terms of workforce composition (such as sectors with a high presence of migrant workers).

Moreover, the role played by the organisational culture of labour organisations may matter. For instance, grassroots unions usually operate primarily on the basis of a logic of membership rather than a logic of influence (see Vandaele 2021). The 'logic of membership' implies, among other things, emphasis on workers' direct participation and democratic control. This emphasis might make grassroots unions more responsive to platform workers' specific attitudes. At the same time, it is possible that mainstream labour actors use other capabilities over time, such as learning (Lévesque and Murray 2010), and adapt their tactics of action in the platform economy.

Contextual aspects mediate the capabilities necessary to intervene effectively in the platform economy. We highlight the role of two very diverse but equally influential contextual factors: one more institutional, the other more informal. Notably, we conceive of the former as the key specific features of the national industrial relations context in which mobilisations take place (Jesnes et al. 2021; Marà et al. 2023), and the latter as the various social communities of support into which couriers are embedded (Cini et al. 2022; Atzeni and Cini 2023).

In terms of the institutional aspects, in those contexts where platform workers enjoy or come to obtain classification as employees, or obtain access to and coverage from institutionalised channels of workers' voice, such as works councils, mainstream unions might be equally, if not better, equipped to intervene effectively in organising gig workers by taking advantage of established institutions (see Vandaele 2021; Schmalz et al. 2023). Conversely, where low institutional resources are available to workers and unions, workers are more likely to resort to alternative repertoires of action like short, spontaneous outbursts of protests and wildcat strikes (Cini and Tassinari 2022; Schmalz et al. 2023).

The second, less formal, contextual aspect we identify as relevant is the presence of groups and communities (Nowak 2019, 2021; Atzeni and Cini 2023) in which couriers are embedded and/or from which they are able to draw some help of various kinds. These communities are primarily understood here as the social contacts that workers exploit in their mobilisation efforts. Atzeni and Cini call them 'supportive communities', which they define as (2023: 7–8):

> a web of social relations supportive of worker mobilisations, travelling across either time or space: the persistence and the mutualistic support of movement infrastructural networks in a worker's locality are a case in point of the former, whereas the logistical and emotional backing that a migrant workforce receives from its ethnic community is an emblematic case of the latter.

In our view, the relevance of such communities for couriers' mobilisations may depend on the level of institutionalisation of the industrial relations system in which their working settings are located. In the absence or marginal presence of interventions by established actors and rules, the influence of various communities of support may be amplified by playing a crucial role in the mobilisation.

GERMANY: FROM GRASSROOTS TO MAINSTREAM TRADE UNIONISM

The German industrial relations system is characterised by two features. First is a high degree of institutionalisation of trade unions and their forms of representation, reflected in the legal provisions, namely the Betriebsverfassungsgesetz, that regulate the rights of workers at the company level and enable them to install works councils independently of the stance of employers. These statutory rights also come with a certain independence of company-based representation with respect to unions, allowing works councils to take either more confrontational or more moderate positions than unions. Second, there is a large low-wage sector and a coverage of collective bargaining agreements that is higher than in the UK and Ireland but much lower than in Italy. For this reason, industrial relations experts see Germany as a country with a high degree of legal institutionalisation that has been hollowed out from within (Baccaro and Benassi 2017).

A difference from other countries in our sample, however, is that food delivery couriers are more likely to be hired as employees than as self-employed. Three factors have been identified in explaining this exceptional situation, namely: a stable and competitive labour market, forcing platforms to remain attractive to employees; the business model of market leader Lieferando, which includes employing workers as regular employees; and criticism of platforms in the media (ETUC 2023).

The food delivery sector in Germany has seen two different phases, dominated first by competition and then by mergers and acquisitions among the main platform companies. In the first phase, Foodora and Deliveroo competed for market dominance. This phase ended with the acquisition of Foodora by Lieferando and the subsequent withdrawal of Deliveroo from the German market. After a short phase in which Lieferando was the only major operator, new companies have entered the scene since 2020, some acting in subsegments of the market, like the delivery of groceries or beverages, although there is a tendency among the major players to diversify into all subsegments.

Lieferando has, since 2017, seen a slow but steady growth of works councils, at present numbering 14. At the end of 2022, the DGB-affiliated union NGG organised rallies and protests at Lieferando, and in April 2023, it staged the first strike at the company, which, at present, has about 7,000 employees (Ewen 2023: 290). The launching of strikes in various cities was the first national action of workers at a delivery company encompassing several workplaces in one campaign. Gorillas, active in the market for delivering non-cooked food and groceries, saw intense mobilisation and wildcat strikes in 2021. The protests at Gorillas were directed against dismissals and payment arrears and for better equipment, seen as crucial to avoid accidents. At the end of November 2021, the first works council at Gorillas was installed in Berlin after the company failed in court to impede its formation. Gorillas was, however, subsequently taken over by competitor Getir. Getir and Flaschenpost – the latter focused on drinks delivery – have faced frequent conflicts about the installation of works councils, while new market entrant Wolt, active in food delivery, encountered protests by workers who had not been paid for months by the subcontractor.

The first instances of worker organisation in the German food delivery industry were dominated by local worker collectives at workplace level, which then made contact with NGG, the other DGB-affiliated service union Ver.di, or the small anarchist union FAU. In some cases, there was cooperation between worker collectives across workplaces in different cities or joint mobilisations of workers from different companies in the same city. The larger organising body was, at the beginning, predominantly FAU. Over time, it has increasingly been NGG. NGG is a rather small union within the DGB, often taking more grassroots-based approaches and with a mostly low-wage constituency working mainly in hotels and restaurants but also in food production and breweries, for example.

The Leeds Index counts that, in 62 per cent of all cases of labour protest held between 2017 and 2022, NGG or other established unions were involved, while in 43 per cent, it was worker collectives, and in 30 per cent, grassroots unions (Neumann 2023).[1] In general, in the first wave of mobilisation, there was a tendency towards FAU organising couriers in eastern Germany and a representation by NGG in the west, where the presence of FAU is much weaker. In some cases, worker collectives cooperated with both NGG and FAU, as in Cologne.

One main aim of couriers' mobilisations has been the establishment of works councils, as these allow workers to intervene in various ways in the actions of management – for example launching requests for information, establishing routines of consultation or raising demands without being persecuted. Office holders in works councils are protected by law from dismissal and can use part of their working time for engagement with workers. Timid success in installing works councils in Foodora has been followed by the establishment of 14 works councils in Lieferando over the past few years.

This strategy follows the general orientation of NGG: first, install enough work councils, and then use these as a basis to launch further demands. The second part of this strategy began in April 2023 with strikes at Lieferando. Hence, the long-term strategy does seem to be paying off, facilitated by the market dominance of one company. If NGG is successful in organising further strikes here, this could consolidate its position. Lieferando is used by 79 per cent of all customers in food delivery in Germany, followed by Domino's Pizza with 23 per cent. Competitors to Lieferando have hitherto taken a rather small market share. The grassroots union FAU is increasingly focusing on smaller companies, which are often based in particular cities, or on companies operating in similar areas, like courier company EcoCarrier that does not supply food. Thus, the dominance of FAU in mobilising food delivery workers seen between 2016 and 2019 has given way to NGG as a more established actor.

IRELAND: SPORADIC AND REACTIVE MOBILISATIONS ON STREET SAFETY

Ireland is one of the two cases we deal with in this chapter, along with the UK, whose industrial relations system is based on the voluntary model (Maccarrone et al. 2019). In principle, this means that the state tends not to intervene directly in matters of industrial relations but lets parties organise themselves, while the government may play a background role where mediation is required. Collective bargaining takes place primarily at the firm level, with the exception of a few low-paid industries in which minimum-wage-setting mechanisms are in place but do not include food delivery couriers, who are primarily classified as self-employed.

In Ireland, food delivery couriers' mobilisations have been sporadic, and workers have remained as yet unorganised either by mainstream or rank-and-file unions, the latter playing a very minor role in Ireland overall (Maccarrone and Erne 2023). In their episodic instances of collective action, couriers – mostly migrants from South America or south-east Asia – have been able to build only provisional, informal and loose, self-organised networks. In doing so, they have relied on ties with couriers of the same country of origin . In the absence of an established organisational infrastructure, the online chats of various social networks, such as WhatsApp, Telegram and Messenger, have played a key role in the communication and organisation of discontent among couriers. At the same time, the adoption of these networks has contributed to – and reinforced – organisation along nationality by creating a segmentation of mobilisation potential.

The few cases of mobilisation have all been self-organised, short-term and mostly reactive, triggered either by a change in pay, such as the reduction in pay per delivery in Deliveroo, or issues of health and safety, such as the episodes of xenophobic attacks and street accidents in which some couriers have been involved.

To date, only three episodes of protest have been organised in Dublin on the issues of pay and working conditions. The first protest was held in February 2019 when about 50 Deliveroo couriers, mostly Brazilians, organised through WhatsApp to challenge unpaid waiting times and the distance travelled for deliveries. The second event was in January 2021 when several groups of Deliveroo couriers organised a two-hour strike to challenge the drop in per-delivery pay that the company had unilaterally decided to implement. Unlike the 2019 protest, food delivery couriers this time also sought to exert some forms of 'societal power' (Schmalz et al. 2018): they gained support from some restaurants, which stopped using the Deliveroo app during the strike, while workers also carried out a campaign on social media to ensure that customers realised the importance of their work. On the 14th of February 2024, food couriers in Ireland joined an international strike on Valentine's Day along with colleagues in the UK and the US, to protest over low rates of pay. To date, these protests remain the only cases of mobilisation in Ireland in which couriers addressed a platform company as a protest target, and no positive outcome was achieved.

The most compelling issue in the episodes of courier mobilisation has to do with the problem of safety on the streets. Indeed, food delivery workers in various areas of Dublin have, since 2018, been a constant target of street violence and xenophobic attacks from gangs of youths (Redmond 2021). This violence worsened during the Covid-19 pandemic and periods of lockdown. The situation created various tensions in the community between locals and migrant workers, leading to the manifestation of some collective reactions from the couriers' side.

The major episode of mobilisation among couriers in Dublin took place in early September 2020 to draw attention to the safety situation on the streets, especially in certain areas of the city. This followed the death of a Brazilian courier, 28-year-old Thiago Cortes, who was killed at the end of August in a never-clarified traffic incident in Dublin's East Wall area while working for Deliveroo. In response, a demonstration, joined by about 2000 people, mostly Brazilian, was organised by the couriers as a tribute to their colleague as well as a demand for better security on the streets.

The only Irish organisations participating in and contributing to the event were a few pro-migrant associations and the English Language Students' Union of Ireland (ELSU).[2] Specifically, ELSU, the union for foreign students in Ireland, has been one of the few Irish pro-labour organisations since the arrival of the pandemic to provide considerable support to couriers in carrying out their campaign on street safety. ELSU has assisted workers in reaching out to and meeting with various Irish government officials and members of An Garda Siochána (the Irish police force), as well as politicians from opposition parties.

Until the death of Thiago Cortes, no Irish trade union considered the representation of couriers as an issue falling within its remit. In most unions' view, couriers are foreign students and not migrant workers. Such a widespread (mis)conception of platform workers' conditions is the main cause of unions' lack of intervention. By and large, relations between the food delivery migrant workforce and the established actors in the Irish industrial relations system have been sporadic and filled with mutual incomprehension (Doherty and Franca 2020), most of them occurring only when prompted by external events. This highlights the absence so far of any specific plan or strategic intervention in app-based food delivery by the unions. Since the entry of food delivery platforms to the Irish market, there has been only one national meeting between government officials and delivery riders, in March 2021, that also involved representatives of the Services Industrial Professional and Technical Union, ELSU, and other associations working on migrant rights. At the time of writing (Autumn 2024), there is no process of institutionalisation of the industrial relations system in relation to the platform economy. It remains to be seen whether the implementation of the Platform work directive will bring any improvement in that respect.

ITALY: FROM SELF-ORGANISATION TO A MIXED FORM OF INSTITUTIONALISATION

Alongside the UK, Italy was a forerunner of the mobilisation of food delivery couriers in Europe. The life-course of these mobilisations in the Italian context can be divided into two phases, reflecting an evolution in terms of workers' organisational forms and their degree of institutionalisation. A first phase, proceeding roughly from 2016 until 2019, can be described as a period of emergence and experimentation, typified primarily by the grassroots self-organisation of couriers through autonomous worker collectives. A second phase, starting from 2019, can in turn be looked at as a period of partial formalisation of couriers' organising dynamics, with more traditional institutional channels of industrial relations and mainstream trade unions acquiring greater relevance, alongside grassroots unionism, in structuring labour conflict and the regulation of work in the sector (see Marà et al. 2023 for a similar periodisation).

To understand these trends, couriers' organisational forms must be contextualised within Italian industrial relations. Italy presents, compared to other European countries, a fairly resilient, institutionalised system of industrial relations, marked by a predominance of industrial collective bargaining that maintains high levels of coverage, with three large union confederations of historically distinct ideological traditions acting as the main representative actors on the side of labour, both as signatories of industrial collective bargaining agreements and as interlocutors of the government on matters of labour law and social policy. Those confederations are Confederazione Generale Italiana del Lavoro (CGIL; Italian General Confederation of Labour), Confederazione Italiana Sindacati Lavoratori (CISL; Italian Confederation of Workers' Unions) and Unione Italiana del Lavoro (UIL; Italian Labour Union).

The regulatory and representative efficacy of unions affiliated with the main confederations, as well as that of the country's collective bargaining institutions, have increasingly been called into question over the last two decades. The rapid growth of atypical, low-paid work fostered by neoliberal labour market reforms since the late 1990s, pressures for collective bargaining decentralisation and unions' difficulties in resisting and adapting to an increasingly hostile political context and employers' liberalisation offensives have all reduced the regulatory reach and value of collective bargaining agreements as well as the representativeness of union confederations among 'outsider' segments of the workforce, such as young, migrant and precarious workers (Politi et al. 2021). At the same time, over the last decades, there has been a growth of independent, small rank-and-file unions like Unione Sindacale di Base (USB; a grassroots trade union) and Sindacato Intercategoriale Cobas (SI-Cobas; Inter-sectoral Self-organised Workers' Union) in industries such as logistics, which call into question mainstream unions' bargaining strategies and agendas.

This context has had its impact on the mobilisation dynamics of food delivery couriers in Italy. Once food delivery platforms arrived, they tended to hire workers on a self-employed basis, so, without access to collective bargaining rights. In the original phase of mobilisation, from autumn 2016, couriers of platforms such as Foodora, Deliveroo and Glovo started a process of autonomous organising through worker collectives (Marrone and Finotto 2019). These started operating in Turin (Deliverance Project), then also in Milan (Deliverance Milano) and Bologna (Riders' Union Bologna), the main northern cities where platforms had first established. The initial protests and strike episodes over 2016–18 focused on contesting the application of piecework payment systems, the arbitrariness of the algorithmic system of performance tracking and delivery assignment, the lack of adequate health and safety protection, and workers' misclassification as self-employed. These self-organised mobilisations attracted widespread media attention, thrusting the couriers' protests into the limelight in Italian political debate (Quondamatteo 2021). In this phase, the collectives attached great importance to their practices of self-organisation and independence from mainstream unions, which they considered an important marker of their strategic autonomy (Cini et al. 2023) and in their recognition as autonomous political subjects (Quondamatteo and Marrone 2023). Such a sceptical attitude towards mainstream unions, which, in this first phase, remained almost completely absent from couriers' mobilisations, was influenced in large part by the ideological and militant background of many key courier-activists who had prior experience of grassroots social movements, including precarious worker movements, and valued the conflictual tactics that their independence allowed them to adopt (Cini et al. 2023).

This first phase of mobilisation resulted in important outputs, including a landmark legal case against the classification of couriers as 'self-employed' in Turin – as well as some concessions on health and safety – promoted by some former Foodora riders and supported by the local worker collective. Local attempts at regulation of platforms' operating practices – such as the Riders' Charter of Fundamental Rights at Work in the Digital Context, signed in Bologna in 2018 by the local courier collectives, city-based officials of the three main union confederations and two local delivery platforms, and setting some minimum protections for couriers (Martelloni 2018); followed, most significantly, by an attempted regulatory intervention in platform work by the national government – marked the passage from a phase of 'emergent' mobilisations in the sector to one of more 'institutionalised' conflict dynamics.

Indeed, as the catch-all Five Star Movement ascended to government in 2018, originally in coalition with right-wing Lega and then, from 2019, with the centre-left Partito Democratico, the labour ministers affiliated with the party (first Di Maio in 2018–19, then Catalfo over 2019–21) repeatedly encouraged formalised bargaining between the courier collectives, food delivery platforms and union confederations to delineate a regulatory agenda for the sector. This eventually resulted (Carella and Marenco 2022) in Law 128/2019 in November 2019. The courier collectives participated at the negotiating table with the ministry as an autonomous collective subject, but the three main confederations at the national level were also included in the process, thus de facto gaining a significant role in the process of regulation of the sector despite having been only marginally involved in any grassroots mobilisations up to then.

The 2019 law established that, in the absence of a collective agreement signed by the most representative social partners, couriers would be subject to the provisions regulating wages established in the national sectoral agreement in comparable sectors. At this point, the process took a contorted turn: in testimony to the contemporary fragmentation of collective bargaining dynamics in the Italian industrial relations landscape, a disadvantageous collective agreement was signed in September 2020 by the food delivery employers' association Assodelivery and the right-wing union Unione Generale del Lavoro (UGL; General Labour Union) that had no relevant representativeness among the couriers. The agreement re-introduced self-employed working status for couriers and a pay-per-delivery system. It was resolutely contested by the courier collectives and by the other union confederations, which decided to form a coalition creating the nationwide organisational network Riders per i diritti (RxD; Couriers for Rights). The coalition's actors became actively involved in the process of negotiating an alternative, firm-level collective agreement with the platform Just Eat Takeaway, which had left Assodelivery, stating its intention to apply more protective labour standards. In early 2021, the parties agreed on the 'Just Eat contract', which identifies subordinate open-ended employment as the main hiring practice, although it gives the platform the possibility of using more precarious contracts within the limits established by the collective agreement, and extends to employees the provisions of national collective agreements in logistics. Overall, this is a more advantageous outcome than other options (Quondamatteo 2021). For the company, flexibility is granted by the use of part-time labour, which the contract identifies as the most common form of work.

In this process of collective bargaining, the courier collectives that had animated the first phase of mobilisation – and which were by then incorporated in the network of RxD, in which, after some months, CGIL more openly took the lead – played a relatively marginal role, as the institutionalisation of the regulatory process initiated by the government called more directly on the union confederations in their 'official' representative capacity. At this stage, the unions themselves – CGIL and UIL in particular – also engaged in a process of catching up and learning. They started to take a more active interest in organising couriers on the ground, setting up organising campaigns and courier union branches in a number of smaller cities and towns all over Italy where self-organised collectives had not been set up, taking advantage of the intervention space opened by the new Just Eat agreement. Interestingly, the dynamic between the informal courier collectives and the established unions has remained one of complementarity rather than possessing a conflictual nature: the self-organised courier collectives and the courier union branches affiliated with the union confederations established the RxD to contest the UGL-Assodelivery agreement and to support the process of negotiating the Just Eat agreement. In addition, grassroots unions such as USB and SI-COBAS, which, over the last few years, have been highly active in organising workers in the peri-urban logistics sector, have also started to organise food couriers in various Italian cities. Hence, different organisational forms of couriers co-exist in the Italian landscape, featuring a mixed form of institutionalisation.

UK: WAVES OF MOBILISATION AIDED BY RANK-AND-FILE UNIONS

After the Thatcher-driven neoliberalisation of industrial relations, British collective bargaining and employment protection legislation have offered little support to trade union action (Waddington 2019). Among the four countries that we analyse, the UK has the lowest collective bargaining coverage and union density. Multi-employer bargaining in the private sector is basically non-existent (Waddington 2019) and negotiations over pay and working conditions are often individualised. Moreover, food delivery couriers tend to be legally excluded from the basic rights still available to employees and 'workers',[3] such as the minimum wage and sickness and holiday pay, as platform companies hire them as self-employed.

To our knowledge, the UK was the first European county where food delivery couriers collectively mobilised. The earliest manifestations took place in London in the summer of 2016 and were organised by Deliveroo food couriers who mobilised against the company's announced policy change from an hourly wage to a piece-rate payment system. In August 2016, around 150 moped riders gathered outside Deliveroo's head office in London demanding the restoration of the hourly wage and were soon joined by many of their cyclist colleagues. The couriers were mostly of Brazilian origin, and community ties played a role in the organisation of the strike. The gathering turned into the first strike of Deliveroo workers in the UK, which continued for six days (Woodcock and Cant 2022; Chapter 5 of this volume).

Whereas this first episode was self-organised, the Independent Workers Union of Great Britain (IWGB), a rank-and-file independent union, intervened to support Deliveroo workers during the protests and then started a longer-term campaign of unionisation. In doing so, the IWGB benefitted from the previous experience it had gathered in organising bicycle couriers through its Couriers and Logistics Branch (Cini et al. 2022; Woodcock and Cant 2022). As Woodcock and Cant (2022: 226) note: 'A layer of workers from the strike were recruited into the CLB [Couriers and Logistics Branch], becoming active union members and continuing to organize after the strike.'

After the summer of 2016, the mobilisation extended to other platforms, such as Uber Eats and Just Eat, and other cities across the UK, including Leeds and Brighton. Other waves of strikes took place in the spring and winter of 2017. Couriers were supported in these protests by either the IWGB or another rank-and-file union, the Industrial Workers of the World (IWW). Neither the IWGB nor the IWW is affiliated with the Trades Union Congress (TUC) and are among the small 'indie' unions (Però 2019) that emerged in London in the mid-2010s to organise low-paid migrant workers (Weghmann 2022). Differently from the IWGB, however, the IWW did not launch a campaign of unionisation, but established a Couriers Network for couriers from various cities. This was, in the words of an IWW organiser, a 'loose structure that could unite couriers as workers without them having to formally join the IWW and pay union dues', although lead organisers were encouraged to join the union (Davies 2022).

Outbursts of mobilisation and attempts at union organising have continued ever since, with uneven success. The IWW Couriers Network appears to have been dormant since 2020 (Davies 2022), but the IWGB's organising drive has proven more resilient despite the challenges posed by high workforce turnover and platforms' counter strategies (Tassinari and Maccarrone 2020). The IWGB's strategy has included a mix of collective action and legal challenges, such as those pursued against Deliveroo on workers' employment status and the right to collective bargaining. To date, however, these challenges have been unsuccessful, and the courts have ruled that Deliveroo's couriers are self-employed. The IWGB has sought new points of leverage, such as contacting potential institutional investors in advance of Deliveroo's initial public offering (IPO) in 2021 and organising a strike on the day of the IPO itself (Woodcock and Cant 2022). The strategy of the union has further involved broadening the target of contention to restaurants and local administrations on issues such as waiting times and safe and adequate parking spaces (Woodcock and Cant 2022).

In recent years, mainstream unions, have also attempted to organise food delivery couriers, most notably the GMB, a general trade union affiliated with the TUC,. In the food delivery sector, the GMB has followed the approach adopted in the platform economy more broadly, trying to reach recognition agreements with some platforms. This happened with Hermes (parcel delivery) in 2019 and Uber (ride hailing) in 2021.[4] In May 2022, the GMB and Deliveroo signed a recognition agreement which maintains Deliveroo workers' self-employed status while providing a platform for collective bargaining on pay and for consultation rights on benefits and on health, safety and well-being (Deliveroo-GMB Voluntary Partnership Agreement 2022). The union will also be able to represent members in individual dispute cases, such as in the unilateral termination of accounts by the platform. This might help raise GMB membership numbers. Deliveroo has committed to paying couriers the national living wage, but only while they are delivering an order, thus excluding the time spent looking for and waiting for an order. Maintaining self-employment status also means that couriers will not be entitled to statutory sick pay and holiday leave. In turn, the IWGB has criticised the agreement, not least because it undermines its own current legal challenge against Deliveroo on collective bargaining rights (McGurdy 2022).

Despite these recent developments in Deliveroo, the picture for food delivery courier organising in the UK is thus, so far, one of limited institutionalisation. Most companies hire couriers as self-employed and do not recognise trade unions. Nevertheless, as reported by the Leeds Index of Platform Labour Protest, food delivery couriers in the UK continue to be rather strike-prone. While over the last few years the IWGB has led many of these strikes, instances of initial mobilisation continue frequently to be the result of self-organisation by loose networks of workers (Joyce and Stuart 2021). This was the case also with the strike held on Valentine's day 2024.

DISCUSSION AND ANALYSIS: ASSESSING THE DIVERSITY OF COURIERS' ORGANISATIONAL PRACTICES

Across all cases, the first wave of mobilisation in the food delivery sector was characterised by a high degree of spontaneous labour organising, and the role of mainstream trade unions remained marginal, if not altogether absent. In this phase, mainstream unions seemed unable to interpret the specificities of platform work and adapt their strategies accordingly, while the contextual absence of any form of regulation of the sector also acted as an obstacle to action.

In two of the four countries (the UK and Germany), however, rank-and-file unions outside the main union confederations were able to intervene relatively early to support and organise workers' struggles. Having experience of operating outside, or on the margins of, the institutional channels of industrial relations, these actors are generally more willing than established unions to employ disruptive, conflictual and innovative tactics of contention – such as wildcat strikes, public-facing creative campaigns and public protests – and are more experienced at doing so. This derives from their specific logic of action, ideological orientation and organisational practices that allow for easier experimentation with diverse action repertoires. These features may have made such actors more capable of intervening in the first phase of mobilisation within food delivery, a sector marked by low institutionalisation and a lack of established channels of voice (see Joyce et al. 2023).

Rank-and-file unions and their capabilities are relevant in explaining the developments in both the UK and Germany, where the first period of mobilisations was symbolised by an active role for these actors, with their relatively conflictual orientations towards platforms and their radical action repertoires. In other words, and considering our agential factor, this first wave was substantially informed by bottom-up organisational experience: the prominent set of political skills and capabilities supporting couriers' organisational practices was built in the universe of independent and rank-and-file unions. In both countries, such unions could draw on their capabilities derived from prior expertise in organising precarious workers in contexts similar to the platform economy, in terms of location or workforce composition, or both. The capabilities of the IWGB in the UK were acquired in the pre-platform economy urban logistics sector, as well as in organising outsourced migrant cleaners in British universities (Però 2019); in 2014–15, FAU in Germany organised migrant workers, mostly from Romania and Bulgaria, in the construction industry in a dispute around the non-payment of wages for the construction of a shopping mall in Berlin.

In Italy and Ireland, however, in the first phase of mobilisation, neither the established trade unions nor the grassroots unions managed to organise the couriers. In Italy, despite the presence of grassroots unions organising in the peri-urban logistics sector, workers opted for self-organisation, creating their own collectives in various Italian cities. Here, specific communities of support – the second contextual factor we identified – played a major role. Indeed, couriers in Italy relied on the key support of political activists and social movements present in the urban context in which these experiences of self-organisation emerged and developed. As the scholarly literature has widely highlighted (Cini et al. 2022; Politi et al. 2021), the support of the 'social movement infrastructure' for organisational practices among precarious workers is not a new phenomenon in Italy. Here, the intervention of movement activists in labour mobilisations dates back to the early 2000s when various groups of political activists helped to organise precarious workers within different sectors and workplaces (Borghi et al. 2021). In turn, the accumulation of these experiences and expertise in activism over time has favoured the proliferation of new labour actors – be they grassroots unions or worker collectives operating in various Italian cities – whose presence constituted the organisational backbone for the recent mobilisations of food delivery couriers (Cini et al. 2022). This 'militant urban space' (Cini and Goldmann 2021: 959) played a decisive role in the Italian case, at least in the first years. Such a space was absent in the case of the UK where, instead, other communities of support played a role; namely, workers' communities along national background. Such a community, providing the affective and organisational backing of fellow migrants, friends and families – a 'community of struggle' (Però 2019) – was particularly relevant in the first episodes of couriers' collective actions.

Unlike the UK, in Ireland, no grassroots union took the lead in organising food delivery couriers in the sporadic mobilisations that have taken place, nor did mainstream unions manage to intervene effectively. Here, the most relevant element accounting for workers' mobilisations has been the support of specific communities, primarily substantiated in the national ties of a mostly Brazilian workforce. Yet, if this factor has favoured the emergence of solidarity and collective action, it has also contributed to further segmenting the mobilisation potential of these workers along country lines. It is not by accident that, thus far, the only organisations taking part in courier mobilisations have been pro-migrant associations.

Albeit heterogeneously across our cases, we have seen the consolidation of food couriers' mobilisation and organising, with mainstream unions coming to play a relatively larger role. In Italy and Germany, they have undergone a process of learning (Lévesque and Murray 2010), adapting and updating their strategies and accordingly managing to start recruiting and organising food delivery couriers. More recently, mainstream unions have started to play a bigger role in this sector in the UK, while, in Ireland, couriers remain – as yet – unorganised.

These interventions by established trade unions did not happen in a vacuum but were built on previous capabilities gained in organising precarious workers. For instance, in Italy, one of the most active CGIL federations organising platform workers is Nuove Identità di Lavoro (NIdiL; New Work Identities), which was established in 1998 with the aim of promoting the rights of atypical workers such as self-employed, parasubordinate[5] and temporary workers (Pulignano et al. 2016). These contractual forms are the most common within food delivery. Within the UIL, food couriers are organised by Turismo Commercio Servizi (UILTuCS; Tourism Commerce and Service), particularly within the umbrella of the initiative Sindacato-Networkers, founded in 2011 to offer union consulting services to ICT workers. In Germany, food couriers are supported by Ver.di but more especially by NGG. The latter often takes more grassroots-based approaches and its rather low-wage constituency means that it is familiar with the reality of workforces on low wages, under adverse conditions and in sectors with a large number of workers with a migrant background. Thus, NGG has the necessary prerequisites to organise platform workers who share many characteristics with the existing NGG membership.

Beyond these actors' capabilities, however, contextual factors are important in explaining the faster catching-up process by mainstream trade unions that we observed in Germany and Italy, in comparison to Ireland and the UK. Here, the legal provisions, in particular the protections offered to collective bargaining rights, are of central relevance. In both Germany and Italy, mainstream unions could leverage some resilient institutional power resources within their respective industrial relations systems. In the Italian case, regulatory initiatives led first by local institutions (such as the Charter of Rights signed in Bologna), and then at national level (including Law 128/2019), provided an opening for the three main union confederations which were called to the negotiating table due to the central role they still play within social dialogue (Marà et al. 2023). In turn, the three confederations signing a firm-level collective agreement with Just Eat Takeaway – extending to most couriers the provisions of the logistics industry as a whole – has offered unions more space for intervention and has fostered organising among couriers, albeit with some obstacles due to high turnover and the predominance of part-time labour. In Germany, the legal protection offered to the institution of works councils at company level could be used by unions as a basis for further mobilisation where they are able to maintain links to activists in the councils. In food delivery, DGB affiliates have followed a strategy already employed in other sectors, based on the installation of a sufficient number of works councils, then using these as a basis to launch further demands. While this strategy proved difficult at Foodora, it has been quite successful in Lieferando, although it still encounters significant legal resistance from the food delivery platform, which often delays the implementation of works councils.

In Ireland and the UK, these institutional features are absent. There have been no significant legislative initiatives at national level to regulate food delivery or platform labour more generally, while social dialogue institutions are, overall, weak in both countries (although slightly stronger in Ireland). In both countries, there is no sectoral collective bargaining[6] and firm-level channels of worker voice are weak. Arguably, these features offer fewer avenues for intervention by mainstream trade unions. It remains to be seen whether attempts at organising by the GMB in the UK will be successful, while no union has yet been able to intervene in the Irish food delivery industry.

CONCLUSIONS

The upsurge of labour mobilisations in the platform economy has engaged scholars and labour supporters in a debate as to whether and how novel forms of action, grievance and actors are emerging in reaction to the transformations of this new world of work. Addressing some of these issues, this chapter analyses the diversity of food delivery couriers' organisational practices across Europe, focusing on four cases: Germany, Ireland, Italy and the UK.

Scholarly literature has highlighted how the initial process of mobilisation in food delivery has been driven mostly from below (Quondamatteo and Marrone 2023) and especially by informal processes of worker self-organisation (Bessa et al. 2022; Atzeni and Cini 2023). Case study research has documented this trend by stressing forms of informal resistance (Tassinari and Maccarrone 2020; Maccarrone et al. 2023Woodcock 2021) and its prevalence has recently been featured in quantitative studies as well (see Joyce et al. 2020; Stuart et al. 2020; Chapter 5? EDITORS, PLEASE CHECK of this volume).

Our analysis of these four European countries has presented a complex picture, uncovering heterogeneous forms of organising across the cases. While mainstream unions initially remained on the sidelines in all four, the study of Italy and Germany has shown, for instance that stressing the relevance of grassroots mobilisations as an important channel for workers' grievances does not mean discarding the role of the institutional context. Indeed, certain features of the regulatory framework – such as the protections offered to worker representatives by German works councils or the primacy of national sectoral bargaining within Italian industrial relations – may facilitate the intervention of traditional unions. At the same time, factors beyond institutions, such as various informal groups and communities from which couriers have drawn resources and support for their mobilisations, have been important in sustaining workers' self-organisation and in explaining different organising patterns.

Despite increasing attempts at regulation, both at the national and EU level (see Chapter 11), many workers in the platform economy in general, and in food delivery in particular, are still far from being granted essential rights. Workers' actions and unions' interventions often face tough opposition from platforms, for whom the deregulation of workers' rights and low wages are key in a low-value-added sector where competition is based on cost. Thus, even when collective agreements are signed, there are still tensions and sources of grievance. In this scenario of a still relatively low institutionalisation of industrial relations, it is likely that the co-existence of mainstream unions and other forms of workers' collective representation will continue to characterise the landscape of organising among food delivery workers for some time to come. Organising might take on different configurations, depending on diverse factors, such as national institutional and political contexts, local political and social movement legacies, union cultures, ideologies, power resources and capabilities. In other words, even if the rise of platform labour produces common pressures regarding industrial relations, these are likely to produce uneven trajectories of regulation and workers' organising. Therefore, our study highlights the need for scholarly work to deepen knowledge around the dynamics, processes and factors explaining the complexity of protests and protesting in the platform economy worldwide.

NOTES

1. The total does not add up to 100 because multiple actors can be involved in one protest.
2. This is because most migrant couriers are also enrolled as students in language schools to learn English. Indeed, the fastest channel for non-European migrants to access the country is to demand a student visa (Stamp 2), which allows non-EU people to study for a certain period in Ireland and work for up to 20 hours a week, except as freelancers or self-employed workers. Stamp 2 is, therefore, the legal status that most non-European citizens hold when living in Ireland, especially during their first years of stay. Most people need to work more than 20 hours a week to live in Ireland, however. Hence, as they are formally prohibited from working for the platforms, they are compelled to sub-rent platforms' official accounts from Europeans, or from Stamp 4 visa holders, in an informal market of account rentals built into several chats and marketplaces on social media networks.
3. Within UK labour law, 'worker' is a third category between employee and self-employed.
4. The agreement with Uber excluded riders at Uber Eats.
5. Of which there are several types, including 'employer-organised work' (collaborazioni continuative organizzate, or co.co.org) and 'employer-coordinated work' (collaborazione coordinata e continuativa, or co.co.co).
6. In Ireland, there exist minimum wage setting mechanisms at the sector level which, however, are limited to a few sectors and which do not currently include the platform economy (Maccarrone et al. 2019).

REFERENCES

Almond P. and Connolly H. (2020) A manifesto for 'slow' comparative research on work and employment, *European Journal of Industrial Relations*, 26 (1), 59–74.

Atzeni M. and Cini L. (2023) New theories and politics for working class organising in the gig and precarious world of work, *Economic and Industrial Democracy*, 45 (3). https://doi.org/10.1177/0143831X231201009

Baccaro L. and Benassi C. (2017) Throwing out the ballast: growth models and the liberalization of German industrial relations, *Socio-Economic Review*, 15 (1), 85–115.

Baccaro L. and Howell C. (2017) *Trajectories of neoliberal transformation: European industrial relations since the 1970s*. Cambridge University Press.

Bessa I. et al. (2022) *A global analysis of worker protest in digital labour platforms*, ILO.

Bieler A. (2021) *Fighting for water: resisting privatization in Europe*, Bloomsbury.

Borghi P., Murgia A., Mondon-Navazo M. and Mezihorak P. (2021) Mind the gap between discourses and practices: platform workers' representation in France and Italy, *European Journal of Industrial Relations*, 27 (4), 425–443.

Carella B. and Marenco M. (2022) Inclusionary populism in office: what consequences for precarious work? Five Star Movement, Podemos and the case of food-delivery platform workers, *Stato e Mercato. Rivista Quadrimestrale*, 2, 261–285.

Cini L. and Goldmann B. (2021) The worker capabilities approach: insights from worker mobilisations in Italian logistics and food delivery, *Work, Employment and Society*, 35 (5), 948–967.

Cini L. and Tassinari A. (2022) Trade unions in the gig economy, in Snow D., della Porta D., McAdam D. and Klandermans B. (eds.) *The Wiley-Blackwell Encyclopedia of Social and Political Movements*, 2nd edn, Wiley Blackwell, 1–3.

Cini L., Maccarrone V. and Tassinari A. (2022) With or without u(nions): understanding the diversity of gig workers' organising practices in Italy and the UK, *European Journal of Industrial Relations*, 28 (3), 341– 362.

Davies P. (2022) 'Flamme Rouge': reflections on the IWW Couriers Network. https://iww.org.uk/news/flamme-rouge-reflections-on-the-iww-couriers-network

Doherty M. and Franca V. (2020) The (non/) response of trade unions to the 'gig' challenge, *Italian Labour Law e-Journal*, 13 (1), 125–139.

ETUC (2023) *Platform Reps. Germany: country report 2022*. www.etuc.org/sites/default/files/page/file/2023–05/ETUC_country%20report_Germany-EN.pdf

Ewen J. (2023) Schluss mit ausgeliefert? Tarifpolitik in der plattformvermittelten Lieferarbeit, *Prokla*, 53 (2), 289–304.

Gandini A. (2019) Labour process theory and the gig economy, *Human Relations*, 72 (6), 1039–1056.

Jesnes K., Neumann D., Trappmann V. and de Becdelièvre P. (2021) The role of worker collectives among app-based food delivery couriers in France, Germany and Norway: all the same or different?, in Drahokoupil J. and Vandaele K. (eds.) *A modern guide to labour and the platform economy*, Edward Elgar Publishing, 258–273.

Joyce S. and Stuart M. (2021) Digitalised management, control and resistance in platform work: a labour process analysis, in Haidar J. and Keune M. (eds.) *Work and labour relations in global platform capitalism*, Edward Elgar Publishing, 158–184.

Joyce S., Stuart M. and Forde C. (2023) Theorising labour unrest and trade unionism in the platform economy, *New Technology, Work and Employment*, 38 (1), 21–40.

Lévesque C. and Murray G. (2010) Understanding union power: resources and capabilities for renewing union capacity, *Transfer: European review of labour and research*, 16 (3), 333–350.

Maccarrone V. and Erne R. (2023) Ireland: trade unions recovering after being tipped off balance by the Great Recession?, in Müller T., Vandaele K. and Waddington J. (eds.) *Trade unions in the European Union: Picking up the pieces of the neoliberal challenge*, Peter Lang, 585–624.

Maccarrone V., Erne R. and Regan A. (2019) Ireland: life after social partnership, in Müller T., Vandaele K. and Waddington J. (eds.) *Collective bargaining in Europe: towards an endgame*, ETUI, 315–335.

Marà C., Pulignano V. and Stewart P. (2023) Dynamics of unionism in the platform economy: the case of the food delivery sector in Bologna, Italy, *The Economic and Labour Relations Review*, 34 (3), 395–412.

Marrone M. and Finotto V. (2019) Challenging Goliath: informal unionism and digital platforms in the food delivery sector: the case of riders union Bologna, *Partecipazione e Conflitto*, 12 (3), 691–716.

Martelloni F. (2018) Individuale e collettivo: quando i diritti dei lavoratori digitali corrono su due ruote, *Labour and Law Issues*, 4 (1), 16–34.

McGurdy C. (2022) Deliveroo-GMB deal: a closer look, *The Social Review*, 7 August.www.thesocialreview.co.uk/2022/08/07/deliveroo-gmb-deal-a-closer-look

Neumann D. (2023) *Five years of platform labour protest in Germany, Leeds Index Country Report 2*, January.

Nowak J. (2019) *Mass strikes and social movements in Brazil and India: popular mobilisation in the long depression*, Palgrave Macmillan.

Nowak J. (2021) From industrial relations research to global labour studies: moving labour research beyond Eurocentrism, *Globalizations*, 18 (8), 1335–1348.

Però D. (2019) Indie unions, organising and labour renewal learning from precarious migrant workers, *Work, Employment and Society*, 34 (5), 900–918.

Politi E. et al. (2021) Mobilizing precarious workers in Italy: two pathways of collective action intentions, *Social Movement Studies*, 21 (5), 608–624.

Pulignano V., Ortíz Gervasi L. and De Franceschi F. (2016) Union responses to precarious workers: Italy and Spain compared, *European Journal of Industrial Relations*, 22 (1), 39–55.

Quondamatteo N. (2021) Eppur si muove: il difficile cammino della contrattazione collettiva nel settore del food delivery, *Labour and Law Issues*, 7 (1), 92–113.

Quondamatteo N. and Marrone M. (2023) Struggle for recognition, a lever to establish industrial relations from below: reinterpreting couriers' mobilisations in food delivery sector in Italy, *Partecipazione e Conflitto*, 16 (2), 252–267.

Redmond C. (2021) Faced with assault, Deliveroo couriers are boycotting parts of Dublin, *Wired*, 21 April.

Schmalz S., Ludwig C. and Webster E. (2018) The power resources approach: developments and challenges, *Global Labour Journal*, 9 (2), 113–134.

Schmalz S. et al. (2023) Varieties of platform unionism: a view from the Global South on workers' power in the digital economy, *Work in the Global Economy*, 3 (2). https://doi.org/10.1332/27324176Y2023D000000001

Tassinari A. and Maccarrone V. (2020) Riders on the storm: workplace solidarity among gig economy couriers in Italy and the UK, *Work, Employment and Society*, 34 (1), 35–54.

Vandaele K. (2021) Collective resistance and organisational creativity amongst Europe's platform workers: a new power in the labour movement?, in Haidar J. and Keune M. (eds.) *Work and labour relations in global platform capitalism*, Edward Elgar Publishing, 206–235.

Waddington J. (2019) United Kingdom: a long-term assault on collective bargaining, in Müller T., Vandaele K. and Waddington J. (eds.) *Collective bargaining in Europe: towards an endgame*, ETUI, 605–624.

Weghmann V. (2022) Theorising practice: independent trade unions in the UK, *Work in the Global Economy*, 2 (1), 132–147.

Woodcock J. (2021) *The fight against platform capitalism: an inquiry into the global struggles of the gig economy*, University of Westminster Press.

Woodcock J. and Cant C. (2022) Platform worker organising at Deliveroo in the UK: from wildcat strikes to building power, *Journal of Labor and Society*, 25 (2), 220–236.

All links were checked on 13 November 2023.

5. The changing composition of app-based food delivery couriers and the consequences for collectivism

Cosmin Popan and Kristin Jesnes

INTRODUCTION

Less than a decade after Deliveroo, Foodora, Glovo, Uber Eats and others launched their operations in Europe, platform food deliveries are today one of the most visible, dynamic and contested forms of work in the platform economy. Couriers on bikes or mopeds, or in cars, carrying bulky, brightly coloured thermal bags, have become a standard visual feature of urban environments across the world, especially since the onset of the Covid-19 pandemic.

Two observations regarding the social composition of these workers have been advanced by existing scholarship. The first is that most couriers in western Europe are young and male and have a migrant background (Altenried 2021; Popan and Anaya-Boig 2022; van Doorn 2017). The second unpacks the previous one and highlights a gradual transition from a labour force comprised mostly of students working part-time to a majority of racialised male couriers (Altenried 2023; van Doorn et al. 2023). Moreover, in recent years, many irregular (also called undocumented)[1] migrants have joined the ranks, often working excessive and irregular hours (Lebas 2020; Mendonça and Kougiannou 2023).

The changing socio-demographic composition of the workforce in app-based food delivery requires further analysis. This is important in understanding to what extent an increasing migrant contingent has an impact on food couriers' capacity to organise and protest. Migrant workers across Europe have started to engage in struggles over rights and recognition since the late 1970s, and the past 20 years have marked a significant surge in political activism and mobilisation among migrant communities on every continent. The demands of vulnerable migrants encompass a wide spectrum, including the recognition of human rights, freedom of movement, opportunities to enter labour markets, a more open asylum procedure and criticisms of deportations and migrant fatalities at borders (Steinhilper 2021). Given this context, it is important to assess whether this pattern also pertains to the newer cohort of migrant platform couriers.

Several other reasons warrant a closer investigation of the socio-demographic (re)composition of the workforce within app-based food delivery. First, reports of this transition have been made based on research conducted mostly in western European countries (Vandaele 2021) and it does not provide a comprehensive overview for the entire continent. Second, the reasons for this demographic change over time are rarely explored. This transition within the workforce has, so far, with only a few exceptions, been acknowledged merely as a fact. Third, little work has been done to account for how the transition from students to (irregular) migrants influences the propensity to organise collectively. Recent research shows that the social composition of the courier workforce, largely represented by young and/or migrant workers, can shape patterns of collective action in terms of industrial struggle or organisation in trade unions or other collectives. Among migrants, mobilisation takes the shape of grassroots, community and independent unions or self-representation through worker-led collectives, and often occurs along ethnic lines. This, in turn, can result in a segmentation of the mobilisation potential (Tassinari and Maccarrone, 2020). Overall, while migrant food couriers have often engaged in collective action against platforms, their gains have not been overwhelming across Europe (Alyanak et al. 2023).

This chapter suggests that changes in the social composition of the workforce, in particular the growth in (undocumented) migrants, have had a negative impact on the propensity of app-based food delivery workers to take industrial action or to become members of a trade union. This finding is based on four case studies drawing on ethnographic fieldwork and qualitative interviews in Cluj in Romania, Lyon in France, Manchester in the UK and Oslo in Norway. To explore the synergy between demographic change and collectivism further, the analysis is conducted through the lens of the migration regimes that apply in the studied countries. As an analytical framework, migration regimes help explain the current over-representation of migrants in precarious jobs such as app-based food delivery. They also shed light on the reluctance of these workers to claim their rights, including the rights to protest and to organise in trade unions.

MIGRANTS, MIGRATION REGIMES AND APP-BASED FOOD DELIVERY

The integration of migrant workers into labour markets across the European Union is generally more difficult when compared to the local population: migrants are systematically disadvantaged with regards to career advancement, job prestige and periods of employment and unemployment and in terms of wage levels and forms of contract (Ahmad 2020). Additionally, immigrants of non-European backgrounds, or third-country migrants, are shown to suffer greater employment disparities (Di Stasio and Larsen 2020). As a consequence, the employment rate for migrants as a whole in the EU is 15 per cent lower than for non-migrants (Eurostat 2023b). This section considers the differentiated access to work opportunities for migrants across the EU: it highlights the role played by the common European migration regime in enabling the current socio-demographic (re)composition of the platform food delivery workforce.

The interplay between app-based food delivery companies and migrant work can be understood in terms of pull and push factors. The pull factors are generally linked with the quick onboarding provided by the platforms: they offer migrants an accessible job opportunity that requires little training and no language proficiency, and only necessitates a bicycle and mobile phone (Newlands 2022). Platforms are able to organise, control and measure labour digitally in an effective manner, allowing the (semi-)automated management of heterogeneous and migrant workforces without much human involvement. The push factors are related to migrant workers' heightened precarity resulting from information asymmetry regarding local job prospects, the imperfect portability of qualifications and a lack of host-country language skills (Newlands 2022). These are complemented by digital platforms' capacity to renew and reconfigure forms of precarious labour through algorithmic management, hyper-flexible forms of work and new forms of control (Altenried 2021; Lata et al. 2023).

An analysis of the EU migration regime enables a deeper dive into the distinct ways in which these push factors affect various categories of migrant people. 'Migration regime' is a concept that encapsulates the set of formal and informal rules governing international migration movements (Comte 2018). It refers to migration policies and their outcomes that reflect the admission and settlement over time of people born in another country. At EU level, the migration regime is comprised of the immigration policies adopted by different states and the effect those policies have on the consequent movement of people into and out of a country. Thus, on the one hand, there are those workers who have the right to reside and work in European countries; on the other, there are asylum seekers or irregular migrants whose access to the labour market and other welfare benefits is severely restricted or denied.

After the Second World War, countries in the Global North partially opened their immigration policies to appeal to specific foreign workers to assist with post-war reconstruction efforts. However, starting in the 1980s, they have also responded by implementing more stringent immigration measures, such as tighter border security, heightened deportation efforts and the establishment of camps for individuals considered undesirable (Steinhilper 2021). The EU migration regime is characterised by two features which make it unique when compared to similar regimes in North America, south-east Asia or the Middle East: an internal openness and freedom of movement of labour, and an external restrictiveness with protection of the external borders. It is thus considered a relatively liberal regime where regionalism nevertheless plays an essential role (Comte 2018).

The UK used to rely on a similar migration regime as the rest of the EU until 2016. After Brexit, EU citizens migrating to the UK have been subject to the same immigration rules as citizens from the rest of the world. The broader EU migration regime informs national migration policies in each of the four countries studied here. France and Romania, which are part of the EU, as well as Norway, which belongs to the European Economic Area (EEA), allow EU migrants to move freely across their territories. The UK migration regime has, since Brexit, prevented EU migrants without a residence permit from accessing its labour market.

The EU's promotion of regionalism in its migration governance is concerned not only with entry controls but also with the creation of an internal 'multiplication of labour' (Mezzadra and Neilson 2013) which restricts who can get what job (Schaupp 2022). The multiplication of labour entails European borders enabling the functioning of differential regimes of filtering and stratification as well as a means of stratification and control of migrant labour (Mezzadra and Neilson 2008). As such, to work with the concept of the multiplication of labour means 'to recognize such divisions as not merely given but always produced, imposed and reimposed, often in reaction to the movements of migration themselves' (Mezzadra and Neilson 2008: 12). This results in an openness and a restrictiveness in the EU's migration regime which produce substantially different labour experiences among different migrants.

EU nationals can apply to work across the EU and do not encounter barriers to enrolling as platform food couriers. They enjoy freedom of movement across EU borders and their stay in any EU country does not depend on a visa or residence permit. Third-country nationals are, on the other hand, more restricted or prohibited from accessing the labour market and, as such, are more likely than EU internal migrants in many western EU countries to be involved, legally or under an alias, in more precarious work such as platform food deliveries. Temporary work or student visas often allow non-EU migrants to carry out platform work on a self-employed basis part-time or full-time (Metawala et al. 2021; Timko and van Melik 2021). Finally, for the increasing number of irregular migrants from outside the EU making deliveries, the situation is substantially different: their lack of work permits regularly pushes them to further exploitation as their only choice is to work under an alias. Additionally, their chances of having their residence recognised through work are considerably lower as EU countries tend to offer regularisation on the grounds of employment rather than self-employment (Kraler 2019).

Restrictive immigration and refugee laws are the main factor creating irregular migrants in European countries (Bertossi 2008). It is estimated that over two-thirds of irregular migrants live in four countries: France, Germany, Italy and the UK (Pew Research Center 2019). For irregular migrants, informal platform work represents one of the few options in the formal economy. Their lack of documentation nevertheless dictates their capacity to access work, and the only option they have is to rent or buy accounts, a practice of 'identity loan' which is common among unauthorised migrant workers (Andrikopoulos 2023). This leads to what Tsing (2009) calls 'super exploitation', a situation where the rate of exploitation is particularly high and based on non-economic factors such as citizenship, visa, work permits and residency status.

CASE SELECTION, METHODS AND DATA

This chapter is grounded in an ethnographic study of platform food couriers carried out in Cluj, Lyon and Manchester, and arising from qualitative research in Oslo. These four cities have been selected based on several criteria: although having a relatively similar population of under one million inhabitants, each city has a different topography and climate, resulting in different work experiences. They have also been selected based on the authors' mastery of local languages. In addition, and important for the argument developed in this chapter, the countries in which they are located have embraced slightly different migration approaches and have different migration traditions.

In all four studies, research participants were recruited from outside hot-spot restaurants as well as from trade unions and via social media. Accessing migrant workers, especially those who do not speak local languages, proved to be a challenge. Establishing trust, in particular among irregular migrants, was also difficult (Figure 5.1). To protect them from further vulnerability, all the names of the couriers referred to in this chapter have been anonymised.

For the cities in France, Romania and the UK, the fieldwork spanned two years and seven months, from September 2020 to April 2023. The ethnographic work involved participant observation as a food courier in each of the cities. Some 45 in-depth semi-structured interviews were conducted, supplemented by informal discussions with another dozen couriers in each city, as well as following 15 of them at work over one or more days. The profile of the couriers reflects the socio-demographic composition of the workforce. Interviewees were between the ages of 20 and 65; seven are women. Regarding the Oslo case study, the 24 couriers interviewed were between 20 and 60, with five women. More than half have a migrant background, and many of the interviews were conducted in English. Half of the couriers were members of a trade union, and one strike was recorded during our fieldwork. Interviews were also conducted with union representatives and personnel from the food delivery companies and employer organisations in Norway, the UK and France.

Regarding non-EU migration, all four countries embrace the EU's regionalist approach and systematically deny entrance to third-country nationals, thus foreclosing safe and legal routes

Note: 'Are you a cop?'; 'Of course not...'; 'Do you have an Uber account to rent?' (translation).
Source: Letizia Bonanno.

Figure 5.1 Building trust among irregular migrants can sometimes be difficult for researchers

for non-EU migrants into their national territories. This political strategy has led to the creation of an irregular migrant workforce, which is over-represented among platform food couriers. Additionally, the presence of non-EU migrant workers in each of the four countries must be contextualised within the colonial histories of both France and the UK as well as national migration traditions. As such, the profile of the interviewees also provides a good indication of the ways in which the European migration regime forces migrant workers into further vulnerability while largely discouraging them from organising. Thus, the phenomenon of irregular migration is more visible in France and the UK: irregular migrants were encountered only in Lyon and Manchester (five and two, respectively). In those two cities, there were considerably more non-EU migrants, nine and six, respectively, than in Cluj and Oslo: zero and four, respectively. Local couriers were more visible in the latter two cities: 12 in Cluj and 11 in Oslo, compared to nine in Manchester and zero in Lyon. In Cluj and Oslo, there were also four non-EU students. Norway is not situated in the proximity of traditional migration routes, and Romania is not economically attractive to most non-EU migrants. There is thus a considerably smaller contingent of non-EU migrants in Norway and, more especially, in Romania.

CLUJ: A SUDDEN INCREASE IN SOUTH-ASIAN COURIERS

Romania has one of the lowest numbers of internet workers in the EU (19.3 per cent of the total population), while the percentage of foreign-born platform workers in the country is also low compared to the European average (FES 2022; Piasna et al. 2022). Immigration to Romania is less common than to most other EU countries, with the percentage of non-nationals reported in 2022 at only 3 per cent (Eurostat 2023a). This is reflected to a great extent in the workforce composition: the number of migrant food couriers in Cluj is small compared to France and the UK. The few foreign workers are international students working fewer hours than most of their colleagues. They rely on bicycles, which makes them even more vulnerable in a city with very low levels of cycling. The density, militancy and overall influence in society of trade unions have declined massively (Guga and Trif 2023), which might explain why protests among platform food couriers have been rather scarce in recent years (FES 2022).

Food delivery work is mediated by intermediate companies that hire workers on behalf of the platforms. The intermediation of work through third parties dilutes platforms' obligations as employers and makes it harder for workers to claim their rights, yet the practice is likely to become even more prevalent across Europe as more platforms are forced to reclassify workers as employees (Bertolini et al. 2021). Average gross earnings for couriers willing to work more than eight hours per day and seven days per week can be higher than the minimum wage in the country. Consequently, many of the couriers in Cluj are highly educated and praise the opportunities offered by the platform economy.

Breaking to an extent with the restrictiveness of the EU's migration regime, the Romanian government announced in 2022 that 100,000 new migrant workers would be accepted in the country on temporary work visas. This is a doubling of the previous year's number and follows a shortage of local workers. Over 2,000 couriers from southern Asia, often recruited by Romanian-based work placement agencies, are visible across the bigger cities in the country. The presence of third-country nationals among food couriers appears to be more and more common across other central and eastern European countries (Kowalik et al. 2023). Despite having employment contracts, these couriers work more than they are legally allowed, their pay is often deducted if they do not reach set targets and they can have their contracts terminated at any given moment (Meseşan et al. 2023; Şuţu 2023). It is not surprising that organising and striking are the least of these migrant workers' concerns.

Organisation of migrant platform workers is even less frequent, not least because of their reduced representation among couriers. Additionally, the few non-EU workers are often the target of racist abuse. One such example is Mamadou, a Guinean who arrived in Cluj on a study visa. He revealed that he was the victim of frequent racist comments and attitudes and fell prey to fraudsters who took advantage of his being new to the country:

> This person I met negotiated with the umbrella company, so I was not in direct contact with the boss; he was in charge of this. So, when I was supposed to be paid, he received the money and only gave me 500–600 lei (€100–120). Only later did I realise I was supposed to receive at least 2,000 lei.

Non-EU food couriers recently arrived in Cluj and other Romanian cities have often indebted themselves to make it into Europe (Şuţu 2023), something that Mamadou also admits (Figure 5.2).

This economic precarity and lack of Romanian language skills explain why Mamadou has not considered striking a viable option.

Note: 'My sister is in Germany, she left (Cluj) today. We came with a travel agency, and that cost me 8,000 euros. I have to pay 3,000 euros for university fees, 3,000 euros for the travel agency, 3,000 euros to open a bank account. So, I had to borrow 1,000 euros to open this (Tazz) account. Why did I leave my country (Guinea) and come here? I left my mum and dad. And I am in a country where my residence permit is expiring.' (translation).
Source: José Sherwood González.

Figure 5.2 As with many non-EU couriers working in Cluj, Mamadou indebted himself to arrive in Europe

LYON: RENTING ACCOUNTS AND BEING TARGETED BY THE POLICE

Alongside the UK, France has historically been a country of immigration; these were the two largest imperial metropoles in Europe. After the Second World War, changes in both colonial empires led to an active resumption of the recruitment of immigrants that had first begun during the inter-war period. Then, like several other western European countries, starting from the mid-1970s, France suspended salaried work immigration while toughening all legal means of entry into its territory. France remains the second most important country of destination for migrants in Europe, and almost a quarter of its inhabitants are migrants or have a migrant background (Héran 2019). Within this context, the migration regime in France contributes to the increasingly precarious status of irregular migrants. A recent history of tightening controls, an end to the need for justification for detention and the obligation to leave the territory are among the policies which have further contributed to the vulnerability of these workers (Baril 2023b).

Since the mid-2010s, the socio-demographic composition of the platform food delivery workforce has shifted dramatically: the early students have gradually given way to more precarious and older workers, including many migrant workers without residence or work permits (Gomes 2022; Lebas 2020; Rioux 2022). A considerable number of couriers in France are irregular migrant workers. According to figures revealed by trade unions and workers' associations, between a third and half of couriers in France rent or buy accounts (Visseyrias 2021). Estimates of how many irregular migrants work on food delivery platforms are difficult to make because companies are not aware of or are simply not keen to publicise these figures, but also because couriers themselves are not willing to admit their irregular status since this can often lead to deportation. Writing on the work experience of undocumented food couriers in Paris, Baril (2023a: 1) observes that 'the subletting of accounts, the complicit role of the state, the hypocrisy of employers and the interdependency with the "regularised" put undocumented couriers in hyper-precarious situations'.

Despite the significant shift in workforce composition, irregular migrants have managed to organise themselves in recent years. Continuing a recent tradition of other irregular migrants going on union-supported strikes for regularisation (Barron et al. 2011), irregular food couriers have started to voice their anger in the public space. The most emblematic case is that of Frichti, a local platform which came under the spotlight in 2020 for purposefully hiring irregular migrants. That summer, Frichti deactivated 200 of its *sans papiers* couriers without notice, which in turn led to a series of strikes in Paris (Baril 2023b; Gomes 2022; Gomes and Isidro 2020). The workers were supported in their struggle by one of the biggest trade unions in France, Confédération générale du travail (CGT; General Confederation of Labor) and a grassroots organisation for couriers, Collectif des livreurs autonomes de Paris (CLAP; Collective of Independent Couriers in Paris). More recent protests by irregular migrants making food deliveries came in the autumn of 2022 after Uber Eats accused couriers of using fake identities and blocked 2,500 accounts. Hundreds of couriers, supported by CLAP and two other smaller trade unions – SUD Commerce; and Confédération nationale des travailleurs-Solidarité ouvrière (CNT-SO; National Confederation of Workers-Worker Solidarity) – demonstrated for several weeks in Paris although without managing to secure the reinstatement of the suspended accounts.

CNT-SO tried to support similar protests in Lyon at the end of 2022. The union distributed flyers to couriers across the city and organised three preparatory meetings, but interest among couriers was low. Over one-third of the couriers encountered in Lyon were renting accounts, although some believe that the percentage is much higher. One such example is Alpha, a 23-year-old irregular migrant from Gambia who arrived in France in 2018 after an arduous three-year journey across the Mediterranean Sea and the Alps. Alpha had just had his asylum claim rejected and was struggling to hold on to a rented Uber Eats account. Account renting is never a winning game: Alpha pays €130 a week for an account he can lose at any time and for which he needs to meet almost daily with the owner: 'Uber Eats asks for facial recognition, so I need to cycle 7 km from Guillotière to Vénissieux to get a selfie from him.' Living such a hyper-precarious life makes Alpha indifferent, if not reluctant, to striking or seeking union support: 'I've crossed the Mediterranean and the Alps; I've seen people dying around me during this journey. I do not care about the strikes.'

Even when they have documents, platform work is not necessarily possible for these migrants. Abdoulaye, a young Moroccan from Lyon, has secured an Italian residence permit which he can use to get a job in Italy. When he travelled to France, however, he could not open an Uber Eats account: 'Here, you can rent a car, you can spend money, but you cannot work. You see the politics?' This situation is reflective of the ways in which the European migration regime allows internal migrants to move and work across the Union while restricting this right for non-EU migrants. Like Alpha, Abdoulaye resorted in the end to renting accounts: 'Since 2020 it's always been like this: I buy an Uber Eats account for €1,200, I work for six months, then it's blocked. Up to now I have had seven accounts.' In addition to this, the police constantly harass him (see Figure 5.3):

Source: Ionuţ Dulămiţă.

Figure 5.3 *Abdoulaye is regularly stopped and searched by the local police in Lyon*

> I was returning home from work. It was 2 o'clock in the morning and there was a traffic jam in front of me. I took the bus lane, I accelerated a bit, I passed a police car, and they started chasing me. I stopped; they came and pushed me against the wall, as if I had killed somebody. They checked my Italian permit and said it was fake. They checked my pockets and asked where I got the bicycle. I showed them the invoice, but they didn't believe me. They checked the serial number on the bicycle frame and looked it up on their database. In the end, they let me go.

Overall, organisation is increasingly remote for irregular workers: they are afraid of deportation, do not always speak the local language, are not aware of their rights or the institutional resources at their disposal and, above all, do not have access to less precarious jobs without going deeper into unlawful activity.

MANCHESTER: INTERNATIONAL STUDENTS AND IRREGULAR MIGRANTS DO NOT GO ON STRIKE

As of 2017, the UK accounted for the second-largest number of foreign-born citizens of all European nations: 9.5 million (14.4 per cent of the total population). For the previous two decades, the EU was the major source of work-related migration to the UK. After the Brexit referendum in 2016, the UK no longer supported the regionalist approach of the EU migration regime: visa grants to EU citizens dropped sharply, while the large majority of people arriving on work visas in 2022 under the post-Brexit immigration system were from non-EU countries (Sumption and Brindle 2023). There are, at the same time, between 800,000 and 1.2 million irregular migrants in the UK, a larger proportion of the population than in comparable countries such as France, Spain, Switzerland and Portugal, where there are more routes to regularisation (JCWI 2022).

The two main food delivery platforms in the UK, Deliveroo and Uber Eats, rely exclusively on a self-employed workforce, while the third market player, Just Eat, recently (2023) reverted to a similar system after briefly offering couriers worker status.[2] Initially, Deliveroo offered a standard hourly rate and rolled out a shift booking system, which contributed both to an intake of a diverse contingent of couriers in terms of gender and race as well as relative control over the workforce. In 2016, the company changed the payment system, switching to pay-per-delivery piece rates, with no hourly rate. This change led to an influx of couriers, a decrease in pay and an increase in the number of working hours. While young British students riding bicycles and working part-time continued to represent the bulk of couriers, this was gradually changing (Cant 2020); older migrant workers, with limited language skills, working long hours and riding mopeds, were becoming more common.

The first strikes against Deliveroo in the UK occurred in 2016, in London, in direct response to the changes to the payment system. An important role in the organisation of the protests was played by established community networks of Brazilian moped drivers (Tassinari and Maccarrone 2020; Woodcock 2016). A small but militant grassroots union, the Independent Workers of Great Britain (IWGB), helped couriers organise, and some of them (mostly younger cyclists of British or EU origin) joined its ranks. Despite the mobilisation, Deliveroo refused to enter formal negotiations with the IWGB, but, after some delays, eventually changed the payment scheme across London.

The first and only two strikes in Manchester took place a few years later, at a time when the changes operated by Deliveroo had already produced a significant reconfiguration of the workforce. The strikes, organised in February 2019, gathered 40 couriers, mostly migrants, who represented 80 per cent of full-time workers yet were a small fraction of the total of 5,000 couriers in Manchester. Despite media coverage and the support of another independent union, the Industrial Workers of the World (IWW), the strikes in Manchester failed to improve working conditions. The next attempts to organise another round of strikes in Manchester were in December 2020, during the Covid-19 lockdown. An insufficient number of couriers were convinced to log off their accounts, so the strike was eventually called off.

Behind this failure lies the exponential increase in Deliveroo couriers since the beginning of the pandemic when the company hired 15,000 more couriers across the UK. The newcomers, often driving cars away from the city centre and not wearing the Deliveroo turquoise bags and kit, were more difficult to add to the WhatsApp group used in 2019 to organise the strikes. Additionally, language barriers prevented newly arrived migrants from joining an English-based messaging group. This lack of engagement is best illustrated by Lucinda, a 42-year-old Portuguese divorced mother of Mozambican origin whose English is not very fluent: 'One Brazilian person told me about the strike, but we don't have time to talk about strikes, we are so busy. There are many Brazilian people who speak Portuguese; there are Afghani people, we don't talk too much.'

Even those who were committed to striking in the past are aware of the risks of getting organised. Mahmoud, one of the previous strike organisers, says that, for any strike he will join in the future, he needs to make sure he is not as exposed as he had been when he and his colleagues picketed the Deliveroo headquarters in Manchester:

> We will not let Deliveroo know who is going to be on strike. Because they don't care about anything, they block the accounts straight away. You know how they were watching me for more than one year since the previous strike? They were looking for any mistake to block my account. I can't risk it again.

Two groups of migrants are the most reluctant to engage in collective action. The first are international students who have been recently onboarded in considerable numbers. High tuition fees and the increase in the cost of living in the last few years have pushed many foreign students into platform work alongside their studies. Since student visas do not allow them to become self-employed, they often rent Deliveroo accounts. This appears to be a prevalent phenomenon – dozens of YouTube channels set up by Indian and Pakistani students working for Deliveroo offer tutorials in Urdu for prospective couriers. At the same time, the temporary nature of their stay in the UK dissuades them from striking and unionising.

The second group encompasses the irregular migrants who represent an increasing minority among food couriers in the UK. The routes to regularisation available to irregular migrants are long, complicated and expensive (Gardner and Patel 2021), which places them at high risk of exploitation. Fieldwork in Manchester identified several Eritrean asylum seekers and refugees who were renting Deliveroo accounts for £50 per week while waiting for their asylum claims to be processed. Account renting has also been reported among Brazilian migrants working as food couriers in London. There is a certain community solidarity among these workers which means that irregular migrants do not always have to pay commission to those renting them an account. The immigration status of these workers leads, nevertheless, to discrimination by police, customers and other members of the public (Robins 2023). Additionally, this deters them from engaging in collective action, especially since the British government frequently targets them for deportation, as was the case in April 2023, for example, when the police arrested 60 irregular migrants working for Deliveroo, Uber Eats and Just Eat.

OSLO: FROM UNION ORGANISING TO MORE SELF-EMPLOYMENT

Since EU expansion in 2004, Norway, as part of the European Economic Area, has experienced a growing migrant population, mainly from eastern Europe. These workers are EU citizens with the right to work in Norway, thereby reducing their vulnerability compared to irregular migrants in France and the UK. Despite this, stringent labour-market access criteria pose challenges for migrants seeking employment in Norway (Newlands 2022). Platform work is more easily accessible and is in Norway, as elsewhere, consolidated in industries with lower unionisation rates, especially within transportation and logistics where migrant workers abound (Jesnes and Oppegaard 2020). Despite a relatively high unionisation rate of 50 per cent, trade unions have, in general, faced challenges in integrating migrant workers as union representatives (Hagen and Jensen 2019). As a result, the unionisation rate among workers with a migrant background is lower than that of the general working-age population (Nergaard and Ødegård 2022).

Foodora and Wolt are the leading platform companies in this sector in Norway, offering delivery from restaurants as well as grocery delivery from their own warehouses since 2021. Foodora initially hired its couriers as part-time employees with ten-hour contracts in 2015. This suggests that these workers would have needed to possess the necessary documentation to work in Norway. However, since 2022, Foodora's 4,000 couriers work as part-time employees, freelancers or self-employed workers. Similarly, Wolt relies on around 3,500 freelancers and self-employed couriers, many of whom are young and have a migrant background (Jesnes and Oppegaard 2023).

The key difference between employees and freelancers/self-employed lies in the coverage provided by the Working Environment Act and the possibility for the former, but not the latter, of engaging in collective bargaining (Jesnes 2019). This shift in employment contracts to more freelancers and self-employed, especially following the surge in demand for food deliveries during the pandemic, has led to an increase in workers with migrant backgrounds. According to its own figures, Foodora employs couriers of 98 different nationalities. Statistics Norway (Lien 2023) reports that approximately 2,000 couriers earned income from platform-based delivery services each month in 2022; among these, only 25 per cent were born in Norway. Many of the couriers work for both companies (Lien 2023), something also observed in this research.

As Foodora provided workers with employment contracts from the start, there were no legal obstacles to unionisation. Since 2018, Landsorganisasjonen i Norge (LO; Norwegian Confederation of Trade Unions) has explicitly welcomed self-employed workers as members, offering customised insurance and specialist legal advice as alternative options to collective agreements. After a dynamic mobilisation process, a local 'union club' of Norsk transportarbeiderforbund (NTF; Transport Workers Union), affiliated with LO, was established for couriers in 2017. The couriers communicated through channels on the Slack app (Jesnes et al. 2021), actively recruiting union members with a migrant background. The organised couriers used a paragraph in the Working Environment Act to demand extra hours in their contracts, a success that resulted in more members joining the union (Jesnes et al. 2021). In August 2019, following a deterioration in working conditions, about 100 members of the union (out of a total of 600 couriers in Oslo) went on strike, demanding a collective agreement with Foodora. During the same period, NTF merged with Fellesforbundet (United Federation of Trade Unions), the largest private sector union in Norway and also a member of LO, which gave the couriers in Foodora access to additional resources, such as a large strike fund, communications officers and valuable human support during the negotiations and the strike. With these extra resources, the local union was able to recruit new members, many of whom had a migrant background.

The five-week strike was very visible in Oslo, with couriers occupying a central square and offering bike repairs and a soup kitchen. They received support from local politicians, the director general of the International Labour Organization and the leadership of LO Norway. The strikers wore pink T-shirts with the slogans 'collective agreement now' and #rosastreiken (pink strike), which quickly spread on social media. Communication during the strike was in English to reach the many workers who did not speak Norwegian. Many of the migrant workers were nevertheless sceptical of joining the union, like this young student from a southern European country: 'I read that the company is not earning money, so I don't know how much we can ask for things. That is one of the reasons I am not in the union. Because I feel like, if the company is not increasing its profits, I am not so entitled to ask for benefits.' During the strike, however, many migrant workers were eventually convinced to unionise, and the union doubled its members in this period. Strikers received benefits from the union in compensation for income lost from missed deliveries.

The collective agreement, which was renegotiated in 2020 and 2022, included a wage increase, equipment compensation, winter pay and access to a pension scheme. About the same time as the agreement was concluded, however, the Finnish company Wolt entered Oslo and expanded its market share in Norway, paying its freelancers and self-employed couriers on a per-delivery basis. The surge in deliveries during the pandemic and this competitive situation led Foodora to follow suit and recruit independent contractors. This move by Foodora challenged the existing collective agreement, putting downward pressure on working conditions and pay, and the union called on the company to return to the model of a contracted workforce.

After this pressure from the union, independent contractors in Foodora wishing to become employees can request (and generally receive) an employment contract. They often do so in the spring, when demand is lower, to obtain greater job security in terms of guaranteed hours. This also works the other way around; there are also employed couriers opting to become freelancers to be able to earn more on weekends when demand is high. Indeed, the self-employed may be hesitant to see the advantages of union membership given that the Working Environment Act and the collective agreement impose limitations on weekend working hours and cap daily working hours to 7.5. Although the collective agreement allows employees to work additional hours at a higher rate, Foodora instead gives these hours to the self-employed at a lower rate. Consequently, Foodora's strategy in the face of the restrictions in the Working Environment Act also places a limit on potential earnings which might influence the appeal of union membership among these self-employed workers, many of whom have a migrant background.

A THREE-PHASE TRANSITION ACROSS EUROPE?

In many European countries, the increasing deterioration in working conditions, worsened by the Covid-19 pandemic and the energy and economic crises, has led to a gradual transition in platform food delivery from part-time temporary jobs done mostly by students to dependent self-employed male migrants working excessive and irregular hours. This section presents a rough estimation of the phases corresponding to this transition based on our case studies combined with evidence from secondary literature. The different phases may have occurred at different moments in time across countries, indicating the maturity of app-based food delivery as well as the labour relations and the European migration regime specificities of each country. That said, no claim is made here that the periodisation of the phases is the same across countries or that all three phases are occurring in all countries.

In phase 1, local students share making deliveries with migrant workers. This is especially visible in France and the UK. The background here is that the initially generous compensation provided by platforms attracted a workforce that was, in the first place, less precarious and vulnerable, making it more inclined to respond to organisational efforts. A local cohort of students, mainly using bicycles to cover the city centres where platforms initially rolled out their operations, represented the bulk of food delivery couriers during the early-to-mid-2010s. Eventually, platform companies started to drop the pay rate, began changing the contractual status from employed to independent contractors, and proceeded to switch the payment system from an hourly rate to a piece rate. Alongside migrant workers, students led several labour protests that addressed the deteriorating working conditions (Heiland 2020; Pérez Capitan and Ranz 2022). Grassroots unions, rather than traditional unions, although there were a few exceptions, supported the collective action of workers, both in demonstrations and in taking legal cases (Borghi et al. 2021; Cini 2023; Jesnes et al. 2021; Tassinari and Maccarrone 2020). In some countries, court judgments ruled for the reclassification of couriers as employees (Hiessl 2021). In Spain, this was followed by the 'Riders' Law' that forced delivery platforms to hire their couriers as employees and made it easier for traditional unions to organise them.

Phase 2, which can be understood as a transition stage, is marked by a growth in migrant workers and more collective action. While this indicates that migrant status does not necessarily preclude organisation, this often follows distinctive ethnic lines (see, for example, Cant 2020; Vandaele 2020). In the few years before the Covid-19 pandemic, students were gradually replaced by second-generation male migrants on motorcycles, working excessive hours as self-employed.

The growing number of migrants, some irregular, became increasingly involved in collective action which was more prevalent than in the years following the pandemic. In France and the UK, for example, more than half the strikes occurred before 2020,[3] a time when increasing numbers of irregular migrants were starting to join the ranks of food delivery couriers. This happened for several reasons. Working full-time makes migrant workers more dependent on platforms and thus more likely to organise. The number of couriers across most cities was still relatively low during this phase, further facilitating face-to-face meetings and organisation. Finally, in some cases, migrants also organised along racial lines, as in London and in Manchester during the first wave of strikes in 2016 and 2019.

In countries such as Norway, where collective bargaining agreements are in place, platforms are increasingly relying on self-employed workers and often use intermediaries, leaving migrant workers, in particular, outside employment protection regulations (Banasiak 2020). In this phase, as well as in the next, growing competition between the platforms could be witnessed, followed by the sudden exit of companies from certain regional markets, such as Deliveroo in Germany and Spain, highlighting the precarity faced by these workers (Altenried 2021).

Phase 3 is characterised by more irregular migrants and consequently less worker organisation. For the last five years (2020 - 2025), several media reports, further corroborated by academic studies, have highlighted the increasing number of irregular migrants renting accounts to work as food couriers, particularly in western Europe.

This is where the European migration regime started to have a decisive impact on workforce composition. With dwindling revenues, most local students and documented migrants preferred to search for other job opportunities, with their courier places gradually being taken, especially in the UK and France, by irregular migrants without working rights who resort to account buying or renting. In Norway, the relatively smaller influx of irregular migrants can be attributed to the country's less entrenched migration history. It has also been influenced by the prevalence of a strongly unionised job market where employment contracts and collective agreements were more widespread, a scenario that was, until recently, also applicable to app-based food delivery. Romania, which is not a migration destination, has also seen fewer migrants and even fewer irregular migrants. Dwindling revenues have, however, led to an increasing contingent of migrants from south Asia on temporary work visas.

Elsewhere in Europe, reports of irregular migrants making food deliveries are equally frequent (for example in Germany, Portugal, Spain and Belgium; see Altenried 2021; Ma et al. 2023; Vieira 2023; Vinale et al. 2022). In Italy, in 2021, a national scandal revealed the exploitation of irregular migrants, with *caporalato* firms hiring them to shell companies to work on Uber Eats accounts for a fraction of normal earnings (Allaby 2021). In Spain, despite the implementation of the Riders' Law, irregular migrants remain unprotected (Metawala et al. 2021).

In these situations, unions' traditional approach of offering collective bargaining is out of the question, but some, such as Confederazione Generale Italiana del Lavoro (CGIL; General

Confederation of Italian Labour), have nevertheless started to offer legal support to irregular migrants (Iazzolino and Varesio 2023). This has also been followed by an increase in the use of employment contracts by food delivery companies due to court cases and regulatory pressure (Lamannis 2023). Even so, there is a significant overall gap in rights, level of social coverage and resulting vulnerability between local/documented couriers covered by regulation or collective agreements and the newer/irregular ones who are becoming increasingly present in many western countries.

These phases do not entirely reflect the situation across the European continent. There are substantial differences between European countries that complicate this transition, related to local labour market relations and variations in the European migration regime; different traditions and histories of migration; work arrangements that classify couriers either as employees or self-employed; and collective and individual perceptions regarding entrepreneurship and collective organisation. Traditional unions across Europe still experience difficulties in engaging with the increasing contingent of migrant platform workers because of the self-employed status that most of them have and as a result of the temporal and geographical dispersion of the work, as well as the extremely precarious situation in which some of them are found (Altenried et al. 2018; van Doorn 2023; Vandaele et al. 2019). Grassroots unions, on the other hand, have had more success, but have also struggled with how to move their cause beyond demonstrations (Bertolini and Dukes 2021; Joyce and Stuart 2021).

CONCLUSIONS

Despite the institutional differences and varying degrees of maturity of food delivery services across different countries, it is striking how deteriorating working conditions have prompted an influx of migrant workers, many of them irregular, often followed by a decrease in their capacity to organise. This shift highlights the increasing reliance of food delivery platform companies on a 'reserve army of labour' made up of vulnerable and exploitable migrant workers, and a growing division between insiders, covered by more social protection and rights, and outsiders, like independent contractors and irregular migrants, who are not covered.

While recognition of changes in workforce composition is widespread, the situation across Europe is not entirely uniform or generalisable to other cities or countries. This investigation of platform work in France, Norway, Romania and the UK finds that the local specificities of the European migration regime and labour market play a significant role in shaping the socio-demographic profile of food couriers and their propensity to organise. While all four countries follow the continent's regionalist approach and systematically deny entrance to non-EU migrants, the consequent production of irregular workers among food couriers differs from case to case. In France and the UK, countries which share an important colonial past, a strong migrant influx and a certain geographical proximity to migration routes, the number of irregular workers is high. Norway and Romania, on the contrary, have a more recent migration tradition, and, in both places, more formal migration fluxes have a lesser impact regardless of whether from other EU countries (Norway) or from south Asia on temporary work visas (Romania).

Whether the three-phase scenario, and particularly the point on irregular migrant workers, is applicable to all the countries studied is thus an empirical question. Similarly, the three phases highlighted do not successively follow each other in all of them. Nevertheless, this scenario might provide a valuable conceptualisation to capture the general dynamics and stimulate further research. The precarious employment of food courier migrants depends on specific migration regulations as well as certain technical and organisational preconditions at the level of the labour process (Schaupp 2022). It is, therefore, expected that, despite the official rhetoric across Europe, the persistent reliance on cheap labour, coupled with platforms' extraordinary capacity to accommodate foreign workers, will contribute to perpetuating a situation where a substantial body of migrant workers continue to work as couriers but where the courier job itself represents a dead end. This is also increasingly visible in central and eastern European countries where migration has historically been a less common phenomenon.

Several regulatory developments have taken place to cope with the increasingly precarious conditions of food delivery workers, including the proposed EU directive on platform workers and the Riders' Law in Spain (see also Chapter 11), which recognise delivery couriers as employees and provide them with social protections. There are, nevertheless, concerns regarding how these new regulations will apply to migrant workers. It is unclear whether such workers will have equal access to the benefits and protections afforded to other platform workers, which may exacerbate existing inequalities and vulnerabilities within the workforce. Third-country nationals working in the EU for a short period of time are already among the workers most often subject to exclusions from social security coverage or who are not covered for certain risks (Bogoeski and Rasnača 2023).

In the specific case of irregular migrants, the regulatory developments designed to improve the working conditions of platform food couriers actually do little to address the 'super exploitation' they face (Tsing 2009). As shown in the case studies presented in this chapter, even when confronted with deteriorating working conditions, any efforts to engage these workers in collective action remain difficult. There is more and more evidence of this challenge also outside our case studies, as witnessed by the efforts of the CGT to mobilise food couriers in France during the first weekend of December 2023. The union's attempt to organise a general strike using a WhatsApp group was met with dismay by some couriers: 'We have irregular couriers here who are sleeping on the streets or in precarious shelters. It's a different reality. It's challenging to mobilise them as they are constantly chasing money due to the commission taken by account owners.' On some rare occasions, these entirely fitting remarks slipped anyway into verbal abuse and even physical attacks directed against those who continued working during the strikes.

It is thus essential that grassroots organisations and trade unions, during their efforts at support and mobilisation, account for how the EU migration regime has a specific impact on already precarious and vulnerable platform workers. By broadening their agenda to include them, (grassroots) unions can effectively support and empower migrant workers in the fight for better working conditions and pay, ultimately benefiting all workers in the industry.

NOTES

1. Alongside other critical migration scholars, the preference is to use 'irregular', 'undocumented', 'unauthorised' or even 'illegalised' (rather than 'illegal') migrants to draw attention to the institutional and political processes of rendering people illegal.
2. Worker status is a category in British labour law between self-employed and employee, giving access to some labour rights such as the minimum wage and holiday pay (Bertolini and Dukes 2021).
3. According to the Leeds Index of Platform Labour Protest: https://leeds-index.co.uk.

REFERENCES

Ahmad A. (2020) Do equal qualifications yield equal rewards for immigrants in the labour market?, *Work, Employment and Society*, 34 (5) 826–843.

Allaby E. (2021) The rise of Uber Eats gang masters is tearing the gig economy apart, *Wired UK*, 15 February. www.wired.co.uk/article/uber-eats-italy

Altenried M. (2021) Mobile workers, contingent labour: the gig economy and the multiplication of labour, *Environment and Planning A: Economy and Space*. https://doi.org/10.1177/0308518X211054846

Altenried M. (2023) Platforms, labour, and mobility: migration and the gig economy in Ness I. (ed.) *The Routledge handbook of the gig economy*, Routledge, 180–189.

Altenried M. et al. (2018) Logistical borderscapes: politics and mediation of mobile labor in after the of migration, *South Atlantic Quarterly*, 117 (2) 291–312.

Alyanak O. et al. (2023) Platform work, exploitation, and migrant worker resistance: evidence from Berlin and London, *The Economic and Labour Relations Review*, 34 (4). https://doi.org/10.1017/elr.2023.34

Andrikopoulos A. (2023) *Argonauts of West Africa: unauthorized migration and kinship dynamics in a changing Europe*, University of Chicago Press.

Banasiak S. (2020) Raising a new collective voice through Greenfield Union organising the mobilisation and unionisation of workers and the establishment of a collective agreement at Foodora in Sweden, MA Mälardaren University, Sweden.

Baril É. (2023a) *Citizen-rentier-ship: delivering the to labour platforms in Paris Antipode*. https://doi.org/10.1111/anti.13009

Baril É. (2023b) Livraison, migration et résistance au sein des plateformes de travail numériques à Paris et Toronto, in Vultur M. (ed.) *Les plateformes de travail numériques polygraphie d'un nouveau modèle organisationnel*, Presses de l'Université Laval, 265–286.

Barron P. et al. (2011) On bosse ici, on reste ici ! La grève des sans-papiers : une aventure inédite, *La Découverte*.

Bertolini A. and Dukes R. (2021) Trade unions and platform workers in the UK: worker representation in the shadow of the law, *Industrial Law Journal*, 50 (4) 662–688.

Bertolini A. et al. (2021) Towards decent work in the digital age: introducing the fairwork project in Germany, *Zeitschrift für Arbeitswissenschaft*, 75 (2), 187–192.

Bertossi C. (2008) The regulation of migration: a global challenge, *Politique étrangère*, 2008/5, 189–202.

Bogoeski V. and Rasnača Z. (eds.) (2023) *Report on the social security rights of short-term third-country national migrant workers*, ETUI

Borghi P. et al. (2021) Mind the gap between discourses and practices: platform workers' representation in France and Italy, *European Journal of Industrial Relations*, 27 (4), 425–443.

Cant C. (2020) *Riding for Deliveroo: resistance in the new economy*, Polity.

Cini L. (2023) Resisting algorithmic control: the rise and variety of platform worker mobilisations, *New Technology, Work and Employment,* 38 (1) 125–144.

Comte E. (2018) *The history of the European migration regime Germany's hegemony*, Routledge.

Di Stasio V. and Larsen E.N. (2020) The racialized and gendered workplace: applying an intersectional lens to a field experiment on hiring discrimination in five European labor markets, *Social Psychology Quarterly*, 83 (3), 229–250.

Eurostat (2023a) Demography. Population on 1st January 2023. https://ec.europa.eu/eurostat/cache/interactive-publications/demography/2023/00/index.html

Eurostat (2023b) Migrant integration statistics. Labour market indicators. https://ec.europa.eu/eurostat/statistics-explained/index.php?title=Migrant_integration_statistics_%E2%80%93_labour_market_indicators#Overview

FES (2022) *Online platforms and platform work*, Friedrich-Ebert-Stiftung.

Gardner Z. and Patel C. (2021) *We are here: routes to regularisation for the UK's undocumented population*, Joint Council for the Welfare of Immigrants.

Gomes B. (2022) The French platform workers: a thwarted path to the third status Italian, *Labour Law e-Journal*, 15 (1), 143–149.

Gomes B. and Isidro L. (2020) Travailleurs des plateformes et sans-papiers: propos du conflit des livreurs Frichti, *Revue de droit du travail*, 12, 728–741.

Guga Ş. and Trif A. (2023) Trade unions in Romania: walking the thin line between politics and the market, in Waddington J., Müller T. and Vandaele K. (eds.) *Trade in the European Union picking up the pieces of the neoliberal challenge*, Peter Lang, 911–943.

Hagen I.M. and Jensen R.S. (2019) Trade union representatives from ethnic minorities representation revisited, *Transfer*, 25 (4), 437–450.

Heiland H. (2020) Workers' voice in platform labour: an overview, *WSI Study 21*, Hans-Böckler-Stiftung.

Héran F. (2019) Migrations en France et en Europe, *Études*, 2019/4, 45–55.

Hiessl C. (2021) The classification of platform workers in case law: a cross-European comparative analysis, *Comparative Labor Law & Policy Journal*, 42 (2), 465–518.

Iazzolino G. and Varesio A. (2023) Gaming the system: tactical workarounds and the production of antagonistic subjectivities among migrant platform workers in Italy, *Antipode*, 55 (3), 667–984.

JCWI (2022) *Who are the UK's undocumented population?*, Joint Council for the Welfare of Immigrants.

Jesnes K. (2019) Employment models of platform companies in Norway.A distinctive approach?, Nordic Journal of Working Life Studies, 9(S6).

Jesnes K. and Oppegaard S.M.N. (2023) Plattformmediert gigarbeid i Norge:f leksibilitet, uforutsigbarhet og ulikhet, in Kavli H.C., Fløtten T. and Trygstad S. (eds.) *Ulikhetens drivere og dilemmaer*, Universitetsforlaget, 137–153.

Jesnes K. et al. (2021) The role of worker collectives among app-based food delivery couriers in France, Germany and Norway: all the same or different?, in Drahokoupil J. and Vandaele K. (eds.) *A modern guide to labour and the platform economy,* Edward Elgar Publishing, 258–273.

Joyce S. and Stuart M. (2021) Trade union responses to platform work: an evolving tension between mainstream and grassroots approaches, in Drahokoupil J. and Vandaele K. (eds.) *A modern guide to labour and the platform economy, Edward Elgar Publishing*, 177–192.

Kowalik Z., Lewandowski P. and Kaczmarczyk P. (2023) *Job quality gaps between migrant and native gig workers: evidence from Poland*, Institute of Labor Economics.

Kraler A. (2019) Regularization of irregular migrants and social policies: comparative perspectives, *Journal of Immigrant & Refugee Studies*, 17 (1), 94–113.

Lamannis M. (2023) *Collective bargaining in the platform economy: a mapping exercise of existing initiatives*, Report 2023.02, ETUI.

Lata L.N., Burdon J. and Reddel T. (2023) New tech, old exploitation: gig economy, algorithmic control and migrant labour?, *Sociology Compass*, 17 (1), 1–14.

Lebas C. (2020) Comment le confinement a enfoncé les livreurs à vélo dans la précarité, *The Conversation*, 17 May.

Lien H. (2023) *De fleste som tjener penger gjennom digitale plattformer driver med privat eiendomsutleie*, Statistics Norway.

Ma S. et al. (2023) Uncovering gig worker-centered design opportunities in food delivery work, in *DIS '23: Proceedings of the 2023 ACM Designing Interactive Systems Conference*, 688–701.

Mendonça P. and Kougiannou N.K. (2023) Disconnecting labour: the impact of intraplatform algorithmic changes on the labour process and workers' capacity to organise collectively, *New Technology, Work and Employment*, 38 (1), 1–20.

Meseşan D., Ionaşcu D. and Chirea V. (2023) Livratorii din Asia care îţi aduc mâncarea muncesc peste 10 ore pe zi, pentru 2.000 de lei pe lună, deşi firmele le promit altceva. 'E un viitor negru pe bicicletă', *Libertatea*, 20 September. www.libertatea.ro/stiri/livratorii-din-asia-care-iti-aduc-mancarea-muncesc-peste-10-ore-pe-zi-pentru-2–000-de-lei-pe-luna-desi-firmele-le-promit-altceva-e-un-viitor-negru-pe-bicicleta-4593461

Metawala P., Golda-Pongratz K. and Irazábal C. (2021) Revisiting Engels' 'housing question': work and housing conditions of immigrant platform delivery riders in Barcelona, *Human Geography*, 14 (2), 243–257.

Mezzadra S. and Neilson B. (2008) *Border as method, or, the multiplication of labor.* https://transversal.at/transversal/0608/mezzadra-neilson/en

Mezzadra S. and Neilson B. (2013) *Border as method, or, the multiplication of labor*, Duke University Press.

Nergaard K. and Ødegård A.M. (2022) *Organisasjonsgrad blant arbeidsinnvandrere*, Fafo.

Newlands G. (2022) 'This isn't forever for me': perceived employability and migrant gig work in Norway and Sweden, *Environment and Planning A: Economy and Space*. https://doi.org/10.1177/0308518X221083021

Pérez Capitan L. and Ranz R. (2022) *Don't gig up, never! Country update: Spain*, Unión General de Trabajadores.

Pew Research Center (2019) Europe's unauthorized immigrant total peaked in 2016 before leveling off. https://www.pewresearch.org/global-migration-and-demography/2019/11/13/europes-unauthorized-immigrant-population-peaks-in-2016-then-levels-off/

Piasna A., Zwysen W. and Drahokoupil J. (2022) The platform economy in Europe: results from the second ETUI Internet and Platform Work Survey (IPWS), Working Paper 2022.05, ETUI.

Popan C. and Anaya-Boig E. (2022) The precarious work of platform cycle delivery workers, in Norcliffe G. et al. (eds.) *Routledge companion to cycling*, Routledge, 33–41.

Rioux L. (2022) État des lieux, lutte et syndicalisation des travailleurs des plates-formes de livraison, *Le droit ouvrier*, 890, 414–417.

Robins D. (2023) Invisible migration and 'perverse' capital: exploring the experiences of migrant delivery riders, *International Migration Review*, https://doi.org/10.1177/01979183231191746

Schaupp S. (2022) Algorithmic integration and precarious (dis)obedience: on the co-constitution of migration regime and workplace regime in digitalised manufacturing and logistics, *Work, Employment and Society*, 36 (2), 310–327.

Steinhilper E. (2021) *Migrant protest: interactive dynamics in precarious mobilizations*, Amsterdam University Press.

Sumption M. and Brindle B. (2023) Work visas and migrant workers in the UK, Briefing 29 September, The Migration Observatory.

Șuțu C. (2023) Reportaj. 'Muncim și 13 ore pe zi pentru 1.500 de lei pe lună'. Cum trăiesc în România livratorii asiatici care-ți aduc mâncarea la ușă, Digi24, 3 September.

Tassinari A. and Maccarrone V. (2020) Riders on the storm: workplace solidarity among gig economy couriers in Italy and the UK, *Work, Employment and Society*, 34 (1), 35–54.

Timko P. and van Melik R. (2021) Being a Deliveroo rider: practices of platform labor in Nijmegen and Berlin, *Journal of Contemporary Ethnography*, 50 (4), 497–523.

Tsing A. (2009) Supply chains and the human condition, *Rethinking Marxism*, 21 (2), 148–176.

van Doorn N. (2017) Platform labor: on the gendered and racialized exploitation of low-income service work in the 'on-demand' economy, *Information, Communication & Society*, 20 (6), 898–914.

van Doorn N. (2023) Liminal precarity and compromised agency: migrant experiences of gig work in Amsterdam, Berlin, and New York City, in Ness I. (ed.) *The Routledge book of the gig economy*, Routledge, 158–179.

van Doorn N., Ferrari F. and Graham M. (2023) Migration and migrant labour in the gig economy: an intervention, *Work, Employment and Society*, 37 (4), 1099–1111.

Vandaele K. (2020) *From street protest to 'improvisational unionism': platform-based food delivery couriers in Belgium and the Netherlands*, Friedrich-Ebert-Stiftung.

Vandaele K. (2021) Collective resistance and organizational creativity amongst Europe's platform workers: a new power in the labour movement?, in Haidar J. and Keune M. (eds.) *Work and labour relations in global platform capitalism*, Edward Elgar Publishing, 206–235.

Vandaele K., Piasna A. and Drahokoupil J. (2019) 'Algorithm breakers' are not a different 'species': attitudes towards trade unions of Deliveroo riders in Belgium, Working Paper 2019.06, ETUI.

Vieira T. (2023) Platform couriers' self-exploitation: the case study of Glovo, *New Technology, Work and Employment*, 38 (3), 493–512.

Vinale H., Gransard C. and Caudron D. (2022) 'C'est l'anarchie': Ismaël et Christophe, livreurs Deliveroo, dénoncent un marché déloyal où sévissent de nombreux faux comptes, RTL info, 2 May.

Visseyrias M. (2021) Les coursiers sans-papiers d'Uber Eats et de Deliveroo, nouveaux forçats de la livraison de repas, *Le Figaro*, 12 December.

Woodcock J. (2016) #Slaveroo: Deliveroo drivers organising in the 'gig economy', Novara Media, 12 August.

All links were checked on 22 January 2024.

PART II

MOBILISATION AND ISSUES

6. Patterns of labour unrest among app-based food delivery workers in Europe: the surprising persistence of industrial relations regimes

Mark Stuart, Vera Trappmann, Denis Neumann, Simon Joyce, Ioulia Bessa and Charles Umney

INTRODUCTION

Labour unrest among app-based food delivery workers has been increasing. Protests by platform workers – food delivery couriers in particular – have become common in many major European cities. To some extent, this should come as no surprise, as the business models of online platforms are typically predicated on disrupting not only established economic markets but also labour markets. Thus, there has been an ongoing concern about the lack of social protection for platform workers, who are often hired on a self-employed basis and lack both job security and wider representational and employment rights (Forde et al. 2017). Against this backdrop, there have been numerous high-profile legal battles around the employment status of platform workers (Aloisi and Gramano 2019) as well as, often spontaneous, strikes and demonstrations by platform workers. Despite the seemingly inhospitable environment that platform work poses for trade unions (Vandaele 2018), there is evidence of increasing union activity targeted at supporting platform workers and, in selected cases, the establishment of new bargaining arrangements and agreements (see Lamannis 2023).

Such developments have been captured to date mainly by case study work that explores the dynamics of particular disputes; either a single protest event or selected protests against a company, with comparative research limited to a few countries (Cant 2020; Heiland 2021; Tassinari and Maccarone 2020; Vandaele 2020). In previous work, in contrast, we have taken a more quantitative approach to show that platform worker protest is a global phenomenon, with important similarities as well as differences across different sectors and countries (Bessa et al. 2022; Joyce et al. 2020; Stuart et al. 2023; Trappmann et al. 2020; Umney et al. 2024).

Building on our previous work, this chapter examines platform worker protests in the app-based food delivery sector in Europe, based on a sample of 430 protests from 2017 to 2023. While labour unrest among platform workers is now an established feature of contemporary industrial relations in Europe, the extent to which such unrest may be shaped by national specificities of collective action or established 'institutional logics' remains unclear. Prima facie, such a possibility might seem unlikely: after all, the industrial relations of platform work scarcely exhibit any degree of institutionalisation and, as noted, platform workers lack employment rights, while union membership is low and collective bargaining rare. Nevertheless, we know that institutions are not entirely absent. Platform workers have turned to the law in efforts to claim or enforce employment and other rights, and there have been some institutional gains. For example, collective agreements have been signed in the Nordic countries, the Netherlands, Italy and Spain (Ilsøe and Jesnes 2020; Kilhoffer et al. 2018; Lamannis 2023), as well as in Germany, where the first works councils in platform work were established by food delivery workers in 2017, and Austria (Herr 2017; Neumann 2023). Furthermore, even where industrial relations institutions have little direct impact, it is plausible that the institutional context can influence actors by framing issues and shaping expectations.

The chapter asks, therefore, to what extent distinct patterns of platform worker unrest are discernible across Europe, considering whether specific patterns of labour unrest in app-based food delivery work share similarities with and can be explained by existing industrial relations frameworks. To address these questions, the analysis draws on a unique dataset – the Leeds Index of Platform Labour Protest. While the dataset is global, the focus of this chapter is specifically on food delivery in Europe. Conceptually and methodologically, we employ Visser's (2009) typology of industrial relations regimes. This allows for an assessment of the extent of the variation in platform labour unrest across five different regimes: liberal pluralism, social partnership, organised corporatism, and both fragmented and polarised state-centred regimes.

The next section considers pertinent issues in relation to platform labour unrest in Europe and shows how Visser's typology frames the analysis. Following this, the data method and analytical approach is described prior to the presentation of the empirical findings. A broad discussion follows, as a result of which the clear conclusion is that distinct patterns of labour unrest in the food delivery sector may be emerging across different industrial relations regimes, though the findings at this stage are tentative and not all the variation is fully explained by the Visser model.

EMPIRICAL OVERVIEW AND CONCEPTUAL FRAMEWORK

Collective action by app-based food delivery workers now features in a wealth of studies from Europe and beyond. Initially, the role of social media in promoting solidarities seemed novel (Soriano and Cabañes 2020; Vallas and Schor 2020), but more familiar methods, such as demonstrations and strikes, have also featured in platform labour unrest (Cavallini and Avogaro 2019; Tassinari and Maccarrone 2020). In some countries, we have even seen the signing of collective agreements and the establishment of works councils, specifically in the food delivery sector (Ilsøe and Jesnes 2020; Neumann 2023; Schreyer 2021).

Informal networking between workers has been a crucial dynamic (Maffie 2020) and studies highlight the prevalence of, often spontaneous, worker-driven mobilisations from below (Cini 2022; Heiland 2020; Vandaele 2020; Woodcock 2021). Nevertheless, viewed globally, unions are involved in over a third of platform worker protests (Bessa et al. 2022), rising to over half for European food delivery worker protests, with roughly equal representation of established, mainstream unions and newer, grassroots unions (Trappmann et al. 2020). The literature features case studies investigating the diversity of organisational forms of worker mobilisation (Cini et al. 2022). Comparative studies have looked at grassroots unions and self-organised protest (Tassinari and Maccarrone 2020), as well as worker cooperatives (Jesnes et al. 2021), but far less attention has been paid to mainstream trade unions (Vandaele 2021). Indeed, some researchers have questioned the role of mainstream unions, at least in the UK (Cant 2020; Woodcock and Cant 2022).

Looking at the issues and grievances driving worker unrest in app-based food delivery, pay is by far the most important, followed by employment status (Trappmann et al. 2020), with algorithmic management and wider regulatory issues seemingly of lesser significance. Direct gains from platform worker protests have been limited and uneven, but evident. Action by platform workers has forced concessions from platform companies and has made the conditions of platform work a topic of considerable public and political debate, leading to state and regulatory interventions, often in the form of new laws that seek to alleviate some of the more blatant injustices of platform work (Joyce and Stuart 2021; Rolf et al. 2022).

Research to date thus provides considerable empirical detail about platform work in general, and app-based food delivery work in particular, including how, why and where workers engage in collective protest (see Umney et al. 2024). Less common in the literature is any attempt to develop an overall conceptual framework for understanding these developments, especially in terms of the comparative institutional analysis commonly found elsewhere in industrial relations research. This chapter seeks to address this gap by assessing the feasibility of applying such comparative frameworks to the new sector of platform work.

Following Visser (2009), five industrial relations regimes, each associated with a particular European region, are distinguished. Social partnership, associated with the centre-west region (including Austria, Belgium, Germany, Netherlands, Slovenia, Switzerland), is characterised by strong sectoral collective bargaining and co-determination through works councils at company level. Liberal pluralism, associated with the western region (Cyprus, Ireland, Malta, UK), features low union density and company-based bargaining and tends to be dominated by employers, with conflict-driven industrial relations and low levels of state intervention. The fragmented state-centred regime, associated with eastern Europe (including Croatia, Czechia, Estonia, Lithuania, Poland), is marked by tripartite social dialogue, a strong state, and (sometimes highly) fragmented trade unions, beholden to state or business interests, commonly operating at company level. Organised corporatism, associated with the north or Nordic region (Denmark, Finland, Norway, Sweden), features strong trade unions and employer organisations, high trade union density and high collective bargaining coverage, with the main bargaining being at national and sectoral level rather than company-based. Finally, the polarised state-centred regime, associated with southern Europe (including France, Greece, Italy, Spain), is characterised by weak and fragmented social partners alongside a strongly interventionist state in the field of employment relations.

The model is not without its limitations, as each regime ignores, by definition, within-regime national variations (Visser 2009). For instance, there is a long-standing debate concerning the best way to describe industrial relations in eastern Europe (Bluhm and Trappmann 2010; Bohle and Greskovits 2019). Significant reductions in trade union membership in Slovenia, for example, raise questions about the future of social partnership. Even traditional German industrial relations have been eroded by increasing dualisation and the significant growth of insecure employment (Dörre 2016). Nevertheless, Visser's (2009) categorisation has been retained because the aim of this chapter is not to test the overall framework but to assess whether this type of institutional analysis can offer any insights into contemporary developments in labour relations in platform work.

DATA COLLECTION AND METHODS

Our database records instances of labour unrest in platform work.[1] We collect data from online news media sources via the GDELT Project.[2] GDELT monitors worldwide news in over 100 languages, gathering reports from the world's largest news agencies combined with the Google News algorithm. Limitations of news reports as a source of data include potential under-reporting (Davenport 2009) and selection bias (Hocke 1996; Jeanis and Powers 2017). However, selection bias is mitigated by GDELT's extensive range of coverage, including national and local publications in each country (Nam 2006). Utilising GDELT enables the identification of a large number of potential protests by platform workers across national territories.

Protest events have been selected as the unit of analysis to overcome the specific problems of measuring labour unrest in the platform sector. As a new area of paid work, with novel employment relations and few of the standard attributes of industrial relations – such as conventional trade union membership and recognition, established employer organisations, collective bargaining and agreements, formal strikes and strike data – new measures of worker organisation and contestation are needed. Industrial relations scholars have noted recent shifts in workers' repertoires of action and contestation, especially among more precarious sectors of employment, and this is particularly relevant in platform work (Atzeni 2021; Chesta et al. 2019; Chinguno 2019; Schmalz et al. 2023; Wood et al. 2021). The methodology for this chapter was therefore adapted from social movement research: specifically, protest event analysis (for an overview, see Opp 2009).

Our database includes classic forms of worker protest, such as strikes and demonstrations, and other methods, such as legal action. Opp (2009: 44) defines protest broadly as the 'joint (collective) action of individuals aimed at achieving their goal or goals influencing decisions of a target'. Legal action certainly meets these criteria and is consequently included here. Indeed, action as a form of labour contestation has been noted by several recent studies of platform work (Aloisi and Gramano 2019; Bertolini and Dukes 2021; Haidar and Keune 2021; Joyce et al. 2020). 'Institutionalisation' as a form of worker protest has also been included to capture the establishment of a new trade union or new works councils.

The database records relevant factors pertaining to a protest event, including: platform name, date and location of protest, platform sector (here, food delivery), key drivers of protest, type of protest, and labour actors involved. The classification of labour actors is designed to capture the specific characteristics of labour unrest in platform work. Thus, recognising that most worker protests involve no trade union or any other formal organisation and are often spontaneous, 'informal group of workers' is recorded as a key category. Mainstream trade unions are also differentiated from more grassroots unions. In addition, platform worker protest often involves non-trade union forms of organisation – often highly informal – which are termed 'worker collectives'. In practice, it should be noted that platform worker protests often involve a combination of actors.[3]

Initial searches of the database were organised by platform company, including all the large international brands and specific national-level platform leaders. Keywords for protest and labour unrest were then searched, eliciting a large number of news articles. Refined searches, through automated and manual means, substantially reduced the number of valid articles, with these then being coded by hand (for full details of the sampling method, see Umney et al. 2024). A final stage of review reduced the sample further. Notably, articles were excluded where they referred only to a planned protest and where there was no further means of verifying if the protest had actually taken place. For a limited number of articles, there was simply insufficient evidence to confirm that a protest had occurred. Again, if the protests could not be verified by secondary searches, they were excluded from the dataset.

The final dataset includes 430 protest events in app-based food delivery in Europe, across 23 countries (see Table 6.1). The largest concentration of protests is in the UK, with 118, which accounts for 27 per cent of the sample. Five further countries have a significant number of cases, each accounting for over five per cent of the sample: Spain (18 per cent of total cases); France (15 per cent); Germany (13 per cent); Belgium (6 per cent); Italy (5 per cent). Together, these six countries contribute more than 84 per cent of all protest events.

Table 6.1 Protest events by industrial relations regime (n = 430)

Industrial relations regime	Number of events	Percentage of total events
Social partnership (centre-west): Austria, Belgium, Germany, Netherlands, Slovenia, Switzerland	111	26%
Liberal pluralism (west): Cyprus, Ireland, Malta, UK	124	29%
Fragmented state-centred (east): Croatia, Czechia, Estonia, Lithuania, Poland	23	5%
Organised corporatism (north): Denmark, Finland, Norway, Sweden	9	2%
Polarised state-centred (south): France, Greece, Italy, Spain	163	38%

Note: Percentage figures do not total 100 due to rounding.
Source: Leeds Index of Platform Labour Protest. Categorisation adapted from Visser (2009).

EMPIRICAL FINDINGS

The Form and Motivation of Protests and the Actors Involved

The highest proportion of protests occur in southern polarised state-centred regimes (38 per cent). Social partnership makes up 26 per cent of the sample and liberal pluralism 29 per cent, while fragmented state-centred regimes and organised corporatism have proportionally lower levels of protest (5 per cent and 2 per cent respectively). Descriptive analysis is included in what follows across all five industrial relations regimes, though the low number of responses for fragmented state-centred regimes and organised corporatism should be noted and the findings treated with caution. That said, irregular protests can often lead to significant outcomes: for example, a strike in Norway that lasted eight weeks, supported by the Fellesforbundet union, led to a collective agreement (see Chapter 5).

Protests are typically brief and involve a small number of workers. They are often spontaneous, with groups of couriers responding to an immediate grievance or incident (such as an accident) by grouping together to demonstrate or by calling on other couriers to observe a 'log-off'.[4] In nearly a quarter of cases (24 per cent) it was not possible to discern the length of the protest. For events where the length of the protest could be verified, eight in ten lasted less than 24 hours (typically just for a couple of hours), although a small proportion lasted more than eight weeks or were ongoing. The most obvious form of ongoing or lengthy protest relates to a legal case, though there are also some clear examples of lengthy strike action by platform workers – for example, the strikes by Deliveroo couriers in Sheffield in the UK that continued for many months. Given that larger actions require coordination and planning, it is perhaps no surprise that these spontaneous protests are mostly smaller in scale, although it is not always possible to verify participant numbers: such information is missing in 45 per cent of all cases. There are also some very large protests involving more than 1,000 workers (but just 3 per cent of the sample).

The most common motivation for protest is pay – in line with previous research (Bessa et al. 2022) – which is present in 61 per cent of cases. Protests often focus on several different issues, however. The frequency with which other types of protests are articulated in protestors' demands is: employment status (29 per cent); working conditions (23 per cent); health and safety (9 per cent); union representation (8 per cent); deactivation (7 per cent); running costs (5 per cent); working hours (4 per cent); non-pay benefits (4 per cent); other regulatory issues (4 per cent); and other issues (7 per cent).

There are two main types of protest action: strikes and demonstrations. In many cases, it took a careful reading to differentiate the two. Strikes account for 41 per cent of events, while demonstrations account for 36 per cent. The next most common form of protest is legal action, present in 15 per cent of cases. Institutionalisation is much less common, defining the protest in just 6 per cent of events, while other forms of action occur in only 2 per cent.

Four main types of labour actors were coded in the dataset: mainstream unions, grassroots unions, informal groups of workers and worker collectives. Around two-thirds of cases (66 per cent) involve informal groups of workers. It is important to recognise, however, that protests often involve a mix of labour actors, with informal groups of workers supported by or receiving advocacy from other actors. Mainstream unions are involved in 38 per cent of cases and grassroots unions in 22 per cent. There is also strong representation from worker collectives, which are involved in around a quarter of protests (24 per cent). Early examples of worker collectives include the Couriers Collective from Belgium, CLAP (Collective of Autonomous Platform Deliverers) from France, the Riders Union from Italy, and RidersxDerechos (Couriers' Rights) from Spain. Collectives including the Gorillas Workers Collective or the Lieferando Workers Collective have also emerged in Germany. Worker collectives often appeal to couriers because they operate in many cases with a grassroots orientation and are independent of established actors.

Law firms are involved in only three per cent of cases. The significance of these varies, often because of differences in how trade unions organise legal matters. In some countries, unions employ lawyers directly, while, in others, they work with lawyers from specialist labour law firms. Some progressive law firms are proactive in representing platform workers (among others) and, as a result, these are included in the classification. A category of 'other' actors is involved in eight per cent of cases. This diverse group includes parliamentarians, civil society organisations and campaigning and leftist political groups. In this category, there are also three employer-associated 'unions' that have played a major role in protests against the Spanish 'Riders' Law'.

A range of coalitions is also possible in platform worker protests. Most typically, these occur when more formal actors (such as trade union organisations) support more informal groups of workers. Thus, 18 per cent of all protests involve an informal group of workers supported by a mainstream trade union. Similar proportions are apparent for the support of informal groups of workers by a grassroots union (13 per cent) or a worker collective (17 per cent). Coalitions between mainstream and grassroots unions are negligible, occurring in just two per cent of cases. The findings suggest that trade unions are quite heavily involved in protests by platform workers, despite the lack of formal recognition. This is indicated by the lower proportion of protest events initiated and led solely by trade union actors. Where this does take place, it is more likely to be mainstream unions (15 per cent) that take the lead actor role rather than grassroots unions (5 per cent).

The following empirical section presents an analysis of platform worker protests, categorised by industrial relations regime. The analysis focuses on three issues: involvement of labour actors, motivations for protests and forms of protest. The analysis aims to show the extent to which different industrial relations regimes are characterised by specific constellations of platform worker protests.

ROLE OF LABOUR ACTORS

Table 6.2 presents findings on the involvement of different labour actors in app-based food delivery worker protests across the five industrial relations regimes, drawn from cross tabulations of labour actors by industrial relations regime. Global data suggests that informal groups of workers tend to be proportionally the dominant actor, and the findings of this chapter across Europe are broadly similar. The exception to this relates to platform worker protests in social partnership countries and in fragmented state-centred regimes: 67 per cent of protests in social partnership and 61 per cent of those in fragmented state-centred regimes involve mainstream unions. Mainstream unions are also quite active in organised corporatism countries (44 per cent) and polarised state-centred regimes (41 per cent), although to a lesser degree. A distinctive finding is the almost total absence of mainstream union involvement in liberal pluralism: present in just three per cent of protest events.

Table 6.2 Industrial relations regimes and labour actors (percentages)

Labour actors	Social partnership	Liberal pluralism	Fragmented state-centred	Organised corporatism	Polarised state-centred
Mainstream union	67%***	3%***	61%*	44%	41%
Grassroots union	18%	52%***	13%	11%	3%***
Worker collective	27%	6%***	13%	33%	36%***
Informal group of workers	57%*	77%**	39%**	78%	67%

Note: The table includes cross-tabulated associations, and the data do not add to 100 – all figures are rounded. Chi-square significance = *.05; **.01; ***.001.
Source: Leeds Index of Platform Labour Protest.

This does not mean, however, that trade unions are not involved in liberal pluralist countries. Where they are involved, it is much more likely to be grassroots unions, which are present in 52 per cent of protest events. This finding is influenced by the large number of protests in the UK and the highly active role of grassroots unions like the Independent Workers' Union of Great Britain (IWGB), which supported the first uprisings in the food delivery industry in Europe in 2016 and has been influential in shaping strategies in other countries. Grassroots unions have a much lower presence in the other regimes, although they were involved in 18 per cent of protests in social partnership countries.

The involvement of worker collectives also varies significantly across the different industrial relations regimes. They are much more likely to have been involved in platform protests in polarised state-centred regimes (36 per cent) as well as countries featuring organised corporatism (33 per cent) and social partnership (27 per cent), being much less visible in liberal pluralism and fragmented state-centred regimes.

As noted, app-based food delivery worker protests often involve more than one group of labour actors working together to support the claims of platform workers. More granular analysis confirms this. Mainstream unions are more likely to support informal groups of workers in their protests in social partnership countries, while grassroots unions are more likely to support informal groups of workers in liberal pluralist ones. Worker collectives are most likely to support informal groups of workers in polarised state-centred regimes. There are, nonetheless, some subtle differences when looking at protests where there is a singular labour actor. As expected, grassroots trade unions are most likely to be the only labour actor involved in app-based food delivery worker protests in liberal pluralist countries. However, mainstream unions are more likely to be the only labour actor in protests in fragmented state-centred regimes, while worker collectives are proportionally more likely to be the only labour actor in organised corporatist countries.

MOTIVATIONS FOR PLATFORM WORKER PROTESTS

The motivations for platform worker protests across the different industrial relations regimes are detailed in Table 6.3. Global analysis spotlights pay as the primary driver of such protests (Bessa et al. 2022; Umney et al. 2024). These findings are confirmed across all European industrial relations regimes, with pay being the primary driver, to varying degrees, within each one. Nearly all protests in fragmented state-centred regimes include pay as a motivator, recorded in 96 per cent of protests. Disputes over pay are also extensive in liberal pluralism (82 per cent) and organised corporatism (78 per cent) countries. Just under half (43 per cent) of disputes in social partnership countries include demands around pay. The wide disparity in the proportion of disputes articulating pay as a central grievance is illustrative of a wider set of demands being identified in some regimes.

The second key motivator of platform worker protest is employment status. While there has been much attention in the UK around legal test cases of employment status – for example, in the Uber rulings – protests around employment status are less frequent in liberal pluralism countries, where just 16 per cent of protest events focus on this issue. Employment status as a motivator of protest is much more common in social partnership countries (39 per cent of events) and polarised state-centred regimes (36 per cent). Almost half of the protests recorded over employment status happened in Spain, which has become a key site of legal battles over

Table 6.3 Industrial relations regime and motivation for protests (percentages)

Issues	Social partnership	Liberal pluralism	Fragmented state-centred	Organised corporatism	Polarised state-centred
Pay	43%***	82%***	96%***	78%	52%***
Working conditions	34%**	19%	26%	11%	18%
Employment status	39%**	12%***	17%	33%	36%*
Union representation	16%***	4%	13%	0%	4%*
Deactivation	4%	5%	0%	11%	12%**
Health and safety	5%	16%***	0%	0%	8%
Running costs[5]	10%**	2%	0%	11%	3%

Note: The table includes cross-tabulated associations, and the data do not add to 100 – all figures are rounded. Chi-square significance = *.05; **.01; ***.001.
Source: Leeds Index of Platform Labour Protest.

the classification of couriers (La Voz de Asturias 2018; Mirón Parra 2019; Europa Press 2020), notably, in struggles for and against the Riders' Law which compels delivery platform companies to consider their workers as employees (see Chapter 11). Following the introduction of the Riders' Law, Deliveroo has withdrawn from Spain, having previously left Germany and the Netherlands due to judicial headwinds.

Working conditions are most likely to be cited as a motivator in social partnership countries, where 34 per cent of protests identify working conditions as a grievance. A similar finding is evident in fragmented state-centred regimes, where 26 per cent of protests cite working conditions. For other regimes, this seems to be less important.

While several other issues are cited as motivators for protests, these are less frequently cited overall. Union representation is associated primarily with protests in social partnership countries but is cited in fewer than one in five (16 per cent) protest events. Deactivation is most commonly a motivator in polarised state-centred regimes, cited in 12 per cent of protest events. Globally, there is evidence of a significant upsurge in platform worker protests over health and safety during the Covid-19 pandemic, notably in Latin America and Africa (Umney et al. 2024). Looking at Europe, health and safety is most likely to be a motivator in liberal pluralist countries, cited in 16 per cent of protests. Finally, running costs are generally not mentioned as frequently as other motivators and are most noteworthy in countries featuring social partnerships and in organised corporatist regimes (cited in 10 per cent and 11 per cent of events respectively).

FORMS OF PROTEST

There are notable differences in how app-based food delivery workers protest across the various industrial relations regimes, shown in Table 6.4. Strikes are the most typical form of protest in liberal pluralist countries and fragmented state-centred regimes, recorded in around two-thirds and three-quarters of events, respectively. The lowest incidence of platform worker

Table 6.4 *Industrial relations regime and form of protest (percentages)*

Form of protest	Social partnership	Liberal pluralism	Fragmented state-centred	Organised corporatism	Polarised state-centred
Strike	21%***	64%***	74%***	44%	33%**
Demonstration	49%***	25%**	22%	22%	37%
Legal action	11%	7%**	0%*	22%	25%***
Institutionalisation	19%***	1%**	4%	11%	1%***

Note: The table includes cross-tabulated associations, and the data do not add to 100 – all figures are rounded. Chi-square significance = *.05; **.01; ***.001.
Source: Leeds Index of Platform Labour Protest.

strikes by regime is in social partnership countries, where just over a fifth of protests by platform workers take the form of strike action. The most common form of protest action in social partnership, in contrast, is public demonstrations: nearly half of all protests in such countries take this form. The notable differences in forms of protest between social partnership and liberal pluralist countries raise an intriguing question about the role of trade unions in supporting platform worker protests. It appears on the face of it to be the case that there is some association, at least in these two regimes, between demonstrations and mainstream unions and strikes and grassroots unions.

Other forms of protest are much less common, though a notable minority of protests in polarised state-centred regimes and in organised corporatism take the form of legal action, rising to a quarter in polarised state-centred regimes. The majority of protests and legal actions against food delivery platforms like Deliveroo, Glovo and Uber Eats in France, Italy and Spain primarily revolve around the misclassification of workers as independent contractors instead of employees. This misclassification, coupled with poor working conditions, is a key driver of disputes and is especially prevalent in Italy and Spain. Few protests (7 per cent) take the form of legal action in liberal pluralism, again possibly reflecting few protests being motivated by claims of employment status.

Institutionalisation as a form of protest is not that frequent across all industrial relations regimes, except in social partnership. Here, nearly a fifth of all protest events take the form of institutionalisation. This can largely be explained by the establishment of works councils in Germany and Austria, especially in the former, where a works council structure has been established throughout the country since 2017, making use of co-determination rights. This finding may be a reflection of higher levels of involvement by mainstream unions in supporting platform worker protests and/or a higher level of protests motivated by a desire to achieve union representation (Neumann 2023).

COMPARATIVE ANALYSIS OF PLATFORM LABOUR PROTEST ACROSS INDUSTRIAL RELATIONS REGIMES

The analysis has thus far explored descriptive associations between various factors pertaining to platform worker protests and different industrial relations regimes. This suggests that particular constellations of protests may take place in particular industrial relations regimes. Multivariate analysis allows us to interrogate these findings still further. Accordingly, a logistic regression was run for each industrial relations regime – with each regime dummy-coded – against our variables for labour actors, the motivations for worker protest and the different forms of protest. This offers an initial analysis into whether different models of platform worker protest are evolving across industrial relations regimes. Table 6.5 presents the summary findings, identifying those variables that are significant and indicating whether any association is negative or positive. Given the low number of protest events within organised corporatism, this is omitted from the analysis.

Regression analysis offers some confirmation of the analysis detailed here. Platform worker protest in social partnerships is thus positively associated with the involvement of established trade unions, with protests typically actioned either via demonstrations or institutionalisation. Protests are most typically associated with claims over working conditions; pay and

Table 6.5a Platform worker protest characteristics by industrial relations regime, actors (n = 421)

Labour actors	**Social partnership**	**Liberal pluralism**	**Fragmented state-centred**	**Polarised state-centred**
Mainstream union	+***	–***	–	–
Grassroots union	–	+***	–	–***
Worker collective	–	–***	–	+***
Informal group of workers	–	–	–***	–
Law firm	–	+*	–	–

Note: The table includes only statistically significant findings at *.05; **.01; ***.001.
Source: Leeds Index of Platform Labour Protest.

Table 6.5b Platform worker protest characteristics by industrial relations regime, motivations (n = 421)

Motivations for protest	**Social partnership**	**Liberal pluralism**	**Fragmented state-centred**	**Polarised state-centred**
Pay	–***	–	+**	–
Working conditions	+*	–	–*	–
Employment status	–	–***	–	–
Union representation	–	–	–	–
Deactivation	–*	–	–	+*
Health and safety	–	+**	–	–

Note: The table includes only statistically significant findings at *.05; **.01; ***.001.
Source: Leeds Index of Platform Labour Protest.

Table 6.5c Platform worker protest characteristics by industrial relations regime, forms (n = 421)

Form of protest	**Social partnership**	**Liberal pluralism**	**Fragmented state-centred**	**Polarised state-centred**
Strike	–	–	–	–*
Demonstration	+*	–	–	–*
Legal action	–	–	–	–
Institutionalisation	+**	–*	–	–***

Note: The table includes only statistically significant findings at *.05; **.01; ***.001.
Source: Leeds Index of Platform Labour Protest.

deactivation are less likely to be motivators for protests when all other factors are included in the model.

In contrast, the involvement of established trade unions is negatively associated with liberal pluralism. Worker collectives are also negatively associated with this regime. Rather, independent trade unions are most typically associated with protests in liberal pluralist countries. There is also a positive association with law firms. Looking at motivations for protest in this regime, it is health and safety that is most positively associated, taking all other factors into account, and there is less of an emphasis on protests around employment status. Liberal pluralist countries do not appear to have characteristic forms of protest, although those on institutionalisation are negatively associated.

The key defining characteristic of fragmented state-centred regimes is protests over pay. There is not a very clear picture in terms of the role of labour actors, although the part played by informal groups of workers, as an element of an overall model of protest, is negatively associated with this regime. As with liberal pluralism, there is no clearly defined form of protest associated with this regime. It should be noted, however, that the modelling for this regime is based on a relatively small number of observations, which suggests that these findings should not be taken as conclusive.

Finally, protests around deactivation and involving worker collectives are positively associated with polarised state-centred regimes. There are few other significant associations, although, notably, protests are less likely to have taken place through the means of institutionalisation and are less likely to involve grassroots trade unions.

DISCUSSION AND CONCLUSIONS

This analysis of platform worker protests in the food delivery sector in Europe offers a first attempt to map quantitatively the patterns of labour unrest by industrial relations regime. The disrupting effects of platform companies on economic markets and in the labour market context are now well established, and this has spurred increased interest in policy circles around issues related to social protection, as well as academic interest in how platform workers have sought to respond. The Leeds Index is a novel dataset that chiefly captures public forms of protest by platform workers. The findings reported in this chapter detail the extent and nature of platform worker protest across the food delivery sector in Europe and reveal potentially intriguing patterns of protest across different industrial relations regimes.

The most notable finding is the seemingly different patterns of protest that are emerging across liberal pluralism and social partnership countries. These highlight distinctive patterns of involvement by trade union actors. Mainstream unions are more prevalent in protests in social partnership countries. In contrast, they have a less notable presence in those taking place in liberal pluralist ones. These findings offer some support for the Visser model, reflecting the greater institutional role of mainstream unions in wider employment relations in social partnership countries compared to liberal pluralist ones. What is less readily predicted from the Visser framework is the significant role of grassroots unions within liberal pluralism and the role of worker collectives in polarised state-centred regimes.

Nevertheless, Visser-derived explanations remain within reach. It is possible that industrial relations regimes may exert an influence not only because of the features that are present but also because of those that are missing. So, we might find (partial) explanations by focusing on the gaps between industrial relations regimes. Looking at the three for which we have the most data – social partnership, liberal pluralism and polarised state-centred regimes – as expected, all three show a considerable (if varied) presence of the most informal form of worker organisation: informal groups of workers. Moving to more formal organisation, social partnership countries, as noted, are characterised by mainstream unions. Under liberal pluralism and polarised state-centred regimes, however, the presence of mainstream unions is reduced, with the resulting representation gap appearing at first glance to be filled by more informal actors in the form of grassroots unions (liberal pluralism) or worker collectives (polarised state-centred). Thus, we can hypothesise that the presence here of non-traditional forms of worker organisation results from, at least in part, what these types lack rather than from what positive features they exhibit.

The predominance of grassroots unions in liberal pluralism is a recent historical development but one that started before the advent of the gig economy, focused on representing workers in a variety of precarious sectors. Notably, the IWGB and other independent unions have been at the forefront of representing workers who are not adequately represented by mainstream unions (such as the bogus self-employed, migrants and sex workers). Led or co-led initially by precarious migrant workers, they have emerged to represent and organise low-paid workers in sectors characterised by high precarity and subcontracting. Since then, they have since expanded and started to represent non-migrant sectors of the precariat, demonstrating an effective approach to organising and bargaining for workers in challenging conditions (Però 2020).

In polarised state-centred regimes, there may be even more reliance on the state and established unions as their resources may sometimes be called upon (especially in France and Italy). Here, worker collectives are independent forms of worker representation that do not need to become official unions as they can temporarily access the resources of unions and are more able to offer grassroots support for the organisation of platform worker protests.

As for the forms of worker protest and the issues driving them, there is also evidence of differences on the basis of the industrial relations regime. In respect of forms of protest, the descriptive findings show that strikes are dominant in liberal pluralist countries and in fragmented state-centred regimes, which, in the former case, may reflect an increase in more general strike activity in countries such as the UK. Strikes are much less common in social partnership countries, where demonstrations are more typical. Institutionalisation as a form of protest is most frequent in countries featuring social partnership and organised corporatism, while legal action is reported most commonly in fragmented state-centred regimes.

Intuitively, specific national institutional logics may account for these differences. However, it should be noted that many differences attracted less significance in our multivariate modelling. The strongest finding is related to social partnership, with a distinctive emphasis on forms of protest via demonstration and institutionalisation. Few findings are significant for the other regimes, although it is notable that protests via institutionalisation are less significant in liberal pluralist countries and polarised state-centred regimes. The positive association with institutionalisation in social partnership countries may reflect ongoing attempts by mainstream unions to establish works councils in the platform economy, as this is seen as a major power resource to determine working conditions. Conversely, the negative association of institutionalisation with liberal pluralism and in polarised state-centred regimes reflects a lack of success in establishing collective initiatives and agreements more generally.

Turning to the motivations for platform labour protest, there is, at first sight, some statistically significant variation between industrial relations regimes, although this is less clear in the multivariate modelling. Of these, the strong negative association of employment status as a driver of protests in liberal pluralism – despite the high profile of some cases – probably reflects the relative lack of employment rights in those countries, which means there is less opportunityfor workers to press for changes to employment status. The same is true for fragmented state-centred regimes, in Poland for example, where striving to become self-employed entrepreneurs is a strong feature (Polkowska 2021; Trappmann 2013), although here the low number of data points does not provide statistical significance.

It is interesting to note a qualification of the earlier findings that pay is the most dominant cause of protest. While pay is an important driver of worker protest in all regimes, it is much less so in social partnership countries and polarised state-centred regimes, and highest in fragmented state-centred regimes. This may be related to contextual factors, with workers mostly on state-regulated minimum wages that are quite high compared to earnings in fragmented state-centred regimes.

It is unclear why health and safety should figure relatively highly as a motivation for protest in liberal pluralism. Previous research shows that protests over health and safety increased across the globe during the Covid-19 pandemic, but it is difficult to explain why the distribution should vary in the way found in this research.

Finally, it is important to acknowledge a limitation to the findings. Although the analysis presented in this chapter is based on a unique database of platform worker struggles, the size of the sample – 430 protest events – means that the number of cases for each industrial relations regime, while giving useful insights, is insufficient for strong empirical generalisations. This problem will be alleviated over time as the continued accumulation of protest data will allow stronger conclusions to be drawn concerning issues such as the size and duration of protests and how particular constellations of protests are associated with particular industrial relations regimes.

The conclusions of this chapter are fairly clear. The data show a distinct pattern of variation in labour unrest among app-based food delivery workers, which fits Visser's analysis of industrial relations regimes in Europe. There are also variations in the issues driving worker protests, the methods used to pursue grievances and, in particular, in the collective actors involved in protests. The chapter thus demonstrates – somewhat surprisingly – that analysis in terms of institutional logics has traction even in this most un-institutionalised area of industrial relations. With this research on the differences in platform worker protest, the chapter thus contributes to the frontline of comparative employment relations debate on how technological change in workplaces and industries is experienced and contested, looking at the role of institutional regulation and union strategies (Doellgast and Wagner 2022; Howcroft and Taylor 2014; Lloyd and Payne 2019, 2021).

A couple of provisos are required. First, some parts of the findings fit Visser's model better than others. For actors, the pattern is well-defined, at least in those regimes for which there is most data. For protest issues and forms of protest, matters are less clearly defined, which suggests the need for further research and also points towards the need to incorporate qualitative research into subjective factors influencing the development of specific patterns of labour protest in different countries, sectors and industrial relations regimes. We would strongly recommend the future development of mixed methods research in this area, alongside the development of explanations that combine an understanding of the subjective dynamics in the development of worker organisation and contestation with an understanding of the relevant structural and institutional factors.

Despite the huge research effort of recent years, which has greatly improved comprehension of the dynamics of worker organisation and contestation in platform work, systematic data is still lacking. We therefore look forward to empirical and theoretical discoveries yet to come.

NOTES

1. The Leeds Index of Platform Labour Protest captures instances of protest by platform workers across the world. It is a unique resource for all those seeking to understand global patterns in the industrial relations of the platform economy. It is an initiative of the Digital Futures at Work Centre and the Centre for Employment Relations Innovation and Change (CERIC). For more information, please visit https://leeds-index.co.uk
2. www.gdeltproject.org
3. For a more detailed discussion of our methodology and the rationale behind our classifications of forms of worker organisation and forms of protest, see Bessa et al. (2022).
4. A log-off is a coordinated action where platform workers log off from the platform app, thereby making themselves unavailable for work. As such, it represents a form of collective action by the workers.
5. Running costs refer to the costs expended in order to keep and use a vehicle, such as a motorbike or a bike, and/or other work equipment such as helmets, outdoor clothing and so on. Especially during the Covid-19 pandemic, these included face masks, sanitisers and similar. Who should pay these costs has been a common issue of contention between couriers and platforms.

REFERENCES

Aloisi A. and Gramano E. (2019) Workers without workplaces and unions without unity: non-standard forms of employment, platform work and collective bargaining, in Pulignano V. and Hendrickx F. (eds.) *Employment relations in the 21st century: challenges for theory and research in a changing world of work*, Kluwer Law International.

Atzeni M. (2021) Workers' organizations and the fetishism of the trade union form: toward new pathways for research on the labour movement?, *Globalizations*, 18 (8), 1349–1362.

Bertolini A. and Dukes R. (2021) Trade unions and platform workers in the UK: worker representation in the shadow of the law, *Industrial Law Journal*, 50 (4), 662–688.

Bessa I. et al. (2022) A global analysis of worker protest in digital labour platforms, Working Paper 70, ILO. https://doi.org/10.54394/CTNG4947

Bluhm K. and Trappmann V. (2010) Spielarten des Kapitalismus in Ostmitteleuropa (Varieties of capitalism in Central Eastern Europe), *Osteuropa*, 1 (6), 61–74.

Bohle D. and Greskovits B. (2019) *Capitalist diversity on Europe's periphery*, Cornell University Press.

Cant C. (2020) The warehouse without walls: a workers' inquiry at Deliveroo, *Ephemera: Theory & Politics in Organization*, 20 (4), 131–161.

Cavallini G. and Avogaro M. (2019) Digital work in the platform economy: the last (but not least) stage of precariousness in labour relationships, in Kenner J., Florczak I. and Otto M. (eds.) *Precarious work: the challenge for labour law in Europe*, Edward Elgar Publishing, 176–196.

Chesta R., Zamponi L. and Caciagli C. (2019) Labor activism and social movement unionism in the gig Economy: food delivery workers struggles in Italy, *Partecipazione e Conflitto*, 12 (3), 819–844.

Chinguno C. (2019) Power dynamics in the gig/share economy: Uber and Bolt taxi platforms in Johannesburg, South Africa, *Labour, Capital and Society*, 49 (2), 31–65.

Cini L. (2022) Resisting algorithmic control: understanding the rise and variety of platform worker mobilisations, *New Technology, Work and Employment*, 38 (1), 125–144.
Cini L., Maccarrone V. and Tassinari A. (2022) With or without u(nions)? Understanding the diversity of gig workers' organizing practices in Italy and the UK, *European Journal of Industrial Relations*, 28 (3), 341–362.
Davenport C. (2009) *Media bias, perspective, and state repression: the Black Panther Party*, Cambridge University Press. https://doi.org/10.1017/CBO9780511810985
Doellgast V. and Wagner I. (2022) Collective regulation and the future of work in the digital economy: insights from comparative employment relations, *Journal of Industrial Relations*, 64 (3), 438–460.
Dörre K. (2016) Die neue Konfliktformation: Klassen-Kämpfe in fragmentierten Arbeitsbeziehungen, *Industrielle Beziehungen*, 23 (3), 348–365.
Europa Press (2020) El TSJC reconoce la relación laboral de los repartidores con Glovo en la empresa, Europa Press, 10 March. www.europapress.es/catalunya/noticia-tsjc-reconoce-relacion-laboral-repartidores-glovo-empresa-20200310102354.html
Forde C. et al. (2017) *The social protection of workers in the platform economy*, European Parliament.
Haidar J. and Keune M. (eds.) (2021) *Work and labour relations in global platform capitalism*, Edward Elgar Publishing.
Heiland H. (2020) Workers' voice in platform labour: an overview, WSI Study 21, Hans-Böckler-Stiftung. www.econstor.eu/handle/10419/225444
Heiland H. (2021) Controlling space, controlling labour? Contested space in food delivery gig work, *New Technology, Work and Employment*, 36 (1), 1–16.
Herr B. (2017) Riding in the gig-economy: an in depth-study of a branch in the app-based on-demand food delivery industry, *Kammer für Arbeiter und Angestellte für Wien*. https://emedien.arbeiterkammer.at/viewer/api/v1/records/AC14491034/files/source/AC14491034.pdf
Hocke P. (1996) Determining the selection bias in local and national newspaper reports on protest events, Discussion Paper FS III 96–103, Wissenschaftszentrum Berlin.
Howcroft D. and Taylor P. (2014) 'Plus ca change, plus la meme chose': researching and theorising the 'new' new technologies, *New Technology, Work and Employment*, 29 (1), 1–8.
Ilsøe A. and Jesnes K. (2020) Collective agreements for platforms and workers: two cases from the Nordic countries, in Jesnes K. and Oppegaard S.M.N. (eds.) *Platform work in the Nordic models: issues, cases and responses*, Nordic Council of Ministers, 53–67.
Jeanis M. and Powers R. (2017) Newsworthiness of missing persons cases: an analysis of selection bias, disparities in coverage, and the narrative framework of news reports, *Deviant Behavior*, 38 (6), 668–683.
Jesnes K., Neumann D., Trappmann V. and de Becdelièvre P. (2021) The role of worker collectives among app-based food delivery couriers in France, Germany and Norway: all the same or different?, in Drahokoupil J. and Vandaele K. (eds.) *A modern guide to labour and the platform economy*, Edward Elgar Publishing, 258–273.
Joyce S. and Stuart M. (2021) Trade union responses to platform work: an evolving tension between mainstream and grassroots approaches, in Drahokoupil J. and Vandaele K. (eds.) *A modern guide to labour and the platform economy*, Edward Elgar Publishing, 177–192.
Joyce S., Neumann D., Trappmann V. and Umney C. (2020) A global struggle: worker protest in the platform economy, Policy Brief 2/2020, ETUI.
Kilhoffer Z. et al. (2018) *Study to gather evidence on the working conditions of platform workers*, European Commission. https://data.europa.eu/doi/10.2767/26582
Lamannis M. (2023) *Collective bargaining in the platform economy: a mapping exercise of existing initiatives*, Report 2023.02, ETUI.
La Voz de Asturias (2018) Lo dice el juez: no son repartidores, son falsos autónomos, *La Voz de Asturias*, 5 June. www.lavozdeasturias.es/noticia/actualidad/2018/06/05/dice-juez-repartidores-falsos-autonomos/0003_201806G5P28992.htm
Lloyd C. and Payne J. (2019) Rethinking country effects: robotics, AI and work futures in Norway and the UK, *New Technology, Work and Employment*, 34 (3), 208–225.
Lloyd C. and Payne J. (2021) Fewer jobs, better jobs? An international comparative study of robots and 'routine' work in the public sector, *Industrial Relations Journal*, 52 (2), 109–124.

Maffie M.D. (2020) The role of digital communities in organizing gig workers, *Industrial Relations: A Journal of Economy and Society*, 59 (1), 123–149.
Mirón Parra E. (2019) El TSJ de Asturias concluye que los 'riders' de Glovo son falsos autónomos, *LegalToday*, 3 November. www.legaltoday.com/practica-juridica/social-laboral/laboral/nuevo-pronunciamiento-sobre-los-riders-el-tsj-de-asturias-concluye-que-los-riders-de-glovo-son-falsos-autonomos
Nam T. (2006) What you use matters: coding protest data, *PS: Political Science and Politics*, 39 (2), 281–287.
Neumann D. (2023) *Platform labour protest: Germany, Leeds Index Country Report #2*. https://leeds-index.co.uk/index-county-report-germany
Opp K.-D. (2009) *Theories of political protest and social movements: a multidisciplinary introduction, critique, and synthesis*, Routledge.
Però D. (2020) Indie unions, organizing and labour renewal: learning from precarious migrant workers, *Work, Employment and Society*, 34 (5), 900–918.
Polkowska D. (2021) Unionisation and mobilisation within platform work: towards precarisation – a case of Uber drivers in Poland, *Industrial Relations Journal*, 52 (1), 25–39.
Rolf S., O'Reilly J. and Meryon M. (2022) Towards privatized social and employment protections in the platform economy? Evidence from the UK courier sector, *Research Policy*, 51 (5). https://doi.org/10.1016/j.respol.2022.104492
Schmalz S. et al. (2023) Varieties of platform unionism: a view from the Global South on workers' power in the digital economy, *Work in the Global Economy*, 3 (2), 201–224.
Schreyer J. (2021) Algorithmic management versus organising protest and co-determination? The case of Foodora/Lieferando in Germany, *Studi Organizzativi*, 1, 105–128.
Soriano C. and Cabañes J.V. (2020) Entrepreneurial solidarities: social media collectives and Filipino digital platform workers, *Social Media + Society*. https://doi.org/10.1177/2056305120926484
Stuart et al. (2023) Labor unrest and the future of work: global struggles against food delivery platforms, *Labor Studies Journal*, 48 (3), 287–297. https://doi.org/10.1177/0160449X231178780
Tassinari A. and Maccarrone V. (2020) Riders on the storm: workplace solidarity among gig economy couriers in Italy and the UK, *Work, Employment and Society*, 34 (1), 35–54.
Trappmann V. (2013) *Fallen heroes in global capitalism: workers and the restructuring of the Polish steel industry*, Palgrave MacMillan.
Trappmann V. et al. (2020) *Global labour unrest on platforms: the case of food delivery workers*, Friedrich-Ebert-Stiftung. https://library.fes.de/pdf-files/iez/16880.pdf
Umney C. et al. (2024) Platform labour unrest in a global perspective: how, where and why do platform workers protest?, *Work, Employment and Society*, 38 (1), 3–26. https://doi.org/10.1177/09500170231209676
Vallas S. and Schor J.B. (2020) What do platforms do? Understanding the gig economy, *Annual Review of Sociology*, 46 (1), 273–294.
Vandaele K. (2018) Will trade unions survive in the platform economy? Emerging patterns of platform workers' collective voice and representation in Europe, Working Paper 2018.05, ETUI.
Vandaele K. (2020) *From street protest to 'improvisational unionism': platform-based food delivery couriers in Belgium and the Netherlands*, Friedrich-Ebert-Stiftung.
Vandaele K. (2021) Collective resistance and organisational creativity amongst Europe's platform workers: a new power in the labour movement?, in Haidar J. and Keune M. (eds.) *Work and labour relations in global platform capitalism*, Edward Elgar Publishing, 206–235.
Visser J. (2009) The quality of industrial relations and the Lisbon strategy, in European Commission (ed.) *Industrial relations in Europe 2008, Office for Official Publications of the European Communities*, pp. 45–72.
Wood A.J., Martindale N. and Lehdonvirta V. (2021) Dynamics of contention in the gig economy: rage against the platform, customer or state?, *New Technology, Work and Employment*, 38 (2), 330–350.
Woodcock J. (2021) *The fight against platform capitalism*, University of Westminster Press. https://doi.org/10.16997/book51
Woodcock J. and Cant C. (2022) Platform worker organising at Deliveroo in the UK: from wildcat strikes to building power, *Journal of Labor and Society*, 25 (2), 220–236.
All links were checked on 8 March 2024.

7. Assessing the quality of food delivery platform work: towards a conceptual framework for job quality in the platform economy

Agnieszka Piasna and Wouter Zwysen

INTRODUCTION

The emergence and rapid expansion of the platform economy have had a profoundly transformative impact on traditional markets and actors. Despite the diversity of types of work and occupations organised by platforms, there are some common characteristics of platform work that position it close to precarious employment and informal work. The platform economy can thus be viewed as the next stage in the ongoing process of the individualisation of risk and the proliferation of low-quality and precarious work which has emerged since the deregulation of the standard employment relationship and the weakening of workers' rights and bargaining power (Grimshaw et al. 2017; Stone and Arthurs 2013). In this sense, labour platforms risk exacerbating many existing inequalities by making those most in need of protection more vulnerable to market pressures and exploitation. This creates a need for a better understanding of the quality of jobs in the platform economy, including in relation to those offered in the traditional economy, and the impact of the new digital technologies used to organise and manage work.

In attempting to measure and analyse the quality of food delivery platform work, one can draw on a rich literature on job quality in the conventional economy which identifies and organises key features of jobs conducive to worker well-being within a multidimensional framework (Burchell et al. 2014; Gallie 2013; Green and Mostafa 2012; Leschke et al. 2008). Over time, a considerable consensus has emerged as to which features of jobs should be included in such job quality measures and, in the context of developed countries, there is currently a notable conceptual consistency in including dimensions such as earnings, job security, skill requirements and development, autonomy, working time, the physical and social environment and representation and voice (Muñoz de Bustillo et al. 2011).

Looking at the issue from a historical perspective, this consensus is only very recent and the approach to the qualitative aspects of work has evolved considerably alongside changes in labour markets and in scientific knowledge on the key determinants of well-being at work (Burchell et al. 2014). Early interest was fuelled by quality-of-life studies advocating the importance of non-economic factors in measuring the progress of societies which were developed in a period of post-war economic prosperity (Land 1975). Job satisfaction as a measure of job quality dominated in this early period. However, with the effects of deindustrialisation and deregulation on employment conditions in developed countries, the emphasis shifted towards the role of job insecurity. The growing importance of work-life balance prompted the introduction of working time arrangements into the job quality framework, while new health hazards and a developing understanding of psychosocial risks directed attention to health outcomes and control over the work process (Burchell et al. 2002; Karasek and Theorell 1990). This shows that changing conditions prompt the adaptation of frameworks used to understand and measure the quality of jobs.

This chapter argues that the platform economy, largely due to its specific business model and the use of algorithmic management, represents an important shift in work organisation. It is therefore useful to adapt further our current job quality frameworks to better capture, measure and ultimately understand job quality outcomes in this emerging segment of work (see also Gundert and Leschke 2023).

In particular, platform work renders some dimensions of job quality particularly salient, while creating important linkages between the others (Piasna 2022). For instance, job quality indicators applied to the traditional economy implicitly assume that their particular dimensions contribute independently to the overall level of quality and thus tend to be added together in an overarching measure. In contrast, in the platform economy, several key aspects of work are closely interlinked and interact, producing particular outcomes in terms of job quality. This is explained in more detail in the following section. Moreover, platform work is marked by self-employment, which is excluded from the dominant job quality frameworks. In the case of dependent employment, it is easy to separate the characteristics of a job which is created, organised and provided by an employer from the characteristics and responsibilities of a worker. In the platform economy, this distinction becomes more challenging. Delineating a job, such as for the purpose of measuring working time, part of which is when a worker is logged in on the platform but a large part of which escapes unaccounted for as unpaid work, is also more difficult in the platform economy (Pulignano et al. 2021). Similarly, measuring income is problematic because earnings might still require deductions to cover the costs of work equipment, while an assessment of job tasks and skill content is complicated in that many platform tasks are effectively chosen by a worker. Finally, the understanding of workplace autonomy and control needs to be revised in the acknowledgement of algorithmic management and the sanctions faced by workers when they attempt to exercise notional control.

To better reflect the reality of work in the platform economy, this chapter therefore proposes a conceptual framework that integrates the literature on job quality and precariousness with emerging research on digitally mediated labour markets. While it focuses on the food delivery sector, the proposed framework can also be applied in the wider platform economy context as there are many commonalities in this model of organising work despite the variety of tasks that are carried out and the differences in the format of their delivery. The chapter then addresses the different aspects of this conceptual framework, using, as far as possible, new cross-national survey data on platform workers in Europe to compare food delivery courier work with other types of platform work and with similar jobs in the traditional economy.

DEVELOPING A CONCEPTUAL FRAMEWORK FOR ASSESSING JOB QUALITY IN THE PLATFORM ECONOMY

While jobs in the platform economy should, in principle, lend themselves to being characterised along the dimensions of job quality used in the analysis of traditional labour markets, in practice, this proves more challenging and risks overlooking some key aspects of this type of work. One example is job security, commonly present in job quality indices. In traditional dependent employment, workers' perceptions of job security are expected to reflect the likelihood of them losing a current job in the near future. While the application of this concept to self-employed or gig workers is problematic in general, it is even less informative in the context of the platform economy where tasks and, hence, income – either through having no tasks or because no shifts are available – may dry up due to labour oversupply or the rerouting of tasks away from workers by an algorithm, even though they formally remain registered on the platform. At the same time, other aspects of work organisation become particularly salient in the context of platform work, such as economic insecurity and economic dependence on a platform. Both of these have been found to be among the key determinants of individual job quality outcomes in various of the other dimensions of platform work, including work-life balance and working time flexibility (Piasna and Drahokoupil 2021; Schor et al. 2020).

The chapter proposes to organise the analysis of job quality in platform work along four key dimensions, using food delivery as a starting point due to particularly abundant empirical evidence on its work and employment conditions. These four dimensions are flexibility, fragmentation, economic insecurity and the shifting of the costs and risks to workers (see Figure 7.1). Two dimensions – flexibility and economic security – largely correspond to those traditionally used in job quality frameworks for the conventional economy (see, for example, Green and Mostafa 2012; Muñoz de Bustillo et al. 2011), although the emphasis and interpretation need to be adjusted to the realities of platform work. The two other dimensions – fragmentation and the shifting of costs and risks – differ from these dominant frameworks and, while particularly closely linked, are somewhat more abstract and less easily operationalised and measured, yet they are crucial in understanding job quality outcomes in this type of work. In this framework, there is a close interdependence between all four dimensions such that outcomes in one have an impact on outcomes in the others.

Finally, the question of the balance of power between actors in the workplace, which has been an integral part of labour process analysis (Burawoy 1979; Edwards 1979; Thompson 1967), is here reintroduced into the job quality framework. Previous studies have brought to light the inherent power imbalance between workers, platforms and clients in digitally

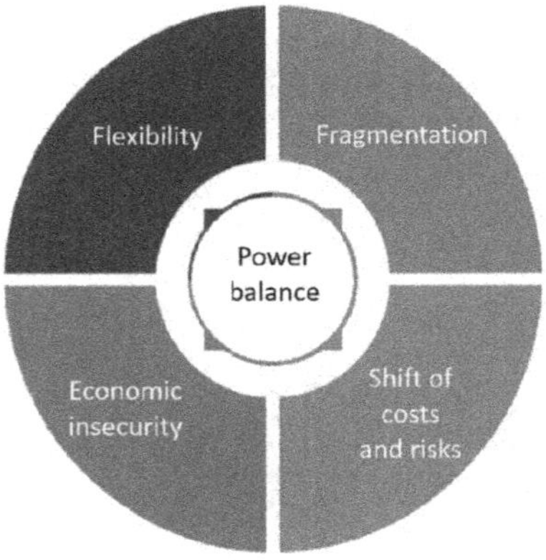

Source: Own elaboration.

Figure 7.1 *Conceptual framework for analysing job quality in app-based food delivery*

mediated labour markets (Berg 2016; Bergvall-Kåreborn and Howcroft 2014; Edwards and Hodder 2022; Prassl 2018), but it has not been explicitly considered in the context of job quality. In particular, the chapter argues that job quality outcomes in platform work influence, and are influenced by, the balance of power between the actors.

The remainder of this section discusses the proposed framework for analysing job quality, focusing on the individual dimensions and highlighting their interactions. This conceptual ambition is then made specific via an empirical analysis of comparative European data.

The first dimension we consider is flexibility, the hallmark of platform work, especially as emphasised by platform companies. This extends to many aspects of work, including contractual arrangements, working time and place and, in the case of food delivery, the choice of route. Platforms argue that they offer this highly flexible work model in response to the needs and preferences of workers, and deploy a narrative of individualisation, entrepreneurship and freedom to substantiate the attractiveness of the model. The flexibility offered is presented as incompatible with an employment relationship but in line with workers' alleged preferences to work as independent contractors rather than as employees (see discussion in Dubal 2020; Prassl 2018). There is nothing fundamentally new about structuring the workforce as a pool of self-employed micro-entrepreneurs, but technology makes such models easier and more efficient for the engagers of labour (Adams et al. 2018).

In theory, a highly flexible work model, where the time and place of work are not fixed, may lend itself to being combined with other activities or sources of income, with workers typically having one or more paid jobs in addition to the work they obtain through platforms (Drahokoupil and Piasna 2019; Hall and Krueger 2018; Ilsøe et al. 2021; Urzí Brancati et al. 2020). Such flexibility may also play a positive labour market integrative function. Low entry barriers and a lack of a standard recruitment process could constitute an advantage for, and provide employment opportunities to, individuals facing discrimination in hiring or who might otherwise be excluded from the labour market, such as migrants, persons with disabilities or those with care obligations (see Rani and Furrer 2021).

However, considering flexibility as a good-quality feature of platform work is at odds with the growing number of cases brought by workers dissatisfied with the misclassification of their employment status and arguing for the restoration of an employment relationship with all its rights and benefits and the responsibilities accruing to the employer (Kirchner and Schüßler 2020). This is largely due to the notional flexibility in platform work tending to materialise as a form of employer-led flexibility, rather than the worker-led flexibility claimed by the platforms (Lehdonvirta 2018; Wood et al. 2019a). Empirical studies indeed reveal a preference for employee status and related protections among food delivery couriers (Piasna and Drahokoupil 2021), as well as among non-standard workers in general (Datta 2019). Similarly, bottom-up collective struggles for better employment conditions point to the inadequacy of the current flexible system for many platform workers (Tassinari and Maccarrone 2017; Vandaele et al. 2019).

The second dimension in our job quality framework is fragmentation. A lack of stable and continuous employment and the intermittent nature of work create fragmented employment patterns among the platform workforce. Spells of work on one or more tasks are simultaneously intertwined with extensive periods of job search, either in the form of watching for tasks to appear online or waiting for orders or clients (Berg 2016). Spells between deliveries, or other gigs, are not remunerated, so, in this sense, resemble periods of unemployment or inactivity in the traditional economy. Moreover, tenure in the platform economy is often very short; in food delivery, it is a range of several months (Piasna and Drahokoupil 2021).

To smooth this intermittent activity, platform workers often have other jobs in the traditional, non-platform economy, but these are more likely to be in the form of non-standard employment (Ilsøe et al. 2021; Piasna et al. 2022), creating particularly precarious conditions among workers having little to no access to any form of protection or safety net. This may also lead to the accumulation of labour market disadvantage over time, and, as experiences of job insecurity tend to lower expectations and change behavioural strategies in future job searches, they also tend towards reproducing fragmented employment patterns and poorer job quality outcomes throughout a working life (Dieckhoff 2011; Mills et al. 2006).

Digital labour platforms do not rely on a continuous employment relationship to secure appropriate levels of labour supply; instead they attract a large pool of readily available workers that exceeds the number of tasks on offer to ensure that there is always someone available to provide a service on request. Low entry barriers, with the recruitment process usually reduced to a straightforward registration, as well as gamification mechanisms encouraging workers to stay logged in longer, are some of the inexpensive strategies used by platforms to build and maintain such a labour buffer. For workers, however, this translates into insufficient availability of work, with many unable to access enough paid tasks to make ends meet (Shapiro 2018; Wood et al. 2019a). Labour oversupply also negatively affects the market power of workers vis-à-vis a platform, propagating feelings of replaceability and job insecurity (Lehdonvirta 2018; Wood et al. 2019b).

Fragmentation is closely connected to the further two dimensions in our job quality framework: economic insecurity and the shifting of costs and risks to workers. Indeed, the model of organising and managing labour in the platform economy usually translates into very low earnings and economic insecurity for workers. Platforms argue that they are lowering the transaction costs of matching labour supply and demand, but what they are actually doing is substantially displacing the transaction costs and associated risks. In a situation where neither platforms nor clients assume the role of an employer, it is clear that the risks, responsibilities and costs are effectively shifted to workers (Drahokoupil and Piasna 2017). Risks such as a drop in demand, equipment failure and incapacity for work due to sickness or an accident at work all tend to be shouldered by workers. This became particularly apparent in the Covid-19 crisis, which forced food delivery couriers to choose between sustaining income and protecting their health (Fairwork 2020).

In addition to the transfer to workers themselves of those costs and risks related to the avoidance of an employment relationship and forms of worker protection, the shifting of costs is directly visible in terms of earnings. The main logic of efficiency maximisation in the platform economy is similar to that in low-level non-standard work in traditional services, achieved by closely matching staffing levels, and thus the amount of effectively paid working time, to fluctuations in demand (Lambert et al. 2012). This introduces instability and income insecurity into workers' lives. Digital technologies and the artificial intelligence used to allocate tasks in food delivery platform work potentially allow for an even closer match between labour demand and supply, reducing paid working hours to a minimum and shifting all inefficiency in time use entirely to workers (Piasna 2023).

Economic insecurity and the shifting of costs and risks are, however, also closely related to flexibility, the first discussed dimension of job quality. The use of self-employment allows workers to be paid below statutory minimum wage levels or the collectively agreed wage in a given sector. Moreover, as most institutions of worker protection, including minimum wages and collective rights offering the capacity to voice concerns and seek support, as well as social insurance, are linked to the presence of an employment relationship, this leaves platform workers excluded from these safety nets and in a position of particular vulnerability vis-à-vis a platform. Platforms are thus effectively shifting to workers the costs associated with health, unemployment and retirement insurance, as well as training and the provision of work equipment.

At the same time, the loss of protection is not compensated by the autonomy of workers to set pay levels or prices for their own services, as should be the case for self-employed or independent contractors (see discussion in Dubal 2020). This issue is particularly relevant in food delivery, where information about prices, and hence earnings, is often withheld from workers prior to task acceptance (Goods et al. 2019; Rosenblat and Stark 2016; Shapiro 2018). This is coupled with a significant burden of unpaid hours, as platform workers are generally only paid for the tasks they complete, while securing these necessitates a significant amount of time and effort that is not paid for (Berg 2016; Pulignano et al. 2021; see also Chapter 8 of this volume). All this translates into very low, unpredictable and erratic earnings (Berg 2016; Piasna et al. 2022; Wood et al. 2019a).

However, economic security in platform work plays a larger role in the quality of work framework beyond the purely economic value of earnings for workers' livelihoods. Recent evidence shows that outcomes for workers in terms of their experiences of working and employment conditions are shaped by the extent to which they are economically dependent on the platform economy (Piasna and Drahokoupil 2021; Schor et al. 2020). Workers who do not rely on platform work to pay their basic living expenses are found to be more selective in the tasks they perform, work less on a platform and only when it is truly convenient for them, or they spend less unpaid time searching and waiting for tasks (Kuhn and Maleki 2017; Lehdonvirta 2018). It follows that, for such workers, platform work is associated with better job quality, greater satisfaction, more autonomy and, in some cases, higher hourly wages (Piasna and Drahokoupil 2021). In contrast, those who try to make a living from platform work experience greater overall precariousness (Schor et al. 2020).

Finally, the relationship between the four dimensions of job quality unfolds in the context of the power imbalance between the actors in the transaction, while the poor job quality features of platform work further deepen this imbalance. For instance, the lack of a promise of a continuation of work in the future, even within the shortest time horizon, augments the uncertainty and insecurity faced by platform workers. They can be disconnected by the platform at any time, without a notice period or warning (Drahokoupil and Piasna 2019; Shanahan and Smith 2021). While this is a reality also faced by the solo self-employed or entrepreneurs in the traditional (offline) economy, in contrast to these groups, algorithmic management limits platform workers' scope for self-determination of the terms and conditions of employment, including the prices of their services (De Stefano 2018; Wood et al. 2019a). Moreover, in many on-location labour platforms, notably in transport and delivery, the choice of clients and the possibility to reject orders are constrained or negatively sanctioned. Furthermore, one important means of control and discipline used by food delivery platforms is client ratings (see Wood et al. 2019a), which can be biased or unfair, but can hardly be disputed by workers, thus adding to their powerlessness vis-à-vis a platform. Despite their importance and the efforts invested in securing positive ratings, they are not portable between platforms, thus locking workers into a particular platform on which they become increasingly dependent.

Overall, then, employment conditions in the platform economy generate power asymmetry between the actors. The various dimensions of job quality should be considered in the context of this inherent power imbalance between workers and platform companies, which operates in favour of the latter. This power imbalance is largely rooted in the architecture of the platforms, particularly in information asymmetry, the lack of transparency of algorithmic management and the invisibility of the employer and manager, as well as the maintenance of labour oversupply (De Stefano 2018; Piasna 2022; Schor et al. 2020; Wood et al. 2019a). Algorithmic management is used to optimise workers' coordination and task allocation, but it is a powerful disciplining and monitoring tool, limiting and sanctioning any deviation in workers' actions that is not conducive to increasing productivity and lowering costs (Shanahan and Smith 2021). Finally, the organisational model of platforms, through various means, including a fragmented and highly volatile workforce, economic insecurity and the threat of disconnection or the limitation of access to tasks, hinders workers' participation rights and voice, further solidifying the conditions of power imbalance.

METHODOLOGY: DATA, DEFINITIONS AND MEASUREMENT

To map the quality of work among food delivery platform workers, this chapter uses data from the dedicated Internet and Platform Work Survey (IPWS) conducted by the European Trade Union Institute (ETUI) (for details, see Piasna et al. 2022). The IPWS is a representative cross-national survey of a simple random sample of the working population aged 18–65. The fieldwork was harmonised and coordinated by Ipsos, with interviews conducted by computer-assisted telephone interviewing. The data presented in this chapter are pooled from two survey waves, conducted in spring and autumn 2021, with a total of 36,124 respondents from 14 countries in the European Union: Austria, Bulgaria, Czechia, Estonia, France, Germany, Greece, Hungary, Ireland, Italy, Poland, Romania, Slovakia and Spain.

While it is not possible to operationalise in full the conceptual framework outlined in the previous section with the IPWS data, or other existing datasets, the dimensions can be approximated. Many of these have already been borne out by in-depth qualitative work with platform workers, highlighting the dual aspects of flexibility for platform workers alongside the fragmentation and economic uncertainty which pushes them into a subordinate position (Schor et al. 2020; van Doorn and Vijay 2021). However, using comparable quantitative data across different countries provides a way to test how platform work compares to other types of work and to highlight the differences and similarities, thereby allowing for a multidimensional comparison of precariousness.

To capture flexibility, we compare the key contractual arrangements in workers' main jobs and their working time on platforms. Ideally, this dimension would also require information on employment status in platform work and the extent to which this is combined with other activities, but these data are not available. The fragmentation of work is more adequately captured through measuring the extent to which platform workers make use of several platforms and their tenure on any specific one. Economic insecurity and dependence on platforms can be directly measured by analysing the earnings made through platform work and the contribution of these to total annual income. An important aspect of economic insecurity is the volatility of earnings, but this cannot be captured with the available data. The shifting of risks is inherent in the short tenure and contractual employment status of workers. With the availability of new data in the future, information on insurance status could also be added to the measurement of this dimension. Finally, power asymmetry, as a contextual factor, is used in the interpretation of results but is measured only indirectly via an analysis of workers' socio-demographic positions and vulnerabilities. Such vulnerabilities indicate the lower bargaining position of platform workers and the risk of their exploitation.

The IPWS allows comparisons between the general working-age population and various types of platform workers, including food delivery couriers. The latter are defined as those who responded that they delivered food or other goods where: they received orders through an app, online platform or website; they had done so in the last 12 months; and they named an app or website that they used for this work that corresponds to an actual labour platform. In total, 393 respondents in the analysed sample are (food) delivery couriers. In addition, there are 1,702 remote platform workers, including micro-taskers and professionals doing more complex activities, and 638 respondents doing other types of on-location platform work such as ride-hailing or tasks in clients' homes (such as handyperson work, tutoring, caregiving). All platform workers were asked what applications or websites they use for each activity, such as food delivery. Those who reported more than one application within the same type of activity are classified here as doing multi-apping. Platform workers are differentiated not only by the type of tasks they perform but also by the degree of attachment to platform work, measured by the share of income derived from this work and the number of hours worked per week. We thus define 'main platform workers' as those who work more than 20 hours per week in this job or derive at least 50 per cent of their annual income from it.

The aim of the analysis is to map the profile of food delivery couriers in Europe, together with the quality of their work along the dimensions proposed in the conceptual framework,

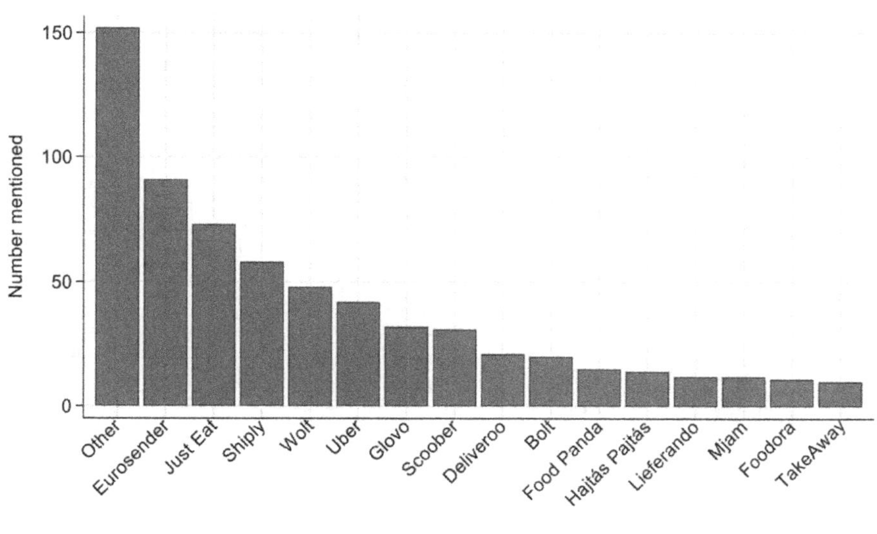

Note: Responses of both 'Uber' and 'Uber Eats' reported as delivery platforms are shown here as 'Uber'.
Source: IPWS 2021.

Figure 7.2 *Delivery platforms most frequently reported in IPWS*

contextualising these findings by comparing couriers to other platform workers and relatively similar workers in the traditional economy. To this aim, we also use the 2021 Labour Force Survey (LFS) to compare food delivery couriers with two other population groups, namely: (a) workers with delivery services as their main job, captured by occupational code 832 'Motor-vehicle drivers', which includes delivery but also taxi or lorry driving; and (b) those who work in the broader transport or food services sector as their second job. Platform workers rarely carry out this work as their main activity, so it is appropriate to compare them to those doing it as a secondary activity. This group may potentially include some platform workers but is assumed predominantly to capture multiple job holders in the traditional economy due to the construction of the survey (see discussion in Piasna 2020).

It is important to recognise that food delivery platform work is not a homogeneous sector. Figure 7.2 shows the main platforms used by couriers in the 14 analysed countries. The top five platforms (Eurosender for parcels, Just Eat, Shiply, Wolt and Uber/Uber Eats) account for 307 (51 per cent) of the 599 named platforms (there are more platforms mentioned than there are platform workers as workers may mention the use of several platforms). When adding in Glovo, the number rises to 335 workers (56 per cent) across six platforms. This high level of fragmentation in the market not only indicates a highly dynamic segment with potential

Table 7.1 Delivery platforms most frequently reported in IPWS, by country

	Most used		**2nd most used**		**3rd most used**	
Country	Platform	N	Platform	N	Platform	N
Austria	Mjam	6	Google	3	Deliveroo	3
Bulgaria	Just Eat	26	Eurosender	14	Glovo	14
Czechia	Hajtás Pajtás	14	Eurosender	14	Shiply	7
Estonia	Eurosender	50	Wolt	36	Shiply	33
France	Uber	18	Just Eat	6		
Germany	Scoober	19	Foodora	9	Lieferando	7
Greece	Glovo	3				
Hungary	Wolt	9	NetPincér	6		
Ireland	Just Eat	10	Deliveroo	5	Taxify	3
Italy	Just Eat	11	Glovo	3		
Poland	Pyszne.pl	5	Uber	3		
Slovakia	Eurosender	12	Shiply	9		
Spain	Uber	16	Just Eat	12	Glovo	9

Note: The most frequently mentioned delivery platforms with at least three respondents naming it per country.
Source: IPWS 2021.

for further growth; it also means that the analysis presented here represents averages across potentially diverse work contexts. Moreover, there is a sizeable variation between countries in which platforms are used, as shown in Table 7.1. Uber was among the most used platforms in Spain, France and Poland; Just Eat was among the top platforms in Spain, France, Ireland, Italy and Bulgaria; and Eurosender was heavily used in Bulgaria, Czechia, Estonia and Slovakia.

PORTRAIT OF FOOD DELIVERY COURIERS IN EUROPE

Before embarking on an analysis of the quality of platform work, it is useful to understand better who is carrying out this type of work and what traits are shared by this group of workers. The individual characteristics of platform workers, and food delivery couriers in particular, are considered within our framework as an important feature of their vulnerability vis-à-vis platforms and, hence, a contributing factor to the power imbalance.

The IPWS data show that app-based food delivery couriers differ from both the general population and other platform workers in several important ways, but they are still a very diverse group. As shown in Table 7.2, couriers are by far the least feminised group in the platform economy, with 39 per cent being women compared to 42 and 48 per cent for the two other types of platform work and half of the working-age population. They are also the youngest on average, with 28 per cent aged 18–24, but with a strong representation of all older age groups. Platform workers are generally more highly educated than others, with food delivery couriers having the lowest proportion of those with only a low level of education (10 per cent). The majority of platform workers (60 per cent) have an intermediate level of education, while those with a tertiary education are by far the most common among remote platform workers (43 per cent), with graduates being around 30 per cent of each of the other groups. The slightly younger age of couriers may explain the lower share taken by parents with a child below the age of 12, but the differences in this respect are small. A higher proportion of couriers (60 per cent) live in big cities or suburbs than is the case for remote platform workers (52 per cent) or the general population (42 per cent); delivery work is also more of an urban phenomenon as regards place of work.

In line with the literature, we find a higher proportion of couriers born outside the country of residence (25 per cent) compared to both the general population and other platform workers (van Doorn and Vijay 2021; see also Chapter 5 of this volume). Around 17 per cent of couriers are born in a non-EU country, although this is very likely to be an underestimate since the IPWS data were collected through random digit dialling in the main language of the country, and migrants, especially undocumented ones, may have been less likely to respond. This percentage of foreign-born couriers nevertheless reflects the relatively lower barriers to entry into this type of platform work, both legally and in terms of connections and social networks. Reflecting the discussions on employment status, we find that embeddedness in the traditional economy follows different patterns for platform and non-platform workers. High numbers of couriers report their main activity as self-employment (23 per cent), which is substantially higher than in the population of working age (11 per cent). Couriers are also more likely than the general working-age population to be on temporary contracts (15 per cent as opposed to 13 per cent) and quite a bit less likely to be on open-ended ones (39 per cent compared to 46 per cent). Finally, they are less likely to be inactive. This indicates that couriers, along with other

Table 7.2 *Food delivery platform workers compared to other platform workers and to the general population*

	Delivery platform workers	Other on-location platform workers	Remote platform workers	All working age population
Women	39%	42%	48%	50%
Average age	36.0	38.4	38.1	42.7
Age				
18-24	28%	20%	20%	11%
25-34	23%	25%	24%	20%
35-44	20%	21%	24%	23%
45-54	18%	19%	17%	23%
55-65	11%	15%	15%	23%
Education				
Low	10%	16%	11%	18%
Intermediate	60%	54%	46%	53%
Tertiary	30%	29%	43%	30%
Child under 12	30%	34%	33%	32%
Big city/suburbs	60%	55%	52%	42%
Place of birth				
Country of residence	75%	82%	87%	87%
Other EU/EFTA country	9%	6%	4%	5%
Third country	17%	13%	9%	8%
Labour market status				
Employee – open-ended	39%	32%	41%	46%
Employee – temporary	15%	15%	13%	13%
Self-employed	23%	25%	19%	11%
*Other**	23%	28%	26%	30%

Note: *Not working; inactive; students.
Source: IPWS 2021.

platform workers, are found more often in forms of work featuring non-standard employment contracts.

A comparison between food delivery couriers and workers doing similar types of jobs in the traditional economy (Figure 7.3) shows that, as expected, the platform workforce shares more characteristics with those having a second job in these sectors than those making deliveries as a main paid activity. What mainly differentiates platform couriers from traditional drivers is their younger age, higher educational attainment and higher concentration in big cities, in line with food delivery platforms being mostly an urban phenomenon.

While much of the power imbalance between actors in the platform economy has to do with the architecture of the platforms, where algorithmic management and information asymmetry weaken the position of platform workers, many such workers are also (as previously reported) more vulnerable in general because of their individual characteristics. This is most visible in the high number of migrant workers that are often found to engage in on-location platform work. Indeed, the low formal entry barriers and skill requirements which make it possible to start earning through platforms, and rather quickly, make this form of work particularly attractive to workers with fewer alternatives. As we have seen, a larger proportion of platform couriers than other types of worker are migrants, with a large fraction born outside the EU. They are, furthermore, on less secure contracts in general and are relatively young. These are examples of a structural power imbalance that results from the particular organisational model combined with traditional patterns of labour market segmentation.

MAPPING JOB QUALITY AMONG FOOD DELIVERY COURIERS WITHIN THE PROPOSED FRAMEWORK

As postulated in the conceptual framework of job quality set out at the beginning of the chapter, the employment patterns of platform workers are, indeed, generally more fragmented and flexible than those of the rest of the workforce, and delivery couriers are no exception. As already highlighted, platform workers are less likely to have standard employment contracts. A similar picture emerges when food delivery couriers are compared with delivery workers in the traditional economy (shown in Figure 7.4). Platform couriers are much more likely than other drivers to be non-standard workers in their main job (are either temporary employees or freelancers) and are correspondingly much less likely to have open-ended contracts. The same, but somewhat less pronounced, differences are observed between couriers and those doing delivery work as their second job in the traditional economy.

Food delivery couriers in the IPWS sample work much shorter hours than average workers or drivers in the traditional economy, with their weekly working hours being more comparable to those of multiple job holders who drive as a second job (Figure 7.4, panel d). However, compared to other platform workers, they actually work relatively long weekly hours on platforms (Figure 7.5, panel c). For instance, those for whom food delivery is a main paid activity spend around 30 hours per week on it compared with just over 20 hours reported by other on-location platform workers for whom this work is also their main paid activity. This highlights that, while flexibility in hours may be an attractive aspect of platform work, the need to be active to get orders and earn money renders this advantage more hypothetical, resulting in a working week which approximates to full-time engagement.

Notes: The figure shows estimated differences of food delivery couriers compared to those working as van drivers and deliverers (ISCO 832) in the traditional economy (panel a); and those with a second job in the transportation or traditional food service sectors (panel b). Differences are shown as percentage points, with 95% confidence intervals.
Source: IPWS 2021 and LFS 2021.

Figure 7.3 *Food delivery couriers compared to the traditional workforce*

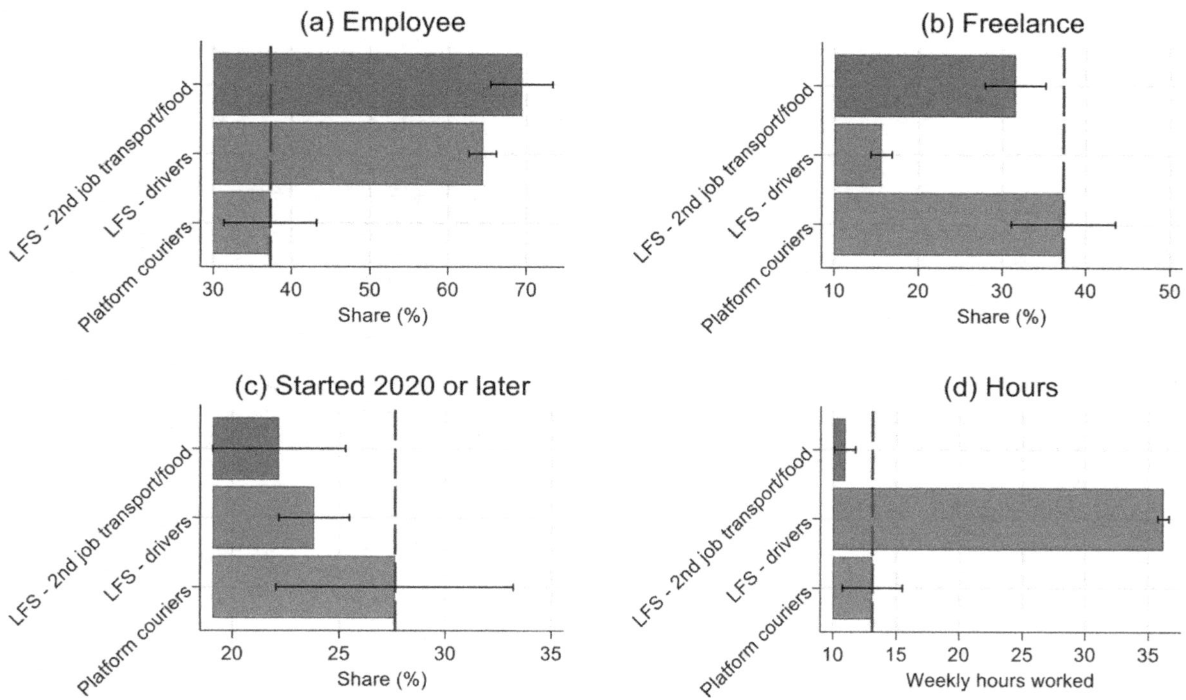

Note: Results of regression analysis, controlling for urbanity of place of residence, educational level, age in categories, gender, country of residence and country of birth. The figure compares platform (food delivery) couriers in the IPWS to different groups in the LFS. The data are weighted.
Source: IPWS 2021 and LFS 2021.

Figure 7.4 *Fragmentation, flexibility and economic insecurity among food delivery couriers: comparison with other delivery workers in the traditional economy*

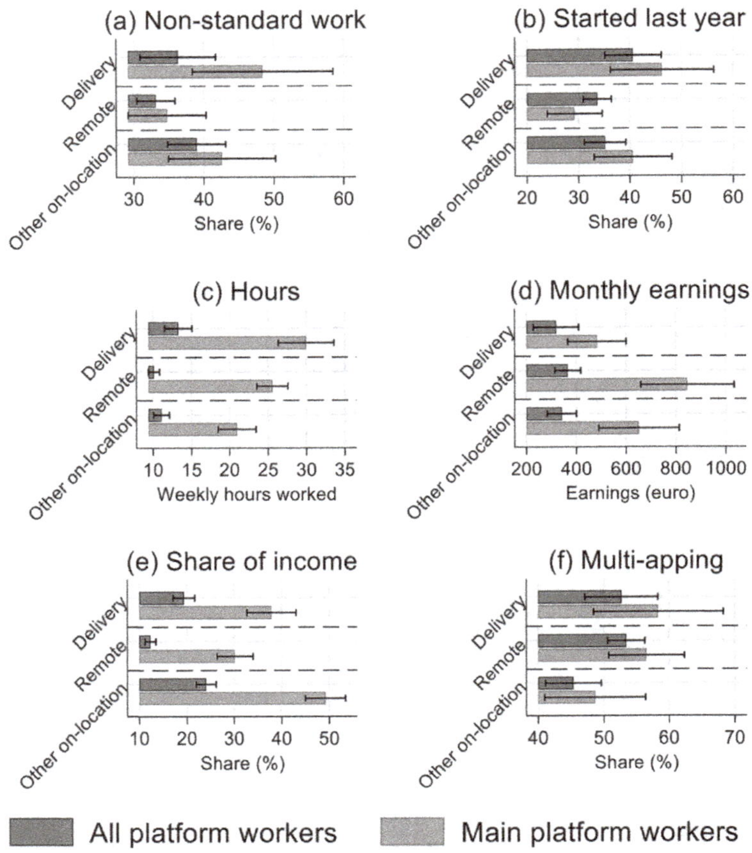

Note: The share or value for each outcome by type of platform work and by degree of attachment to platform work (main platform workers are defined as those working more than 20 hours per week or deriving at least 50% of annual income from platform work). The data are weighted.
Source: IPWS 2021.

Figure 7.5 *Fragmentation, flexibility and economic insecurity among food delivery couriers: comparison with other types of platform work*

Food delivery couriers also experience more fragmented work patterns characterised by short tenures and high turnover (Figure 7.4, panel c). While almost a third of couriers (28 per cent) had a tenure of one year or less, this was the case for fewer than one in four drivers (24 per cent for delivery workers in the traditional economy and 22 per cent for those driving as a second job). This may reflect the low barriers to entry and flexibility in opting in and out of this type of work, but it also reflects the high levels of job insecurity or poor working and employment conditions forcing workers to look for alternative paid activities.

Platform work is generally a low-paid activity and therefore rarely provides enough income to be a sole source of revenue. Several further reasons for this are proposed in the literature, notably that workers spend short hours on platform tasks in order to fit this work around their other activities and commitments, as well as that hourly earnings and task availability are simply too low to be able to make a living from a single platform (Berg 2016; Piasna and Drahokoupil 2021; Schor et al. 2020).

As shown in Figure 7.5 (panel d), the monthly earnings of delivery couriers are low compared to other types of platform work, especially for those who are more economically dependent on this type of work. That probably also explains why there is a relatively high level of multi-apping among delivery workers compared with other types of on-location platform work (panel f). These low earnings contrast problematically with the relatively long working hours of couriers, which may indicate low pay rates but also the high burden of unpaid hours (spent, for example, waiting for new orders or for food to be ready from restaurants). Given that couriers tend to bear the costs of work equipment or lost income due to accidents at work, which are not uncommon in food delivery, the extent of cost and risk shifting in this segment of the platform economy appears to be significant.

Food delivery couriers also emerge as relatively dependent on and attached to platform work. On average, they derive a higher share of their total income from platform work than higher-earning remote platform workers, but lower than other on-location platform workers (Figure 7.5, panel e). Food delivery couriers also tend to use more than one platform to search for orders more often than other on-location platform workers (panel f). This multi-apping may be a strategy to cope with low income level and insecurity and the insufficient or unpredictable availability of orders when using only one platform.

Overall, the analysis provides evidence of the economic insecurity and associated shifting of risks, revealing a relatively more vulnerable position of food delivery couriers compared to other platform workers.

CONCLUSIONS

The framework for the analysis of job quality in food delivery platform work proposed in this chapter is helpful in identifying the specific challenges faced by workers in this sector. However, it could also be applied to platform work more broadly, responding to calls for a dedicated conceptualisation of job quality in the platform economy (Gundert and Leschke 2023). Although labour platforms operate in different sectors and organise both blue- and white-collar occupations (Pesole et al. 2018; Piasna et al. 2022), there is a clear commonality in many of the features of platform work in general; notably, irregular and low earnings, a lack of labour and social protection and job instability (Berg 2016; Bergvall-Kåreborn and Howcroft 2014; Scholz 2016). These characteristics are commonly used to identify precarious employment (Kalleberg 2009; Kalleberg and Vallas 2017), and they are largely the result of platforms shifting the risks and costs of doing business to workers. While platforms cede most of the responsibilities of being employers to workers, depriving them of employment rights and protections, algorithmic management and the prominence of customer ratings block genuine autonomy and the self-determination of employment conditions (De Stefano 2018; Piasna and Drahokoupil 2021).

The conceptual framework developed in this chapter for analysing the quality of work in the platform economy – centred around flexibility, fragmentation, economic insecurity and the shifting of costs and risks to workers in the context of the inherent power imbalance between the parties – usefully highlights the interlinkages between different aspects of the model of work organisation in the platform economy. It also demonstrates the importance of taking a comprehensive view of the issue when designing and implementing any regulation in this area. The introduction of employee status may address some of the issues related to protection, income and workers' rights. However, in the context of the inherent power imbalance and vulnerability of workers, employer prerogatives exercised by hegemonic platforms may further erode workers' autonomy and flexibility, potentially increasing surveillance, control and subordination, and thus having a negative impact on various dimensions of the quality of work. Therefore, beyond striving to establish the presence of an employment relationship for food delivery couriers, close scrutiny is needed of the terms and conditions included in such contracts, where clauses limiting voice mechanisms and dissent, or which restrict working for other platforms, are particularly problematic.

Overall, the growth of the platform economy, and delivery services in particular, should be considered more generally in view of its implications for employment, particularly at the margins. This is not only because of the increasing adoption across many traditional sectors and workplaces of the technologically mediated forms of work organisation pioneered by the platform economy, but also because of the embeddedness of couriers in the traditional labour market, particularly in its more precarious segments. Therefore, frameworks developed to analyse the quality of work in digitally mediated labour markets should recognise and account for such intersectionality and complexity.

REFERENCES

Adams A., Freedman J. and Prassl J. (2018) Rethinking legal taxonomies for the gig economy, *Oxford Review of Economic Policy*, 34 (3), 475–494.

Berg J. (2016) Income security in the on-demand economy: findings and policy lessons from a survey of crowdworkers, *Conditions of Work and Employment*, Series 74, ILO.

Bergvall-Kåreborn B. and Howcroft D. (2014) Amazon Mechanical Turk and the commodification of labour, *New Technology, Work and Employment*, 29 (3), 213–223.

Burawoy M. (1979) *Manufacturing consent: changes in the labor process under monopoly capitalism*, University of Chicago Press.

Burchell B., Ladipo D. and Wilkinson F. (2002) *Job insecurity and work intensification*, Routledge.

Burchell B., Sehnbruch K., Piasna A. and Agloni N. (2014) The quality of employment and decent work: definitions, methodologies, and ongoing debates, *Cambridge Journal of Economics*, 38 (2), 459–477.

Datta N. (2019) Willing to pay for security: a discrete choice experiment to analyse labour supply preferences, CEP Discussion Papers dp1632, Centre for Economic Performance, LSE.

De Stefano V. (2018) *'Negotiating the algorithm': automation, artificial intelligence and labour protection*, ILO.

Dieckhoff M. (2011) The effect of unemployment on subsequent job quality in Europe: a comparative study of four countries, *Acta Sociologica*, 54 (3), 233–249.

Drahokoupil J. and Piasna A. (2017) Work in the platform economy: beyond lower transaction costs, *Intereconomics*, 52, 335–340.

Drahokoupil J. and Piasna A. (2019) Work in the platform economy: Deliveroo riders in Belgium and the SMart arrangement, Working Paper 2019.01, ETUI.

Dubal V.B. (2020) An Uber ambivalence: employee status, worker perspectives, and regulation in the gig economy, in Das Acevedo D. (ed.) *Beyond the algorithm: qualitative insights for gig work regulation*, Cambridge University Press, 33–56.

Edwards P. and Hodder A. (2022) Conflict and control in the contemporary workplace: structured antagonism revisited, *Industrial Relations Journal*, 53 (3), 220–240.

Edwards R. (1979) *Contested terrain: the transformation of the workplace in the twentieth century*, Basic Books.

Fairwork (2020) *The gig economy and Covid-19: looking ahead*, The Fairwork Project.

Gallie D. (ed.) (2013) *Economic crisis, quality of work, and social integration*, Oxford University Press.
Goods C., Veen A. and Barratt T. (2019) 'Is your gig any good?' Analysing job quality in the Australian platform-based food-delivery sector, *Journal of Industrial Relations*, 61 (4), 502–527.
Green F. and Mostafa T. (2012) *Trends in job quality in Europe*, Publications Office of the European Union.
Grimshaw D., Fagan C., Hebson G. and Tavora I. (eds.) (2017) *Making work more equal: a new labour market segmentation approach*, Manchester University Press.
Gundert S. and Leschke J. (2023) Challenges and potentials of evaluating platform work against established job-quality measures, *Economic and Industrial Democracy*, 45 (3). https://doi.org/10.1177/0143831X231199891
Hall J.V. and Krueger A.B. (2018) An analysis of the labor market for Uber's driver-partners in the United States, *ILR Review*, 71 (3), 705–732.
Ilsøe A., Larsen T.P. and Bach E.S. (2021) Multiple jobholding in the digital platform economy: signs of segmentation, *Transfer*, 27 (2), 201–218.
Kalleberg A.L. (2009) Precarious work, insecure workers: employment relations in transition, *American Sociological Review*, 74 (1), 1–22.
Kalleberg A.L. and Vallas S. (2017) Probing precarious work: theory, research, and politics, in Kalleberg A.L. and Vallas S. (eds.) *Precarious work*, Emerald Publishing, 1–30.
Karasek R. and Theorell T. (1990) *Healthy work: stress, productivity, and the reconstruction of working life*, Basic Books.
Kirchner S. and Schüßler E. (2020) Regulating the sharing economy: a field perspective, in Maurer I., Mair J. and Oberg A. (eds.) *Theorizing the sharing economy: variety and trajectories of new forms of organizing*, Emerald Publishing, 215–236.
Kuhn K.M. and Maleki A. (2017) Micro-entrepreneurs, dependent contractors, and instaserfs: understanding online labor platform workforces, *Academy of Management Perspectives*, 31 (3), 183–200.
Lambert S.J., Haley-Lock A. and Henly J.R. (2012) Schedule flexibility in hourly jobs: unanticipated consequences and promising directions, *Community, Work & Family*, 15 (3), 293–315.
Land K. (1975) The role of quality of employment indicators in general social reporting systems, *American Behavioral Scientist*, 18 (3), 304–332. https://doi.org/10.1177/000276427501800302
Lehdonvirta V. (2018) Flexibility in the gig economy: managing time on three online piecework platforms, *New Technology, Work and Employment*, 33 (1), 13–29.
Leschke J., Watt A. and Finn M. (2008) *Putting a number on job quality? Constructing a European Job Quality Index*, ETUI-REHS.
Mills M., Blossfeld H.-P. and Klijzing E. (2006) Becoming an adult in uncertain times: a 14-country comparison of the losers of globalization, in Blossfeld H.-P., Klijzing E., Mills M. and Kurz K. (eds.) *Globalization, uncertainty and youth in society*, Routledge, 393–411.
Muñoz de Bustillo R., Fernández-Macías E., Antón J.-I. and Esteve F. (2011) *Measuring more than money: the social economics of job quality*, Edward Elgar Publishing.
Pesole A. et al. (2018) *Platform workers in Europe*, Publications Office of the European Union.
Piasna A. (2020) Counting gigs: how can we measure the scale of online platform work?, Working Paper 2020.06, ETUI.
Piasna A. (2022) Precariousness in the platform economy, in Choonara J., Carmo R.M. and Murgia A. (eds.) *Faces of precarity: critical perspectives on work, subjectivities and struggles*, Bristol University Press, 130–145.
Piasna A. (2023) Algorithms of time: how algorithmic management changes the temporalities of work and prospects for working time reduction, *Cambridge Journal of Economics*, 48 (1), 115–132. https://doi.org/10.1093/cje/bead017
Piasna A. and Drahokoupil J. (2021) Flexibility unbound: understanding the heterogeneity of preferences among food delivery platform workers, *Socio-Economic Review*, 19 (4), 1397–1419.
Piasna A., Zwysen W. and Drahokoupil J. (2022) The platform economy in Europe: results from the second ETUI Internet and Platform Work Survey (IPWS), Working Paper 2022.05, ETUI.
Prassl J. (2018) *Humans as a service: the promise and perils of work in the gig economy*, Oxford University Press.

Pulignano V. et al. (2021) Does it pay to work? Unpaid labour in the platform economy, Policy Brief 2021.15, ETUI.
Rani U. and Furrer M. (2021) Digital labour platforms and new forms of flexible work in developing countries: algorithmic management of work and workers, *Competition & Change*, 25 (2) 212–236.
Rosenblat A. and Stark L. (2016) Algorithmic labor and information asymmetries: a case study of Uber's drivers, *International Journal of Communication*, 10, 3758–3784.
Scholz T. (2016) *Uberworked and underpaid: how workers are disrupting the digital economy*, Polity Press.
Schor J.B. et al. (2020) Dependence and precarity in the platform economy, *Theory and Society*, 49, 833–861.
Shanahan G. and Smith M. (2021) Fair's fair: psychological contracts and power in platform work, *International Journal of Human Resource Management*, 32 (19), 4078–4109.
Shapiro A. (2018) Between autonomy and control: strategies of arbitrage in the 'on-demand' economy, *New Media & Society*, 20 (8), 2954–2971.
Stone K. and Arthurs H. (2013) *Rethinking workplace regulation: beyond the standard contract of employment*, Russell Sage Foundation.
Tassinari A. and Maccarrone V. (2017) The mobilisation of gig economy couriers in Italy: some lessons for the trade union movement, *Transfer*, 23 (3), 353–357.
Thompson E.P. (1967) Time, work-discipline, and industrial capitalism, *Past and Present*, 38, 56–97.
Urzí Brancati M.C., Pesole A. and Férnandéz-Macías E. (2020) *New evidence on platform workers in Europe: results from the Second COLLEEM Survey*, Publications Office of the European Union.
Vandaele K., Piasna A. and Drahokoupil J. (2019) 'Algorithm breakers' are not a different 'species': attitudes towards trade unions of Deliveroo riders in Belgium, Working Paper 2019.06, ETUI.
van Doorn N. and Vijay D. (2021) Gig work as migrant work: the platformization of migration infrastructure, *Environment and Planning A: Economy and Space*. https://doi.org/10.1177/0308518X211065049
Wood A.J., Graham M., Lehdonvirta V. and Hjorth I. (2019a) Good gig, bad gig: autonomy and algorithmic control in the global gig economy, *Work, Employment and Society*, 33 (1), 56–75.
Wood A.J., Graham M., Lehdonvirta V. and Hjorth I. (2019b) Networked but commodified: the (dis) embeddedness of digital labour in the gig economy, *Sociology*, 53 (5), 931–950.
All links were checked on 29 January 2024.

8. The problem of unpaid labour in food delivery platforms in Europe: understanding the role of socio-technical and employment contract effects

Valeria Pulignano and Damian Grimshaw

INTRODUCTION

Unpaid labour is a major feature of digital labour platforms (for example, Pulignano and Mará 2021; Rani et al. 2021) and a key feature of platform workers' experience of 'algorithm insecurity' (Wood and Lehdonvirta 2023). It exists in a proximate relationship with paid work, unlike unpaid domestic work or care work, for example, and is defined as unremunerated working time that contributes directly to the completion of platform tasks (D'Cruz and Noronha 2016). Research already demonstrates that proximate unpaid labour is often a gateway to accessing paid work on a digital platform (Wood et al. 2019). It can be instrumental in enabling the worker to conform to algorithmic performance metrics that require workers to spend time undertaking qualification tests, searching for tasks or researching clients, for example (Casilli and Posada 2019). There are gaps in our understanding of why pressures to undertake unpaid labour vary across different platforms, however. This line of enquiry is relevant given parallel debates about the convergent and divergent characteristics of platforms' algorithm technologies which suggest potentially differentiated worker experiences (Vallas and Schor 2020) as well as differentiated institutional responses establishing diverse employment contractual statuses of platform workers across diverse country settings (Ametowobla and Kirchner 2022; Koutsimpogiorgos et al. 2023).

This chapter examines unpaid labour in two food delivery digital labour platforms, Deliveroo and Takeaway, in three countries: Belgium, France and the Netherlands. It focuses on how platforms design and operationalise diverse 'socio-technical systems' to govern labour by enabling or hindering key aspects of worker autonomy. The chapter interrogates two interrelated features that constitute the socially embedded character of algorithm-based technologies; that is, the platform's socio-technical approach to labour governance, and the contractual employment form, and relates both to the diverse patterns of unpaid labour.

A socio-technical system of digital technologies encompasses aspects of management mediation that may cushion some of the techno-centric performance consequences of algorithmic technologies (for example Guest et al. 2022). This socio-technical effect interacts with an employment contract effect, which ascribes self-employed or employee status to platform workers in specific institutional settings. The argument is made that unpaid labour has emerged in new forms as a result of digital platform technologies, yet significant variety is explained by these interrelated socio-technical and employment contract factors that shape workers' experiences of autonomy and employment status in different platforms and different countries.

STRATEGIES OF LABOUR GOVERNANCE IN DIGITAL PLATFORMS

Platforms are 'multi-sided markets' (Eisenmann et al. 2006) which enable the purchase and sale of labour-intensive services by matching clients, or users, and workers, or service providers, thus acting as 'digital intermediaries' (Lehdonvirta et al. 2014). The ability to match clients directly with workers offers a key advantage, but it also poses challenges for platforms, such as information asymmetry, which could constrain their capacity to ensure service quality for users (Rosenblat and Stark 2016). Moreover, the fragmentation of tasks among a geographically dispersed population of providers increases the difficulty for platforms to monitor and control their services (Kässi and Lehdonvirta 2018).

Platforms pretend to alleviate these problems by operating as the 'invisible hand' (Goldman 2011) by rewarding good service providers while sanctioning others. This occurs via monitoring worker performance using a variety of ratings aggregated by algorithm technologies, including clients' reviews of completed tasks or automated tracking of worker performance, such as location availability. In operationalising algorithm technologies to rank workers' performance, platforms create incentives for workers to act in accordance with company objectives, especially to maximise economic transactions. On private ride-hailing platforms, for example, drivers who fall below a certain rating can be removed from the platform (Rosenblat and Stark 2016). In this way, ratings stimulate drivers to improve their performance, reinforcing behaviours aligned with platform objectives and creating a powerful stimulus for various forms of unpaid labour (Gandini 2016; Pulignano et al. 2023a).

Nevertheless, there is a need for more detailed knowledge about platforms' potentially differentiated socio-technical strategies that influence how algorithm technologies pressure workers to undertake unpaid labour while building and defending their performance on platforms. In particular, to understand the varied forms of unpaid labour, one needs to investigate how ostensibly similar algorithm technologies are implemented by platforms for different strategies of labour governance. Such strategies interact with the use of standard and non-standard forms of employment. The dilution of the institutional protections of the traditional standard employment relationship has, in many countries, facilitated employer experimentation in multiple variants of precarious, on-demand and independent work arrangements (Rubery et al. 2018). Casual and irregular part-time employment forms do not provide minimum guaranteed working hours – for example zero hours and on-demand work – and therefore create precarious work by transferring to individuals the responsibility for financial costs (having enough income to make ends meet) and social ones (such as sickness and holiday provision and pensions). Moreover, declining labour power in many settings means workers sometimes lack the collective strength to contest the misuse of flexible employment measures or reverse their negative effects on precarity (Doellgast et al. 2018).

Running counter to these trends, however, some European countries, regions and cities are re-regulating platform work, using judicial decisions and administrative reforms that oblige platforms to define workers as employees rather than as self-employed (Kocher 2022). Hence, there is also a need to understand the different institutional circumstances in which platform workers with different employment statuses experience the need to undertake unpaid labour in platform contexts characterised by diverse socio-technical systems.

'OPEN' AND 'CLOSED' REGIMES FOR WORKER AUTONOMY

The analysis of algorithm technologies in this chapter builds on research recognising that 'technology is not neutral' (Bélanger and Edwards 2007: 717) and 'offers a more or less favorable ground for job autonomy, control over work, and power' (Bélanger 2006: 336). From this perspective, therefore, the design and implementation of a given technology are likely to shape the balance of coercion and legitimation used by management to govern labour in a way that reflects the social and regulatory context in which technologies are socially embedded.

Evidence from digital workplaces points to the potential of platform work to undermine workers' autonomy through algorithmic control systems. How platforms enable or foreclose worker choice and autonomy is key to understanding platform control (Maffie 2020). While platform workers in certain contexts may be considered 'technically free' and 'independent' to choose their schedule or switch platforms, intense competition for tasks means that it is often customer demand that dictates a worker's schedule instead (Shapiro 2020). Moreover, the algorithms that determine client or customer matching and task remuneration potentially reduce workers' autonomy to accept or reject work assignments due to information asymmetries (Woodcock 2020). Hence, algorithmic control systems incorporate a variety of more or less subtle control strategies for influencing workers' behaviour even when there is ostensibly a high degree of autonomy.

Considerations of the social embeddedness of a specific technology within a workplace mean interrogating the effects on labour of a seemingly uniform technology. The concept of embeddedness draws on Polanyi's understanding of economic activity as always 'embedded and enmeshed in institutions economic and non-economic' (Polanyi 1944/2001: 250). Technologies developed and applied in a work setting are necessarily bounded by a set of social institutions which, in Polanyi's terminology, continuously act to de-commodify labour by insulating workers from pure market exchange. In other words, the social aspects of the employment relationship, no matter how much reconfigured by advanced digital technologies, endure.

Moreover, platform research highlights the 'malleability' of digital technologies (Schüßler et al. 2021) as platforms design and remodel their strategies depending on context (Vallas and Schor 2020). Context embodies varied strategies of labour governance, reflecting distinctive social relationships of control (Tubaro 2021) and varied modes of production (Frenken and Fuenfschilling 2020).

Burawoy's (1985) concept of a workplace 'regime' refers to a diverse set of socio-technical relationships organised around production, labour control and worker autonomy. We extend Sørensen and Kalleberg's (1981) analysis of the variation in control and autonomy over work conduct to a digital platform setting to examine the socially embedded character of algorithm-based technologies and relate them to the diverse patterns of unpaid labour. In our framing of ideal types, we borrow Sørensen and Kalleberg's (1981) distinction of 'open' and 'closed' worker regimes that describe two aspects of worker autonomy related to access to the job and control over job activities. An 'open' regime features relatively high access to the job and relatively high control over work activities. It also reflects relatively unstructured 'entry channels' that have different impacts on workers depending on the skills required. For jobs requiring few skills, a 'closed' regime brings structured entry channels that shelter workers from competition with other workers (Maurice et al. 1982).

Unlike non-digital workplaces, however, where management typically exercises close physical supervisory control over contractually subordinated employees, platform workers are often self-employed and more likely to have to comply with the control strategies dictated via algorithmic technologies. Moreover, the idea of worker autonomy concerning access to the job needs to distinguish between: (a) access to the platform, including freedom to sign up to other platforms and/or seek other jobs in the labour market; and (b) access to paid tasks once on the platform. With respect to worker control over the conduct of work, we need to differentiate between: (c) control over working time; (d) how to do the work; and (e) the choice of task, including the (im)possibility of task rejection. These five variables are analysed in the empirical section of the chapter. Given the opportunities for distinctive social embedding of algorithmic technologies, the chapter hypothesises that 'open' and 'closed' socio-technical regimes are both theoretically possible on digital platforms. These regimes are further contextualised within an institutional setting that regulates the employment form as employee or self-employed. What remains to be empirically investigated, therefore, is the significance of 'open' and 'closed' socio-technical regimes under the adopted contractual employment form in shedding light on the different patterns of unpaid labour.

RESEARCH DESIGN AND CASE SELECTION

The research consists of a comparative qualitative case study research design (Eisenhardt and Graebner 2007), involving narrative interviews and working diaries collected from workers on two food delivery platforms, Deliveroo and Takeaway, operating in three countries: Belgium, France and the Netherlands. Country selection is based on the rate of penetration of platform work. The Flash Eurobarometer (European Commission 2018) reports that platform work penetration is relatively similar across the three selected countries: 11 per cent of citizens in France state that they have provided a service via a platform at least once, compared to 9 per cent in the Netherlands and 6 per cent in Belgium. Two considerations guide platform selection: (1) the variety of platform control strategies which monitor worker performance and influence the degree of worker autonomy (Table 8.1a and 8.1b; see also Griesbach et al. 2019); and (2) the presence of platform operations in more than one country in order to explore differences in employment forms. We are aiming to achieve a conceptual fit, such that the sample is representative of the phenomenon under investigation (Miles and Huberman 1994).

In addition, there are some cross-country specificities regarding how each platform manages employment status. Deliveroo hires couriers as self-employed workers in all three countries, but, in Belgium, it also hires couriers who are still students or who fall under 'peer-to-peer' status (P2P). This, introduced by law in 2017, in what was then termed the 'collaborative economy', differs from self-employment status as such couriers are exempt from social security contributions but are entitled to a special, favourable tax regime for income earned from working on officially licensed platforms, up to a ceiling of €7,170 in 2023. Deliveroo's use of P2P status in Belgium has recently been contested. Initially, (student) self-employed and P2P workers in Belgium received a variable fee per delivery, consisting of a fixed amount for delivering the food and a distance-based amount dependent on client distance. When the Belgian

Table 8.1a *Selected platforms' operations and employment status: the 'open' regime in Deliveroo*

Categories	Explanation
Socially embedded technologies	Algorithmic locational availability
Employment status	Self-employment (including P2P status)
Platform operation	Dimensions
Access to platform	Login system with free entry and exit
Access to tasks	Algorithm governs access to tasks (the 'best order-to-rider fit') according to constant worker availability (being 'in the right place at the right time')
Worker control over task conduct	Workers decide when to start and finish the work, but they do not decide on the number of orders and pay (pay per delivery). They can decline orders, but if cancellation occurs during delivery, the courier is not compensated

Source: Own elaboration.

Table 8.1b *Selected platforms' operations and employment status: the 'closed' regime in Takeaway*

Categories	Explanation
Socially embedded technologies	Algorithmic management-mediated performance metrics
Employment status	Employees either directly employed, or indirectly via a temporary employment agency. Some self-employment, including P2P status
Platform operation	Dimensions
Access to platform	Conditioned by shift assignment by the platform: a minimum of 2 shifts for a total of 6 working hours per week
Access to tasks	Metrics and assessment by middle-range management govern worker access to tasks
Worker control over task conduct	Platform controls working time, the deployment and the timing of tasks, and pay. Workers are paid per hour and retain an employment relationship either with the platform or the employment agency

Source: Own elaboration.

tax authorities challenged the P2P classification of couriers in 2019, Deliveroo switched to a fixed delivery fee to justify 'self-employment' contracts, claiming that the client 'directly' pays the worker,[1] although self-employed Deliveroo workers' fees remained distance-related. This change went hand in hand with eliminating the possibility for P2P workers to see the client's location before accepting an order and to receive financial rewards (bonuses) from the platform. Conversely, Deliveroo discloses locational information about the client and the restaurant to self-employed workers in all three countries because distance-based fees still apply.

Conversely, Takeaway employs couriers either directly or through an employment agency as employees in Belgium, France and the Netherlands, paying them an hourly wage, including overtime. At the time of collecting the data, agency workers had daily or weekly contracts, but could be offered monthly contracts and direct employment after three months of work provided they had good performance ratings. Working under a shift-based system, Takeaway couriers are supervised by 'driver captains' and/or 'hub coordinators'.

Deliveroo assigns orders through an algorithm which calculates the best order-to-rider fit on the basis of the expected pick-up time and the location of the worker by using data on workers, clients and restaurants ('algorithmic locational availability'). Workers are 'independent contractors' (self-employed) who can freely access the platform by logging in through the app ('free login system') and are paid per delivery. The algorithm models the data to optimise the delivery process; however, the platform uses a worker's availability to assess performance, which is translated into access to orders. Workers' task conduct is characterised by the worker having control over when to start and finish work, but they do not decide on the number of orders or the rate of pay. Workers can decline orders, but if cancellation occurs while an order is in delivery, the courier is not compensated. Since the payment for those with P2P self-employment status in Belgium is fixed, Deliveroo does not inform workers of the client's location in order to prevent them from choosing only short-distance deliveries. This pattern is not followed for those with normal self-employment status.

Takeaway collects performance ratings through automated metrics which are then combined with assessments by supervisory managers who incorporate their daily decisions about sanctions, pay rises, career progressions or dismissals ('algorithmic management-mediated performance metrics'). Workers can access the platform through a login system which is not 'free' in the sense that workers are assigned orders in accordance with a shift system to which they are asked to be available and which, under normal circumstances (good weather conditions, for example), workers cannot decline. Workers need to complete a minimum of six hours per week and at least one day on the weekend in order to be assigned additional shifts by the platform. The assignment of shifts is automated, but managers can still intervene manually. Workers are paid per hour and are employed either directly (more often in Belgium and France) or indirectly through a temporary employment agency (more often in the Netherlands). At the time of conducting the research, only a minority of workers remained self-employed.[2] Workers are informed of the restaurant's and client's addresses, but Takeaway does not disclose data on restaurants' waiting times. Workers do, however, use the app to self-report information about restaurant waiting times to other co-workers.

DATA COLLECTION AND DATA ANALYSIS

The primary method of data collection is narrative interviews. Working diaries are the secondary method, complementing the interviews by validating them and providing further analytical insights (Morse and Niehaus 2009). Data collection included 34 narrative interviews and 21 working diaries with food delivery couriers (15 in Belgium, 10 in the Netherlands, 9 in France) in the period April 2020 to January 2021. Respondents were recruited via snowball sampling and through grassroots and traditional unions. They reported different employment statuses (self-employed, employed via temporary employment agency, employed directly by the platform) and had worked on one or several platforms. While some respondents consented only to an interview, others agreed to both a narrative interview and a working diary.

Narrative interviews were used to capture the workers' lived experiences, especially their sense-making practices concerning autonomy and ways of relating these to their overall work and life situation. Working diaries consisted of audio recordings of work experiences over ten successive working days, with a focus on autonomy over access to the platform, platform tasks and task control, and the form and frequency of unpaid labour. Frequencies were calculated by examining per platform the number of working days in which a respondent mentioned a form of unpaid labour or autonomy, dividing this by the total number of working days completed in the diary. Respondents recorded work activities via their smartphones and sent them to the research team via the Belnet secure transfer network. Thematic analysis was used to interpret the interview and diary data. Data analysis was thematic and proceeded in three sequential steps: (1) open coding of interviews and diaries; (2) selective coding of interviews and diaries, where the prevalence of each code was identified in the diary data; and (3) comparative analysis of both data sources, moving from codes through themes to concepts.

AUTONOMY IN A RELATIVELY OPEN SOCIO-TECHNICAL WORKER REGIME: DELIVEROO

The main feature of openness in Deliveroo's socio-technical system concerns workers' autonomy to enter and exit the platform, which appears to complement the self-employment form: 'We are self-employed and therefore we are free to move in and out at will' (NLMF01). Crucially, this feature means workers are free to decide when to start and finish work each day; they can register easily via the app (for example, 'If you have a bike and a phone you can start immediately' – NLMF01), log in when they wish and receive payment for each task they complete. The relatively 'open' socio-technical system also enables workers to decide their own routes (38 per cent of Deliveroo respondents) and combine rides with work elsewhere: 'When there are no deliveries on Deliveroo, I work for Uber Eats' (NLLV12); 'I did my first three months with Deliveroo until Fetch arrived; I also worked with them' (FRCM21). Diaries confirm that workers freely log in and off on the vast majority of working days (86 per cent). Moreover, on around half of the recorded workdays, neither commissions nor sanctions were imposed when workers declined tasks (51 per cent) (Table 8.2).

Table 8.2 *Measures of worker autonomy in the two case study food delivery platforms (% of working days)*

Measures of autonomy		Example quote	Percentage of working days on which the form of autonomy was mentioned by workers	
			'Open' regime: Deliveroo	**'Closed' regime: Takeaway**
Access to platform and task	Autonomy related to access to work outside the platform	*'I called the platform today and they told me that I can't work for them and for another platform.'* (BECM09)	13%	13%
	Autonomy related to access to platform (login/logoff or open shifts)	*'I can choose myself when I login and when I logout'* (BEMF40)	86%	2%
	Autonomy related to access to paid work on the platform	*'I am always paid by the hour – more or less around €11 per hour gross'* (BECM17)	10%	90%
Task control activities	Autonomy related to control over work time: what to do or when to take a break	*'If you have nothing to do in between orders, then you can quickly go to a waiting space'* (NLMF02)	0%	30%
	Autonomy related to control over how to do the job	*'I was free to choose my routes'* (NLMR02)	38%	28%
	Autonomy related to task rejection	*'I can turn down orders if I want to.'* (NLMR03)	51%	2%

Note: Sample size = 70 working days in Deliveroo, 80 working days in Takeaway.
Source: Own elaboration.

Open access to the platform does not necessarily correspond to having open access to paid work, however, as not all workers who log in are assigned an order immediately. The diaries illustrate a huge discrepancy between workers exercising autonomy to access paid work (just 10 per cent of working days) versus accessing the platform (86 per cent) (Table 8.2). Workers log in to the app and then remain inactive on the platform until they receive an order. This is because the Deliveroo algorithm ('FRANK') monitors workers' performance and assigns orders on the basis of the temporal and spatial efficiency of each delivery – as one driver put it, being 'in the right place at the right time' (FRCM14). The algorithm calculates the optimal

Table 8.3 *Measures of unpaid labour in the two case study food delivery platforms (% of working days)*

Forms of unpaid labour	**Example quote**	**Percentage of days on which this form of unpaid labour was mentioned by workers**	
		'Open' regime: Deliveroo	**'Closed' regime: Takeaway**
1. Waiting time because of a lack of orders	*'In a period of 15 minutes it can be that there aren't any orders and then you're just waiting.'* (BEMF16)	64%	0%
2. Searching time in case of errors and delays at restaurant	*'I had to wait four times for 10 minutes in different restaurants. That is waiting time you are not paid for.'* (BEMF40)	47%	2%
3. Travel time to and from work	*'I got an order and then cycled from the customer's house back to the centre waiting for an order. After that I cycled home, which was also unpaid.'* (NLMR02)	39%	12%
4. Travel time between orders	*'Between the orders I always had to wait for about 10 minutes for a new order. That is also unpaid.'* (BEMF38)	23%	0%
5. Time invested in dealing with conflicts (restaurants/clients)	*'I tried to call the customer but he did not answer. I then contacted the platform with the chat. After 5 minutes they answered but they could not reach them either.'* (BEMF16)	11%	0%
6. Compulsory unpaid breaks and shortening of shifts	*'It was a bit frustrating that they made me finish my shift earlier than I should. Which is something that they constantly do'* (NLMR05)	2%	44%

Note: Sample size = 70 working days in Deliveroo, 80 working days in Takeaway.
Source: Own elaboration.

delivery distance using data collected from restaurants, workers and clients so that 'there is always a worker waiting and ready to take an order' (FRCM21). Workers thus need to allow for periods of unpaid waiting time between available orders (Table 8.3).

Deliveroo workers try to reduce waiting time by collecting as many orders as possible in a row, through 'frequent login and avoiding cancelling orders' (BEMF35). They expressed powerlessness over the decisions as to whether and when they are assigned paid work, however: 'Often there are no orders and you're just waiting. You don't get paid for that. You're only paid when you're picking up an order' (BEMF16). Thus, despite the relatively 'open' socio-technical regime, workers declare a lack of autonomy resulting from the high frequency of unpaid labour they undertake waiting to access orders through the platform. Indeed, diaries report that Deliveroo workers experienced no working days when they exercised autonomy over working time despite them being classified as self-employed. As a consequence, workers' remuneration is highly uncertain: 'It is impossible to use Deliveroo as a main source of income' (NLMF01) (Table 8.2).

Moreover, Deliveroo's open platform access, absence of recruitment checks, and piece-rate payment system mean it can rely on a 'reserve army' of labour to fill low-skill jobs: 'Everyone can connect at any time' (FRCM14), 'including no checks of visa or work permit' (BEMF39). Drivers must compete for orders on the basis of locational availability, which is calculated and imposed on workers by the algorithm despite the fiction of autonomy that self-employment status would normally imply. The 'free login' system, with workers ostensibly paid directly by clients, allows the platform to legitimise the use of self-employment status in so far as workers can claim to have freedom over accepting or cancelling orders based on the information they have about the client's location.

While Deliveroo workers experience autonomy over task rejection on around half their working days (51 per cent), their autonomy over work conduct in the course of those days is far less (38 per cent) (Table 8.2). Workers also often live in the suburbs, and it takes them up to 'an hour of cycling to reach the city centre, where they can check in and start working' (BEMF38). Thus, when someone works, they earn 'just a little money considering how long you have to wait before receiving an order... and in between orders... or how long you have to cycle to reach the point you need to be' (BEMF39).

AUTONOMY IN A RELATIVELY CLOSED SOCIO-TECHNICAL WORKER REGIME: TAKEAWAY

A 'closed' regime refers to various features that restrict workers' autonomy to access the platform and paid work through it. Takeaway workers' access to paid work is strongly conditioned by the assignment of shifts on the platform – a minimum of two shifts for a total of six hours per week. Takeaway workers thus rarely experience autonomy to access the platform (only 2 per cent of working days). Once on the platform, however, Takeaway workers report high autonomy to access paid work – experienced on 90 per cent of working days – as they are paid per hour (Table 8.2).[3]

The socio-technical system in Takeaway is based on algorithmic metrics that measure and monitor workers' performance and then determine the assigned orders. Workers are employed directly, or indirectly via a temporary employment agency, with few being self-employed. Workers who indicate their availability in advance are granted working hours, subject to country-specific working time rules and their individual metrics: 'You have statistics that allow you to reserve your shifts. People with the best statistics can reserve first' (BEMF16). Workers who reject orders once working hours have been stipulated are penalised by the platform; diaries indicate workers experience relatively low autonomy (2 per cent of working days) in relation to task rejection. Performance metrics include worker availability, on-time delivery, 'food in bag time' (the time from pick-up to delivery), and 'wrong app usage' (late pick-up). Assignment of a minimum of six hours work each week grants workers some control over when to take a break (30 per cent of days).

Worker performance is measured through a combination of statistics – generated by algorithmic technologies using client reviews – and the evaluations of supervisors who have daily face-to-face contact with workers. This means there is some space for negotiation as workers can contest bad statistics and potentially avoid sanctions by talking directly to their supervisors. As reported by a mid-level Takeaway manager:

> We have performance reviews, a milestone review every three months and check-in reviews in between. We have the data generated by the app and we have the captain on site who will actually conduct the evaluations with the couriers face to face. It could be that a worker scores poorly on the app, but the captain may still say that this person is doing well. Then it's up to the coordinator to do the final evaluation (BEMF45).

On the basis of this mixed (algorithmic-management mediated) appraisal, decisions are made about the type of contract, pay rise, promotion and dismissal. Workers who are employees and who perform best are awarded a pay increase of almost €0.50 per hour every three months. This means that high-performing workers, after a year of platform work, earn around €12 per hour while other workers earn around €10 an hour (BEMF17; BEMF18; FRCM25; BEMF04). Good statistics are also rewarded with promotions, which often consist of prolonging the contract via the employment agency. For example, Takeaway upgrades workers in Belgium 'from daily to weekly and thereafter monthly contracts' (BEMF18). Moreover, workers with good statistics move up the career ladder 'from rider through to captain who delivers food and supervises workers' (BECM09) and receive bonuses, while workers with bad statistics receive a 'warning' followed by a 'performance talk' and, if necessary, 're-training' (BECM09).

As workers are hourly paid, Takeaway sends as many orders as possible to them and requires orders to be delivered within the time workers are paid for: 'At the very moment you've delivered an order, *bam*, you get a new one' (BEMF18). Workers who depend on good statistics and a good relationship with captains tend not to refuse. Those who are slower or who regularly reject orders risk being sanctioned: 'If a rider keeps getting less than two deliveries per hour, they'll receive a warning from me and we'll talk... If the worker carries on along this path there will be another warning and eventually they will be kicked out' (NLMF03) – unless a legitimate reason is provided by the worker (such as sickness) within the terms established by national law.

As such, Takeaway workers cannot reject orders as they need to deliver at full speed to guarantee good scores and to access paid work:

> I need to be fast with picking up the order and delivering it. If I'm not fast enough, I may face some trouble. I may even lose my job. And you don't know how many orders you may have. You may do in a 4-hour shift more than 30 or 35 km, so in the whole day you may do 70 km (NLMR05).

Nevertheless, there is a degree of 'human mediation' of the algorithms. Workers contact captains and coordinators directly when they experience problems and/or accidents. In this way, workers may avoid performance sanctions and reduce the risk of losing income or their job for events beyond their control: 'Once I fell during my shift and my bike broke down. I took screenshots and sent them to the hub, explaining what had happened. In this way, I avoided bad statistics' (BEGIGMF19).

COMPARING AUTONOMY AND UNPAID LABOUR IN RELATIVELY OPEN AND CLOSED WORKER REGIMES

Overall, Deliveroo's self-employed workers experience far greater autonomy in accessing the platform than Takeaway workers (86 per cent and 2 per cent of working days, respectively). Self-employment status allows them to hop on and off the platform and sublet their accounts in case of longer absences due to sickness, travel or family issues: 'When I want to see my family in Pakistan, I stop working and rent my account to somebody else, for a month or longer' (BEMF36). Yet, the capacity to access paid work is much lower in Deliveroo (10 per cent, versus 90 per cent in Takeaway) (Table 8.2), which increases uncertainty for Deliveroo workers and drives them to engage in more unpaid labour. 'You don't have any control over your pay. You don't know how long you'd wait for an order; restaurants are often busy so you might end up doing just two deliveries an hour, which means €7 before tax' (NLLV12).

Deliveroo's self-employed workers spend considerably more unpaid time waiting to access a task than Takeaway workers (64 per cent and zero per cent, respectively; Table 8.3). As one Deliveroo worker reported: 'Often you have to wait and, when you wait, you earn nothing. Then you don't know how much you're going to make by the end of the day' (BEMF39). In addition, while workers for both Deliveroo and Takeaway report working outside the platform (13 per cent of working days in both cases), this represents the need to compensate for lost income at Deliveroo or the opportunity to top up income at Takeaway as the guaranteed shifts may not always be sufficient: 'The contract they [Takeaway] proposed at the beginning was interim only. This was good to keep me employed as when I didn't get enough shifts on Takeaway I went to work for other platforms' (BECM09).

Unpaid search time in case of errors and delays at restaurants is mentioned far more frequently in Deliveroo (47 per cent) than Takeaway (2 per cent). Both groups of platform workers reported unpaid travel time from customers to restaurants (Table 8.3); however, this was considerably more often at Deliveroo as workers in Takeaway are paid by the hour. Unpaid time spent addressing conflicts, both with restaurants and clients, prevailed only among Deliveroo workers (11 per cent), reflecting the absence of human mediation of the algorithms observed at Takeaway. One exception to this pattern of unpaid labour concerns Takeaway workers experiencing greater frequency of unpaid compulsory breaks or reduced shifts than Deliveroo workers: respectively, 44 per cent and 2 per cent. The explanation is that Deliveroo workers choose to skip unpaid breaks whenever possible due to their self-employed status and being paid on a piece-rate basis.

Unsurprisingly, given the higher frequencies of unpaid labour under self-employment, Deliveroo workers report higher income insecurity than Takeaway workers. As the platform adjusts per-delivery pay according to demand, pay is low and unpredictable. While the average net income per working day, as reported in diaries, is €70.89 in Takeaway; in Deliveroo, it is €38.71. Deliveroo workers say they cannot plan their incomes adequately, thereby perpetuating insecurity: 'I can go to work this lunchtime and earn €5, €10, maybe €15 for two or three hours. And then the next day, there won't be many deliveries and I will maybe earn half. So, it's really hard to predict' (FRCM21). In Takeaway, less frequent unpaid work under a more secure employment status and more predictable income means workers can calculate their earnings on the basis of the number of scheduled working hours: 'I got a contract for 15 hours a week. I saw the salary; it seemed to me average, like for 15 hours they give us €605 per month as a gross salary' (FRCM22). Moreover, workers report that the Takeaway captain and hub coordinators are accessible and helpful in ensuring they received promotional pay rises and avoided sanctions: 'You get assistance for every problem you might have – accidents or anything else. For instance, [when] people who ordered the food are not there, you contact the dispatchers and they advise you what to do.' (BECM09). Workers with either a direct or indirect employment contract report that their employment status helps them build a relationship of trust with Takeaway management which, in turn, supports improved pay and working conditions, consequently reducing unpaid labour: 'I have an employment contract and this is why I can establish such a trusting relationship with those in the hierarchy. It is much easier for me!' (FRCM22).

DISCUSSION

This chapter critically investigates how platforms' socio-technical worker regimes, alongside different rules governing the employment relationship, contribute to explaining the extent and forms of unpaid labour. Drawing on our empirical evidence in food delivery, we identify three contributions to our understanding of this growing sphere of employment in Europe. We note that the findings reflect the specificities of on-location food delivery; in related research, we have found that the results for online freelance work, requiring higher skills, are quite different (Pulignano et al. 2023a, 2023b).

A first contribution builds on studies that document how unpaid labour results from algorithmic performance pressures (for example, Gandini 2016; Shapiro 2020) and mutually shapes experiences of insecure work (Wood and Lehdonvirta 2021). We interrogate in more detail the antecedents shaping the variety of relationships between unpaid labour, algorithmic performance management and the contractual form of the employment relationship. Our complementary approach of focusing on 'open' and 'closed' worker regimes brings to the foreground theoretical insights from the sociology of work that consider management control strategies as socio-technically embedded (Burawoy 1985), alongside explanatory frameworks of control and autonomy that intersect with standard and non-standard employment forms (Sørensen and Kalleberg 1981).

Accordingly, an 'open' regime allows self-employed workers to: enter and exit the platform freely (including remaining inactive on the platform without incurring sanctions or fees), control access to (and refuse) tasks and exercise discretion over the conduct of platform tasks. Conversely, a 'closed' regime restricts workers' autonomy to access the platform and tasks, as well as to exercise control over tasks. These are 'ideal' types that do not map neatly to the two case studies; nevertheless, they provide a valuable heuristic for distinguishing the key drivers of worker autonomy and unpaid labour. Moreover, they are useful in discerning the complexity of the relationship between diverse systems of socially embedded algorithm technologies, employment contracts and the consequences for unpaid labour.

Whereas unpaid labour is relatively extensive in both 'open' and 'closed' regimes, our evidence points to significant differences that reflect diversity in the extent and form of unpaid labour between the two platforms. Takeaway is more characteristic of a 'closed' regime than Deliveroo and appears better at mitigating unpaid waiting time than Deliveroo's relatively 'open' regime. This also reflects the employment status designated to Takeaway workers as employees versus the self-employed status of Deliveroo workers. In other words, the relatively 'closed' regime at Takeaway provides employees with a degree of market shelter from the risk of being easily replaced in a relatively overcrowded sector, given the high numbers of people able to undertake platform tasks that require limited training or experience. Nevertheless, it is the case that compulsory unpaid breaks and unpaid time caused by a reduction in shifts assigned to the worker by the platform, for example due to low ratings based on performance, as well as an intensification of work, can still unfold for Takeaway employees. This suggests that standardisation of employment status is a necessary, but not sufficient, reform in combating unpaid platform work.

A second contribution relates to the persistence of the 'human element' in shaping performance pressures on workers. By examining the influence of management-mediated algorithmic technologies at Takeaway, our findings contribute to conceptualisations of platforms as 'contested relational structures' (Schüßler et al. 2021) by revealing the structuring conditions which offer distinct sources of autonomy to platform workers – potentially within both 'open' and 'closed' regime types. Other studies highlight the 'subordinated' nature of the employment relationship in platform work (Wood and Lehdonvirta 2021). Our theorisation of 'open' and 'closed' regimes provides a means to analyse how the socio-technical relationship among workers, clients and platform managers shapes the extent and form of unpaid labour and helps explain the extent to which workers are left at the mercy of platform algorithms. Our findings demonstrate that the 'social structure' within which digital technologies are embedded, which includes a socio-technical effect (at the level of the platform) and a contractual employment effect (concerning rules fixed at a city or national level), is still a significant force in shaping the strategic 'economic action' of platforms (Vallas and Schor 2020). This enhances, or otherwise inhibits, worker autonomy and influences the resulting pressures to undertake unpaid labour. Thus, rather than assuming workers undertake unpaid labour solely as a result of the need to build their digital platform reputations, it appears that differences in platform regimes and employment status contribute to a more rounded explanation.

The third contribution concerns the implications for precarious digital work. Unpaid labour is a significant feature of precarious working and living conditions as it affects the capacity of workers to make a living in terms of both the pathway to paid work and the costs associated with accomplishing unpaid platform tasks. Our evidence of precarious work illustrates that platforms are key architects of precarity because they mould a worker's platform dependency around unpaid work. Therefore, we argue that both 'open' and 'closed' regimes shape workers' dependency on platform income by affecting platforms' capacity to exploit workers' unpaid labour. The extent to which, and how, platforms can do this depends on the embeddedness of digital technologies within a context of the triadic ties between workers, clients and platform management. Our findings therefore challenge a representation of worker dependency on platforms based only on income (for example, Schor et al. 2021) and show how the platform can enact dependency (for example, Wood and Ledhonvirta 2023) by illustrating how the 'human' or 'management-driven element' of the technology, which may reflect the 'human-centred' supervision of platform workers and/or legally mandated employee status, helps workers gain partial autonomy despite the overriding power of algorithmic technologies to control worker performance.

CONCLUSIONS

The theoretical insights presented in this chapter suggest that no simple correspondence exists between unpaid labour and digital platform work. Instead, we need to understand the way platforms' socio-technical strategies of labour governance steer unpaid labour by enabling or constraining key aspects of worker autonomy. Moreover, it is clear from our evidence that platform reliance on self-employment exacerbates unpaid labour in comparison to the use of employee status. Combined with a relatively 'open' worker regime (Deliveroo), self-employed food delivery platform workers experience diminished market shelter and can be easily replaced in a relatively overcrowded sector that requires few skills. Conversely, the use of the employee contractual form can mitigate unpaid labour within a relatively 'closed' regime (Takeaway). It cannot eliminate unpaid labour completely, however. The risk of unpaid labour persists under an hourly paid system since the worker is subordinated to work faster (work intensification) and is also subject to short-term changes in working time arrangements.[4]

With these headline findings in mind, this chapter has raised an additional concern, namely that platforms can worsen precarious working conditions even when a contractual employment relationship is in place. Recent studies illustrate that some platforms sidestep their regulatory obligations through exploiting institutional loopholes, involving practices of subcontracting, flexible employment oriented around irregular hours (such as marginal part-time and short-term employment forms) (Niebler et al. 2023) and/or different 'third status' self-employment solutions. A 'third status' self-employment/worker category blurs the boundary between employee and self-employed (for example peer-to-peer status in Belgium, para-subordinate status in Italy and civil law contracts for mandate in Poland) (Muszyński and Pulignano 2023). This means that, while the proposal for an EU directive on platform work addresses employment reclassification, it is unclear whether reclassification will be applicable to situations of workers with these types of 'third status'. Moreover, it still remains to be seen how countries will guarantee reclassification for undocumented migrants (who constitute the majority of workers on food delivery platforms) and what strategies are required of trade unions, especially concerning how to develop proactive labour solidarity with under-represented groups (Marino et al. 2017).

Overall, this chapter argues for the need to examine the organisational labour governance arrangements shaping platform work within different national regulatory settings. By framing the comparison of platforms against the twofold typology of 'open' and 'closed' socio-technical worker regimes, and considering the influence of distinctive contractual employment forms, the findings shed light on the fact that the contractual employment form is certainly a necessary but not entirely sufficient condition to combat unpaid and precarious labour within the platform economy.

ACKNOWLEDGEMENT

The research underlying this article is funded by a European Research Council Advanced Grant under the European Union's Horizon 2020 research and innovation programme (Grant agreement No. 833577) and the Flemish Research Council FWO (Project Number G073919N) (PI: Valeria Pulignano).

NOTES

1. Between 2018 and 2020, P2P workers were tax-free and exempt from social contributions up to an annual ceiling of €6,340 in 2020. The Belgian Constitutional Court overturned the tax-free scheme, meaning that a tax rate of 10.7 per cent on platform earnings has applied since January 2021.
2. At the time of writing, Takeaway employs all workers in Belgium either directly, or indirectly via a temporary employment agency.
3. It is also relevant that Takeaway had, at the time of our fieldwork, taken further steps to regulate employment in other countries by concluding collective agreements in Italy, Spain and Denmark (Hadwiger, 2022).
4. At the time of writing, Takeaway wishes to increase the number of direct employees even further over the number of indirect (via temporary agency) employees. However, the hourly paid system endures under the platform's consistent use of daily contracts to respond to volatile demand, even though it risks jeopardising pay rights for workers.

REFERENCES

Ametowobla D. and Kirchner S. (2022) The organization of digital platforms, *Zeitschrift für Soziologie*, 52 (2), 143–156.

Bélanger J. (2006) Technology and work, in Korczynski M., Hodson R. and Edwards P.K. (eds.) *Social theory at work*, Oxford University Press, 325–355.

Bélanger J. and Edwards P. (2007) The conditions promoting compromise in the workplace, *British Journal of Industrial Relations*, 45 (4), 713–734.

Burawoy M. (1985) *The Politics of production: factory regimes under capitalism and socialism*, Verso.

Casilli A. and Posada L. (2019) The platformization of labor and society, in Graham M. and Dutton W.H. (eds.) *Society and the internet: how networks of information and communication are changing our lives*, Oxford University Press, 293–306.

D'Cruz P. and Noronha E. (2016) Positives outweighing negatives: the experiences of Indian crowdsourced workers, *Work Organisation, Labour and Globalisation*, 10 (1), 44–63.

Doellgast V., Lillie N. and Pulignano V. (eds.) (2018) *Reconstructing solidarity: labour unions, precarious work, and the politics of institutional change in Europe*, Oxford University Press.

Eisenhardt K.M. and Graebner M.E. (2007) Theory building from cases: opportunities and challenges, *Academy of Management Journal*, 50 (1), 25–32.

Eisenmann T., Parker G. and Van Alstyne M.W. (2006) Strategies for two-sided markets, *Harvard Business Review*, 84 (10), 92–103.

European Commission (2018) Flash Eurobarometer on illegal content. https://digital-strategy.ec.europa.eu/en/library/flash-eurobarometer-illegal-content

Frenken K. and Fuenfschilling L. (2020) The rise of online platforms and the triumph of the corporation, *Sociologica*, 14 (3), 101–113.

Gandini A. (2016) Digital work: self-branding and social capital in the freelance knowledge economy, *Marketing Theory*, 16 (1), 123–141.

Goldman E. (2011) Regulating reputation, in Masum H. and Tovey M. (eds.) *The reputation society: how online opinions are reshaping the offline world*, MIT Press, 51–62.

Griesbach K., Reich A., Elliot-Negri L. and Milkman R. (2019) Algorithmic control in platform food delivery work, *Socius*, 5, 1–15.

Guest D., Knox A. and Warhurst C. (2022) Humanizing work in digital age: lessons from socio-technical systems and quality of working life initiatives, *Human Relations*, 75 (8), 1461–1482.

Hadwiger F. (2022) *Realizing the opportunities of the platform economy through freedom of association and collective bargaining*, ILO.

Kässi O. and Lehdonvirta V. (2018) Online labour index: measuring the online gig economy for policy and research, *Technological Forecasting and Social Change*, 137, 241–248.

Kocher E. (2022) *Digital work platforms at the interface of labour law: regulating market organisers*, Hart Publishing.

Koutsimpogiorgos N., Frenken K. and Herrmann A.M. (2023) Platform adaptation to regulation: the case of domestic cleaning in Europe, *Journal of Industrial Relations*, 65 (2), 156–184.

Lehdonvirta V., Barnard H., Graham M. and Hjorth I. (2014) Online labour markets-levelling the playing field for international service markets?, Paper presented at IPP2014: Crowdsourcing for Politics and Policy conference, 25–26 September, Oxford, UK.

Maffie M.D. (2020) Are we 'sharing' or 'gig-ing'? A classification system for online platforms, *Industrial Relations Journal*, 51 (6), 536–555.

Marino S., Roosblad J. and Penninx R. (eds.) (2017) *Trade unions and migrant workers: new contexts and challenges in Europe*, Edward Elgar Publishing.

Maurice M., Sellier F. and Silvestre J.-J. (1982) *Politique d'éducation et organisation industrielle en France et en Allemagne: essai d'analyse sociétale*, Presses universitaires de France.

Miles M.B. and Huberman A.M. (1994) *Qualitative data analysis: an expanded sourcebook*, 2nd edn, Sage.

Morse J.M. and Niehaus L. (2009) *Mixed method design: principles and procedures*, Left Coast Press.

Muszyński K. and Pulignano V. (2023) Regulating platform work in the EU, *Medium*, 16 May. https://medium.com/@reshaping_work/regulating-platform-work-in-the-eu-158e38043532

Niebler V., Pirina G., Secchi M. and Tommassoni F. (2023) Towards 'bogus employment?' The contradictory outcomes of ride-hailing regulation in Berlin, Lisbon and Paris, Cambridge Journal of Regions, Economy and Society, 16 (2), 289–301.

Polanyi K. (1944/2001) *The great transformation*, Beacon Press.

Pulignano V. and Mará C. (2021) *Working for nothing in the platform economy: forms and institutional contexts of unpaid labour*, Solidar.

Pulignano V., Grimshaw D., Domecka M. and Vermeerbergen L. (2023a) Why does unpaid labour vary among digital labour platforms? Exploring socio-technical platform regimes of worker autonomy, *Human Relations*, 77 (9), 1243–1271.

Pulignano V.Delete Marino S., Johnson M., Domecka M. and Riemann ML. (2023b) 'Digital Tournaments': the colonisation of freelancers' 'free' time and unpaid labour in the online platform economy, *Cambridge Journal of Economics*, 48 (1): 133–150.

Rani U. et al. (2021) *The role of digital labour platforms in transforming the world of work*, ILO.

Rosenblat A. and Stark L. (2016) Algorithmic labor and information asymmetries: a case study of Uber's drivers, *International Journal of Communication*, 10 (27), 3758–3784.

Rubery J., Grimshaw D., Keizer A. and Johnson M. (2018) Challenges and contradictions in the 'normalising' of precarious work, *Work, Employment and Society*, 32 (3), 509–527.

Schor J.B. et al. (2021) Dependence and precarity in the platform economy, *Theory and Society*, 49 (5), 833–861.

Schüßler E., Attwood-Charles W., Kirchner S. and Schor J.B. (2021) Between mutuality, autonomy and domination, *Socio-Economic Review*, 19 (4), 1217–1243.

Shapiro A. (2020) Dynamic exploits: calculative asymmetries in the on-demand economy, *New Technology, Work and Employment*, 35 (2), 162–177.

Sørensen A.B. and Kalleberg A.L. (1981) An outline of a theory of the matching of persons to jobs, in Berg I. (ed.) *Sociological perspectives on labor markets*, Academic Press, 49–74.

Tubaro P. (2021) Disembedded or deeply embedded? A multi-level network analysis of online labour platforms, *Sociology*, 55 (5), 927–944.

Vallas S. and Schor J.B. (2020) What do platforms do? Understanding the gig economy, *Annual Review of Sociology*, 46, 273–294.

Wood A. and Lehdonvirta V. (2021) Platform precarity: surviving algorithmic insecurity in the gig economy. http://dx.doi.org/10.2139/ssrn.3795375

Wood A. and Lehdonvirta V. (2023) Platforms disrupting reputation: precarity and recognition struggles in the remote gig economy, *Sociology*, 57 (5), 999–1016.

Wood A., Graham M., Lehdonvirta V. and Hjorth I. (2019) Networked but commodified: the (dis) embeddedness of digital labour in the gig economy, *Sociology*, 53 (5), 931–950.

Woodcock J. (2020) The algorithmic panopticon at Deliveroo: measurement, precarity, and the illusion of control, *Ephemera*, 20 (3), 67–95.

All links were checked on 12 October 2023

PART III

OUTCOMES AND REGULATION

9. Platforms, wages and individual bargaining power: assessing labour market competition among Swedish couriers

Carl Fredrik Söderqvist

INTRODUCTION

Early narratives promoting the nascent 'gig' or platform economy often drew parallels to the atomistic labour markets found in most entry-level microeconomics textbooks. By matching consumers and workers using digital platforms, drawing labour from a contingent, flexible and self-employed workforce, the platform economy would increase economic efficiencies by better matching latent supply with demand in an array of services. For workers, the narrative offered unparalleled flexibility to switch between platforms. By unshackling workers from single-employer exclusivity, which we often associate with regular employment, platform workers could take up work at whichever platform where demand (and pay) was highest. This would then improve the wage bargain for workers by improving between-platform competition for scarce labour. And, just as in the textbooks, workers could punish misbehaving platforms by simply switching to better outside options if platforms deviated from market-clearing wages.

Such narratives formed an integral part of many platforms' global rollout strategies, which included political lobbying, urging legislators to provide exemptions or adaptations or to deregulate to allow such 'modern' supply- and demand-driven labour markets to flourish (Rogers 2015; Pasquale 2016; Baccaro and Howell 2017). Unsurprisingly, such strategies have often resulted in clashes with national institutions (for example Thelen 2018).

The underlying assumption that deregulation would improve the efficiency and competitiveness of labour markets – and thus the wages of platform workers – does not necessarily fit well with a growing consensus among labour market economists that it is primarily firms, not markets, that set wages (Card 2022). The notion that firms have wage-setting power rests on empirical observations of human behaviour: workers simply do not quit and move on to other (better) jobs in response to employers paying below-market wages – which neoclassical models predict – allowing employers to pay workers less than the market-clearing wage (for example Manning 2021; Naidu and Carr 2022). This finding also seems to hold in the platform economy, despite the theoretical cost of switching platforms being very low compared to other forms of employment (Caldwell and Oehlsen 2018).

We thus have two competing narratives with variable outcomes. If the entry of digital labour platforms improves the efficiency of labour markets while shedding or evading worker power-leveraging institutions, as proposed by the platforms themselves, the wage bargain should improve for workers. But, if digital labour platforms have wage-setting power and succeed in shedding or evading power-leveraging institutional arrangements, as proposed by the emergent monopsony literature, the wage bargain should worsen. What, then, has been the net effect on worker wages and incomesfrom digital platforms entering an established labour market?

This chapter explores how wages, working time, labour income, labour market mobility and the characteristics of companies that employ couriers developed in Sweden between 2014 and 2020. Couriers are defined as everyone who does a courier job, either in the platform economy or the conventional economy, including food delivery and other types of delivery tasks. Although the study is limited to couriers within a broader occupational group than just food delivery couriers, the data speak of significant changes within the relevant labour market that coincide with the entry of digital labour platforms: the number of couriers has doubled over the observed six-year period, and there are significant shifts in industry composition that suggest increased platformisation.

Although employer concentration decreased by nearly 35 per cent between 2014 and 2020, which is analogous to a 53 per cent increase in the number of employers hiring couriers – a remarkable rise in the number of available outside options – the overall wage bargain for couriers has worsened, primarily driven by decreased working time resulting in stagnant labour incomes. This stands in stark contrast to developments in other comparable occupations in logistics and transportation. Furthermore, over half of all couriers who stayed in the occupation between these years saw reduced year-on-year real incomes. On average, couriers who changed to other occupations received both lower real wages and incomes in their outside occupation options, indicating a relatively weak individual bargaining position of couriers. This supports similar qualitative conclusions regarding worker agency in the Swedish platform economy (Weidenstedt et al. 2023).

Assuming that the significant reduction of employer concentration relates to the entry of digital labour platforms, this development has incurred negative trends in wages and incomes. Together with the relatively poor outside options offered to couriers by other occupations, there is tentative evidence that the bargaining position of couriers weakened – rather than strengthened – between 2014 and 2020. Organising couriers and integrating platforms into the Swedish collective bargaining system is therefore central to improving the wage bargain.

THE SWEDISH INSTITUTIONAL BACKGROUND

As in most European settings, app-based food delivery platforms started appearing in Swedish cities around 2014 to 2017. Swedish institutional responses were somewhat atypical in a European comparative perspective, however, resulting in the employment classification of food delivery couriers and the creation and signing of a collective agreement at industry level.

In 2015, the Swedish Tax Authority performed proactive audits of digital labour platforms to assert tax compliance, including employment classification from a tax law perspective. Compared to other platform companies, which provided more marketplace-like activities where customers and workers could negotiate tasks and prices, couriers on food delivery platforms were classified as employees largely due to the standardised tasks provided by, and the payment grades set by, the platforms. As a result, the platforms were obliged to ensure that employers' social contributions were paid in respect of workers (Skatteverket 2016). In 2021, Foodora, the largest food delivery platform in Sweden, signed a collective agreement with Svenska Transportarbetareförbundet (Swedish Transportation Workers' Union), likely as a result of union litigation and organising pressure, thereby benefiting from first-mover advantage by being able to set sectoral standards in collective bargaining and gaining access to public procurement tenders (Ilsøe and Söderqvist 2022). These institutional interventions are perhaps not as significant as one might expect, however, on two accounts.

First, gaining employment classification in only the tax law dimension implied that platforms could contract couriers from umbrella companies who employ, invoice and pay employer contributions for the couriers. As a result, many food delivery couriers are employed by these umbrella companies – staffing companies that were originally modelled as freelance invoicing service providers but have expanded to subcontract gig workers to platforms. Umbrella companies operate outside the Swedish temporary work agency framework, which is regulated in collective agreements between unions and employer associations (Söderqvist and Bernhardtz 2019).

Second, the Foodora collective agreement only covers bicycle and moped couriers. Although Foodora stands out among the competition by directly hiring its couriers, the relatively large share of workers who deliver by car (particularly common in less densely populated markets) are not covered by the collective agreement. Foodora initially promised that a separate, already existing sectoral collective agreement covering their car-driving couriers would be signed, but this has yet to materialise. The bicycle and moped collective agreement has improved wage levels and benefits, and sets guaranteed hourly rates, among other things, but it has not eliminated the extensive use of fixed-term contracts, nor does it guarantee workers full-time employment. And, although the agreement is technically a sectoral collective agreement, it has yet to be ratified by the other major food delivery platforms. Uber Eats and Wolt are the two other major food delivery platforms currently operating in Sweden, Bolt having ceased its food delivery services in June 2023, citing 'business reasons'. All three competitors use, or have used, the umbrella company set-up to hire subcontracted couriers (Ilsøe and Söderqvist 2022).

Operating outside the Swedish collective bargaining system can give employers significant levels of flexibility, not least because there is no legislated minimum wage. Furthermore, trade union density is estimated to be very low in the app-based food delivery sector. This lack of union presence is likely to mean less enforcement of laws and regulations, which may give unorganised employers like the food delivery platforms even more one-sided flexibility (Ilsøe and Söderqvist 2022).

These considerations are aggravated because food couriers represent a growing set of precarious occupations in Sweden (Jonsson et al. 2019). Labour market precarity has, in turn, been linked to several negative health outcomes (Matilla-Santander et al. 2023).[1] The precarity has been partially attributed to Sweden's voluntarist industrial relations system, which provides relatively poor institutional protections for non-union members in unorganised firms (Weidenstedt et al. 2023).

Thus, the Swedish experience of app-based food delivery couriers presents similar vulnerabilities and levels of precarity observed in other European settings, despite the apparent institutional differences suggesting otherwise.

WAGE-SETTING POWER, LABOUR MARKET COMPETITION AND FISSURISATION

From a neoclassical economic perspective, a digital labour platform entering a labour market may represent a form of market entry that expands workers' outside options; by allowing workers to switch freely to better alternatives, platforms could provide workers with additional leverage through the exit channel (Hirschman 1970; Freeman and Medoff 1984). A key assumption of this argument is that improvements in outside options also increase competition for labour, which then improves workers' wage bargaining. If the platform's entry also implies a weakening of employment protections, however, will the increased leverage provided by this enhanced exit channel make up for such institutional losses?

The belief that competitiveness and efficiency in labour markets can be improved by eliminating regulatory 'frictions' has informed neoliberal policymaking for decades. From the 1970s to the 1990s, there has been much focus on the inefficiencies derived from institutions – such as minimum wages or trade unions – raising wages above market-clearing natural rates (Oswald 1982; Lindbeck and Snower 1986). The notion that institutional interventions imply inefficiencies rests largely on the assumption that modern labour markets are inherently competitive and will thus tend towards efficiency (Stigler 1946); if firms are left unhindered, competition will force them to set wages according to market rates, making firms price-takers in the market. Outside actors interfering in wage setting create market distortions, often represented as 'wedges' hindering the socially optimal outcomes produced by a 'purer' market mechanism.

The assumption that modern labour markets are inherently competitive is largely based on theoretical research and conjecture. However, a recent and growing body of empirical evidence finds that firms seem to have considerable wage-setting power in many labour markets, suggesting that these theories and assumptions stand on rather shaky ground. Thus, it is largely firms, and not markets, that set wages (Card 2022).

Profit-maximising firms can therefore set wages below the rates predicted in more perfectly competitive markets, with the simple economic reasoning that modern labour markets, when left to their own devices, are far from perfectly competitive. The notion that firms have market power was famously formalised by Robinson (1933). In perfect competition, no profit-maximising firm can set a price above the market price. If it were to pursue such a strategy, the firm would lose all business to competitors, but, if there are no competitors and the market is dominated by a single seller, the profit-maximising monopoly firm can sell goods at prices that are higher than the perfectly competitive case. Then, because there are no alternatives to the monopoly firm, buyers have no outside options to punish this deviation from market prices. The symmetrical sister of the better-known monopoly case is a market with a single buyer, which allows a monopsony firm to buy goods at prices below perfectly competitive levels from sellers in the market. In both cases, a lack of competition results in firms with buying or selling power capturing economic rents while producing fewer quantities, resulting in reduced economic welfare compared to the competitive case, and they can do so because the market does not punish such behaviour. In labour markets, oligopsonistic or monopsonistic competition implies firms having wage-setting power, which is predicted to lead to both lower wages and lower employment (e.g. Manning 2011).

Empirically assessing the competitiveness of labour markets has generated a large and growing literature, as such findings have significant implications for both economic theory and labour market policy. If firms have wage-setting power, raising wages through collective bargaining or legislation can increase wages and *raise* (rather than lower) employment, as was the economic prediction of yesteryear.[2]

One popular approach to assessing labour market competitiveness is to study worker behaviour in response to wage shocks. If workers are relatively insensitive to wage reductions (or increases) and are not punishing (or rewarding) employers to the extent that economic theory would predict, employers have wage-setting power. Worker insensitivity to wage shocks can come from a variety of sources, including search frictions, implying that, at a given time, there are fewer vacancies than jobs; information asymmetries, which can arise when workers are uninformed about their outside labour market options; unobserved job amenities, implying that workers may like their current job, but such preferences are unrelated to wages; or contractual restrictions, such as non-compete covenants, which may ban workers from going to the competition. The more insensitive the labour supply is to wage changes, the greater the potential wage-setting power of the employer (for a recent review, see Manning 2021).

Another approach, utilised in this chapter, is to assess the hypothetical outside options available to workers by estimating the concentration of employers within a particular labour market and then assessing the effect on wages of this estimated employer concentration. From this, we can draw tentative conclusions about labour market competitiveness (for example Azar et al. 2022; Schubert et al. 2022).

The difference between the two approaches is that the former looks at worker responses to wage shocks, while the latter looks at where workers could go in response to a wage shock. In concentration-based assessments of labour market competitiveness, we expect a higher concentration of employers to decrease the value of the wage bargain. This rationale is similar to the static model case raised by Robinson (1933); if all hires are made by one or a few dominant employers in a labour market, implying that concentration is high, the wage bargain will be worse than if there were several employers hiring in the same labour market. But does this also mean that increasing the number of employers will always improve the wage bargain? Are large – and thus concentrated – employers always bad when it comes to labour markets? Or, can a plethora of small employers also have a negative impact on the wage bargain?

Using a similar wage-concentration model to Schubert et al. (2022) on Swedish administrative data, Söderqvist and Eklund (2023) find a negative, but comparatively modest, effect of employer concentration on the wage bargain in aggregate labour markets. However, when regressing blue-collar occupations separately,[3] we find that increased employer concentration has a positive impact on the wage bargain. This rather surprising result is largely driven by low wages in smaller firms that tend to operate in less concentrated labour markets where collective bargaining coverage and union density are lower. Their study also assesses Schubert et al.'s (2022) measure of outside occupation options by estimating the mean wages received by workers who move from the observed occupation to another in the studied time period. This measure provides a flexible means to address concerns over labour market definitions; in an occupation where workers are observed receiving relatively poor wages when they switch to other occupations, the effect of employer concentration will be larger compared to an occupation where the wages received in outside occupational options are (observably) better. Taken together, the two measures thus provide an intuitive assessment of labour market competitiveness within specific occupations in different labour market regions.

How can we reconcile that a rather higher concentration implies higher wages for Swedish blue-collar workers? One possible explanation, with major relevance to the platform economy, is the role of domestic outsourcing or the fissurisation of Swedish labour markets (Weil 2014). Firms outsourcing tasks can have negative implications for the wage bargain. If a larger firm outsources tasks to a subcontractor, the workers performing those tasks may lose the wage premia gained from working for the larger firm. If the larger firm has price-setting power, operating surpluses (and wages) at the smaller subcontracting firm will be squeezed. Finally, if the subcontracting firm has wage-setting power over the worker, the wage bargain may be reduced even further (see, for example, Dube and Kaplan 2010; Card et al. 2013; Goldschmidt and Schmieder 2017; Card et al. 2018).

Given that many food delivery couriers in the Swedish labour market are not directly employed by the platform itself but by a subcontracted umbrella company, both the entry of platforms and their usage of umbrella companies imply that employer concentration will be lower than if all couriers were directly employed by the platform. If all couriers were to become self-employed, labour market concentration for couriers would be reduced manifold. However, if this has a negative impact on the wage bargain, the fissurisation assumption provides an intuitive explanation for the counter-intuitive result of wages decreasing with concentration. Thus, in the platform economy, decreasing concentration might negatively impact the wage bargain, despite conventional economic theory predicting the opposite.

USING ADMINISTRATIVE DATA TO ESTIMATE EMPLOYER CONCENTRATION, OUTSIDE OPTIONS AND WAGES

To assess how digital labour platforms in app-based food delivery have affected the competitiveness of food delivery labour markets in Sweden, we draw on employer-employee matched administrative data for the years 2014 to 2020, covering both employed and self-employed workers. This data allows the observation of worker and firm characteristics over time and, to some extent, the assessment of the impact on wage bargaining competitiveness among delivery couriers.

To capture workers in the food delivery labour market and their characteristics, occupational code 8329 'Motorcycle, bicycle drivers and other automobile drivers not elsewhere classified' (henceforth couriers) is selected from Standard för svensk yrkesklassificering (SSYK; Swedish Standard of Occupational Classification), which includes tasks relating to the delivery of goods and parcels, and which is equivalent to EU standard ISCO08 codes 83210, 83211, 83221 and 83222. Using this occupational code attaches a limitation to a study of food delivery platforms as it also includes non-food delivery work; but, assuming that it sufficiently captures a similarity in the tasks of all the occupations it contains, implying that food delivery workers can also do other forms of parcel delivery, aggregate measures within the occupation over time still provide validity to the defined labour market.

Occupational codes are assigned by employers to correspond to their primary tasks and primary sources of income. In the case of workers having multiple sources of income, an individual will be assigned the occupation which is their primary source of labour income during the year.[4] This also includes self-employed workers. Considering that a relatively large share of app-based food delivery couriers have been estimated to do such work as a supplementary source of income (Piasna et al. 2022), this constitutes a second limitation to the study, implying that the data only consider workers who are most dependent on their courier incomes.

Nonetheless, this is a valid and interesting group to study, not least when considering more direct effects on the wage bargain from platformisation.

Looking at components that represent the wage bargain, labour income, wages and working time, two different sources are used. First is yearly taxed labour income, which is the full gross labour income reported to the tax authority in November each year. Labour incomes are then divided by 12, yielding monthly average incomes, which improves comparability with the wage variable. Second, wages and working time are taken from wage structure statistics, collected from pay slips and surveys made in September or October each year. Wages represent full-time equivalent monthly income, including both fixed and variable components, while the working-time percentage approximates working time as a percentage of full-time employment (100 per cent). The wage, working time and income metrics have been chosen as being assigned sufficient hours of work is a well-known and salient constraint on workers wanting to improve their income in precarious jobs.

Firm characteristics are taken from the Business Registry and include workplace location and industry classification. To define the spatial size of labour markets, the 2015 'functional labour market' definition set by Tillväxtverket (2023), which uses mobility statistics to define regional commuting zones, is used. A salient limitation to the study is that data which risk identifying individual firms or workers are not presented out of ethical considerations. Presenting statistics based on firm size, for example, is not possible due to this limitation.

To assess the competitiveness of labour markets from the worker perspective, estimates from Söderqvist and Eklund (2023) are used to establish occupational employer concentration, providing an estimate of the number of firms that employ or hire couriers in a regional labour market; while outside occupation statistics provide an estimate of the mean wages or income that couriers receive when switching to other occupations. Occupational employer concentration is measured using a standard Hirfendahl-Hirschman Index (HHI), which is estimated by first calculating each firm i's market share s_i in the regional labour market r at time t. Two measures of the concentration of market share within an occupation are used – the market share of hired employees (stocks) and the share of yearly new hires (flows):

- The market share of stocks of workers, which is the regional share of occupation o employed at firm i divided by the sum of all those employed in occupation o in the region:

$$s_{i,o,r,t}^{stock} = \frac{\text{Sum employees in occupation o at firm i, region r, time t}}{\text{Sum workers in occupation o, region r, time t}}$$

- The market share of flows of workers, which is the regional share of newly observed hires in occupation o in firm i, divided by the regional sum of all new hires in occupation o:

$$s_{i,o,r,t}^{flow} = \frac{\text{Sum of new hires in occupation o at firm i region r, time t}}{\text{Sum of new hires in occupation o, region r, time t}}$$

Hires are estimated as any person observed working at occupation o in firm i not observed in this occupation in the previous year.

The HHI is attained by taking the square value of each firm's market share and summarising each squared market share to the regional labour market for a specific year. The resulting concentration index will yield a number between close to 0 and 1: a market dominated by a single firm will result in an HHI of 1; a labour market with two equally large firms results in an HHI of 0.5; and a market with ten equally large actors results in an HHI of 0.1. Thus, an HHI value approaching 0 approximates perfect competition, whereas a value of 1 indicates monopsony.

$$HHI_{o,r,t} = \sum_{i=1}^{N} s_{i,o,r,t}^{2}$$

The second estimate from Söderqvist and Eklund is an adapted value of Schubert et al.'s (2022) outside occupation option index (OOI). This is attained by observing job changes from observed occupation o to alternative occupation p, and calculating a weighted mean wage among those who made the transition between years $t-1$ and t. Thus, the estimate provides the mean wage of workers that were previously employed in occupation o but who are now working in occupation p.

$$OOI_{o,r,t} = \sum_{p \neq o}^{N_p} \sigma_{o \rightarrow p} w_p$$

Looking at the limitations of the data, we can only observe workers with an identification number, implying that we cannot capture irregular migrant workers, for example. Those who work for a platform using someone else's identification number will inflate courier labour incomes for the individual 'subcontracting' their phone to the illegal worker, for example. Further, the administrative data does not provide any information on subcontracting, and thus we cannot tell which couriers are subcontracting for platforms that do not hire their couriers directly.

DYNAMICS IN THE SOCIO-DEMOGRAPHIC AND OCCUPATIONAL PROFILES OF COURIERS AND THE COURIER SECTOR

This section presents data on the characteristics of the couriers and the growth of the courier sector between 2014 and 2020. Panel a of Figure 9.1 shows the age and sex distribution of couriers in 2020. The courier occupation is almost entirely male-dominated with a relatively young age profile. Panel b looks at worker tenure. In 2014, 45 per cent of workers had been employed in the same firm for two years or less.[5] Panel c reports the primary citizenship of couriers, where the share of third-country, such as non-Nordic or EU, citizens rises steadily from 3 to 12 per cent of workers between 2014 and 2020. Finally, panel d accounts for the share of workers who are registered in education or training programmes in the autumn term of each year.

Although the share of non-students is roughly 90 per cent, the data reflects findings by the Swedish Migration Authority, which raised warnings in 2022 that student visas were being used as de facto work visas,[6] observing large numbers of students having their residences in cities different from their affiliated universities while not attaining the credits associated with their education (Migrationsverket 2022). As food delivery work is popular among students from non-EU countries (Weidenstedt et al. 2023), this metric is salient in understanding the characteristics of couriers.

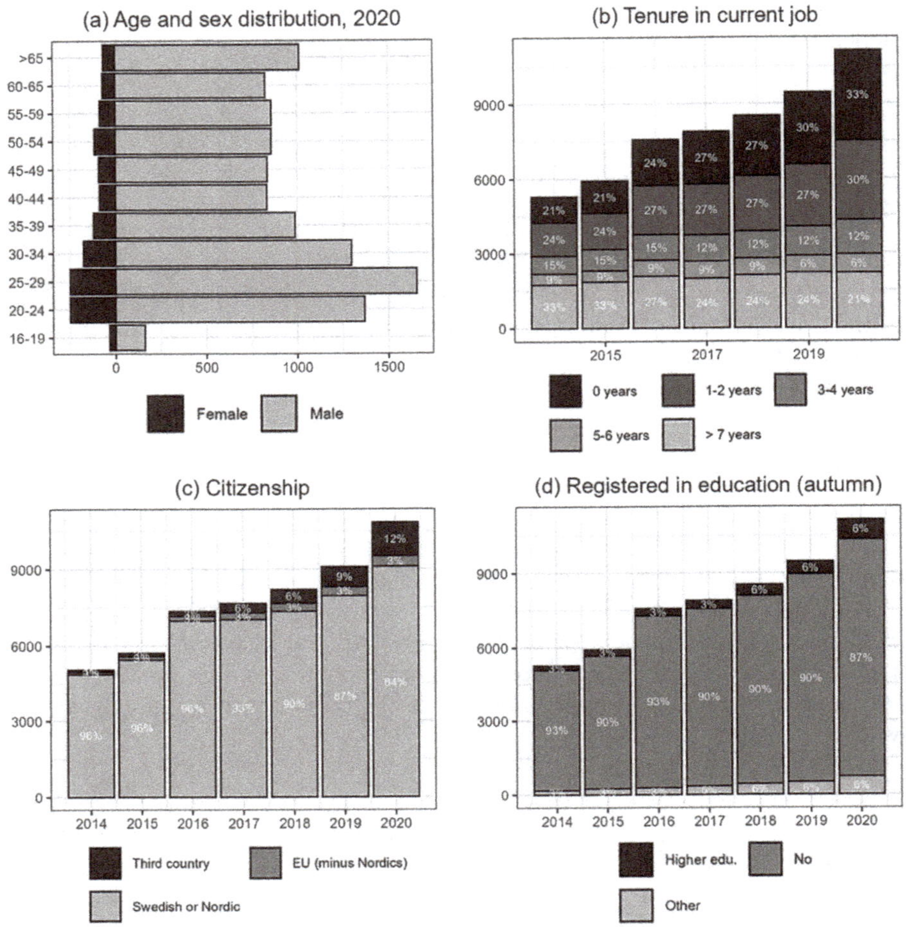

Note: All diagrams show distributions of the characteristics of couriers. A shows the age and gender distribution in 2020. B shows how job tenure (number of years at the same employer) is distributed among all workers from 2014 to 2020. C shows the distribution of citizenship among all couriers. D shows the share of workers registered in some form of education in the autumn term.
Source: Based on data from Statistics Sweden.

Figure 9.1 Characteristics of couriers

Based on the Figure 9.1, it is fair to say that the social composition of couriers in Sweden is highly similar to the profile of app-based food delivery couriers in other countries (see Chapters 5 and 7).

Turning to the dynamics in the courier sector, first of all, significant growth can be noted since app-based food delivery and other delivery platforms entered Swedish markets. In Figure 9.2, we can trace these developments from 2014 to 2020. We find that the number of workers observed working as couriers has more than doubled: from 5,281 in 2014 to 11,139

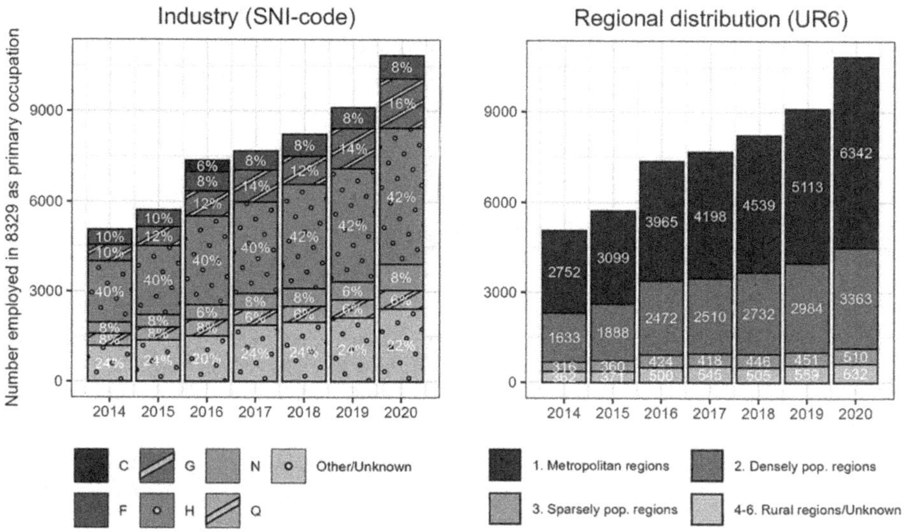

Note: Industries and their share of all workers are shown in the first panel, including (C) manufacturing, (F) construction, (G) wholesale and retail, etc., (H) transport and storage, (N) administrative and support service activities, and (Q) human health and social work activities. Other/Unknown represents any other industry codes that have a share smaller than 5 per cent of total employment in each year. The second panel shows the number of couriers per region. Regions are classified by the Swedish Agency for Growth Policy Analysis and represent functional labour market regions according to the UR6 definition. Metropolitan regions represent the Stockholm, Gothenburg and Malmö functional labour market regions.
Source: Based on data from Statistics Sweden.

Figure 9.2 *The number of observed workers and their distribution across industries and regions for couriers (SSYK occupation 8329), 2014–20*

in 2020. The rapid growth of couriers in 2020 is likely to be an effect of the Covid-19 pandemic (OECD 2021): between 2019 and 2020, the number of workers in the occupation grew by 15.6 per cent, which is the sixth largest growth in any four-digit occupation between 2019 and 2020.

Second, the growth of couriers is largely being driven by new companies. In 2020, 67 per cent, or 7,546 of all 11,139 couriers, worked for firms that did not employ any couriers in 2014.

Third, looking firm size in 2020,[7] 12 per cent are self-employed, 66 per cent work for small enterprises (between 2 and 50 employees), and 22 per cent work for medium-to-large enterprises (more than 50 employees). The shares of employment taken by self-employed and medium-to-large enterprises have both increased by around 5 percentage points since 2014.

Figure 9.2 is broken down by industry and the geographical location of principal. Regionally, couriers are most present and have grown most in Sweden's three metropolitan regions (Stockholm, Gothenburg and Malmö) and other relatively densely populated regions (second panel of Figure 9.2). From a sectoral perspective, 62 per cent of employers were in private industries in 2014, increasing to 68 per cent in 2020 (the rest being public employers). We are most likely to find food delivery platform workers in transport and storage (H) and in administrative and support service activities (N), the latter encompassing temporary work agencies and thus the umbrella companies discussed earlier. Together, these two industries hire over half of the observed couriers.

WAGES AND LABOUR MARKET MOBILITY

This section analyses the impact of the entry of digital labour platforms on the resulting wage bargain and competitive dynamics in the courier labour market. The three panels in Figure 9.3 represent mean wages, labour income and working time, where the shaded areas represent the tenth and ninetieth percentiles within the distribution. Couriers (occupation 8329) are compared with other transportation occupations in the same occupational family (83). These include a broad range of occupations, including taxi drivers, bus drivers, heavy equipment operators and train drivers. Although skills and qualifications are heterogeneous within this occupational family, it does hold some occupational proximity while also providing income-related comparisons with occupations in the Swedish labour market with more regular forms of employment. The tenth and ninetieth percentiles are included for each metric to give an impression of distribution and heterogeneity within the occupational group.

Panel a reports the gross real equivalent wage (at 2021 prices) from the wage structure survey. The measure captures the monthly, full-time equivalent wage, including variable payment forms such as overtime and bonuses. The wage measure thus attempts to provide a metric that is consistent and comparable between occupations. An increase in wages in both occupational groups (although at a slower pace for couriers) can be noted, alongside couriers being paid, on average, between 2,500 and 3,000 SEK (approximately €215–260) less per month than in other transportation occupations.

Panel b is also from the wage structure survey and reports the mean working time percentage of each worker as a share of full-time employment; thus, 50 per cent roughly corresponds to a 20-hour working week. Here we find a large divergence from other transportation occupations, where over 90 per cent of the population reports 100 per cent working time. The mean working time for couriers drops sharply in our observed period, from 95 per cent to 85 per cent, indicating that full-time work is becoming less prevalent in the occupation.

Because the wage survey covers less than 40 per cent of the population in a given year, and because precariousness may also imply difficulties getting enough work, panel c considers the yearly gross income reported to the tax authority for all observed individuals. This number is divided by 12 to obtain a monthly figure, which is more comparable to the monthly wage in panel a. Mean income for couriers are increasing at a lower rate than in other occupations, expanding the income gap between the groups.

On average, courier incomes are stagnant between 2014 and 2020. Could this be explained by reduced competition for labour in the courier labour market? Although the standard economic prediction would be 'yes', estimates of employer concentration within the occupation do not support this prediction. The first panel in Figure 9.4 shows developments in within-occupation employer concentration in the courier labour market. Concentration in terms of both flows (concentration of hires) and stocks (concentration of employed workers) is relatively low, with a maximum HHI of 0.11 and a minimum value below 0.05. The United States

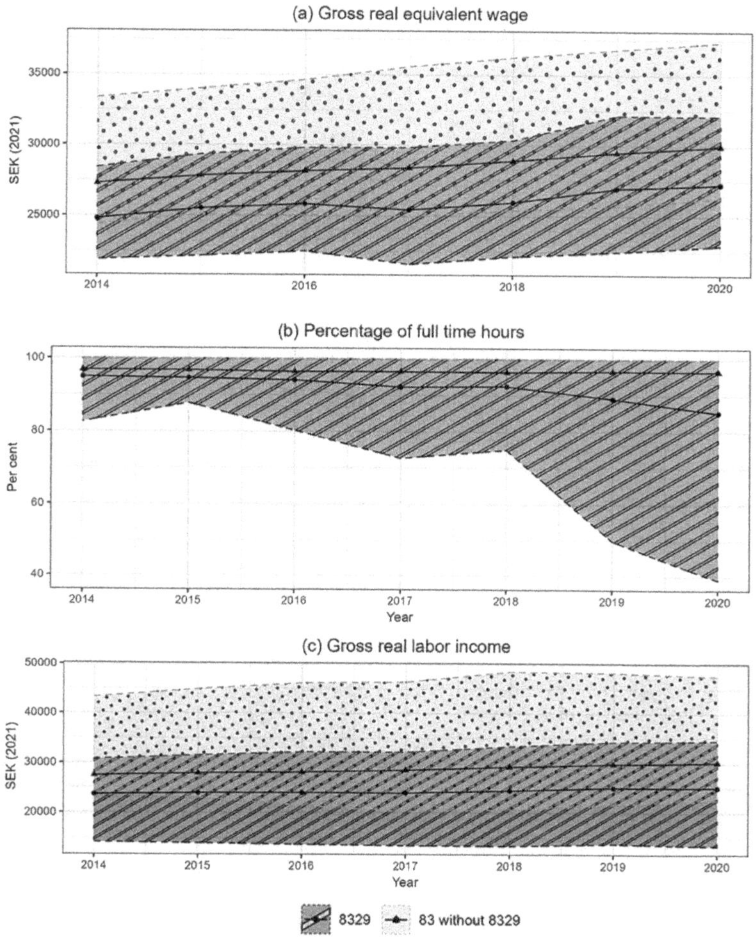

Note: The dashed limits of the shaded bands indicate the tenth and ninetieth percentiles within the observed distribution. The three panels compare yearly mean values for occupation 8329 (striped) and the wider group of transportation occupations in the corresponding 83 occupational group (circles). Panel a estimates the mean full-time equivalent wage (including variable compensation such as overtime and commission). Panel b shows mean individual employment expressed as a percentage of full-time hours (100 per cent). Panel c shows mean monthly gross labour income (based on the yearly filed figure reported to the tax authority divided by 12).
Source: Based on data from Statistics Sweden.

Figure 9.3 *Mean wage, mean working time and observed mean monthly labour income for couriers (8329) and all other occupations within the same 2-digit occupational family (83, other than 8329)*

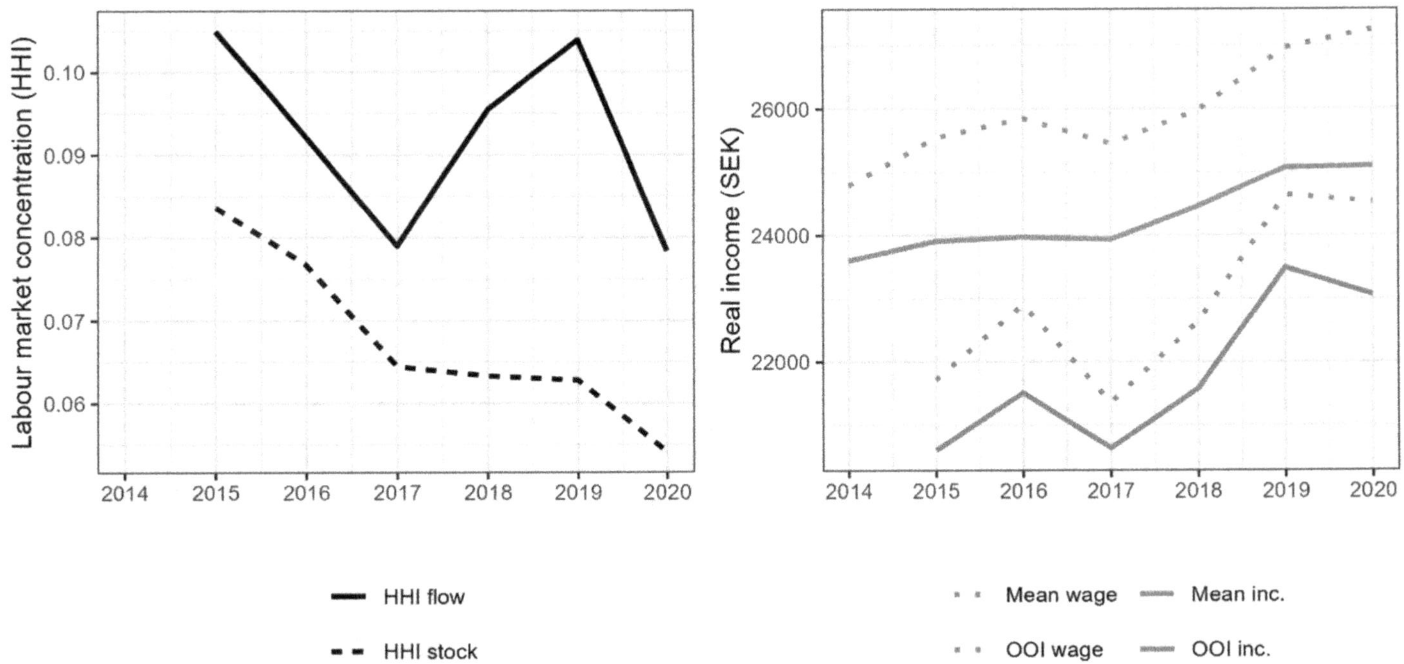

Note: The first panel shows the weighted mean regional employer concentration for couriers based on hires/flows (solid line) and for stocks (dashed line). The second panel shows the mean wage (black dotted line) and mean income (black solid line) for couriers , as well as the new wages and incomes received in outside occupations (OOI, grey) for those who had been couriers in the previous year.
Source: Based on data from Statistics Sweden.

Figure 9.4 *Labour market concentration (HHI) and mean wage and monthly labour incomes compared to outside occupation option (OOI) wages*

Fair Trade Commission sets an HHI value above 0.25 (where 1 implies a single buyer) as problematic from a competition perspective. Further, we find that the concentration of stocks has reduced significantly (the solid black line in Figure 9.4) since 2015, implying that a larger number of unique firms are employing couriers over time. The fluctuation in the concentration of flows or new hires is higher (the dashed black line), but displays a similar downward trend. A likely explanation for this fluctuation relates to a relatively high turnover of firms (including in the self-employed).

Having determined that income and, to some extent, wages are decreasing with concentration between 2014 and 2020, it would appear that the wage bargain has not improved, on average, with the introduction of labour platforms. Given these poor developments in the courier occupation, what outside options exist for couriers in other occupations? The second panel of Figure 9.4 compares the wages (dashed line) and income (solid line) of couriers and of workers who were couriers in the previous year. This is the outside occupation index presented earlier, which tells us how strong the wage bargain is for couriers who have switched to other occupations. It can be concluded that couriers taking up outside occupational options are paid lower monthly wages and receive considerably lower incomes compared to those who stayed on as couriers. This suggests that the outside occupation options are statistically worse than continuing to work as a courier.

Thus far, the data illustrate a poor, and worsening, wage bargaining for couriers. Taking up outside options in other occupations appears worse, on average, implying that, in terms of the wage bargain, most couriers are likely to be better off staying on as couriers. But, against this background of having relatively poor outside options and, in essence, low individual bargaining power, what happens to workers who continue to work as couriers? Figure 9.5 uses an alluvial diagram to illustrate year-on-year inflows to the courier occupation and gross income effects. The diagram thus illustrates the mean income effects of staying on or becoming a courier between 2015 and 2020.

The first column in Figure 9.5 represents the origin of workers employed as couriers in the current year based on their occupation in the previous year: 71.7 per cent were employed as couriers in the previous year, 18 per cent held some other occupation, 4 per cent were unemployed, and 6.3 per cent had an unknown occupation or employment status. The second column compares changes in gross (real) incomes between the current and previous year. If gross incomes were greater in the current year compared to the previous year, the individual is coded as having a 'higher' change of incomes, whereas, if the current year's figure is lower or equal to that of the previous year, the individual is coded as having 'lower or 0' income change. Binding both columns with the grey ribbons, we find that all couriers from unemployed or unknown origins improved their incomes by taking work as a courier. However, nearly half the workers that remained as couriers or had held some other occupation in the previous year experienced reduced or stagnant gross incomes between 2015 and 2020.

CONCLUSIONS

Between 2014 and 2020, we observe a doubling of couriers in the Swedish labour market and a growing number of firms hiring such workers. However, wages and labour incomes are either relatively stagnant or decreasing within the occupation during the observed time period. Stagnant incomes are largely explained by significant reductions in average working hours.

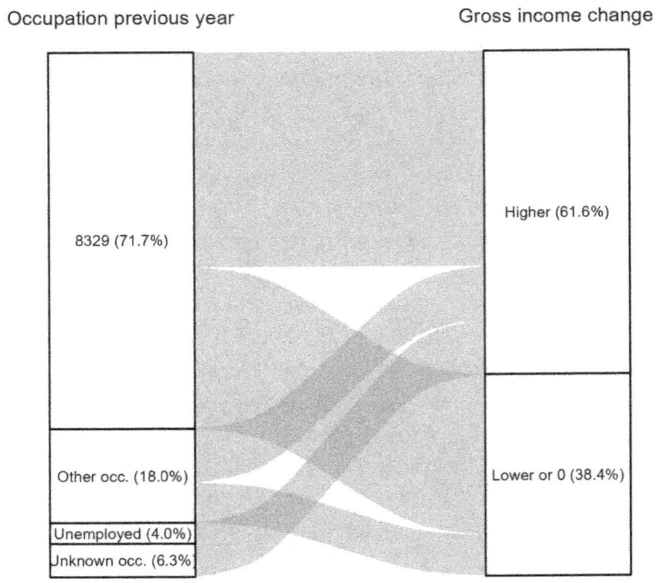

Note: The left column summarises the previous year's (*t*–1) occupation or status for all couriers (8329) in year *t* between 2015 and 2020. 8329 indicates that they were also couriers in the previous year (so stayed in the occupation). The right column compares income levels in year *t* with year *t*–1, reporting how incomes changed between the years for the groups in the first column. For example, nearly half of those who were also couriers (8329) in *t*–1 had smaller gross incomes in year *t* compared to *t*–1.
Source: Based on data from Statistics Sweden.

Figure 9.5 Year-on-year inflows to occupation 8329 and changes to gross labour incomes, 2015–2020

Considering that courier work is often precarious and paid by the hour or by piecemeal rates, getting jobs – or gigs – is central to the outcomes for the worker, and so labour ubcines is arguably a better-suited variable for assessing the position of the wage bargain. Consequently, the wage bargain of couriers appears to be worsening, despite a large entry of new firms, as indicated by a significant reduction in employer concentration in the courier occupation. Couriers thus provide an example where incomes decrease with decreased concentration. This may be explained by poor individual bargaining power – couriers taking outside occupational options see even worse outcomes in wages and incomes.

A salient shortcoming of this study relates to not being able to discern digital platforms from 'regular' employers. Nor can we identify the contractual relationships that may exist between the relatively large group of self-employed workers and platforms or other principals. However, by assuming that the tasks associated with the occupational group (couriers delivering goods or parcels) are relatively similar, and these developments coincide with the entry of digital labour platforms, it is likely that the platform economy, not least food delivery platforms, has had a significant impact on the wage bargain.

Assuming these developments are largely driven by the platforms, they have certainly not lent themselves to improved incomes over time, as was promised by early sharing/gig economy narratives. Rather, the data imply a rather large increase in precarity in the seven-year time period over which we can follow these developments.

All in all, the reduction of concentration alongside a worsened wage bargain for couriers runs contrary to the neoclassical prediction of increased outside options improving individual bargaining power. There are two related explanations for this discrepancy. The first is quite simple: concentration is not a good approximation of competition, and thus we should not draw conclusions on its effects on wages (prices) (Miller et al. 2022). The second explanation considers the concentration metric within the context of other outcome-related variables, which may tell us something about individual bargaining power. If concentration is decreasing while wages are stagnant over time, and outside options in other occupations are (statistically) worse, it might be indicative of fissurisation – employers leveraging their bargaining power through subcontracting. Platforms' use of umbrella companies as subcontractors of couriers, for example, implies that they can subcontract 'non-core' business activities, avoiding the rent-sharing associated with traditional employment or even the social costs, such as investing in proactive work safety measures. Domestic outsourcing events observed in the past have implied large penalties on workers' wage bargains (for example Dube and Kaplan 2010; Goldschmidt and Schmieder 2017). If outsourcing reduces employer concentration, which is likely (with one big employer being replaced by a plethora of service sector firms), and wages go down, we should expect wages to decrease as concentration decreases.

What can be done to turn these developments around? A central finding is that Swedish outcomes are likely to be similar to those found in other European labour markets, which – importantly – do not boast the same levels of unionisation or collective bargaining coverage. Platforms do pose a challenge to the Nordic models (Ilsøe and Söderqvist 2022). Given the Nordic social partners' weariness of legislative intervention, the only 'true' Nordic response rests on union organising to address the identified asymmetries in individual bargaining power. Organising is, however, challenging, given that many couriers have various reasons to be reluctant to join unions: low incomes, relatively high union fees (in relation to incomes), temporary visa statuses and differing cultural attitudes towards unions are among a few of the examples often discussed in the Swedish trade union movement. Further, the identity of the employer might cause difficulties – unions may be unwilling to bargain with the umbrella companies subcontracting couriers lest they risk legitimising a highly irregular form of employment: temporary work agencies employing 100 per cent of the 'temporary' group of workers in a given occupation. Thus, fixing this highly irregular form of subcontracting might require legislative or judicial intervention rather than traditional collective bargaining regulation.

Looking ahead, there are developments that may have a positive impact on couriers' wage bargaining. Among Swedish food delivery platforms, three major actors now remain in a market that previously boasted up to six competing food delivery platforms. The ongoing consolidation process among food delivery platforms might be positive for the wage bargain if it means that such platforms can attain some comfortable level of profitability and thus generate larger economic rents, which may be distributed either as higher dividends and/or as wages. If this scenario plays out, market consolidation should lead to increased concentration. Effects on the wage bargain, however, are uncertain. Decreased concentration correlates with a worsened wage bargain, but whether increased concentration will result in an improvement in the wage bargain comes down to worker bargaining power. The employment arrangements of those employing couriers and utilising subcontractors to avoid employer classification can be viewed as a fissurisation strategy that deleverages both the individual and collective bargaining power of couriers, allowing firms to capture larger rents. If the wage bargain does not improve with consolidation, fissurisation provides a highly plausible explanation. Thus, using employer concentration on its own as a metric to understand labour market competition and the impacts on the wage bargain does not provide us with much predictive power unless we also consider more complex institutional arrangements, including platforms redefining the boundaries of their firms in order to gain economic rents.

Another positive development is that employment among migrants, who are assumed to make up the lion's share of the food delivery courier workforce, has increased significantly in 2023 (SCB 2023). If increased employment among migrant groups also implies better outside occupation options for couriers, their individual bargaining power will improve and might force food delivery platforms to improve wages and terms and conditions of employment, for example by signing sectoral collective agreements. Further, Sweden has tightened its migration policy and plans to continue to do so in the coming years. The pool of cheap labour from non-EU countries working for food delivery platforms may therefore dwindle, creating tighter labour markets and further improving couriers' individual bargaining power. Whether this would equally translate into collective power via trade unions or otherwise remains to be seen.

NOTES

1. Matilla-Santander et al. (2023) find that switching from precarious to standard employment reduces the risk of death by 20 to 30 per cent over the 12-year ex-post period.
2. In motivating David Card's Nobel prize in economics, his 'empirical contributions to labour economics' include the finding 'that increasing the minimum wage does not necessarily lead to fewer jobs, as was previously thought'.
3. Using Statistics Sweden's suggested classification of blue- and white-collar occupations.
4. The Swedish Occupation registry covers over 94 per cent of all working individuals in Sweden, including the self-employed. Occupational data is gathered in September or October each year along with the wage structure statistics; this is one to two months before employer taxes are filed in November of each year.
5. In Swedish labour law and practice, fixed-term contracts tend to be converted to open-ended ones after two years, which has been noted as a salient explanation of labour turnover in Swedish firms. See, for example, Arai and Heyman (2004).
6. Swedish student visas permit working for side income.
7. The total number of workers employed within a 'concern number' or, if not available, organisation number.

REFERENCES

Arai M. and Heyman F. (2004) Temporary contracts and the dynamics of job turnover, *Economics Bulletin*, 10 (1), 1–6.

Azar J., Marinescu I. and Steinbaum M. (2022) Labor market concentration, *Journal of Human Resources*, 57 (S), S167–S199.

Baccaro L. and Howell C. (2017) *Trajectories of neoliberal transformation: European industrial relations since the 1970s*, Cambridge University Press.

Caldwell S. and Oehlsen E. (2018) Monopsony and the gender wage gap: experimental evidence from the gig economy, Working Paper, Massachusetts Institute of Technology.
Card D. (2022) Who set your wage?, *The American Economic Review*, 112 (4), 1075–1090.
Card D., Heining J. and Kline P. (2013) Workplace heterogeneity and the rise of West German wage inequality, *The Quarterly Journal of Economics*, 128 (3), 967–1015.
Card D. et al. (2018) Firms and labor market inequality: evidence and some theory, *Journal of Labor Economics*, 36 (S1), S13–S70.
Dube A. and Kaplan E. (2010) Does outsourcing reduce wages in the low-wage service occupations? Evidence from janitors and guards, *ILR Review*, 63 (2), 287–306.
Freeman R.B. and Medoff J.L. (1984) *What do unions do?*, Basic Books.
Goldschmidt D. and Schmieder J.F. (2017) The rise of domestic outsourcing and the evolution of the German wage structure, *The Quarterly Journal of Economics*, 132 (3), 1165–1217.
Hirschman A. (1970) *Exit, voice, and loyalty: responses to decline in firms, organizations, and states*, Harvard University Press.
Ilsøe A. and Söderqvist C.F. (2022) Will there be a Nordic model in the platform economy? Evasive and integrative platform strategies in Denmark and Sweden, *Regulation & Governance*, 17, 608–626.
Jonsson J. et al. (2019) Precarious employment in Sweden: translation, adaptation and psychometric properties of the Employment Precariousness Scale (EPRES), BMJ Open, 9, e029577.
Lindbeck A. and Snower D.J. (1986) Wage setting, unemployment, and insider-outsider relations, *The American Economic Review*, 76 (2), 235–239.
Manning A. (2011) Imperfect competition in the labor market, in Card D. and Ashenfelter O. (eds.) *Handbook of labor economics*, Elsevier, 973–1041.
Manning A. (2021) Monopsony in labor markets: a review, *ILR Review*, 74 (1), 3–26.
Matilla-Santander N. et al. (2023) Causal effect of shifting from precarious to standard employment on all-cause mortality in Sweden: an emulation of a target trial, *Journal of Epidemiology and Community Health*, 77 (11), 736–743.
Migrationsverket (2022) Missbruk av uppehållstillstånd för studier: Analysrapport från enheten för operativ analys. Dnr: 1.3.4–2022–14601.
Miller N. et al. (2022) On the misuse of regressions of price on the HHI in merger review, *Journal of Antitrust Enforcement*, 10 (2), 248–259.
Naidu S. and Carr M. (2022) If you don't like your job, can you always quit? Pervasive monopsony power and freedom in the labour market, *Journal of Law and Political Economy*, (3)1, 131–159.
OECD (2021) The role of online platforms in weathering the COVID-19 shock, *OECD Policy Responses to Coronavirus (COVID-19).*
Oswald A.J. (1982) The microeconomic theory of the trade union, *The Economic Journal*, 92 (367), 576–595.
Pasquale F. (2016) Two narratives of platform capitalism, *Law & Policy Review*, 35 (1), 309–319.
Piasna A., Zwysen W. and Drahokoupil J. (2022) *The platform economy in Europe: results from the second ETUI Internet and Platform Work Survey*, ETUI.
Robinson J. (1933) *The economics of imperfect competition*, Macmillan.
Rogers B. (2015) The social costs of Uber, *University of Chicago Law Review*, 82 (1), 85–102.
SCB (2023) Sysselsättningen fortsätter att öka andra kvartalet 2023. www.scb.se/hitta-statistik/statistik-efter-amne/arbetsmarknad/sysselsattning-forvarvsarbete-och-arbetstider/befolkningens-arbetsmarknadsstatus/pong/statistiknyhet/befolkningens-arbetsmarknadsstatus-kvartal-2–2023
Schubert G., Stansbury A. and Taska B. (2022) Employer concentration and outside options. http://dx.doi.org/10.2139/ssrn.3599454
Skatteverket (2016) Kartläggning och analys av delningsekonomins påverkan på skattesystemet, Report Dnr 1 31 129651–16/113.
Söderqvist C.F. and Bernhardtz V. (2019) Labor platforms with unions: discussing the law and economics of a Swedish collective bargaining framework used to regulate gig work, Working Paper 57, Swedish Entrepreneurship Forum.
Söderqvist C.F and Eklund J. (2023) Employer concentration, outside options, and earnings in Swedish labor markets, PhD Dissertation /(Forthcoming).
Stigler G.J. (1946) The economics of minimum wage legislation, *The American Economic Review*, 36 (3), 358–365.

Thelen K. (2018) Regulating Uber: the politics of the platform economy in Europe and the United States, *Perspectives on Politics*, 16 (4), 938–953.
Tillväxtverket (2023) Funktionella arbetsmarknadsregioner. https://tillvaxtverket.se/tillvaxtverket/statistikochanalys/statistikomregionalutveckling/regionalaindelningar/faregioner.1799.html
Weidenstedt L., Geissinger A., Leick B. And Nazeer N. (2023) Betwixt and between: triple liminality and liminal agency in the Swedish gig economy, *Environment and Planning A: Economy and Space*. https://doi.org/10.1177/0308518X231172
Weil D. (2014) *The fissured workplace: why work became so bad for so many and what can be done to improve it*, Harvard University Press.
All links were checked on 27 November 2023.

10. Judicial creativity in the platform economy: normative insights for broadening the scope of labour law

Silvia Rainone and Christina Hiessl

INTRODUCTION

Over the past decade, scholarly and normative debates on the nature of platform work have intensified, accompanied by a growing body of case law (Adams-Prassl et al. 2022; Hiessl 2021; Menegatti 2022; Moyer-Lee and Countouris 2021). Recently, platform work has drawn increased attention from regulators, with national and European lawmakers introducing provisions to address this evolving form of work. In Europe, this led to a significant milestone with the political consensus on the Platform Work Directive in April 2024 (European Parliament 2024). This shift has moved the labour law discourse towards regulatory options (Aloisi and Potocka-Sionek 2022; Hiessl 2022; Ponce Del Castillo and Naranjo 2022). However, national courts will continue to play a pivotal role in shaping the normative frameworks that define the integration of app-mediated work in national legal and labour systems. This is particularly true in view of the two-year transposition period during which EU member states will have to decide how to implement the Directive in their legal systems.

Even if the case law is far from homogeneous, three distinct key findings have emerged from the judicial rulings. First, there is a pervasive risk of misclassification concerning the employment status of platform workers. Second, and closely linked, platform work has contributed to exposing the limits of national legislative paradigms, which typically rely on the normative concept of subordination, control and direction to afford employment protections, yet struggle fully to encompass the nuanced vulnerabilities arising in the platform economy (see Chapter 11). Third, digital labour platforms often disguise their nature as traditional 'firms', leading to new complexities in determining the appropriate allocation of employer responsibilities among the various involved parties (Hiessl 2023). For instance, it is sufficient for platforms to externalise the hiring and coordination of workers to intermediaries to erect a legal barrier shielding them from the responsibilities of the employer (De Groen et al. 2021; Silberman et al. forthcoming).

So far, only the first aspect, namely the high risk of the misclassification of workers, has actually been addressed by legislators (and, even there, to different degrees of effectiveness) (Aloisi 2022). The European Union and national legislative reforms that clarify the criteria against which platform workers can access employment law aim to facilitate the correct determination of employment status (De Stefano 2022; Chapter 11 of this volume). Regulators have, however, largely overlooked the fundamental challenges the platform economy poses to the normative paradigms that govern the scope of labour law (Rainone 2023a).

This chapter argues that the effective embedding of platform work within labour law systems requires a rethinking of the scope of the normative models that currently informs labour protections. Developing these considerations, the multifaceted normative innovations emerging from national jurisprudence are brought to light, emphasising their potential to inform more inclusive and outreaching regulatory responses.

The chapter is predominantly descriptive in that it proposes an analysis of a rich body of judgments on the platform economy, totalling 531, collected and curated over several years (Hiessl 2024a). The study is approached from three analytical dimensions. The first considers the judicial strategies employed by judges in their deliberations. While all analysed decisions eventually revolve around workers' rights to labour protection, the study also encompasses a consideration of legal demands extending beyond the mere reclassification of employment status. For instance, judicial claims may also include demands for the recognition of joint liability between platforms and their intermediaries regarding employment obligations. Alternatively, legal actions can have a basis that lies outside labour law, such as data protection or criminal law. Consideration of the different judicial strategies provides a full picture of the quest for legal protection pursued on behalf of platform workers. The second analytical dimension looks at the legal arguments considered by judges in employment status cases. Here, the study reveals the emergence of novel normative judicial criteria surpassing the traditional test of control, direction and subordination often relied upon in reclassification cases, and redefining the notion of employer in the digital economy. Finally, the third dimension evaluates the 'success rate', from the perspective of workers, of the various lines of argumentation presented in courtrooms, and ultimately assesses their potential to broaden the application of labour rights and obligations.

THE SUBORDINATION PARADIGM: TOO TIGHT FOR PLATFORM WORK?

Platform work has exacerbated a number of challenges affecting the efficacy of labour law in promoting fairer working conditions (Aloisi et al. 2023; De Stefano 2016). This section explores the difficulties in positioning platform work in relation to the legal construct of the employment relationship and presents the urgent need for an interpretative recalibration of the paradigm of subordination.

Subordination is generally presumed when the principal exercises direction, control and disciplinary authority over the worker (Hepple 2011). Originally, this concept effectively detected imbalanced bargaining power in hierarchical employment relationships characterised by a linear allocation of tasks performed at the employer's premises and within predetermined time frames. However, in today's evolved world of work, a strict reliance on this classical framework results in more workers being left at the margins of traditional employment (Freedland and Kountouris 2011; Stylogiannis 2023), and this is particularly evident in the platform economy. The most prominent paradox of the platform economy in fact is that it draws on sophisticated work performance surveillance tools powered by algorithmic management, yet it relies on a self-employed workforce engaged under civil law contracts (Adams-Prassl 2019). Consequently, platform workers lack contractual autonomy and are excluded from labour protections (Wood 2021). This scenario blatantly contradicts the normative function of labour law, which was designed to promote a fairer redistribution of the risks and benefits between the worker and the business entity for which work is performed (in this case, the platform) (Dukes 2014). The systematic avoidance of labour protection law questions the adequacy of the subordination paradigm in regulating its scope.

At the same time, the decline of labour law coverage is not a phenomenon specific to the platform economy. Amid pressures for deregulation and the creation of 'third' or 'hybrid' categories of workers, access to full labour protection is precluded for all those in a contractual relationship that does not strictly embody the normative model of subordination (Oladeinde 2008). The progressive integration of digital technology into the work environment, epitomised by the platformisation of the economy, has further blurred the lines between subordination and autonomy, and between technological dependency and human agency; and, in turn, has intensified those alarming trends. In fact, among the most debated normative implications of the platform economy is the opacity of algorithmic management and its seeming irreconcilability with the traditional mechanisms of control and direction that generally characterise employment relationships (Adams-Prassl 2019). The free choice of logging in and out and the (formal) possibility of refusing tasks have created a perception of flexibility and autonomy that conveys an image of platforms as supporting the entrepreneurship of freelance professionals (Aloisi 2022).

While the margin of autonomy varies considerably depending on the sector in which platform work is carried out, as well as from one digital labour platform to another (De Groen et al. 2021; Piasna et al. 2022), the main legal question for the judiciary and policymakers remains the same: are individuals working with and through digital platforms, where human managers, if present, operate behind the curtain of algorithmic management, to be subsumed under the normative notion of subordination and thus given access to the full range of labour rights?

There are four possible answers to this conundrum. The first is affirmative, based on the assumption that algorithmic management implies a relationship of subordination as it represents a digitally mediated expression of the power of direction and control (ETUC 2022). In this case, subordination would remain the normative model of reference, albeit broadly interpreted. The second answer is negative, pointing to the various dissonances between the nature of work in the platform economy and in traditional companies, concluding that platform work should be considered a form of self-employment (Gillis et al. 2022). This reading continues to be consistent with the paradigm of subordination which, while rejecting its applicability to platform work, remains the key criterion for access to employment protection. The third possible solution is more nuanced, suggesting that the inclusion of platform work in the subordination paradigm should be determined on a case-by-case basis, depending on the actual identification of elements of control and direction in the execution of the work (De Stefano and Wouters 2020; Hiessl 2021). This option reflects a classical understanding of the notion of subordination, with little scope for evolutive interpretation, and helps to counter the most blatant cases of misclassification of platform workers. Finally, a fourth answer would be that the question is wrongly framed, as the difficulties in placing platform work within the classical legal framework suggest that subordination should not be seen as the only relevant paradigm for regulating the scope of labour law. Instead, alternative normative models and legal requirements should be developed to identify new grounds of protection for vulnerable platform workers (for further reflection, see Rainone 2022 and De Stefano and Countouris 2024).

So far, national regulators have tended to avoid unambiguous positioning, opting for partial legislative reforms that incorporate a number of elements from the first three solutions (Aloisi 2022). Instead, it is more distinctly the third option that has been taken up in the EU Platform

Work Directive (De Stefano 2022) which requires member states to establish effective legal presumptions in order to facilitate the reclassification of platform workers within existing national employment categories (Article 5). It should be noted, however, that in implementing the Directive, national legislators still have the ultimate choice as to how define the national concept of 'worker' and can go beyond the classical requirements of direction and control in determining the scope of employment relationships (Kountouris 2018; Menegatti 2020). So, while the fourth solution – exploring new normative paradigms beyond subordination – has not been openly explored by regulators, recent legislative interventions do not rule it out. Until then, the difficult task of transposing the practical arrangements of platform work into the normative definitions in force is still largely left to the interpretation of judges.

FISSURING AND THE CORPORATE LEGAL VEIL: ANOTHER JURIDICAL OBSTACLE FOR LABOUR RIGHTS

It is not only in relation to the notion of the worker that predominant regulatory paradigms fall short of capturing the platform economy's dynamics. This is also the case when looking at the employer end of the relationship and at the gaps left by the traditional, formalistic understanding of the employing firm, classically identified with the business entity with which workers contractually engage (Aloisi et al. 2023). In particular, platforms have quickly capitalised on the rigidities of labour law structures and have begun to rely on subcontracting schemes (Brave New Europe 2021). They often hire intermediaries which assume the formal role of employer, although these have no agency in defining the terms and conditions of work – a prerogative that remains with the platform (Vieira and Mendonça 2023). This creates another paradox whereby platforms exert overt dominance vis-à-vis their subcontractors, define all the conditions of the service provided by workers and directly profit from their labour, but are absolved from the duties and accountabilities of an employer.

As in the case of non-standard and precarious work, the dilution of employer responsibility through creative and multi-party business arrangements is not a novelty introduced by the platform economy (Rogers 2016). Workplace fissuring has been a fairly common feature of corporate structures for several decades as an effective stratagem to reduce labour, social security and tax costs (Weil 2019). The fragmentation of enterprises leads to increased complexity in the legal structure of the overall economic unit, allowing the employer's obligations to be distributed away from the main contractor and along the subcontracting chain (Hassel and Sieker 2020).

On-location platforms rapidly moved to exploit this fictional corporate disaggregation, which has become a core feature of the platform economy (De Groen et al. 2021), with algorithmic management acting as a facilitator in smoothing the reintegration of atomised economic activities and operations into seemingly linear processes (European Commission 2019). Food delivery platforms, for example, can outsource the hiring and management of couriers to intermediaries without incurring significant additional coordination costs, while still projecting the image of a single corporate provider of food delivery services to the market and customers. Workers hired through intermediaries generally even use the same software (the mobile app) to access work and perform tasks as those working directly for the platform. In other words, delivery services are performed within the same digital ecosystem controlled by the platform, which acts as an 'operational glue' (Weil 2019), in practice reassembling an otherwise legally fragmented business structure into a single economic entity.

As already pointed out by Hiessl (2023), a reliance on intermediaries not only shields platforms from their duties as employers but also permits the fragmentation of the business in dimensional terms, spreading workers across different legally separate business entities. This makes it possible to circumvent the application of collective labour rights that are anchored in dimensional requirements in relation to the workforce (e.g. Directive 98/56/EC on collective redundancies and Directive 2002/14/EC establishing a framework on information and consultation practices) (Borelli 2022), since it reduces the chances of workers reaching the critical mass needed to set up works councils or other representation bodies and to negotiate collective agreements. In addition, the workers' counterpart in collective bargaining would hardly be the platform but rather its intermediaries – formally vested with the role of employer but deprived of genuine contractual and negotiating autonomy in relation to working conditions (Rainone 2024). It can also be problematic in the event of the intermediary's insolvency as workers would not be able to obtain satisfaction of their claims from the platform in the absence of forms of joint liability (Hiessl 2023).

Again, this raises a normative question: what defines a company in the platform economy and, in turn, determines accountability for the obligations of the employer? The answer is largely left to national judges, whose approach may vary. Judicial interpreters can choose to focus on the actual distribution of economic and labour market power, thus emphasising the de facto economic unit and looking beyond fragmented legal structures (Howcroft and Bergvall-Kåreborn 2019). Along with a similarly flexible interpretation, it could be recognised that the intermediary lacks operational autonomy if it is the platform that oversees crucial aspects of the service provision, including the organisation of shifts and the setting of tariffs, and controls the mobile application and the volume of data generated as well as the overall algorithmic management system (OECD 2023). The alternative, more formal and traditional solution is to remain anchored in a legalistic interpretation of the firm in which legal corporate structures delineate the limits of employer accountability. This does not, per se, give complete immunity to digital platforms operating through subcontractors as forms of joint liability can be established. In particular, this option has been implemented in the Platform Work Directive, whose Article 3 on 'intermediaries' requires member states to establish 'appropriate mechanisms, which shall include, where appropriate, joint and several liability systems'.

Confronted with legislative guidance that is still too scattered and often vague (see Chapter 11), judges are thus faced with the challenge of developing coherent normative solutions to nuance or fill existing regulatory gaps.

AN EMPIRICAL LABOUR LAW STUDY: METHODOLOGY AND DATA

Having presented the normative framework, the chapter now turns to examine national jurisprudence on platform work, with the aim of shedding light on judicial reasoning that potentially has profound normative implications. Before proceeding, however, a brief methodological introduction is needed.

The chapter is engaged with an empirical analysis of case law on the platform economy, focusing specific attention on app-based food delivery. In doing so, it adopts a methodological approach that is rather niche for legal disciplines, consisting of a systematic examination of the patterns and trends in a relatively large body of legal documents – in this case, judicial decisions – in order to uncover developments within legal systems. This means that it is not explicitly comparative and does not aim to explore differences between countries nor explain the merits of individual decisions. Rather, the aim is to provide a more general, but coherent, overview.

This methodology has been first employed in sociological labour studies, with the seminal work of Stone Sweet (2004), who examined a large body of EU case law to identify developments in the approach of the Court of Justice towards EU non-discrimination rules. While there is a branch of legal research concerned with the application of empirical methods to jurisprudence (Dyevre et al. 2019; Dyevre et al. 2022; Ovádek 2021; Sadl 2020), this is rarely adopted in labour law studies. In the transnational context, there are examples where labour law scholars have focused on the judiciary (such as Hunt 1998; O'Leary 2002; Prassl 2016; Rainone 2023b; Sciarra 2001) but these contributions tend to focus on EU law and to overlook the national context.

Hiessl (2021) and Potocka-Sionek (2023) were the first to integrate an empirical method into a cross-country analysis of case law in the area of platform work. This chapter aims to add further insights to their work by embedding a systematic study of case law within a broader discourse on labour law theory, namely the adequacy of the key paradigms that regulate the scope of application of labour protection.

The analysis is based on Hiessl's rich dataset of national jurisprudence on platform work, which provides a range of detailed information, including the facts considered by the judge, the decisive reasons that guided the judge's assessment, the counter-arguments raised, and the final outcome of the case. A total of 531 judgments from 17 European countries are considered: Austria (10), Belgium (8), Switzerland (24), Germany (5), Denmark (6), Spain (250), Finland (8), France (124), Hungary (3), Ireland (4), Italy (37), Luxembourg (2), the Netherlands (17), Norway (2), Portugal (2), Sweden (13) and the United Kingdom (24). The data is thus rather skewed to two countries: France and Spain account for 70 per cent of the judgments.

On the basis of the elements provided in the dataset, judicial reasoning has been categorised and coded, taking into account the type of platform work, the judicial outcome and, in the case of decisions on the reclassification of the employment relationship, the supporting legal arguments. The study distinguishes between cases relating to food delivery (which includes delivery from restaurants and fast-food outlets, as well as from grocery stores) and those concerning other platforms. This distinction is justified by the high number of rulings in the sector (274, almost half of the total) and by its relevance to the emergence of innovative normative arguments.

There are several methodological limitations. The main one is that the analysis and coding of the case law were carried out on the basis of the metadata contained in the dataset and not on the basis of the original text of the judgments. Although the database provides a fruitful overview, it is important to stress that it was not created for the purposes of this specific chapter. It is therefore possible that certain relevant aspects of the reasoning may not have been included because they did not pass through the filters with which the dataset had originally been organised. Another limitation is that, although the study also aims to compare the main legal innovations emerging from case law in app-based food delivery with the legal approach that characterises the rest of the platform economy, the overall analysis is de facto limited to on-location platforms. Indeed, online platform work has not yet been the subject of litigation in the jurisdictions considered.

BETWEEN FAMILIAR AVENUES AND JUDICIAL CREATIVITY

Turning to the case law on platform work, among the various issues that have been addressed before national courts, two are of particular relevance in the context of this chapter. The first revolves around the notion of the employment relationship and concerns the legal regime applicable to individuals working through platforms. Should it be labour law or the general civil law governing contracts for services? The second option, which has been explored in a smaller but growing number of judgments, complements the first and relates to the identification of the legal entity that should bear the obligations of the employer. Is it the subcontractor with whom the workers contract, or should it be the platform that actually controls the work and the organisational processes?

This section outlines the main legal approaches adopted by national judges when faced with these legal challenges. Eight judicial strategies can be empirically identified: (A) a reclassification of the worker as an employee; (B) a reclassification of the worker as a third-category worker; (C) confirmation of the worker's status as self-employed; (D) a flexible interpretation of legal structures – employer obligations are not (only) assigned to the formal employer (such as the intermediary and/or the temporary work agency) but (also) to the digital labour platform; (E) a strict interpretation of legal structures – employer obligations are not attributed to the digital labour platform but to third parties alone (such as the intermediary and/or the temporary work agency); (F) an application of data rights, also in light of non-discrimination rules, without specific focus on employment status; (G) an application of collective labour rights, including anti-union behaviour, the right to be covered by a more favourable sectoral collective agreement and the exercise of information and consultation rights, without specific focus on employment status; and (H) criminal charges, without specific focus on employment status.

The first three legal strategies relate to workers' claims that they have been wrongly classified by the platform as self-employed when they should instead be covered by labour law. In both A and B, but particularly in the case of reclassification as employees, the judge is usually presented with legal arguments explaining how the facts of the actual performance of the work, including algorithmic management, indicate a relationship of subordination between the worker and the platform (or possibly the intermediary, if there is one) (Hiessl 2024a). In legal systems where third categories exist, legal claims may also ask the judge to reclassify the worker as belonging to this intermediary group (B) if the legal requirements for access to full worker status are not met. Were the judge not to be convinced by these arguments, the outcome would be confirmation of existing self-employed status (C).

Judicial outcomes D and E reflect two different approaches to identifying the legal entity that exercises the role of employer (for further discussion, see Maran and Chieregato 2022). When adopting a more flexible interpretation of the legal structure (D), the judge looks at the power dynamics between the actors involved and goes beyond the fragmented organisational model of the platform. In line with this judicial stance, workers could claim liability against both the subcontractor and the platform, or even be declared to be in an employment relationship directly with the digital platform. Rulings of this nature have the effect, albeit to varying degrees, of lifting the corporate veil created by the platform to avoid assuming the obligations of an employer.

Category D also includes decisions in which the platform is considered to be a temporary agency and either the client or the intermediary is referred to as the 'user' company. In these cases, workers are placed in a legal regime that is less protective than that applicable to standard (and linear) employment relationships (Ratti et al. 2024). This is also due to the sectoral collective agreements covering temporary agency workers usually being less generous than those covering logistics and transport. Still, from the perspective of employer accountability, these contractual regimes include the platform as a potentially liable subject against which the worker could activate some sort of legal claim.

The opposite result is achieved by strategies that follow a strict interpretation of the legal structures in which the platform business is organised (E). In this category are decisions concerning a multi-party arrangement (platform, intermediary, worker) in which workers are classified as employees, but all the employer responsibilities are attributed to the intermediary, leaving the workers with no legal claim against the platform. Category E also includes cases concerning temporary work agency schemes where only subcontractors are involved, thus excluding any contractual link between the worker and the platform, as well as cases where workers have taken legal action only against the subcontractors without including the platform among the defendants. In all these examples, judgments do not exert legal effects beyond the subcontractors and thus hit the walls of the multi-party legal structure in which the platform has organised its business.

Finally, the last three judicial strategies (F, G, H) do not directly address the question of whether workers should be considered to be in an employment relationship. Instead, they rely on legal provisions that have the effect of providing alternative and more universal grounds of protection for platform workers. Whether based on data protection rights (F), on anti-union busting norms (G) or on criminal provisions sanctioning the exploitation of workers (H), these arguments are a reflection of the limits of the strictly dichotomous paradigms in which legal status determines access (or not) to the available set of workers' rights.

Taken together, the strategies constitute the legal arsenal on which national judges draw in answering the fundamental labour law questions raised by the platform economy. Figure 10.1 provides a picture of the frequency with which each one is reflected in the final judgment and compares the overall case law on platforms with the body of decisions in app-based food delivery.

It appears clear that, in the large majority of cases, judges found that workers had been misclassified as self-employed (A and B, amounting to 280 decisions out of 377, panel A). This rate is even higher when looking only at food delivery (panel B), with 204 judgments out of 243 decisions in favour of reclassification, equalling 84 per cent.

While Figure 10.1 aggregates cases relating to status as employees and as third-category workers, the analysis indicates similar results for each. Reclassification cases concerning third-category status are in the minority (43 out of 388) and are prevalent in the UK and in Italy, where intermediate categories are recognised in the domestic legal systems (Aloisi 2022; Bertolini 2024). The success rate is quite high, albeit with some differences when looking at the case law as a whole and in food delivery alone (70 per cent for all platforms; 62 per cent for food delivery).

Fewer cases concern the allocation of employer obligations in the case of multi-party contractual arrangements (D and E), especially when looking at rulings in food delivery. Furthermore, the vast majority originates in Spain (106), where subcontracting is particularly common and represents an attempt by platforms to escape a clear national trend in favour of employment status (Cardo and Alonso 2022). Differently from what emerges from proceedings on employment status, judicial outcomes here are less likely to meet the demands

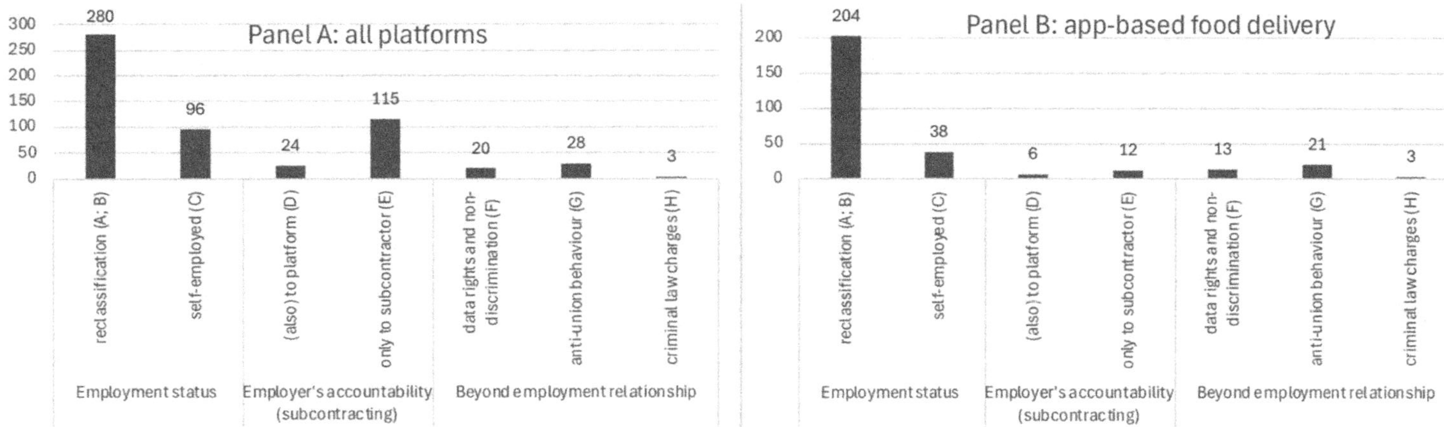

Note: While, generally, each case only reflects one judicial outcome, the analysed findings are not necessarily mutually exclusive. For instance, a legal proceeding may concern criminal charges for workers' exploitation (H) and, at the same time, the judge may decide to limit the legal consequence of the decision to the subcontractors and not to extend liability to the platform (E).
Source: Authors' own elaboration.

Figure 10.1 *Frequency of different judicial outcomes*

for protection against the platform in full. Where there are subcontracting arrangements, the predominant strategy is to recognise the intermediary as the sole employer, with no further or pending claims against the platform itself (E). This is the case for all platforms as well as for food delivery. Still, Figure 10.1 shows that the proportion of judgments in which the judge found forms of joint liability (D) is higher in food delivery (39 per cent) than in platform work as a whole (18 per cent).

Among the decisions attributing forms of liability across the subcontracting chain (D), it is significant that nine rulings held that only the platform and not the intermediaries – formally entrusted with the role of contractual employer – should be identified as the employer. These cases come mostly from Spain (six; two of which in food delivery), one from Switzerland and two from Italy (both in food delivery). Of the 114 cases in which no form of joint liability is established (E), at least 84 concern proceedings in which the platforms were not even listed as a defendant (67 in Spain, 14 in France, two in Italy). This suggests that, during the inception of the proceedings, plaintiffs have renounced expanding their legal claims to the platform.

Legal strategy E prevailing over legal strategy D suggests that the judiciary tends to refrain from reallocating the obligations of the employer, preferring instead to confirm the distribution of responsibilities resulting from the multi-party legal structure established by the platforms. However, the picture is more nuanced when excluding cases in which the legal claim was brought exclusively against the subcontractors and in which the platform was not the defendant, thus considering only those decisions in which the judge had a real option to extend the effects of the decision to the platform. In this case, the proportion of judgments that reflect strategy D is significantly higher (around 45 per cent of all subcontracting-related proceedings).

Finally, Figure 10.1 provides information on the frequency with which judges have ruled in favour of labour-related claims that do not directly depend on employment status. These cases are overall a minority, although their number is not negligible (51 judgments when looking at the entire case law, of which 37 are in food delivery). They include 20 decisions – 13 in food delivery – on data rights and the discriminatory bias built into the algorithm (F). These rulings are prevalent in the Netherlands (7) and Italy (11), and in every one of them the judge found the claims well-founded. A similar picture emerges in relation to judicial claims based on criminal law (H). Here, only three decisions are identified, all from Italy and all concerning forms of exploitation of (migrant) workers perpetuated by subcontractors of food delivery platforms, in which the judge ultimately held that criminal charges were substantiated. The most frequent rulings looking beyond the existence of an employment relationship are those dealing with forms of anti-union behaviour (G). The analysis identifies a total of 37 proceedings that feature a judicial complaint related to the exercise of collective labour rights, formulated independently of workers' status. The number is proportionally slightly higher when considering only food delivery (21). Judges have so far ruled against the platform in all food delivery cases, while the overall success rate is also high, although not as absolute as for legal strategies F and H (28 positive decisions from 37 cases). Again, most of these decisions were taken in Italy (19), followed by Spain (12). The prevalence of procedures that are not strictly dependent on employment status in the Italian context may be explained by the lack of consolidated case law on the reclassification of platform workers as employees in the national landscape (Pacella 2019). In addition, most of the rulings on anti-union and discriminatory practices were closely coordinated by Confederazione Generale Italiana del Lavoro (CGIL, one of the most representative trade union confederations) and aimed at unlocking the 'black box' of the algorithm in order to obtain further evidence for subsequent reclassification cases (de Marchis Gómez 2021).

DISSECTING THE LEGAL ARGUMENTATION: MOVING BEYOND SUBORDINATION?

While the analysis so far has focused on the frequency of the different legal findings, this section concentrates on the role of creative reasoning in reclassification cases. To what extent do judges resort to legal reasoning that goes beyond the classical paradigm of subordination when deciding the employment status of platform workers?

In analysing the case law, it is noticeable that, in order to argue in favour of reclassification, the pleading lawyer or the judge has, at times, resorted to a stretched and more flexible interpretation of the concept of subordination. In particular, two types of creative legal argumentation emerge. This section explores the frequency and impact of these two lines of judicial reasoning, comparing them with the rate of decisions in favour of reclassification emerging from the overall case law.

The first, referred to as 'argument 1', emphasises elements that go beyond traditional notions of direction and control in the performance of work. The identified legal considerations that feed into this line of argument are the following:

> 1) Workers are integrated into the business organisation of the platform; the work is performed in a personal capacity; the platform unilaterally defines the terms and conditions under which the work is to be performed; the platform unilaterally sets the prices for the service provided by the worker, including his/her own remuneration; and there is information asymmetry between the worker and the platform with regard to the organisation and conditions under which the work is performed.

The second type of creative argument, labelled 'argument 2', instead challenges the autonomous (and therefore non-subordinate) nature of platform work by relying on a repurposed definition of the notion of employing firm and productive assets in the digital economy:

> 2) The employer is the owner of the means of production which, in the platform economy, should be identified with the set of technological tools (the software, the mobile app) that enable algorithmic management and that are crucial for organising and delivering the service to customers. These assets, therefore, do not coincide with the tools possessed by worker, such as their smartphone and/or vehicle, but are owned by the platform.

Arguments 1 and 2 can be cumulatively present in the same proceeding as they are not mutually exclusive. It should be noted that the 'total reclassification cases' benchmark is smaller than the number of such cases appearing in Figure 10.1. This is because, in order to provide as accurate a measure as possible of the impact of these creative argumentations, only those rulings for which the database included a summary of the judge's motivations are considered. Furthermore, this section focuses only on cases concerning reclassification as employees (not as 'third category workers') since the aim of the analysis is to measure whether these arguments succeed where standard subordination tests fail in providing full employment protection.

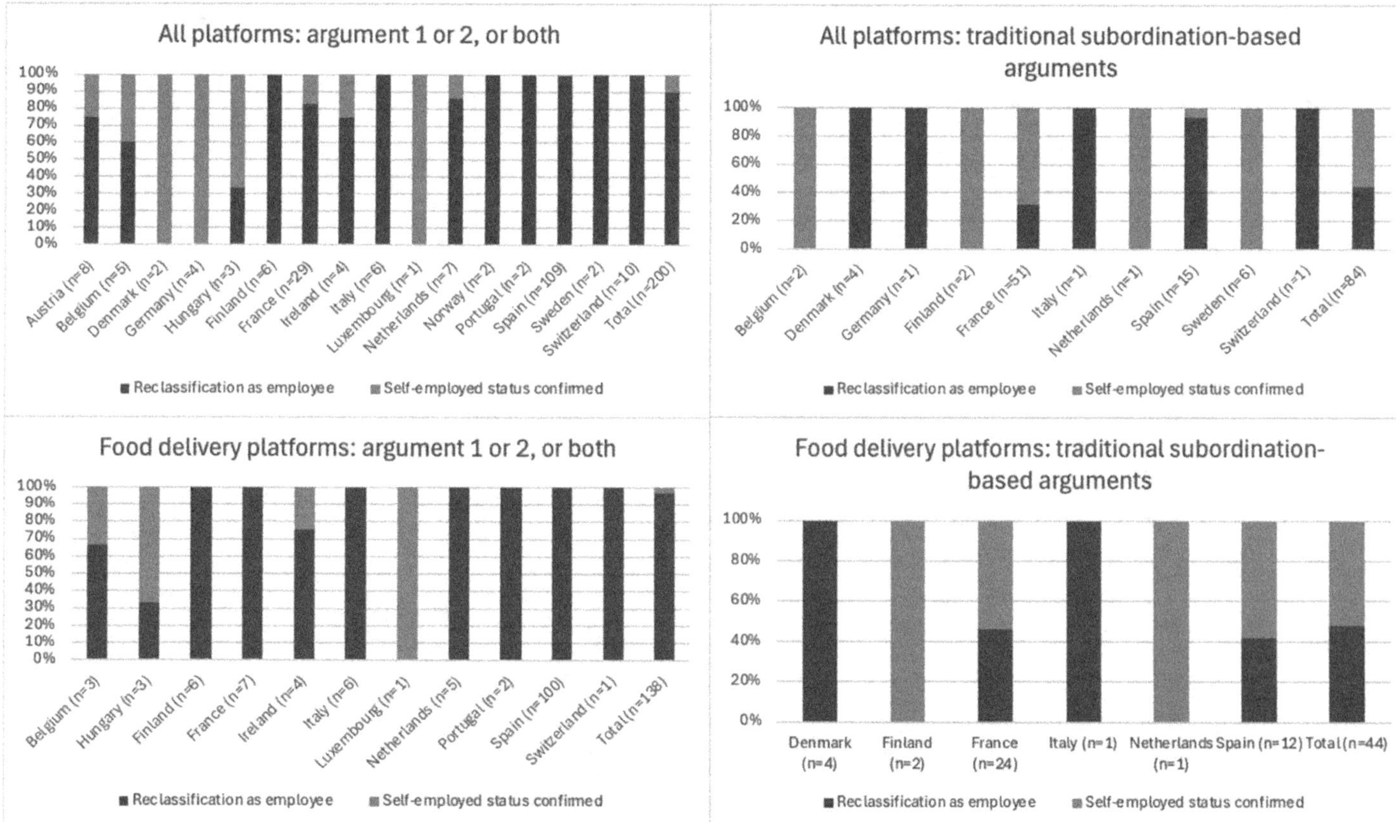

Source: Authors' own elaboration.

Figure 10.2 *Frequency of judicial arguments extending beyond a strict notion of subordination*

Figure 10.2 identifies the impact of both legal arguments on the judge's final decision on reclassification and shows the number of times the dataset reports that arguments 1 and 2 were developed in cases where the judge ultimately found that the worker should be reclassified as an employee, compared to the number of times that self-employed status was confirmed. It should be remembered that, as the study did not rely on textual analysis of the full judgments but on metadata, it could be that the reported data do not reflect all the instances in which the arguments have been proposed by the plaintiff or considered by the judge.

Figure 10.2 indicates clear results. First, judges appear to be relying on these arguments quite extensively, indicating a judicial transition towards a looser notion of subordination. This emerges in relation to overall case law as well as in food delivery. Second, the study suggests that arguments 1 and 2 are particularly conducive to judicial outcomes recognising the existence of an employment relationship. In fact, Figure 10.2 shows that they are much more often associated with decisions in which the judges find in favour of reclassification than with decisions in which self-employed status is confirmed. This is particularly true in food delivery, where the proportions of reclassification decisions featuring argument 1 and argument 2 are 83.7 per cent and 44.8 per cent respectively, compared to other on-location platforms of 73 per cent and 17 per cent. There are a few exceptions, in relation to case law on all platforms (Germany, Denmark, Hungary and Luxembourg) and in food delivery (Hungary and Luxembourg). However, it should be noted that these jurisdictions cover a quite small number of cases (a total of 15 rulings).

The study also indicates that argument 1, which goes beyond the classic requirements of control and direction by considering other signs of vulnerability and unequal bargaining power, can be found in several national jurisdictions. A notable exception is France where, despite a high number of cases, relatively few decisions report such judicial reasoning (see also Hiessl 2024a). Instead, argument 2, which considers ownership and control of digital assets as key criteria in defining the relationship between the platform and the workers, is mostly concentrated in Spanish case law. Nevertheless, here too, French jurisprudence stands out not only because of the lack of relevance given to the digital ecosystem but also because of the opposite tendency of judges to attach considerable importance to the ownership of (ancillary) material assets such as a mobile phone or vehicle. Unsurprisingly, in France the success rate of employment reclassification proceedings (55 decisions in favour; 48 against) is considerably lower than in Spain (136 decisions in favour; just 11 against).

All in all, these findings suggest the inadequacy of the traditional and formalistic interpretation of subordination as a key paradigm for the scope of application of labour protection. There is ample room for the development of innovative and more realistic conceptualisations; the case study showing that valuable guidance can be derived from national judicial reasoning.

JUDICIAL CREATIVITY IN APP-BASED FOOD DELIVERY: A SOURCE OF NORMATIVE INNOVATION

This chapter sheds light on legal developments in relation to the two key challenges that platform work has exacerbated for labour law: overcoming the limits of the subordination paradigm and ensuring a fair allocation of employer responsibilities across fragmented business models.

Three main observations can be made. The first relates to the tension between formal and traditional interpretative approaches vis-à-vis more creative lines of argumentation. With regard to the paradigm of subordination, the analysis clearly shows that judicial assessments based strictly on criteria of control and direction are ill-equipped to grasp the dimensions of vulnerability that characterise platform work. More helpful and successful – from a litigation perspective – are arguments that take into account a broader range of circumstances.

At the same time, these interpretive approaches depart from the established jurisprudential and normative *acquis* and struggle to gain proper regulatory recognition (Aloisi et al. 2023). Indeed, the normative potential of innovative legal reasoning has not (yet) received sufficient attention from policymakers or scholars, despite some notable but rare exceptions (Davidov 2016; Freedland and Kountouris 2011; Georgiou 2022). A telling example can be found in the recent Platform Work Directive, which insists on linking the presumption of employment to the existence of 'facts indicating control and direction'. It remains to be seen whether less orthodox legal reasoning will become more structurally embedded in national jurisprudence, for example by being taken up more systematically by higher courts. Promising developments in this regard can be seen in Spain, where the Tribunal Supremo (Supreme Court) has already issued 17 rulings, 8 of which use as key indicators platforms' unilateral determination of working conditions and their control over the relevant technology, and thus the means of production.

The tension between legal formalism and creativity is instead at an earlier stage in judicial solutions regarding the allocation of employer obligations in multi-party relationships. While a significant number of judgments have the effect of at least partially lifting the corporate veil, the majority of decisions still attribute employer responsibilities exclusively to the legal entity that is formally invested with the role of employer (the intermediary), even if it is deprived of any real autonomy vis-à-vis the platform. It may, however, be noted that, in most of the cases involving an intermediary, the platform does not even appear as a defendant. Once this element is considered, the study suggests that, when judges are given the option to extend the effects of the ruling to the platform, they are not disinclined to do so in a considerable number of cases. It would be interesting to continue monitoring jurisprudential developments in this area. Indeed, it is likely that litigation involving intermediaries will continue to increase as a result of stricter labour regulations being adopted across Europe, which may push more and more platforms towards the subcontracting model in order to avoid directly bearing higher labour costs (Cobo 2023). Moreover, judicial arguments in favour of forms of joint liability between the intermediary and the platform may gain normative strength in light of Article 3 of the Directive, which encourages the establishment of these co-liability mechanisms.

The second observation that emerges is that case law in food delivery plays the role of a normative incubator. Apart from findings concerning the judicial approach to employer liability in case of subcontracting, that are largely in line with the overall case law, app-based food delivery has emerged as a source of modernisation in the interpretation of labour law. Creative arguments stretching the notion of subordination (legal arguments 1 and 2) are mostly developed in cases involving food delivery couriers and slightly less in other on-location platforms. More importantly, the estimated impact of these arguments appears greatest in relation to proceedings in food delivery than in other sectors. Thus, not only has litigation systematically resorted to innovative normative criteria, it also clearly shows that these criteria are leading to a legally sound and much-needed extension of the scope of application of labour protection (Freedland and Kountouris 2011; Georgiou 2022). Moreover, it is prevalently in food delivery that creative lawyers and prosecutors have resorted to alternative legal grounds, such as the principle of non-discrimination, criminal law and anti-union behaviour, to target the abusive dynamics perpetuated by platform companies. The vast majority of these cases ruled against the platform, further suggesting that the vulnerability of platform workers goes beyond the relationship of subordination that traditionally defines reclassification cases.

It is difficult to identify with certainty the reasons for the vivid judicial activity and creativity in food delivery. Possible explanations include almost half of all court cases being in this sector, reflecting the high rate of platform work in the industry (Piasna et al. 2022). Lawyers and judges have therefore had more opportunities to experiment with legal strategies and arguments. In turn, the high rate of litigation may well be linked to the apparent exploitation of food delivery couriers, which creates favourable conditions for strategic litigation (Bidetti et al. 2022). The intrusiveness of the most common algorithmic management systems and their impact in depriving workers of any concrete autonomy in the provision of their services (such as use of geolocalisation data, the inability of couriers to set prices and conditions, sudden deactivation of the account) is quite obvious even to less tech-savvy observers. Furthermore, even more than for other on-location platform work, the widespread presence of couriers in the urban context (see Chapter 2) makes it difficult not to see the contradictions between the arguments put forward by platforms, focused on the enhanced entrepreneurship and flexibility of workers, and the actual circumstances in which workers make deliveries.

Finally, the third observation that can be drawn is that the innovative normative solutions developed in the context of app-based food delivery can be exported not only to platform work in general but also to the conventional economy. Legal arguments that depart from a strict subordination paradigm, as well as those that have led judges to attribute employer obligations to the platform despite the existence of subcontracting agreements, respond to problems that have influenced the effectiveness of labour norms long before the expansion of the platform economy (Aloisi et al. 2023). While app-based food delivery and platform work in general represent the tip of the iceberg of the creeping labour market power of private and highly digitised corporate entities, examples also abound in traditional sectors (see Chapter 14).

As the case law on app-based food delivery demonstrates, the limits of the predominant legal paradigms governing the scope of labour law are now being exposed, and it is time for bold reinterpretation efforts. While this requires a titanic effort, lawmakers are not wandering in the dark; judicial creativity can serve as their guiding light. The consolidation of these normative approaches would significantly contribute to realigning the scope of labour norms in view of the growing need for the protection of the working population, aggravated by the intensive integration of digital technology in the world of work.

CONCLUSIONS

The judiciary is at the forefront of efforts to embed platform work within a coherent regulatory framework. While the academic debate is now beginning to move towards legislative developments, this chapter aims to take a step back and discuss the lessons that can be learned from the rich and still growing body of case law on platform work, with a particular focus on app-based food delivery. The main exploratory question addressed is whether litigation has signalled an opening towards more inclusive labour law paradigms, regarding both the notion of the employment relationship and the allocation of employer accountability in situations of business fragmentation.

Looking first at the issue of the definition of employment relationships, analysis of the case law shows that judicial interpretation has not systematically embarked on an explicit rejection of the subordination model. There is still a widespread attachment to classical interpretive paradigms according to which platform work is observed through the narrow lenses of the control and direction criteria. At the same time, it has shown that judges are less hesitant than legislators to explore innovative normative solutions that depart from traditional and established schemes. Particularly in food delivery, and despite judges not openly advocating a paradigm shift, emphasis is often placed on additional factors, such as being subject to working conditions unilaterally determined by the platform, or that workers do not own any productive assets since the relevant software technology is controlled by the platform. It is not uncommon for these arguments to be developed along with considerations based on more traditional criteria, such as the presence of intrusive surveillance mechanisms enabled by the app, or the exercise of disciplinary power by the platform. Nevertheless, the presence of more creative reasoning has proved to be quite crucial to overall judicial assessments, as suggested by their estimated impact on the success rate of reclassification claims. Indeed, judges are more likely to rule in favour of reclassification when judicial reasoning takes into account the dynamics between workers and platforms that go beyond those indicating subordination, at least in the narrow sense.

Turning to the second key issue – the definition of the role of the employer in a situation of business fragmentation – jurisprudence has not (yet) reached the same maturity as that observed in relation to employees and the employment relationship. The case law in food delivery shows that only a minority of judgments in cases featuring the presence of subcontractors end up attributing (more or less extensive) forms of liability to the platform concerning the obligations of the employer. The same is true when looking at case law on platform work as a whole, indicating that this is not a sectoral trend. Thus, the main judicial approach does not go as far as lifting the corporate veil created by platforms through subcontracting arrangements. However, the existence of exceptions leaves room for future jurisprudential developments in a different direction. In this respect, it is worth noting that the requirement in the Platform Work Directive to establish mechanisms of joint liability between intermediaries and the platform could play a role.

All in all, this chapter reveals a growing judicial dynamism, first and foremost in app-based food delivery, that continues to outpace legislators in terms of normative creativity and constructiveness. Judges are the primary interpreters of how legal frameworks should be applied to actual labour practices and, overall, their reasonings reveal the limits of the normative model that currently defines the scope of labour law. It is now up to legislators to continue to fill these gaps and to translate the interpretative creativity of the judiciary into sound provisions that lay the basis for a more inclusive distribution of labour rights and obligations. The transposition of the Platform Work Directive into national legislation will be a crucial testing ground to assess whether policymakers' ambitions for the future of labour law match the expectations raised by judicial creativity.

REFERENCES

Adams-Prassl J. (2019) What if your boss was an algorithm? Economic incentives, legal challenges, and the rise of artificial intelligence at work, Comparative Labor Law and Policy Journal, 41 (1), 123–146.

Adams-Prassl J., Laulom S. and Maneiro Vázquez Y. (2022) The role of national courts in protecting platform workers: a comparative analysis, in Boto J.M.M. and Brameshuber E. (eds.) Collective bargaining and the gig economy: a traditional tool for new business models, Hart Publishing, 75–98.

Aloisi A. (2022) Platform work in Europe: lessons learned, legal developments and challenges ahead, *European Labour Law Journal*, 13 (1), 4–29.

Aloisi A. and Potocka-Sionek N. (2022) De-gigging the labour market? An analysis of the 'algorithmic management' provisions in the proposed Platform Work Directive, *Italian Labour Law e-Journal*, 15 (1), 29–50.

Aloisi A., Rainone S. and Countouris N. (2023) An unfinished task? Matching the Platform Work Directive with the EU and international 'social acquis', Working Paper 101, ILO.

Bertolini A. (2024) Regulating platform work in the UK and Italy: politics, law and political economy, *International Journal of Comparative Labour Law and Industrial Relations*, 40 (1), 131–154.

Bidetti M.M., Vacirca S. and de Marchis Gómez C. (eds.) (2022) *Quo vadis rider: la lotta umana e sindacale dei ciclofattorini*, Futura editrice.

Borelli S. (2022) Subcontracting: exploitation by design: tackling the business model for social dumping, *The Left*, 7 December. https://left.eu/issues/subcontracting-exploitation-by-design-tackling-the-business-model-for-social-dumping

Brave New Europe (2021) Gig Economy Project: is sub-contracting becoming the new normal in the platform economy?, 22 April. https://braveneweurope.com/gig-economy-project-is-sub-contracting-becoming-the-new-normal-in-the-platform-economy

Cardo I.T. and Alonso D.A. (2022) Multiparty work relationships in Spain: legal provisions and emerging trends, *European Labour Law Journal*, 13 (4), 492–514.

Cobo J.M.D. (2023) Contractual relations between providers and digital platforms: the Spanish 'Riders Law', *European Business Law Review*, 34 (7), 1193–1212.

Davidov G. (2016) *A purposive approach to labour law*, Oxford University Press.

De Groen W.P. et al. (2021) *Digital labour platforms in the EU: mapping and business models, final report*, Publications Office of the European Union. https://data.europa.eu/doi/10.2767/224624

de Marchis Gómez C. (2021) I diritti del lavoro etero diretto, Centro per la Riforma dello Stato, 22 April. https://centroriformastato.it/i-diritti-del-lavoro-etero-diretto

De Stefano V. (2016) The rise of the 'just-in-time workforce': on-demand work, crowd work and labour protection in the 'gig-economy', *Comparative Labor Law and Policy Journal*, 37 (3), 471–504.

De Stefano V. (2022) The EU Commission's proposal for a Directive on Platform Work: an overview, *Italian Labour Law e-Journal*, 15 (1). https://doi.org/10.6092/issn.1561–8048/15233

De Stefano V. and Countouris N. (2024) Lifting the private-law veil: employer authority and the contractual-coating of worker subordination, *Comparative Labor Law and Policy Journal*, 44 (3).

De Stefano V. and Wouters M. (2020) Embedding platforms in contemporary labour law, in Drahokoupil J. and Vandaele K. (eds.) *A modern guide to labour and the platform economy*, Edward Elgar Publishing, 129–145.

Dukes R. (2014) *The labour constitution: the enduring idea of labour law*, Oxford University Press.

Dyevre A., Glavina M. and Atanasova A. (2019) Who refers most? Institutional incentives and judicial participation in the preliminary ruling system, *Journal of European Public Policy*, 27 (6), 912–930.

Dyevre A., Lampach N. and Glavina M. (2022) Chilling or Learning? The effect of negative feedback on inter-judicial cooperation in nonhierarchical referral regimes, *Journal of Law and Courts*, 10 (1), 87–112.

ETUC (2022) ETUC resolution on the proposal of the European Commission of a Directive on improving working conditions in platform work and way forward ahead of the ordinary legislative procedure, Adopted at the Executive Committee Meeting of 16–17 March 2022.

European Commission (2019) *Report of the high-level expert group on the impact of the digital transformation on EU labour markets*, Publications Office of the European Union. https://data.europa.eu/doi/10.2759/586795

European Parliament (2024) Legislative resolution of 24 April 2024 on the proposal for a directive of the European Parliament and of the Council on improving working conditions in platform economy, A9–0301/2022.
Freedland M. and Kountouris N. (2011) The legal characterization of personal work relations and the idea of labour law, in Davidov G. and B. Langille (eds.) *The idea of labour law*, Oxford University Press, 190–208.
Georgiou D. (2022) 'Business risk-assumption' as a criterion for the determination of EU employment status: a critical evaluation, *Industrial Law Journal*, 51 (1), 109–137.
Gillis D., Lenaerts K. and Waeyaert W. (2022) France: lessons from the legislative framework on digital platform work, Policy Case Study, EU-OSHA.
Hassel A. and Sieker F. (2020) The platform effect: how Amazon changed work in logistics in Germany, the United States and the United Kingdom, *European Journal of Industrial Relations*, 28 (3), 363–382.
Hepple B.A. (2011) Factors influencing the making and transformation of labour law in Europe, in Davidov G. and Langille B. (eds.) *The idea of labour law*, Oxford University Press, 30–42.
Hiessl C. (2021) The classification of platform workers in case law: a cross-European comparative analysis, *Comparative Labor Law and Policy Journal*, 42 (2), 465–518.
Hiessl C. (2022) The legal status of platform workers: regulatory approaches and prospects of a European solution, *Italian Labour Law e-Journal*, 15 (1), 13–28.
Hiessl C. (2023) Multiparty relationships in platform work: cross-European case law developments and points of departure for (supranational) regulation, *European Labour Law Journal*, 14 (4), 514–540.
Hiessl C. (2024a) Case law on the classification of platform workers: cross-European comparative analysis and tentative conclusions, Updated to February 2024. https://papers.ssrn.com/sol3/Delivery.cfm/SSRN_ID4768181_code2683432.pdf?abstractid=3839603&mirid=1
Howcroft D. and Bergvall-Kåreborn B. (2019) A typology of crowdwork platforms, *Work, Employment and Society*, 33 (1), 21–38.
Hunt J. (1998) The Court of Justice as a policy actor: the case of the Acquired Rights Directive, *Legal Studies*, 18 (3), 336–359.
Kountouris N. (2018) The concept of 'worker' in European labour law: fragmentation, autonomy and scope, *Industrial Law Journal*, 47 (2), 192–225.
Maran E. and Chieregato E. (2022) Multiparty work relationship across Europe: a comparative overview, *European Labour Law Journal*, 13 (4), 474–491.
Menegatti E. (2020) Taking EU labour law beyond the employment contract: the role played by the European Court of Justice, *European Labour Law Journal*, 11 (1), 26–47.
Menegatti E. (2022) The classification of platform workers through the lens of judiciaries: a comparative analysis, in Gyulavári T. and Menegatti E. (eds.) *Decent work in the digital age: European and comparative perspectives*, Hart Publishing, 105–126.
Moyer-Lee J. and Countouris N. (2021) Taken for a ride: litigating the digital platform model, Issue Brief, International Lawyers Assisting Workers.
OECD (2023) *OECD Employment Outlook 2023: artificial Intelligence and the labour market*, OECD Publishing. https://doi.org/10.1787/08785bba-en
Oladeinde O. (2008) Global capitalism and rise of non-standard employment: challenges to industrial relations, in Blanpain R. (ed.) *The global labour market: from globalization to flexicurity*, Wolters Kluwer, 53–61.
O'Leary S. (2002) *Employment law at the European Court of Justice: judicial structures, policies, and processes*, Hart Publishing.
Ovádek M. (2021) Supranationalism, constrained? Locating the Court of Justice on the EU integration dimension, *European Union Politics*, 22 (1), 46–69.
Pacella G. (2019) Il lavoro tramite piattaforma digitale nella giurisprudenza dei Paesi di civil law, *Labour & Law Issues*, 5 (1), 17–42.
Piasna A., Zwysen W. and Drahokoupil J. (2022) The platform economy in Europe: results from the second ETUI Internet and Platform Work Survey, Working Paper 2022.05, ETUI.
Ponce Del Castillo A. and Naranjo D. (2022) Regulating algorithmic management: an assessment of the EC's draft Directive on improving working conditions in platform work, Policy Brief 2022.08, ETUI.

Potocka-Sionek N. (2023) Platformisation of work: challenges beyond employment classification, PhD thesis, European University Institute.
Prassl J. (2016) The interaction of EU law and national law: between myth and reality, in Bogg A., Costello C. and Davies A.C.L. (eds.) *Research handbook on EU labour law*, Edward Elgar Publishing, 42–63.
Rainone S. (2022) Labour rights beyond employment status: insights from the Competition law guidelines on collective bargaining, in Addabbo T. et al. (eds.) *Defining and protecting autonomous work: a multidisciplinary approach*, Palgrave Macmillan, 167–191.
Rainone S. (2023a) Digital and remote work: pushing EU labour law beyond its limits, in Countouris N., De Stefano V., Piasna A. and Rainone S. (eds.) *The future of remote work*, ETUI, 163–183.
Rainone S. (2023b) *The role of the Court of Justice in EU labour law: a case study on the Transfer of Undertakings Directive*, Wolters Kluwer.
Rainone S. (2024) EU social dialogue revitalisation: between rhetoric, new rights, political commitments and historical caution, *European Labour Law Journal*. https://doi.org/10.1177/20319525241251436
Ratti L. et al. (2024) 'Equal' yet poor: the ineffective protection of atypical workers under EU law, *European Labour Law Journal*. https://doi.org/10.1177/20319525241228980
Rogers B. (2016) Redefining employment for the modern economy, *The Journal of ACS*, 10 (3), 3–12.
Sadl U. (2020) Does the Court of Justice make law in small steps? (Circumstantial) Evidence from the free movement of persons jurisprudence, Paper presented at the EUI Faculty Seminar, EUI.
Sciarra S. (ed.) (2001) *Labour law in the courts: national judges and the European Court of Justice*, Hart Publishing.
Silberman S.M., Rakshita S., Abraha H. and Adams-Prassl J. (Forthcoming) Regulating data-driven management in a fissured world of work, *ILR Review*.
Stone Sweet A. (2004) *The judicial construction of Europe*, Oxford University Press.
Stylogiannis C. (2023) Freedom of association and collective bargaining in the platform economy: a human rights-based approach and an ever-increasing mobilization of workers, *International Labour Review*, 162 (1), 123–145.
Vieira T. and Mendonça P. (2023) Beyond misclassification: algorithmic management as challenge to the standard employment relationship, Paper presented to ETUI conference on 'Future of Work: working with and through digital technology', 14 February, Brussels. www.etui.org/sites/default/files/2023-02/Presentation_Tiago%20Vieira.pdf
Weil D. (2019) Understanding the present and future of work in the fissured workplace context, *RSF: The Russell Sage Foundation Journal of the Social Sciences*, 5 (5), 147–165.
Wood A.K. (2021) *Algorithmic management: consequences for work organization and working conditions*, JRC124874, European Commission.
All links were checked on 17 June 2024.

11. Regulating platform work in the European Union: initiatives, challenges and the ways ahead

Despoina Georgiou

INTRODUCTION

In recent years, the platform economy has been on the rise. While it is difficult to know the exact number of people actively engaged in platform work in the European Union today, in 2021, it was estimated that over 28 million people worked via digital labour platforms, with this number expected to reach 43 million by 2025 (CEPS 2021). The rise in the number of platform workers has reignited the debate over their classification status and working conditions. Platform work can be associated with long and unsociable hours and low and unstable incomes (Eurofound 2021b), leaving many workers exposed to physical and psychosocial health risks (Acemoglu 2021). Platform workers are frequently also exposed to a range of financial and commercial risks since they often have to bear payment-related, material and human capital investment and maintenance, redeployment, health and safety insurance and third-party liability risks (Georgiou 2022c).

Yet, despite shouldering business risks that are in number and nature comparable to those of the self-employed, platform workers do not display the typical characteristics of 'micro-entrepreneurs'. More particularly, they often cannot benefit from the upside pay-offs of their risk-taking activity because they have to work under the control of the platform(s) to which they provide their services (Georgiou 2022c). Platforms control various aspects of the working relationship: they set minimum quality standards for service, strict branding requirements and terms of payment (Aloisi and De Stefano 2022). They also use advanced automated systems to assign tasks, monitor workers and limit (or even terminate) their work through the app (see Chapter 14 of this volume). These methods, commonly referred to as 'algorithmic management', constitute a form of control that can be just as invasive, if not more so, than *stricto sensu* control exercised by managers in a traditional work setting. They may be novel and innovative, but they can generate negative outcomes for workers including increased workload and stress, potentially unfair evaluations and discipline, data privacy concerns and transparency issues.

To add to the precarity of their position, most platform workers do not enjoy the labour and social protections afforded to 'workers' in an employment relationship. The European Commission (EC) estimates that nine out of ten platforms active in the EU today classify people working through them as 'self-employed'. This means that they cannot benefit from protective national and EU legislation regarding equal pay, working time, maternity and paternity leave and pay, health and safety, information and consultation, collective redundancies, and others. It becomes clear, however, that many of these people are 'bogus self-employed'. The EC estimates that there are over 5.5 million platform workers in the EU at risk of employment status misclassification (European Commission 2021b).

Aware of these problems, courts in several domestic jurisdictions have started reclassifying bogus self-employed platform workers as 'workers'[1] (see Chapter 10). The increasing litigation has also inspired legislators in some member states and, more recently, the EU to take regulatory steps to improve conditions in platform work. Are the adopted paradigms adequate to provide greater protection to platform workers?

This chapter analyses how the platform economy, and app-based food delivery in particular, has been approached so far by the EU and national legislators across various member states. It argues that, while recent legislative initiatives constitute steps in the right direction, they do not go far enough in providing rights to all those who are in need of protection. For this reason, the chapter advocates the need to re-examine the predominant normative paradigm according to which labour rights are anchored to the presence of a subordinate relationship between the worker and the employer. Alternative frameworks that have been proposed in the literature are analysed to illustrate how they can be used to guide regulatory intervention in the future.

NATIONAL REGULATORY APPROACHES

This section analyses the measures that EU member states have adopted to regulate platform work. As of 2023, few member states had adopted legislation directly addressing platform work. The first to do so was France. In 2016, France introduced the 'El Khomri' law (Law 2016–1088) which provides basic protections to self-employed platform workers. Accordingly, platforms that determine the characteristics and prices of the service have to provide self-employed individuals who earn a certain minimum income working through them (€5,400 per year) with protection against occupational accidents and pay for their vocational training. Furthermore, the statute establishes a right for self-employed platform workers to form or join a trade union and to go on strike without fear of adverse consequences. As Daugareilh et al. (2019) note, with the 'El Khomri' law, French legislators attempted 'to create a third status without actually naming it'. The result is that self-employed individuals whose working conditions are controlled by a platform are entitled to limited social protection.

On top of the 'El Khomri' law, which captures platforms operating in all sectors, the French parliament introduced in 2019 the Orientation of Mobility law (Law 2019–1428), which applies only to platforms operating in transport and delivery. From this, platforms have to engage in negotiations with platform workers' representatives, as a result of which they can adopt social responsibility charters that address various aspects of the working relationship, including health and safety measures, workers' right to disconnect from the app, training opportunities and social dialogue practices. While the statute stated that these voluntary codes were unable to be used as proof of subordination in classification claims, this provision has since been deemed unconstitutional,[2] and the charters can now be used to prove 'worker' status. Finally, the law accords self-employed drivers and delivery couriers certain limited rights, such as the right to access and share data about their activities on the platform.

A more interventionist approach has been taken in Italy. In November 2019, Italy adopted Law 129/2019, which provides two frameworks of protection for platform workers. First, the law partially reformed the rules introduced by the 2015 Jobs Act package. In line with Article 2 of Legislative Decree 81/2015, individuals who provide 'predominantly personal work organised by the other party', known as *etero-organizzato*, are entitled to labour protection regardless of their employment status. The 2019 law extended the scope of the 2015 Act by broadening the etero-organizzato category explicitly to include technically dependent self-employed platform workers, specifying that self-employed individuals whose work is organised by the platform are entitled to the same labour and social protections as subordinated workers.

Apart from the broad reform addressing organisationally dependent self-employed individuals who work for platforms operating in all sectors, the 2019 law also introduced a specific regime for genuinely self-employed couriers who use bicycles and vehicles to deliver goods for platforms. Platforms must now provide workers with a written contract containing all relevant information regarding their working relationship. The law also stipulates that social partners can conclude collective agreements on wages. In the absence of such a collective agreement, the platforms cannot just pay individuals on a per-delivery basis, but have to provide a fixed wage based on the minimum wage levels established through collective agreements in comparable sectors. Furthermore, platforms must provide additional pay – at least 10 per cent higher than standard pay – for work performed during the night, on public holidays or weekends or in adverse working conditions, as well as insurance for occupational accidents and illnesses. Finally, the law states that platforms cannot penalise couriers for refusing to accept delivery tasks, and includes provisions on anti-discrimination and data protection.

A different approach has been followed in Spain. After a six-month process of tripartite social dialogue, the Spanish government adopted, in 2021, the Riders' Law' (Real Decreto-ley 9/2021). This introduced a presumption of worker status for delivery couriers whose work is organised and controlled, directly or indirectly, through algorithmic management by a platform. These individuals are considered 'workers' and are to be provided with labour and social protections unless the platform proves that they are genuinely self-employed. Moreover, the law introduces a right for workers to be informed about the algorithmic formula that governs their working relationship. In contrast to the legal presumption that applies only to persons who work in delivery, the right to information covers all platform workers, regardless of employment status and sector of work. Crucially though, this right is not accorded to individual workers but to their legal representatives.

A similar approach has been taken up in Portugal. In 2018, Portugal adopted Law 45/2018, which introduced a presumption of employment solely for platform workers engaged in transport. More recently, the Portuguese government has adopted, as part of its Decent Work Agenda (Agenda de Trabalho Digno), a new law that expands the presumption to cover individuals engaged in all areas of platform work. Law 13/2023 establishes a rebuttable presumption of 'worker' status for platform workers engaged in all sectors and provides a list of indicators that would trigger the presumption. It also introduces algorithmic management and information and consultation rights, and establishes a new category – 'economically dependent workers' – to which it bestows certain collective rights. Self-employed platform workers who receive more than 50 per cent of their income from a single platform can now be represented by trade unions and employee councils, which have the power to negotiate and sign collective agreements on their behalf.

A broad legal presumption of employment has also been introduced in Belgium. The 2022 Labour Deal Act made two changes to Chapter 4 of the Belgian Labour Relations Act to improve the protection of platform workers. First, it introduced a rebuttable presumption of worker status for platform workers who are controlled by a platform, providing eight indicators that would denote control. Platform workers who fulfil at least three of these eight, or two of the last five (which correspond to those listed in the EC's proposed Platform Work Directive) are considered 'workers' and are provided with labour and social protections unless the platform proves otherwise. The Labour Deal Act also establishes a legal obligation for platforms to provide self-employed platform workers with insurance against occupational accidents. More particularly, the platforms must now cover all those performing platform work, regardless of their employment status, against bodily harm resulting from accidents occurring during the performance, or on the way to and from, remunerated activities for the platform.

Finally, a broad legal presumption of worker status has been introduced in Greece. Instead of listing the criteria for the legal presumption to apply, as in the other countries, Greek Law 4808/2021 introduces an exhaustive list of 'negative' criteria that must be fulfilled for a service provider *not* to be considered a dependent 'worker'. These criteria include the ability to choose one's hours, the type and amount of work and the freedom to employ subcontractors and to work for other platforms. The law also establishes a series of rights that it bestows on all those providing platform work, regardless of employment status. These include being informed about one's rights and the main parameters of work; being able to form or join a trade union, go on strike, negotiate and conclude collective agreements; algorithmic management rights, health and safety coverage, and others (Articles 70–72).

This analysis demonstrates that legislators in different domestic jurisdictions have adopted diverse policies to address working conditions in platform work. While it is too early to tell which regulatory approach is the most effective and resilient in conferring protection on platform workers, some preliminary comments can be made.

All initiatives aim to increase the level of protection afforded to platform workers by preventing the misclassification of employment status, promoting worker representation and conferring specific rights on the genuinely self-employed. At the same time, they do not come without shortcomings. While the broad presumption of employment introduced in Belgium and Portugal has the potential to cover many online and on-site platform workers, the criteria that platforms can use to rebut the presumption have not been specified. This may imply limited legal certainty and predictability and might lead to lengthy and costly legal disputes. In this respect, the Greek approach, which provides an exhaustive list of 'negative' criteria for rebuttal, might prove more effective.

Although promising, as it ties protection to a broad notion of 'control', the legal presumption of 'worker' status established in Spain has the disadvantage that it only covers couriers operating in the delivery sector. The same applies to laws introduced in France and Italy, which specifically target couriers using vehicles. While these laws increase the level of protection in this area of platform work, they leave uncovered many individuals who provide on-location and online services via platforms operating in other sectors.

These individuals may be able to draw on the residual protection afforded to vulnerable self-employed persons in some jurisdictions. By providing limited rights to genuinely self-employed platform workers, EU member states such as France and Italy have effectively introduced intermediate categories of workers who are entitled to minimal labour and social protection. This approach, however, might have negative unintended consequences. As Aloisi (2022: 8) notes, 'the adoption of third categories – construed around criteria that are less stringent than those underpinning the definition of employment – can lead to widespread arbitrage, favoured by the existence of inexpensive alternatives to employment'. It could also lead to increased levels of litigation and uncertainty caused by these parties now having to litigate over three rather than two employment statuses (Garben 2021). Platform workers in Italy, for instance, have to go to court to prove their etero-organizzato status – just as they have to prove that they are subordinate employees. Similarly, the high-income thresholds established in France and Portugal for the self-employed to be entitled to some labour and social protection mean that many vulnerable platform workers might be left uncovered.

Finally, apart from labour and social protection legislation, certain member states have introduced beneficial tax laws for platform workers. France, for instance, has adopted a law that aims to reduce the administrative burden of tax returns for platform workers providing transportation and food delivery services (Law 2018–898). Platforms operating in these sectors have to inform people working through them about their tax and social security obligations and provide the relevant information to the tax and social security authorities. Similar initiatives have also been taken in Belgium and Estonia (Eurofound 2021a). Laws have been introduced in these countries which establish lower tax rates (up to a certain threshold) for income produced by working through a platform and provide for the automatic transfer of the payable tax by the platform to the tax authorities. While these measures do not directly address working conditions in platform work, they are beneficial to platform workers and help tackle undeclared work, which constitutes a serious problem in this area of the labour market (Public Policy Research Center 2022).

Overall, the measures so far adopted by EU member states to address working conditions in platform work are few and (quite) far between. Considering the precarious working conditions of many of the individuals, it becomes clear that a more robust framework is needed to level the playing field and provide greater protection to vulnerable platform workers.

EU POLICYMAKING INITIATIVES

The EU has, in recent years, taken several steps to address the emergence of platforms and their disruptive effects on the world of work (Georgiou and Barnard 2024). In December 2021, the EC published its proposal for a new Platform Work Directive, with the aim of tackling employment status misclassification, ensuring fairness, transparency and accountability in algorithmic management and improving enforcement of the applicable rules. Unlike some laws introduced in certain member states (France, Italy, Spain) that only cover platform workers operating in a particular sector, such as transport or delivery, this proposed Directive has a broad personal scope, applying to individuals engaged in all forms of work performed through a digital labour platform, whether online or on site.[3]

To tackle employment status misclassification, the proposed Directive introduces a legal presumption of 'worker' status for persons controlled by a platform (Article 4). This is considered to be the case when two of the five following indicators apply:

a) the platform determines, or sets upper limits on, the level of remuneration;

b) the platform imposes specific binding rules with regard to appearance, conduct or performance;

c) the platform supervises performance or verifies the quality of work, including by electronic means;

d) the platform restricts the freedom, including through sanctions, to organise one's work, in particular the ability to choose working time or periods of absence, to accept or to refuse tasks or to use subcontractors or substitutes;

e) the platform restricts the possibility to build a client base or work for any third party.

The presumption is, however, rebuttable. Platforms can do so by proving that the contractual relationship is not an employment relationship according to national laws and the case law of the European Court of Justice (CJEU) (Article 5). In making such an assessment, attention should be paid to what the person actually does in the case in question, rather than to their formal classification in the contract (in accordance with the 'primacy of facts' principle).

To increase transparency and accountability in the use of algorithmic management, the proposed Directive also introduces a series of rights which it bestows on all those providing services through platforms, regardless of their employment status (Article 10).[4] Platforms must disclose to all individuals who provide services through them (including the genuinely self-employed) the types of activities which are monitored by, and the types of decisions taken through, the use of automated decision-making systems as well as the parameters factored in the decision-making and the weight attributed to them (Article 6). Individuals have the right to request a review of such decisions which, therefore, cannot be taken without human oversight (Articles 7 and 8). Moreover, the proposed Directive provides that platforms must inform and consult with workers' representatives before they introduce such systems or make substantial changes to them (Article 9) and they must create contact channels for platform workers' communication with a view to defending their interests (Article 15). Other collective rights introduced include the right of workers' representatives to bring claims and to engage in judicial and administrative procedures on behalf of platform workers. Crucially, the information and consultation rights established under Article 9 are afforded only to workers and not to the genuinely self-employed.

The EC's recent emphasis on collective rights is also evidenced by the adoption of another instrument, namely the 2022 Guidelines on collective bargaining for the solo self-employed (European Commission, 2022),[5] which remove many of the existing competition law restrictions on collective bargaining for self-employed individuals who can now conclude collective agreements without the fear of being found liable for breaching competition law provisions (Georgiou 2022b). Platform workers who cannot benefit from the legal presumption of 'worker' status established under Article 4 of the proposed Directive, or whose status as 'workers' has successfully been refuted (under Article 5) will be considered to be 'solo self-employed persons who are in a situation comparable to that of workers' and will be able to bargain collectively without being captured by Article 101 of the Treaty on the Functioning of the European Union.

The proposed Directive, combined with the 2022 Guidelines, increases the level of protection afforded to those providing platform work. If adopted, the legal presumption of 'worker' status, the reversal of the onus of proof and the recognition of algorithmic management as a form of control would lead to the (re)classification of many platform workers as workers for the purposes of EU labour and social law provisions. The EC, for instance, estimates that, as a result of the proposed Directive, between 1.72 million and 4.1 million people (out of 28 million) who work for platforms will be reclassified as workers.

The breadth of the Directive's coverage will eventually depend, to a large extent, on how it is transposed into domestic jurisdictions and interpreted by the CJEU, which can be activated by means of requests for preliminary rulings to assess the consistency between EU law and the domestic law that transposes it. In the meantime, academics, unions and advocacy groups have called attention to certain aspects that could hamper the proposal's effectiveness. Concerns have, for instance, been raised about the indicators of control, with the proposal promoting a more stringent and formalistic notion of control than that already accepted by employment tribunals in several member states (Aloisi and Georgiou 2022; Rainone 2022; Chapter 14 of this volume), thus precipitating a potential regression in the overall level of protection afforded to platform workers. Furthermore, many have expressed the view that the requirement for two out of five indicators needing to be present for the legal presumption to apply is too restrictive, removing protection from vulnerable platform workers. Other criticisms raised include the indeterminacy of the criteria to rebut the presumption, the number of platforms that can act as employers, the ability to use subcontracting agencies to avoid employer responsibilities, the categories of platforms covered and the carve-out for start-ups (Georgiou and Karanovic 2023).

Many of these criticisms have been addressed in the report on the Platform Work Directive prepared by Rapporteur Gualmini and approved by the European Parliament (EP) in 2023. Here, the members of the EP have taken a more ambitious approach, establishing a broad presumption of employment that is not dependent on certain preconditions. According to the report, workers, trade unions and national authorities should be able to trigger the presumption if they consider that individuals work under the control, direction or supervision of the platform. Certain elements that could indicate control are listed in Recital 25, but this list is not exhaustive and not binding. Hence, other elements could be taken into consideration to classify workers.

The introduction of a broad legal presumption of employment, however, does not mean that all those performing platform work would automatically be reclassified as workers, as the platform always has the possibility to rebut the presumption before a decision of reclassification has been made by the competent administrative or legal authorities. The Parliament's report provides a list of criteria and indicators that platforms can use in rebuttal proceedings to prove that persons are, in fact, genuinely self-employed (Amended Article 5). As with the EC's proposal, the report reiterates that the assessment should be guided by factual elements, not by the parties' characterisation of the contract. At the same time, a broader and more dynamic notion of control is promoted, giving the proposed Directive wider coverage. Finally, provisions are added to help enforce the legal presumption more efficiently. For example, if a person is reclassified as a worker, the relevant authority should, within one month of such recognition, start an inspection rapidly to verify the status of others performing work for the same platform.

Overall, by removing the preconditions for the legal presumption to be triggered, establishing the criteria platforms can use to rebut the presumption, clarifying or removing elements that could hamper the application of the 'primacy of facts' principle and establishing measures that boost the efficiency of the Directive, the EP's approach increases certainty, coverage and predictability, and will help level the playing field across platforms and avoid lengthy and costly judicial disputes. It further clarifies various contentious points in the EC's proposal, thus providing greater protection to platform workers.

Other changes found in the EP's report regarding the EC's proposal include clarification of the number of parties who can act as the employer (Amended Article 3.2), wherein more than one party can assume the obligations of the employer. The report also sets out rules regarding the ability to subcontract (Amended Article 3.2.b) under which member states can introduce legal provisions that deliver joint and several liability, as well as effective access to redress, across subcontracting chains. This should ensure that contractors in a subcontracting chain are held liable to pay wages, social security contributions and financial penalties in addition to or in place of the direct employer. Furthermore, the report makes clear which platforms are captured by the Directive. While the EC's proposal states that only those platforms for which the organisation of work constitutes a 'necessary and essential component' of their activities are included, the report omits this language (Amended Article 2.1.1.c). As a result, all platforms which involve the organisation of work performed by individuals would fall within the scope of the Directive, although here it adds an exclusion: other than those platforms whose primary purpose is to exploit or share assets, platforms which allow private individuals to resell goods are excluded (Amended Article 2.2). The report also clarifies who can act as a 'workers' representative' (New Article 2.1.5a) and removes the exclusion for start-ups and small and medium-sized enterprises.

In general, the EP has adopted a more interventionist approach in relation to platform work regulation. Many of the criticisms raised against the EC's approach are addressed in the EP's report, which, arguably, constitutes a win for workers' rights (Georgiou 2023). While the report clarifies various contentious issues and provides greater protection to platform workers, there is a long way to go before these changes materialise into actual rights for Europe's platform workers. The EP's approval gives Rapporteur Gualmini the necessary mandate to enter inter-institutional negotiations, known as 'trialogue', with the EC and the Council, which typically adopt a more conservative approach. It remains to be seen whether the EU organs will agree on a more worker-protective piece of legislation in the area of platform work.[6]

A NEED FOR A PARADIGM CHANGE

The regulatory developments analysed here demonstrate that legal classification is of utmost importance as it constitutes the vehicle for the delivery of rights and entitlements. Indeed, a key tenet of the proposed Directive is that adequate access to labour and social protection can be achieved domestically through the correct classification of the employment status of individuals performing platform work. This means that those who will be granted 'worker' status for the purposes of the Directive are likely to be given access, at national level, to labour and social security rights such as healthcare, insurance against occupational accidents and illness, and (potentially) access to unemployment and pension benefits. In contrast, individuals who are deemed genuinely self-employed will not be covered by the Directive and will not be entitled to labour and social protections.[7]

The regulation of platform work constitutes an 'ideal testbed for analysing the suitability of the "binary divide" between employment and self-employment' (Aloisi 2022: 8) that can be found in many legal orders. In the EU and, for that matter, in most member states, the distinction between workers and self-employed is made by reference to the concept of 'subordination', understood as referring primarily to elements of control, direction or supervision (Kountouris 2017). While control continues to constitute the main element to ascertain subordination, the

CJEU has also, more recently, been paying increasing attention to two more elements, namely 'integration' and 'business risk-assumption' (Georgiou 2022a, 2022c).

Even though this model of subordination might have been effective in classifying individuals in the past (when most workers were engaged under open-ended contracts of employment for one principal throughout their lives), this is no longer the case. The emergence of new casual forms of work has brought to the surface the difficulty of the current taxonomy to grapple with complex work arrangements. Under many modern-day contracts for platform work, individuals are called upon to shoulder a number of financial and commercial risks and are under various levels of monitoring and control from their principals. On the one hand, these individuals do not satisfy the archetypical paradigm of dependent workers who are under the strict control of their employer and do not assume any business risks. On the other, they are not entrepreneurs free to provide their services in the market in whatever way they please. Since they exhibit some of the characteristics of subordinated working activity but not others, their classification has become increasingly troublesome. Are these quasi-subordinate individuals 'workers' or are they 'self-employed'; and how should we decide?

Apart from the increasing difficulty in classifying individuals, recent changes in labour market structures have also shown that the traditional normative criteria for classifying workers are inadequate to reach all those who are in need of protection. The current paradigm that requires employees to be fully subordinated to their employer to be given workers' rights does not capture many individuals who are in a vulnerable, imbalanced position vis-à-vis their counterparties. For Rainone (2022: 10), 'adherence to this regulatory model compromises the ability of labour law to pursue its emancipatory function effectively'. Therefore, critical reflection is needed on the possible need to re-adapt, transform or even overcome the predominant normative paradigm according to which labour rights are anchored to the presence of a subordinate relationship between the worker and the employer.

FOUR POSSIBLE PARADIGMS BEYOND SUBORDINATION

This section reviews the alternative frameworks that have been proposed in the literature which could guide regulatory intervention in the future.

The first is that of 'predominantly personal work' (Freedland and Kountouris 2011). According to the 'personal work relation' approach, workers' rights should be given to anyone who provides labour and is not genuinely operating a business undertaking on their own account. Two elements indicate that a person does not provide work or services in a predominantly personal capacity: (a) the employment of staff; and (b) making substantial investments in assets, for example capital, equipment or intellectual property rights. Hence, individuals who do not have employees of their own and who have not made substantial investments in assets can, under this approach, be considered workers entitled to national and EU labour and social protection.

An even broader approach is taken with the paradigm of 'imposed acquiescence' (Rainone 2022). According to this paradigm, labour law should be refocused on those situations where the distribution of bargaining power between the contracting parties is so unequal that, in the absence of safeguards, the provision of work risks being commodified and performed under contractual terms that disproportionately reflect the interests of the principal.

How can 'imposed acquiescence' be translated into normative criteria that could guide regulatory intervention in the future? The following suggestions have been made: a criterion based on labour or services being provided to a business and consisting of the performance of predominantly individual and labour-intensive work; a criterion based on the service performed converging in the economic activity of the counterparty because it is an integral part of the core business of the receiver; and a criterion based on the service provider and the contractor being competitors, for example offering the same product or service on the market. According to this theorisation, these criteria (which should be considered separately, not cumulatively) could address situations where there is an imbalance in bargaining power, thus extending the level of labour protection to include individuals who would not be covered under the current subordination paradigm.

The 'personal work relation' approach and the paradigm of 'imposed acquiescence' are partially reflected in the EC's 2022 Guidelines on collective bargaining[8] which apply to 'solo self-employed' persons defined as individuals who are not in an employment relationship and who rely primarily on their personal labour for the provision of the services concerned (para. 2(a)). Individuals are considered not to rely on their own personal labour when they employ staff and when their economic activity consists in the sharing or exploitation of goods or assets (such as housing rental) or the resale of goods or services (for example resale of automotive components). Persons can, however, make *certain* investments in goods or assets to be able to provide their services. A cleaner, for instance, can invest in cleaning materials, and a musician can invest in the purchase of a musical instrument without falling outside the 'solo self-employed' category. As the Guidelines clarify, 'in these instances, the goods are used as an ancillary means to provide the final service' (para. 18), so those concerned are still classified as 'solo self-employed'.

The EC also commits not to take action against collective agreements concluded by the solo self-employed who are in an imbalanced negotiating position vis-à-vis their counterparties. According to the Guidelines (paras. 36–40), two categories of individuals are in an 'imbalanced negotiating position': those who are facing an reduction in bargaining power due to having to negotiate with counterparties of a certain strength;[9] and those who are entitled to bargain collectively by national or EU legislation. As Rainone (2022: 3) notes, 'by giving normative relevance to the imbalance of bargaining power among the parties to a labour relationship, the EC's initiative on collective bargaining and competition law might have, inadvertently, made the first step towards legitimising a much-needed paradigm change on the scope of application of labour law'. Since the 'personal work relation' approach and the paradigm of 'imposed acquiescence' have, to some extent, been used in the competition law context to extend the reach of collective bargaining beyond the narrow confines of subordinate employment, they can also be used in the labour and social law contexts to inspire more worker-protective legislation.

A third approach would be to focus on the criterion of risk and, more particularly, on the 'inability of persons to spread their risks' (Davidov 2002; Georgiou 2022c). I have shown elsewhere (Georgiou 2022c) why risk constitutes an important element for the delineation of the boundaries of the firm and why it plays an important role in the determination of the obligations of the parties to the contract of employment. The criterion of business risk-assumption is consistently and increasingly being used by the CJEU and national courts to classify workers. In the way it is currently being used, however, it leads to paradoxical results as it can render as self-employed many who do not have the ability to benefit from the upside pay-offs of their risk-taking activity. More particularly, the use of this criterion would make self-employed many persons who cannot enjoy the advantages this status offers because they are unable to spread their risks as they often do not determine the price of their services, have to work under the control of the platform(s) and must over-rely on a specific platform for income.

The adoption of an alternative risk-related criterion based on the 'involuntary assumption of business risks', measured by the 'inability of persons to spread their risks', might avoid this. The rationale behind this conceptualisation is that, when people have the ability to spread their financial risks, for example because they can pass them on to consumers/clients through the price mechanism or because they have significant capital, employees of their own and/or multiple sources of income, they come to the negotiating table as unconstrained and fully autonomous adults. In this instance, they can decide what kind, quality and amount of risk(s) they want to undertake – if any. If they have decided to take on business risks, they have accepted the concomitant risk of being classified as self-employed, with the consequent implication of the non-application of labour law protection. Conversely, if they have decided that, being able to spread their risks, they want to be engaged under a contract of employment, the state has no reason to interfere with their choice.

In contrast, those individuals who do not have the ability to spread their risks, for example because they have little capital, have made sunk or job-specific investments, do not have employees and have no alternative sources of income and/or little or no control over business strategy, are not in a position to make truly free choices. Under these circumstances, such persons find their backs against the wall; they really have no option but to accept whatever terms are being offered. Since the individuals cannot be said to have assumed these business risks voluntarily, the state has legitimate reason to interfere with their will, as expressed in the contract, and reclassify them as de facto subordinate workers. Overall, by acting alongside the criterion of control, this risk-based criterion would expand the personal scope of national and EU labour and social law provisions to include casual types of worker that are excluded under the subordination paradigm.

Fourth, I have recently advocated for the adoption of a different paradigm based on the concept of 'integration', as that has been developed through EU competition law cases concerning agents and workers (Georgiou 2022a). In the competition law field, the CJEU and the EC have drawn an explicit jurisprudential parallel between the categories of agents and workers, specifying the criteria that need to be present for an 'agent' to be integrated into their principal's undertaking in the same way that a 'worker' is integrated into their employer's business unit. Following a strictly doctrinal approach, this parallel in case law can be used to develop a refined framework for distinguishing between integrated 'workers' and unintegrated 'self-employed person-undertakings' in EU labour, social and competition law fields (Georgiou 2022a).

Extensive analysis of the case law and the regulatory instruments in place reveals two elements as determinative for the assessment: the assumption of significant business risks, and control over the business strategy and the activities for which the person has been hired. Individuals who assume an insignificant level of business risk and who work under the control of their principals can, under this approach, be presumed to be integrated into their employer's business unit and entitled to labour and social protections.

An advantage of this approach is that it is jurisprudentially consolidated, as it constitutes a by-product of the systematic (re)application of an already established body of law. Consequently, it can readily be used by EU and national judges who do not have to fear exposing themselves to criticisms of 'judicial activism' – a risk that could arise if an alternative normative approach were adopted. Furthermore, this approach has the advantage that it relies on precise criteria and, as such, can act as a blueprint in the hands of judges and legislators in their attempts to classify modern-day workers. The framework that emerges from a systematic re-examination of case law provides detailed guidance on the type, amount and quality of risk[10] persons can undertake and the quality and intensity of control[11] they need to be under in order to be considered integrated into their principal's undertaking.

Finally, apart from being more efficient in classifying workers, the integration framework is also broader than the subordination paradigm. First, it clarifies that certain categories of risk do not count towards the assessment, for example, labour and social market risks, commission-related risks, non-sunk market-specific risks. Second, it permits the assumption of an insignificant level of business risks – 'insignificant' being broadly defined. Third, it recognises more subtle forms of control. Fourth, it provides that exclusivity in the relationship between the parties is not a precondition, so that persons can work for a small number of principals without losing their integrated worker status. Fifth, it stipulates that persons can assume parallel activities as independent contractors in the same (or a different) market on their own account.

Overall, all the alternative paradigms briefly presented here shift the focus away from the concept of subordination towards other normative considerations. In doing so, they allow a larger number of casual and atypical workers to fall under the EU 'worker' category and be entitled to EU and national labour and social protection.

EXTENDING THE LEVEL OF PROTECTION IN PLATFORM WORK

How can the alternative paradigms presented here be used to extend the level of protection afforded to persons engaged in platform work? 'Predominantly personal work' can be used to extend the ambit of protection to capture platform workers who are currently excluded from EU and national labour and social law provisions. Most platform workers perform their tasks themselves, without employing staff, and do not make substantial investments in goods or assets. Hence, if this approach were to be used, these persons would be considered to provide 'predominantly personal work' and would be covered by EU and national labour and social law provisions. More particularly, while parcel and food delivery platform workers usually have to make a certain investment in goods or assets (they may have to buy or rent a vehicle and pay for petrol), this could be viewed as 'ancillary means to provide the final service'.[12] Since they do not usually have employees of their own, and their investments are not substantial enough to negate that their economic activity relies primarily on the provision of personal labour, they could thus be classified as workers entitled to EU and national labour and social protections.

The same applies under an approach based on the unevenness in bargaining power between the parties. If this paradigm were to be followed, parcel and food delivery couriers who make deliveries for digital market platforms which offer delivery as part of their market offer, such as Amazon, would be considered workers and would be entitled to labour protection. Other categories of online or on-site platform workers would also be covered. So long as their services constitute an integral part of the core business of the platform (the platform and the platform workers are competitors in the market for the same goods or services) (Rainone 2022), they would fall under the category of workers and would be provided with EU and national labour and social protection.

Similarly, an increased level of protection would be afforded under a paradigm in which the unevenness in bargaining power was measured on the basis of quantitative criteria – as, for example, in the EC's 2022 Guidelines on collective bargaining for the solo self-employed. An approach, for instance, under which platform workers would be provided with labour and social protections when they work for platforms which represent the whole (or a large part of the) sector or industry, have annual aggregate turnover of over €2 million or employ more than ten members of staff[13] would capture most platform workers engaged in the transportation and food delivery sectors.

An expansive impact would also be detected under an approach based on the 'inability of persons to spread their risks'. As already noted, platform workers today assume a plethora of business risks (Georgiou 2022c) which, under the current paradigm of subordination, would render them self-employed. If the criterion of 'inability to spread risks' were to be used, however, many platform workers who do not have the ability to spread their risks would be (re) classified as workers entitled to EU and national labour and social protection. In particular, this would provide grounds to (re)classify many parcel and food delivery platform workers: besides not having significant capital investment nor employees, they do not determine the price of their services (thus not being able to pass on their risk to consumers); they work for just one, or a small number of, platforms (thus they do not have multiple sources of income) and they have no control over the business strategy of the platforms.

Finally, an expanded level of protection would also be achieved under the integration paradigm. As explained earlier, the framework that emerges from the jurisprudential parallel between agents and workers in EU competition law is very detailed and, as such, can act as a refined toolset in the hands of judges and regulators in their attempts to classify platform workers. Since this framework provides detailed guidance on the type, amount and quality of risk that persons can undertake, as well as on the quality and intensity of control they need to be under in order to be considered integrated into their principal's undertaking, it can help determine with greater ease and clarity the status of individuals who exhibit some characteristics of dependent and some characteristics of independent economic activity (platform workers whose classification is difficult because they assume a certain level of business risks and are under various levels of control from their principal(s)/platforms). This way, greater certainty and predictability would be provided, and lengthy and costly legal disputes would be avoided.

Apart from being more operational in practice, this framework could also be used to provide protection to a greater number of platform workers.[14] More particularly, the breadth of the integration paradigm allows platform workers to assume a certain level of business risk without being deprived of 'worker' status, while it recognises more subtle and indirect forms of control. Furthermore, it allows platform workers to work for a small number of employers and to perform parallel activities as independent contractors in the same (or in a different) market on their own account.

Overall, each of these paradigms could be used to increase the level of protection afforded to those engaged in platform work. It should also be noted that they are not necessarily mutually exclusive. For example, the integration paradigm and that based on the inability of persons to spread their risks could be used alongside the personal work relation approach to elucidate our understanding of when persons perform platform work in a predominantly personal capacity.[15] More particularly, they can be used to determine when persons are genuinely operating a business undertaking on their own account; that is, when their investments in goods or assets are significant enough to preclude a finding of 'predominantly personal' work.

CONCLUSIONS

The emergence of large platforms has disrupted the world of work as we know it. Legislators have struggled to regulate this new area, as exemplified by the fact that few member states have adopted legislation on the topic. The difficulty in regulating platform work is also evident in the variety of approaches that have been adopted by national jurisdictions, the European Council and the European Parliament. While these legislative initiatives constitute steps in the right direction (as they recognise more atypical and indirect forms of control), they are not innovative enough to overcome the dualism between 'autonomy' and 'subordination' that lies at the heart of labour law. Hence, they leave uncovered many vulnerable platform workers who are in need of protection. Therefore, it is paramount that we reassess the suitability of the traditional tests for conferring labour rights on workers.

This chapter argues in favour of a shift away from the subordination paradigm towards a more universalist approach. Alternative paradigms, such as those explored here, could be used to address policy gaps, extending the scope of labour and social protection to cover vulnerable platform (and other categories of casual) workers who are left uncovered under the current paradigm of subordination.

At the same time, it should be noted that the use of these frameworks would not solve all the problems encountered in this area of work. Despite addressing the classification issue, other problems remain, such as transparency issues regarding algorithmic management, enforcement issues and undeclared work. As the platformisation of work exacerbates the shortcomings related to the coverage of labour norms, a more pronounced integration of digitalisation within labour processes risks accentuating the protective gaps and amplifying the weaker bargaining position of workers (see Chapter 7). Furthermore, even under a broader framework, some vulnerable platform workers might be left uncovered because, for example, they have been made to assume a significant amount of business risks. It is thus crucial that, besides continuing the discussion on the expansion of the scope of labour rights, labour law scholarship takes further ownership of the debate on how to address the implications of digital and algorithmic management-based technologies for working conditions.

NOTES

1. In the EU labour law context, the terms 'worker' and 'employee' are used synonymously and interchangeably. The distinction between the terms has legal meaning only in the UK, where there is a tripartite structure ('employees', 'workers' and 'self-employed').
2. Conseil constitutionnel, Décision 2019-794 DC 20/12/2019.
3. The proposed Directive only covers platform workers engaged on platforms in which the organisation of work constitutes 'a necessary and essential component' of their function (Article 2). In contrast, individuals engaged on platforms whose primary purpose is to exploit or share assets, like Airbnb, might not be covered.
4. The limitation introduced by Article 2 applies here as well.

5. The Guidelines explain the EC's approach to the topic but are not binding on national authorities.
6. At the time of writing, EU member states had not struck a deal on the Directive. Agreement was finally reached on 11 March 2024. The final text of the Directive does not include the five indicators of control listed in the Commission's proposal; instead, it introduces a broad presumption of employment for individuals who work under the control and direction of a platform, leaving ample discretion to the member states to determine when this is the case according to their national law, collective agreements or practice in force in their jurisdiction, with consideration of the case law of the CJEU (Article 5). While the solution adopted in the final text partially diverges from the approaches of the Commission and the European Parliament outlined in the chapter, the arguments made therein are still valid (and will be useful in the implementation of the Directive by national legislators and courts), as is the need for a paradigm change.
7. Some member states, such as Estonia and France, provide national frameworks for self-employment. Depending on the national framework, some self-employed and quasi-subordinate platform workers might also be entitled to a level of labour and social protection (see the section 'National regulatory approaches').
8. See the section 'National regulatory approaches'.
9. This is considered to be the case when the counterparties: (a) represent the whole sector or industry; or (b) have an annual aggregate turnover that exceeds €2 million or whose staff headcount exceeds ten workers (individually or jointly) (para. 34).
10. The risks individuals cannot undertake are divided into three main categories: (a) contract-specific risks; (b) market-specific risks; and (c) risks related to other activities undertaken in the same product or services market to the extent that the employer has required the worker to carry these risks without compensation for the costs. There are multiple indicators of 'forbidden risks' as well as many examples of instances when working persons can be presumed to assume such risks. Furthermore, there is methodological guidance on how to assess these risks. For an analysis of the type, amount and quality of risk individuals can undertake without losing 'integrated worker' status, see Georgiou (2022a: 166–176).
11. Control is divided into: (a) direct or indirect; (b) positive or negative; (c) *de facto* or *de jure*; and (d) actual or potential. For an analysis of these categories and the quality and intensity of control individuals need to be under to be considered 'integrated workers', see Georgiou (2022a: 176–179).
12. By analogy to the 2022 Guidelines on collective bargaining for the solo self-employed, para. 18.
13. 2022 Guidelines on collective bargaining for the solo self-employed, para. 34.
14. For the benefits of using the 'integration' framework in the EU free movement, equal pay, labour and social law fields, and for its application to the facts of the Yodel (C-692/19) and Uber (C-434/15) cases (CJEU 2017, 2020) (i.e., a demonstration of how these cases would have been decided had the 'integration' framework been used), see Georgiou (2022a: 205–218).
15. They are not, however, compatible with the second and third criteria used to guide regulatory intervention under the 'imposed acquiescence' paradigm.

REFERENCES

Acemoglu D. (2021) Harms of AI, Working Paper 29247, National Bureau of Economic Research.

Aloisi A. (2022) Platform work in Europe: lessons learned, legal developments and challenges ahead, *European Labour Law Journal*, 13 (1), 4–29.

Aloisi A. and De Stefano V. (2022) *Your boss is an algorithm: artificial intelligence, platform work and labour*, Hart Publishing.

Aloisi A. and Georgiou D. (2022) *Two steps forward, one step back: the EU's plans for improving gig working conditions*, Ada Lovelace Institute, 7 April. www.adalovelaceinstitute.org/blog/eu-gig-economy

CEPS (2021) *Digital labour platforms in the EU: mapping and business models*, Publications office of the European Union.

CJEU (2017) Asociación Profesional Élite Taxi v Uber Systems Spain, SL, Case C-434/15.

CJEU (2020) B v Yodel Delivery Network Ltd, Case C-692/19.

Daugareilh I., Degryse C. and Pochet P. (2019) *The platform economy and social law: key issues in comparative perspective*, ETUI.

Davidov G. (2002) The three axes of employment relationships: a characterization of workers in need of protection, *University of Toronto Law Journal*, 52 (4), 357–418.

Eurofound (2021a) *Initiatives to improve conditions for platform workers: aims, methods, strengths and weaknesses*, Publications Office of the European Union.

Eurofound (2021b) *The digital age: implications of automation, digitisation and platforms for work and employment*, Publications Office of the European Union.

European Commission (2021a) *Proposal for a Directive of the European Parliament and of the Council on improving working conditions in platform work*, COM(2021) 762 final, 09.12.2021.

European Commission (2021b) Impact assessment accompanying the Commission's Proposal, SWD(2021) 396.

European Commission (2022) *Communication from the Commission: Guidelines on the application of Union competition law to collective agreements regarding the working conditions of solo self-employed persons* (2022/C 374/02).

European Parliament (2023) *Report on the proposal for a Directive of the European Parliament and of the Council on improving working conditions in platform work*, COM(2021) 0762, 21 December.

Freedland M. and Kountouris N. (2011) *The legal construction of personal work relations*, Oxford University Press.

Garben S. (2021) The regulation of platform work in the European Union: mapping the challenges, in Drahokoupil J. and Vandaele K. (eds.) *A modern guide to labour and the platform economy*, Edward Elgar Publishing, 145–161.

Georgiou D. (2022a) Devising a refined framework for distinguishing between 'workers' and 'self-employed persons-undertakings' in the EU labour and competition law fields: lessons from the EU agency acquis, Doctoral Thesis, University of Cambridge.

Georgiou D. (2022b) An assessment of the EU's draft Guidelines on the application of EU Competition Law to collective agreements of the solo self-employed, Competition Policy International, 20 July. www.competitionpolicyinternational.com/an-assessment-of-the-eus-draft-guidelines-on-the-application-of-eu-competition-law-to-collective-agreements-of-the-solo-self-employed

Georgiou D. (2022c) 'Business risk-assumption' as a criterion for the determination of EU Employment status: a critical evaluation, *Industrial Law Journal*, 51 (1), 109–137.

Georgiou D. (2023) Analogies and differences between the European Commission's and the Parliament's approaches to the new Directive on platform work, Medium, 6 May. https://medium.com/@reshaping_work/the-presumption-of-employment-revisited-46418d386643

Georgiou D. and Barnard C. (2024) EU developments in the labour and social field: jurisprudential and regulatory responses to the digitalisation of work, in De Vos M., Verhulp E. and Anderson G. (eds.) *Cambridge handbook of technological disruption in employment and labour law*, Cambridge University Press.

Georgiou D. and Karanovic J. (2023) The EU Directive clearing new paths to decent platform work, in Karanovic J. and Sapic J. (eds.) *Back to what truly matters: platforms, AI, and youth at workplace*, Reshaping Work, 6–15.
Kountouris N. (2017) The concept of 'worker' in European Labour Law: fragmentation, autonomy and scope', *Industrial Law Journal*, 47 (2), 192–225.
Public Policy Research Center (2022) Gigmetar: Gig workers in the region, May 2022. http://gigmetar.publicpolicy.rs/en/region-en-2022-1
Rainone S. (2022) Labour rights beyond employment status: insights from the Competition Law Guidelines on collective bargaining, in Addabbo T. et al. (eds.) *Defining and protecting autonomous work: a multidisciplinary approach*, Palgrave, 167–191.
All links were checked on 17 October 2023.

PART IV

BEYOND EUROPE AND FOOD DELIVERY

12. Challenges in advocating recognition and protection among delivery platform workers across the Americas: cases from Argentina, Chile, Mexico and the US

María Figueroa and María Eugenia Rodríguez

INTRODUCTION

The global expansion of app-based food delivery has sparked renewed collective action by grassroots organisations aiming to ameliorate the precarious conditions of workers in this burgeoning industry. In the US, the market reached sales of $26.1 billion in 2022 and is expected to reach $46.5 billion by 2028, at an annual growth rate of 10 per cent (IMARC 2023); in Latin America, the market is $6.5 billion and this is also expected to grow at about 10 per cent during 2023 to 2028 (theorg.com 2023).

The top platform companies in the US are DoorDash, Uber Eats and Grubhub, which is owned by Just Eat Takeaway (based in the Netherlands). Together, these three companies have captured 98 per cent of the US market by order volume (IMARC 2023). Uber Eats operates in seven Latin American countries, including Costa Rica, the Dominican Republic, Ecuador, El Salvador, Guatemala, Panama and Chile (UberEats.com). Uber also owns Cornershop, an on-demand grocery delivery service that started in Chile and Mexico in 2015 and operates in five Latin American countries and Canada.[1] The top Latin American platforms are Rappi (headquartered in Colombia), Pedidos Ya (headquartered in Uruguay but owned by Delivery Hero since 2014) and Ifood (based in Brazil). Together, these three companies outcompete Uber Eats and DiDi Food (established in China) in platform delivery market share across the region (Beyer 2023). Like their US and European peers, the Latin American platforms have expanded thanks to the growth of financial investment in the industry, especially venture capital, which surpassed $15 billion in the region in 2021. Pedidos Ya operates in 15 countries in Latin America, and Rappi in nine (Andonova et al. 2023). Ifood operates in Brazil, which is the biggest market in the region.

This chapter delves into the strategic approaches employed by trade unions and worker organisations in advocating fair labour conditions among platform food couriers. The focus extends across the US and three Latin American countries – Argentina, Chile and Mexico. The analysis aims to identify how institutional frameworks and industry structures shape worker strategies while examining potential sources of worker power. Additionally, the chapter explores the impact of exogenous factors, such as migration and the Covid-19 pandemic, on the industry and how this influences collective action and representation, particularly given the pandemic's role in magnifying unemployment and migration while amplifying the demand for socially distanced food services. The assessment includes how immigration status is shaping the regulatory initiatives and worker organising dynamics in Latin America and the US.

The chapter seeks to contribute to the ongoing discourse on the role of new technology in shaping work dynamics and collective action. The primary objectives revolve around identifying the commonalities and variations in worker organisations' strategic approaches. Specifically, the chapter aims to comprehend how such approaches are shaped by the institutional framework, industry structure and workforce composition in each country.

To address the research questions, we draw upon the fissurisation of work framework (Weil 2014) as well as associational and structural power frameworks (Joyce et al. 2023; Maffie and Gough 2023; Vandaele 2018). Fissurisation manifests as the classification of couriers as independent contractors, pivotal to the platforms' business model, shifting labour and social protections burdens to workers. This classification also determines the policies and legal approaches pursued by advocates in each country. The legal enactment approach, which consists of obtaining improvements in labour conditions through policy or legal changes rather than collective bargaining, has been identified as a fitting strategy for platform workers due to their lack of structural power resulting from geographic dispersion (Joyce et al. 2021). Additionally, potential sources of workplace power have been identified in the disruptive capacity of couriers within the just-in-time food delivery system (Vandaele 2018) and in workers' ability to withdraw labour from multiple competing platforms (Maffie and Gough 2023).

This chapter integrates these frameworks to explore sources of associational and structural power among couriers in the selected countries, emphasising the potential leverage that couriers hold through multi-apping and disruption in the production-distribution chain. Further, it hypothesises that collaboration between courier organisations and unions campaigning in the fast-food sector could significantly enhance workers' structural power. The empirical evidence base includes regulatory reviews, ethnographic research, worker interviews and observations at worker gatherings, demonstrations and public hearings. Case selection was based on the level of regulatory activity and data accessibility.

DELIVERY PLATFORMS IN THE AMERICAS: MIGRATION AS LABOUR SURPLUS AND THE EVOLUTION OF CONSUMER PREFERENCES SINCE THE PANDEMIC

The success of platform-based food delivery companies hinges on leveraging network effects, driven by an ever-expanding base of consumers and couriers. The industry's growth on the continent has largely been driven by two main factors, initially induced by the onset of Covid-19. First and foremost is the increase in the supply of labour which resulted from pandemic-related migration and unemployment in other sectors; second are changes in consumer preferences. In both the US and Latin America, the pandemic triggered the fast growth of demand for food services without human contact. In the US, the industry in 2021 was four times larger than at the start of 2018 (Ahuja et al. 2021). Additionally, the growth in demand for delivery services has been aided by the increased use of internet technology by the overall population and, specifically for Latin America, by the increase in consumer buying power in large urban centres.

In terms of the labour supply factor, platform couriers represent a small fraction of the employed population in most countries, but this workforce is expected to grow in the coming years. Pandemic unemployment triggered mass migration, which also increased the supply of labour for the food delivery platforms. As a result of its low entry barriers, the industry has become a quick source of income for thousands of immigrant workers across the continent, including Venezuelan migrants in South America and in US cities such as New York (Silverstein 2023).[2] For example, in Santiago (Chile), 71 per cent of platform couriers were immigrants in 2019, with 87 per cent of them originating from Venezuela (Asenjo and Coddou 2021). In Argentina, in 2018, 80 per cent of migrant couriers had migrated from Venezuela. In 2019, the platforms Rappi and Glovo engaged 83.6 per cent and 65.7 per cent of their workforces as recent migrants, respectively (Madariaga et al. 2019). The profound economic and political crisis in Venezuela has triggered the second-largest displacement in the world such that, in March 2023, there were over 6 million Venezuelan migrants and refugees residing in Latin America and the Caribbean, and another hundred thousand in the US (UN IOM 2023). Although Argentina, Chile and Mexico are not the largest host countries, they have still experienced a considerable inflow of Venezuelans in recent years.

Another characteristic that increases workers' vulnerability in this industry is that platform work often represents the primary income source, with many workers being heads of households. Of surveyed couriers, eighty-one per cent in Mexico, 61.3 per cent in Argentina and more than 80 per cent in New York report that platform work is their main occupation and primary source of income (Alba Vega et al. 2021; Figueroa et al. 2021; Madariaga et al. 2019). In Santiago, 53 per cent of couriers have dependants (Asenjo and Coddou 2021). This dependency on courier work might represent a deterrent for workers to participate in organising activities and, consequently, to face potential deactivation.

Fuelled by a rich reserve of often undocumented migrants through which it has easy access to the labour market, platform delivery work has profited from these workers' vulnerability and further exacerbated their precarious working and living conditions. Because of the lack of documentation, thousands of immigrant workers can only work as independent contractors in the US if they are able to obtain a tax identification number or otherwise rent a platform account in the informal economy (Alba Vega et al. 2021; Figueroa et al. 2021; Madariaga et al. 2019). Some Latin American countries have labour regulations that work in favour of the platforms' business strategy of hiring couriers as independent contractors – such regulations limit the percentage of foreign employees that companies can hire (SUSESO 2023). Since couriers are categorised as self-employed, most of them work in the informal sector and do not have access to social protection and other benefits that regular employees enjoy. In Mexico, for instance, the self-employed represent 23 per cent of the employed population, but only 0.1 per cent of them have access to social security (Martinez 2022).

Thus, platform companies have contributed to the expansion of precarious and informal work across the continent and especially in Latin America, which exhibits high levels of economic informality (ILOSTAT 2023a). Recent assessments in Argentina, Chile and Mexico have found no robust evidence of platforms adhering to the Fairwork organisation's principles of fair platform work (Fairwork 2022, 2023a, 2023b).

The following section develops the US case, starting from an analysis of the specific way in which platforms benefit from the grey areas of regulatory frameworks and how they actively resist regulatory changes that would favour workers.

THE INSTITUTIONAL CONTEXT AND PLATFORMS' POLICY AGENDA IN THE US

Platform couriers, along with other platform workers in the US, are classified as independent contractors and, as such, are excluded from all federal and state-level labour and employment laws. Independent contractors are not covered by the National Labor Relations Act (NLRA), which grants collective bargaining rights to workers classified as employees. Additionally, anti-trust laws prohibit independent contractors from engaging in collective bargaining over pay and other conditions of work (Sherman Anti-trust Act 1890, 2004; Clayton Anti-trust Act 1914). This legal framework is the key factor explaining the focus of trade unions, worker centres and other worker advocates in adopting legal enactment approaches to improve the working and living conditions of all platform workers, including food delivery couriers.

Platform companies, in turn, have fiercely resisted pro-worker policy changes by spending hundreds of millions of dollars to defeat such initiatives and to promote regulation that would advance their business strategies. Just one example of the platforms' aggressive approach to policymaking is their successful campaign to pass Proposition 22 in California and thereby achieve exemption from the AB5 Law, which would have required them to classify drivers and couriers as employees (Dubal 2022). The platforms spent more than $200 million to convince voters that California's new AB5 Law was going to hurt platform workers by taking away their scheduling flexibility and ultimately their source of income. Platform companies have also built political influence by donating abundantly to both the Democratic Party and the Republican Party at federal and state levels as well as founding the Flex Association, which proclaims itself as the voice of the platform economy in policy advocacy, especially in Washington DC, to advance their policy priorities more effectively. The delivery platforms DoorDash, Uber, Grubhub, and Gopuff are among the eight founding members of Flex (PR Newswire 2022).

One of the main legislative strategies implemented by the platforms since 2014 has consisted of seeking exemptions from state labour and employment laws to avoid platform workers being classified as workers. This exemption strategy has involved codifying independent contractor status for platform workers, thereby exempting them from the coverage of such laws (Pinto et al. 2019). Platform companies have concentrated their legislative efforts on the ride-hailing sector, but these have, nonetheless, had reverberations across the delivery industry. Uber, for example, has actively lobbied for laws that would classify ride-hailing drivers as independent contractors and has achieved such regulations in at least half of US states (NELP 2022). In New York State, the platform companies promoted legislation that would codify independent contractor status for platform workers in all sectors in exchange for bargaining rights. In 2019, when an independent worker proposal was introduced, it was halted by a coalition of unions and worker advocates who argued that platform workers would have had to negotiate pay, benefits and all other rights without any existing minimum standards being applicable to them. In 2021, the platform companies promoted a modified version of this legislation, including additional provisions on unionisation rights, but the initiative was again defeated because of opposition by worker advocates and some unions (Scheiber 2021).

In many markets, ride-hailing and food and grocery delivery platforms engage workers as drivers and couriers at the same time. Thus, in Massachusetts, Uber and Lyft joined with DoorDash and grocery delivery Instacart to fund a ballot initiative that would have declared in state law that drivers are independent contractors, while providing them with some new benefits, although this was ultimately declared ineligible (Ruckstuhl 2021; Young 2022).

Even when they do not cover food delivery couriers, new policies established for ride-hailing drivers usually set a model that is replicated in the food delivery sector. This is the case with the municipal laws passed in New York and Seattle (discussed immediately following), as well as a legislative initiative in Massachusetts, promoted by Local 32BJ of the Service Employees International Union (SEIU) and the Independent Drivers Guild of the International Association of Machinists (IDG-IAM). The Massachusetts initiative focuses on ride-hailing platforms only and, as such, is not applicable to couriers on food delivery platforms. It is interesting to note, however, that the state legislators sponsoring the proposal explicitly stated that they hoped its passage 'will create a model that can extend to other sectors' (Lisinski 2023).

At federal level, initiatives to extend labour rights to platform workers have received widespread support from the politically powerful national unions and the worker advocacy community. Such initiatives include the Protecting the Right to Organise Act (PRO Act), which was first introduced in 2019 and reintroduced in 2021 and 2023 (HR 2474 2019; HR 842 2021; HR 20 2023), as well as a recent regulation issued by the Department of Labor. While the PRO Act has not yet been passed, the Department of Labor regulation was issued in January 2024, establishing more strict legal tests to prevent the classification of platform workers and other on-demand workers as independent contractors, thereby granting them rights under federal labour and employment laws (US DOL 2024). This new regulation is likely to intensify the lobbying efforts of the platforms, which have been actively campaigning against these federal policy changes through their lobbying organisation, Flex.

While the platforms have been able to forge a cohesive and coherent policy agenda, the labour movement, including unions, worker centres and advocates, is far from reaching a unified policy strategy to advance platform workers' protections and rights to organise. Platforms have actively promoted this persistent division among worker organisations by funding platform worker unions, as Uber and Lyft did in the ride-hailing sector in New York City in 2016 with the Independent Drivers' Guild, an affiliate of the International Association of Machinists (Scheiber 2021). Another divisive tactic that platforms are using is to establish alliances with unions and state labour federations to promote legislation that would provide bargaining rights to platform workers without classifying them as employees. This is their strategy for a 'third way' worker category, which would deliver collective bargaining rights and some benefits (such as portable health and pension funds) without employee classification (Sumagaysay 2022). In New York State, the platforms gained the support of the Machinists Union and the NY State Labor Federation to advance their 2019 and 2021 legislative proposals for bargaining rights and limited benefits for platform workers. On both occasions, the proposals were halted by the efforts of coalitions of worker centres, advocates and SEIU Local 32BJ, which opposed the legislation, arguing it would codify independent contractor status for platform workers, providing them with sub-standard protection (Scheiber 2021).

Most legal protections achieved for platform workers in the US have been at local or municipal level rather than via state laws. As long as state laws do not pre-empt the enactment of local protections for workers, municipalities and other local governments can establish worker protections for independent contractors, including platform workers. Thus, local governments do not need to overrule or contradict existing federal or state labour and employment laws as they are not granting independent contractors the protections provided to regular employees. Rather, local governments could create new protections for independent contractors because their legal framework does not stop them from doing so. This has been the case for protections established for platform workers in New York City, Seattle, Philadelphia and some cities in California (NELP 2022). New York and Seattle were the first US cities to establish basic protections and minimum pay for ride-hailing workers in 2018 and 2020 respectively, and more recently for app-based food delivery couriers in 2021 and 2022. In New York City, ordinances were enacted to set minimum pay standards for ride-hailing drivers in 2018 and platform food couriers in 2021. However, the platforms have actively (and often successfully) lobbied to close this narrow window of opportunity by preventing the enactment of municipal laws that would provide labour protections to platform workers. Currently, only nine states allow the passage of municipal laws protecting platform workers, while another handful allow such policy changes only in certain cities (NELP 2022).

In addition to pursuing the same policy strategy (municipal laws), the New York and Seattle cases involve key commonalities, including the presence of progressive local governments featuring elected officials from the Democratic Party, the influence of politically powerful unions such as the SEIU (which has supported policy efforts in both cities), the ability of worker organisations to leverage their symbolic power and, no less importantly, the impact of the pandemic on worker conditions and organising. New York and Seattle were ground zero for the Covid-19 pandemic on the US east and west coasts in early 2020. Largely because of the pandemic, the platform-based food delivery industry grew exponentially in both cities, leading to the concentration of tens of thousands of delivery workers in a delimited urban area (New York with 65,000 workers and Seattle with 40,000). Furthermore, in both cities, there was a precedent for establishing local protections for platform workers as ride-hailing worker advocates had successfully implemented policy initiatives for minimum pay and other protections.

US CASE STUDY 1: NEW YORK'S COURIERS FIGHT FOR A MINIMUM PAY RATE

As everywhere else, the pandemic exacerbated the already precarious conditions that low-wage workers were facing, including members of the Workers' Justice Project (WJP), an alt-labour organisation founded in 2010. Before the pandemic, WJP represented low-wage, mostly immigrant, workers in the construction and house-cleaning industries in New York City (NYC). By the summer, WJP leaders had learned that many of their members who had lost their jobs in the construction industry were working as platform food couriers and facing severe challenges in terms of low pay and health and safety risks, even becoming victims of crimes such as bike thefts and physical assaults. Studies conducted by Cornell University and the NYC Department of Consumer and Worker Protection (DCWP)[3] found that the average hourly pay of food couriers was approximately $7, excluding tips and net of operating costs such as vehicle maintenance (Figueroa et al. 2021). This hourly rate was well below the legal minimum wage of $15 per hour for all workers in NYC (NYC DCWP 2022).

To address these severe conditions, WJP started a worker mobilisation campaign to achieve municipal-level policy changes that would grant basic protections to food couriers, organising a series of highly successful worker actions including two marches to City Hall with thousands of workers. These mobilisations revealed the presence of a grassroots movement, largely sustained by natural networks and self-organising structures. Of important note is that

NYC couriers are a largely immigrant workforce, with the majority having migrated from Latin American countries (Figueroa et al. 2021; NYC DCWP 2022). This characteristic of the workforce might explain the formation of self-organising structures based on social or family networks imported from the workers' countries of origin. These successful actions led to the formation of Los Deliveristas Unidos (Delivery Workers United; LDU), with WJP as its home base, which emerged as the face of the advocacy campaign, receiving wide attention and support from progressive elected officials as well as SEIU 32BJ and Local 100 of the Transport Workers Union (TWU). These two unions, especially SEIU 32BJ, provided support by participating in rallies and demonstrations, and having their leaders speak at them.

More than a year of grassroots organising and policy advocacy efforts by WJP/LDU culminated in the passage of a set of municipal ordinances in September 2021, the first of their kind in the US delivery courier industry, providing basic protections such as access to toilet facilities, trip distance limits, safeguards against unfair banking fees and, most importantly, minimum pay (Meyer and Hicks 2021; Yakas 2021).

Among these municipal laws, Local Law 115 (2021) charged DCWP with the production of a study that would help determine the level of minimum pay that digital platforms must provide to food delivery couriers. After completing an industry study in 2022, DCWP issued its first regulatory proposal in November 2022, setting the minimum pay at $23.82 per hour. This first proposal received intense opposition from the platforms, forcing DCWP to issue a second in early 2023. This set minimum pay at $19.96, $3.86 lower, due to the introduction of a multi-apping factor in the calculation of hourly pay. DCWP introduced this in response to criticisms by the platforms that couriers may work for multiple platforms and that they should not pay for the time that workers spend delivering for other apps.

Despite these concessions, once the city mayor had signed the new minimum pay regulation, the three dominant platforms, Uber, DoorDash and Grubhub lodged cases in the state Supreme Court to block its implementation. In September 2023, the Supreme Court judge denied the platforms' requests and allowed the pay increase to take place, but the platforms immediately appealed, requesting a stop on implementation while the appeal was underway (Browning and Ley 2023). The WJP/LDU, along with SEIU 32BJ and the National Employment Law Project (NELP), filed an amici curiae with the court opposing the appeal and making the case for the prompt implementation of the law (NYS Supreme Court 2023). Finally, in early December 2023, the New York Court of Appeals ruled in favour of the implementation of the minimum pay, which went into effect immediately (Wiessner 2023).

Parallel to this year-long legal battle, platforms waged a campaign of fear against couriers, including push notifications encouraging workers to testify against raising their own pay, claiming that this would 'make conditions far worse' for workers and 'negatively impact flexibility' (Hirschfeld-Kroen 2023; Masmoudi 2023). Unfortunately, the campaign succeeded in creating division between workers, significantly diminishing the mobilisation levels seen in previous years, which may have negative impacts on the implementation of minimum pay.

Moreover, the new law itself will require significant resources on the part of WJP/LDU and the DCWP in terms of monitoring compliance, preventing business practices that undermine the pay and safety of workers, including the bundling of multiple orders in one trip and restricting the hours in which workers can connect to the app (Schwartz and Weber 2023). An immediate response by the platforms to the implementation of the law was to allow tipping only after the delivery was completed. This tip policy change created confusion among consumers and frustration among workers as their earnings were negatively affected (Irizarry 2023).

US CASE STUDY 2: ADVOCATING COURIERS' RIGHTS IN SEATTLE

About 4,000 kilometres west of New York, trade unions and their progressive allies in the municipal government of Seattle (in Washington state) have also been at the forefront of policy innovation to provide protections for platform couriers, including the more than 40,000 Seattle couriers who work for restaurant and grocery delivery platforms. Similar to New York, Black and Latinx workers are over-represented among Seattle platform couriers, comprising almost 42 per cent of the platform-based workforce but less than 29 per cent of the overall labour force (City of Seattle 2022).

An organisation that has played a key role in promoting pro-worker policy innovations has been Working Washington (WW), founded in 2011 by leaders from the SEIU and its Local 775 as part of the union's 'Fight for a Fair Economy' campaign. For more than 12 years, Working Washington has waged various successful campaigns for better pay and benefits in the Seattle-Tacoma area, including the first $15 minimum wage in the United States. WW has also led organising and policy initiatives nationally, connecting worker groups through social media campaigns.

WW's first campaign with platform workers took place in 2019, when it ran a social media campaign against Instacart, a grocery delivery platform that operates across the US. Couriers protested extensively in digital forums, such as Reddit and Facebook groups, against Instacart's policy of counting tips toward the guaranteed minimum pay. This national campaign succeeded in getting the company to reverse its policy, and even to grant back-pay to its couriers, and gave rise to WW's national Pay Up campaign, focused on promoting minimum pay and other protections for platform workers (Roose 2019).

At the height of the pandemic in 2020, WW ran a three-day national strike in which platform couriers working for Postmates, which had been bought by Uber, were encouraged not to pick up any orders from the fast-food chain Chipotle. The strike was part of the Pay Up campaign and had the goal of pressuring the platform to provide sick leave, hazard pay (compensation for work that entailed exposure to the Covid-19 virus) and personal protective equipment like masks and gloves (Working Washington 2020). Although in a previous inquiry no evidence was found of its success, the action did serve to highlight platform worker needs during the pandemic and revealed a potential vulnerability in the structure of the industry, fast-food chains having been identified as the platforms' largest clients in large urban markets (Figueroa et al. 2021).

Another union actively engaged in organising and policy campaigns in the platform economy in Seattle and Washington State is Teamsters Union Local 117, which has advocated, along with WW, for the passage of paid sick leave for couriers and other platform workers in Seattle, as well as for Washington State's collective bargaining law for ride-hailing workers (Stiffler 2023).

The other key social actor on Seattle's progressive policymaking stage is the municipal government, which is made up mostly of elected officials from the Democratic Party and which has a long tradition of supporting innovative worker protections. Among these are the scheduling regulations for food-service and fast-food workers, which provide workers with advanced notice of schedules (similar to the Fair Work Week ordinance of New York City),[4] wage theft protections and a Domestic Workers Bill of Rights (Schwartz and Weber 2023). In 2020, the Seattle government issued minimum pay standards for ride-hailing workers engaged by Lyft and Uber, similar to the New York City local law passed in 2018 (Groover 2020).

The dominant platform companies in the Seattle food and grocery delivery market are DoorDash, Grubhub, Uber Eats, Instacart and Gopuff (Working Washington 2022). Unlike in New York, most Seattle food couriers use cars or motorcycles to make deliveries. The mode of transport has an impact on couriers' operating costs and, thereby, the calculation of what fair minimum pay would be: the government agency determining this factors in operating costs to ensure that minimum pay yields an adequate net pay per hour for couriers. In Seattle (and in NYC, too), the lack of transparency on the part of the platforms in releasing workers' pay data has hindered the determination of minimum pay. For instance, DoorDash in Seattle claimed that its delivery workers made $28 per hour (on delivery time) by adding tips to base pay, unilaterally set by the platforms, omitting mileage costs (fuel expenses) and not accounting for waiting time (Working Washington 2022). A survey by WW revealed that, after accounting for mileage and waiting time, the average pay rate for delivery workers in Seattle was $9.58 per hour, below the city's legal minimum wage of $17.27 in 2022 (Working Washington 2022).

To bring the pay level of couriers to legal minimum levels, the Seattle City Council passed the App-Based Workers Minimum Payment Ordinance SMC 8.37 in May 2022 (City of Seattle 2022). The local law went into effect in January 2024, providing a minimum pay rate for delivery workers that would enable them to earn Seattle's minimum wage and receive the standard mileage reimbursement set by the US Internal Revenue Service. The new law also provides for data transparency, most importantly the right of couriers to receive upfront disclosures of information on order offers, as well as receipts and payment records. Another important provision protects couriers from platforms' adverse responses to refusing orders or limiting hours of availability. Lastly, the new law provides flexibility for couriers to connect to the platforms 'at any date, time of day, or for any amount of time', but without exceeding the maximum amount of consecutive working time to protect worker and public safety (City of Seattle 2022).

As a result of the advocacy efforts of WW and Teamsters Local 117, Seattle became the first US city to require sick leave for couriers and other platform workers in March 2023. Through the new rule, these benefits, provided temporarily during the pandemic, became permanent (City of Seattle 2023a). This ordinance provides sick and 'safe' time benefits, including paid time off for illness and preventative health care, unemployment due to a public health emergency or other safety reason, a family member's school closure, and for seeking assistance in cases of domestic violence, sexual assault or stalking (Stiffler 2023).

In August 2023, the City Council passed a further law, again the first of its kind in the country, to protect platform workers from unjustified deactivation. The law covers platform workers who make food and grocery deliveries or carry out other on-demand jobs, and requires platforms to base deactivation on 'reasonable' company policies as well as to provide 14-day advance notice and a 'human review' (City of Seattle 2023b). This is a widespread issue for couriers, who may be deactivated for 'rejecting too many orders, being unavailable during certain days or times, or unknown reasons' (Rolph and Soper 2023). Like the minimum pay and paid sick leave protections, this latest policy victory for platform workers also resulted from WW's Pay Up campaign.

The platforms have not yet challenged Seattle's new laws through litigation, although one industry group, Technet, has expressed opposition to the protection against unfair deactivation, arguing that it would compromise the privacy rights of workers and consumers (Rolph and Soper 2023). Of note is that Seattle's minimum pay law did not call for a study to determine its level, whereas NYC's law had taken the approach of commissioning such a study; this contributed to the implementation delay and gave more room to the platforms to challenge the regulatory initiative. Apart from these differences, the two cities have set historic labour standards for platform couriers in the US and across the rest of the continent.

THE PLIGHT OF DELIVERY WORKERS IN ARGENTINA: LEGAL BATTLES, UNIONISATION EFFORTS AND STRUGGLES FOR RECOGNITION

Delivery workers are not recognised as formal salaried employees in Argentina; instead, they are categorised as self-employed (Elbert and Negri 2021). In this area, there is a lack of regulation by the state that allows platforms to avoid the responsibilities related to health and safety and other labour benefits by which formal employers must abide. Consequently, the Ley de Contrato de Trabajo (LCT; Labour Contract Law) does not regulate self-employment, while the Código Civil y Comercial de la República Argentina (CCCRA; the Civil and Commercial Code of Argentina), in its Article 1251, regulates those activities as contracts for services.

In the second half of the twentieth century, therefore, self-employment has not been covered by labour law in Argentina even though it has become an important part of the employment structure in the country (accounting for 25 per cent of the employed urban population) (Madariaga et al. 2019). However, the labour courts do tend to turn away from the use of contracts for services, replacing them with labour contracts, when they identify the presence of a dependent or subordinate relationship in line with different criteria, such as legal, economic or technical subordination, and where service has accrued over time, the worker follows instructions and orders and there is exclusivity.

As a result, worker organisations in Argentina have sought recognition of the labour relationship as the key element in accessing legal protections. Different political formations proposed no fewer than six draft bills between 2020 and 2021 that attempted to regulate platform workers (ILAW 2022) by defining and qualifying the labour relationship and regulating the working day, as well as demanding data and algorithm transparency, protection against labour accidents, and the right to unionisation.[5] However, these proposals have not yet resulted in new legal provisions being adopted.

Couriers have also sought judicial recognition of their employment status. For example, after the firing (by deactivation) of union leaders, Asociación de Personal de Plataformas (APP; Association of Platform Workers) lodged a case against Rappi on the grounds of its 'anti-trade union' practices. The judge of the first instance ordered re-engagement, but Rappi appealed, and the second instance tribunal reversed the order in July 2019, arguing that it was impossible to determine the relationship between the platform and its couriers. This interpretation suggests that the legal relationship between platforms and couriers is an ex ante requirement in terms of the recognition of the rights of association and collective bargaining (Hartmann Cortes 2021).

Furthermore, local authorities have attempted to regulate platform practices in areas other than their employment status. In 2020, the Ministerio de Trabajo (MT; Ministry of Labour) in Buenos Aires province surveyed 172 delivery workers in different municipalities to assess their labour conditions. As a result, in 2021 and 2022, MT fined Glovo, Pedidos Ya and Rappi for violating the LCT because it identified features of a dependent relationship.[6] In 2023, in an attempt to regulate delivery services, the Senado de la provincia de Buenos Aires (Senate of Buenos Aires province) introduced a bill to create the mandatory registry of platform couriers to keep a record of the delivery activities carried out by motorcycles, bikes and cars (Irungaray 2023).

In terms of the forms of the collective representation of couriers in Argentina, three types of worker organisation have been identified (Menendez et al. 2023), including unions that preceded the arrival of the platforms, those created after their entrance and non-union grassroots organisations. Asociación Sindical de Mensajeros y Motocicilistas (ASiMM), based in Buenos Aires, has represented couriers since before the arrival of the platforms and, in 2017, began representing couriers working for Pedidos Ya. However, this union rejects the idea of the representation of informal workers and has not been receptive to couriers' demands to gain labour rights while retaining flexible working days (Bachoer 2022). Unions formed after the platforms' arrival include APP and Sindicato de Base de Trabajadores de Reparto por Aplicación (SiTraRepA; Union of App-Based Delivery Workers). Formed in 2018, APP has put together collective claims, promoted direct actions such as street mobilisations and received support from labour lawyers with close ties to Central de Trabajadores Argentinos (CTA; Argentine Workers' Central Union). APP's main goal has been to achieve the recognition of the labour relationship (Arias et al. 2021). Formed in 2020, SiTraRepA is also looking for recognition as a union. Lastly, the most active non-union grassroots organisation is Agrupación de Trabajadores de Reparto (ATR; Delivery Workers Collective). The formation of APP and ATR has been broadly documented in the (Argentine) literature (Bachoer 2022; Menendez et al. 2023), so this chapter examines the creation of SiTraRepA.

Working conditions during the Covid-19 pandemic were a key factor in the formation of this union (according to a SiTraRepA leader in interview): being portrayed as essential workers, but without any labour and employment rights, was what motivated workers to join it. Among the challenges workers faced were the lack of personal protective equipment, which the platforms did not provide, as well as social distancing, imposed and enforced with GPS technology by the platforms, which kept them isolated from one another. Additionally, platforms deactivated couriers' accounts and did not pay bonuses even though couriers reached company-set targets. In response, worker leaders took their grievances to platforms' headquarters, but found nobody there, leading workers to refer to them as 'ghost companies'. Consequently, they brought their demands to Ministerio de Trabajo, Empleo y Seguridad Social (MTEySS; Ministry of Labour, Employment and Social Security), which made it clear that it did not have legal jurisdiction because the couriers did not have union representation and had been classified as self-employed. The MTEySS response highlighted the need to challenge the platforms' narrative of workers' autonomy, and the formation of SiTraRepA was the response. Its members believe that having a union is the only way to elevate their voice in public forums and advance regulatory proposals for labour protections.

Currently, SiTraRepA has around 2,500 members (Lutzky 2022) across Argentina. The effective organising tactics that this union has implemented include Paradas Solidarias (Solidarity Hubs) as well as building solidarity networks in Argentina and with organisations of precarious workers in other countries.[7] Solidarity Hubs were established as a form of protest against the platform companies, highlighting couriers' precarious working conditions, including a lack of access to toilet facilities and places to charge their phones and get water or essential tools to repair their bikes. They have been run on a weekly basis, becoming a meeting spot for couriers to grab a hot drink during the winter and 'where the political life of the union takes place', as the SiTraRepA leader revealed.

Nevertheless, it can be observed that delivery workers in Argentina had begun to express their demands prior to the pandemic. For example, in 2018, workers from Rappi, led by APP, held the first digital strike to protest against changes in a platform algorithm that, among other things, assigned deliveries (couriers could not reject more than three deliveries) and reduced delivery payments. The strike was successful due to the strategic time selected for it. Thus, APP leaders were able to meet with the platforms to express their demands but were then blocked from the app, with these undercover dismissals motivating the legal case referred to earlier (Bachoer 2022).

Another conflict before the pandemic was launched at Pedidos Ya between February and June 2019, triggered by the dismissal of 450 delivery workers. Of note is that, in 2017, Pedidos Ya initially hired delivery workers as employees on hourly contracts and with benefits. The union ASiMM represented them. However, after the arrival of Glovo and Rappi in 2018, Pedidos Ya adopted the same practice of freelance or self-employed labour, laying off those hired as employees. This struggle achieved the reinstatement of a small fraction of workers after the intervention of the national minister of labour; moreover, ATR emerged out of the disagreements between delivery workers and ASiMM (Bachoer 2022).

During 2020, ATR delivery workers participated in at least four international strikes to demand improvements in their labour conditions. The articulation of those protests relied on digital channels such as WhatsApp and Zoom. However, delivery workers did not participate to the extent anticipated by the union's leaders because the platforms offered high rates for deliveries subsequent to the announcement of the strikes, while participating in the strike meant not earning any money that day (Bachoer 2022).

Elbert and Negri (2021) highlight two features about worker mobilisations during the pandemic: 'grassroot organizations experienced a rapid growth... and the actions of protest gained an international character'. Moreover, they claim that, during this period, workers guaranteeing the circulation and consumption of goods boosted their structural power which, in turn, translated into increasing associative power. Consequently, their mobilisations and the growth in their membership and geographic coverage stimulated public debate about their working conditions and relationships with the platform companies.

During 2022 and 2023, SiTraRepA actively organised street mobilisations[8] in support of its request for formal recognition by MTEySS. The economic downturn after the pandemic, characterised by high inflation, has hit delivery workers hard. Some couriers continue to earn less than one dollar per delivery, a situation on which the union continues to build. Moreover, it has participated in international forums to strengthen solidarity with other delivery workers globally.[9]

NAVIGATING LEGAL REFORMS AND THE ORGANISING CHALLENGES: THE LANDSCAPE OF PLATFORM WORK IN CHILE

Chile was the first country in Latin America to modify its labour code to incorporate a new framework that regulates the contracts of transport couriers engaged in digital platform work.[10] Before this law, platform workers had attempted to gain recognition of the presence of a labour relationship through two alternative routes: the legal system, via two cases brought before the courts, and the legislative one, through two bills proposed by different political groupings.[11]

The two court cases were lodged in May 2020 by lawyers retained by FIEL.[12] They followed the mass dismissal (of around 50 and 70 delivery workers, respectively, achieved by account deactivations) arising from street mobilisations[13] protesting against changes made the previous month that degraded working conditions in Pedidos Ya. Both cases requested the acknowledgement of the existence of an employment relationship, compensation for dismissal due to union activities, and the payment of other labour benefits. In May 2021, the judge rejected the demands in one of the cases.[14] An appeal was made, but this too was dismissed (Riquelme 2021). Consequently, the group of riders involved in the second case agreed to a deal that included financial compensation with Pedidos Ya before the court decision.

Chile's new law (Law 21,431) was enacted in March 2022 and came into effect in September 2022. It creates a new legal framework that addresses employment status, creating two categories of platform worker: dependent and independent. Furthermore, it entitles platform couriers in the delivery sector, regardless of their employment status, to benefit from some protections regarding transparency and access to information, the prohibition of discrimination by automated decision-making systems, matters of health and safety, and the right of both dependent and self-employed platform workers to organise in trade unions and bargain collectively with their employers (Leyton and Azocar 2022). Law 21,431 is administered by Ministerio del Trabajo y Previsión Social (MiniTrab; Ministry of Labour and Social Security) under Dictamen (Code of Practice) 1831/39, which identifies 'general and common subordination and dependence' factors as evidence of the presence of a labour relationship. Among the factors considered are platforms' mediation of consumer demand in the form of the orders received by workers; control over which tasks must be executed; direct or indirect control over how much money will be paid for the execution of such tasks; direct or indirect control of the execution of the work and the performance of the worker at work; and the evaluation of the work carried out.[15]

MiniTrab's interpretation of the Law has been highly controversial.[16] Uber Eats filed a protective appeal in November 2022,[17] claiming that the Dictamen 'incurs serious illegality' because it established examples of subordination and dependence that the company regarded as contradictory to Law 21,431 (Benavente 2022). In particular, it claimed that this interpretation would imply that the 18,000 people offering their services through Uber's apps would become dependent workers. Consequently, it regarded that the Dictamen violated its constitutional rights to equality before the law, freedom of labour contracting and the right to carry out lawful economic activities (Cárdenas 2022). In April 2023 (Diario Constitucional 2023), the Court of Santiago rejected the protective appeal,[18] arguing that the Dictamen described an abstract interpretation which was not a statement of specific cases and that MiniTrab had acted within the scope of its competence in publishing it.

Nevertheless, Law 21,431 has shortcomings, including in relation to tax collection, the settlement of processes between those who use various platforms to generate income (such as tax and social security payments) and the need for it to encompass new types of platform, not just transport and delivery ones (Azuara et al. 2022), given its exclusion of platforms that act as digital marketplaces (online platforms).

The biggest shortcoming, however, is that the law does not define a priori whether there is a dependent relationship in employment; it determines that this is the duty of the judge and is based on the specific facts of what it is that workers are actually doing – so, on a case-by-case basis. Furthermore, the independent worker is considered something of a hybrid figure because the law does not require economic dependence before some forms of labour protections can be extended to them (such as the right to form a union). However, it does attempt a degree of protection for one group – independent platform workers – by providing them with some rights to which dependent workers are commonly entitled (Arab Verdugo and Frontaura Marzolo 2022).

Focusing on couriers' organising efforts in Chile, it should be noted that these were, as elsewhere, triggered by the pandemic. During casual gatherings and informal conversations (for example while waiting for orders) during the pandemic, couriers realised the different practices that Pedidos Ya used to control its workers, for example and the basic conditions required to carry out the job: schedules, changes in earnings definitions, failures to reimburse unpaid orders, increased delivery distances and so on. Moreover, they identified generally that they received less money than expected and had to travel longer distances than before. As a result, all those concerns, on top of safety issues, motivated the couriers to create WhatsApp groups in several municipalities in order to be in touch and offer network support. They started to put out anonymous statements on social media networks to make their labour conditions visible, and they organised street mobilisations.

Among the organising attempts, mention can be made of Riders Unidos Ya, founded by Venezuelan migrants in Chile, and other groups such as Repartidores Penquistas, located in Concepcion, and Shoppers (in Cornershop). In association with other movements, they set up Mancomunal de Repartidores por App (MAREA), a trade union federation for app-based delivery couriers.[19] There is also Autodefensa Motorizada,[20] a group of riders that have developed different initiatives to address some of the main problems that couriers face which the local authorities or the company do not deal with, such as getting their motorcycles returned in cases of robbery,[21] lobbying activities to support migrants to obtain driving licences, and fundraisers to help couriers who have suffered labour accidents, among other activities.

Most of those groups are not legal entities, nor are they able to negotiate working conditions. This is due to different constraints, one of which is that only those with employment status can exert collective bargaining rights. The only case of a legal union in a platform company is Sindicato de Empresa Cornershop Chile (Cornershop Company Union in Chile)[22] and this is linked to Cornershop initially hiring 'shoppers' as employees. In 2017, 240 of the 350 shoppers formed a union and entered into collective bargaining for the first time.

Another constraint on becoming a legal entity is the profile of the group's members. In the case of Riders Unidos Ya and Autodefensa Motorizada, most are migrants (Asenjo and Coddou 2021). In contrast, in the case of the Cornershop union, the union's president, Angelica Salgado, described in an interview conducted for this research that the first shoppers were actually individuals looking for temporary jobs, students and native Chilean homemakers. This difference is relevant because, although national and migrant workers might face the same problems at work, they have to deal with different challenges that shape whether or not they fight for their rights and seek justice.

MEXICO: LOW TRUST IN UNIONISATION, BUT HIGH HOPES FOR LEGAL ENACTMENT

In Mexico, there are no legal provisions directly regulating digital platforms. Therefore, workers on digital platforms are classified as self-employed individuals and, as such, are not covered by the Ley Federal del Trabajo (LFT; Federal Labour Law), nor are they enrolled in the social security system. The LFT only relates to subordinate workers who are entitled to the rights and protections defined by this law (Bensusán Areous 2020). The discussion of how to regulate platform work in Mexico has been taking place within the context of the implementation of the 2019 labour reform – the staged introduction of which culminated in May 2023.[23]

The 2019 labour reform was linked to the conclusion of the free trade agreement signed between Canada, Mexico and the US,[24] which came into force on 1 July 2020[25] and required compliance with international labour rights. Consequently, the reform strengthened the labour justice system and collective bargaining, explicitly acknowledging explicitly the rights of ILO Conventions 87 and 98 regarding freedom of association and the right to organise and collective bargaining.

However, the reform still faces the challenge of incorporating a special chapter in the LFT and in Ley del Seguro Social (LSS; Social Security Law) to regulate platform workers. In 2022, the secretary of labour and social security claimed to the press that the department had held multiple meetings with stakeholders (platform companies, workers and so on) and was working on a bill proposal that would be submitted at the end of 2022 and enacted during 2023 (Zermeño 2023). This did not happen and was then rescheduled for February 2023, but, by the end of 2023, the debate had clearly been frozen and there is little public information about the content of any bill.[26] Based on public declarations, it seemed that the reform would go in the direction of acknowledging the existence of a labour relationship between platform workers and the platforms and, as a result, grant workers access to social security and employment protection. However, the pause in the debate means that nothing is certain. Besides the labour secretary's proposal, there are no fewer than 21 initiatives (Martinez 2023) waiting to be discussed in Congress.

At the same time, Instituto Mexicano del Seguro Social (IMSS; Mexican Institute of Social Security) signed an agreement in September 2021 with Uber, Beat, DiDi and Rappi to promote the voluntary enrolment of independent workers in Régimen Obligatorio del Seguro Social (ROSS; Mandatory Regime of Social Insurance) (Flores 2021). However, couriers themselves rejected this initiative because voluntary affiliation to social insurance acknowledges the platforms' narrative that they are independent workers. Consequently, platforms and the state do not have to cover social insurance payments for them as they do for employees. Moreover, enrolment as self-employed means a reduction in income (of some 2,000 Mexican pesos (€110) on average per month).[27]

In terms of organising strategies and forms of collective representation in Mexico, it was the 'ghost' liabilities[28] that appeared on delivery workers' accounts – due to alleged payment errors – and the associated deactivations which triggered the first mobilisations against the platforms in 2018. Furthermore, complaints about safety, including robberies, were ubiquitous.

Since then, workers have created many WhatsApp groups to provide a support network in their areas. Different organisations have emerged from these groups, some of which are still active. However, some events triggered organising attempts even before Covid-19. The grassroots organisation Ni un repartidor menos ('Not one fewer courier'), with branches in seven states, is a collective that emerged in November 2018 following the death of an Uber Eats courier who was struck by a refuse truck. The collective provides a support network for emergencies and does not demand affiliation or fees to receive help. It channels assistance through partnerships with different institutions and participates in dialogue roundtables to address issues such as labour rights, violence and harassment and road safety.[29]

Overall, Mexico is characterised by a multiplicity of local grassroots collectives and spontaneous initiatives, such as Repartidores de Ciudad de Mexico (Couriers of the City of Mexico) (Alba Vega et al. 2021) or even less structured Whatsapp groups. These groups share their demands for improvements to labour conditions and join together to raise their voice in public debate. As an example, 25 different grassroots organisations agreed on ten demands called Manifiesto de piso mínimo de las trabajadoras y trabajadores de plataformas digitales (the 'Minimum Floor' manifesto) expressing the minimum requirements that the law needed to address to ensure platform workers' access to labour justice.[30] They submitted this document in August 2022 to the secretary of labour and social security, requesting their demands be incorporated in the bill proposal on which the department was working. Among the demands are the definition of labour categories based on connection time, tax-free tips not being part of salary and the right to receive materials like helmets and other information at work.

However, only a few of the spontaneous organisations that have been created by workers have actively pursued legal recognition as a union. Sergio Guerrero, the general secretary of Unión Nacional de Trabajadores por Aplicación (UNTA; National Union of App-Based Workers), pointed out directly in communications conducted for this research that several of these groups have different priorities and interests and are strongly sceptical about the idea of unionisation. This resistance is rooted in Mexico's entrenched partisan union framework, in which unions are often perceived as corrupt and politically aligned institutions (Marquez et al. 2022). Moreover, here too, workers are not able to bargain collectively unless they have employee status, and this represents a crucial obstacle to forming unions in the Mexican platform economy context.

As an illustration, a collective called Sindicato Independiente de Repartidores por Aplicaciones (SIRA-Apps; Independent Trade Union of App-Based Couriers) has emerged, receiving official acknowledgement as a 'coalition' in September 2019 by the Junta Local de Conciliación y Arbitraje de la Ciudad de México (Local Conciliation and Arbitration Board of Mexico City). Although such recognition fell short of official union registration, SIRA-Apps claimed to function similarly to a union (Márquez et al. 2022).

Sergio Guerrero communicated that riders who supported the idea of unionising then came together and decided to form a union with legal status. The secretary of labour rejected this request, however, because workers needed the acknowledgement of an employment relationship by the platform companies, which the companies denied. A second attempt came with a different strategy: first, the leaders identified the primary activity of Uber and DiDi as the transport of people and goods using federal routes alongside the design of technology for the more efficient allocation of those resources; second, to fulfil the requirements for forming a union, they drew up a template (or model) in the transport sector so that they could register as a trade union because they had members from Uber, DiDi and Rappi. Despite facing many setbacks due to bureaucratic paperwork, they succeeded in forming an independent, authentic, legal and representative union for platform workers, receiving registration number 7405 in April 2021 (Meléndez 2022). Nevertheless, the union has still not been able to bargain collectively because employers do not acknowledge its members as employees.

Since Mexico does not have a legal framework applicable to platform work, UNTA had the choice of following either a legal or a legislative route to seek acknowledgment of the presence of an employment relationship. It attempted to introduce a court case (UNTA 2021) but withdrew it because the paperwork did not meet the formal requirements (which UNTA members adjudged as a deliberate bureaucratic delay). Nonetheless, Sergio Guerrero communicated directly that the legal path was not the best option because of the country's move to implement a new model of labour justice, concluded in May 2023,[31] so the union continued in limbo during the transition. As a result, UNTA has put all its advocating effort and expectations into the legislative project led by the secretary of labour (El Economista 2022).

DISCUSSION: LEGAL ENACTMENT, ROLE OF UNIONS AND POTENTIAL WORKER POWER RESOURCES

The predominant features of courier work do raise questions about whether couriers are immersed in a poverty trap, working in a low-productivity sector without a social safety net and facing limited chances of getting formal employment due to a lack of documents or regular migration status, and being short of time to look for another job. Determining whether platform couriers are in a poverty trap or in a double feedback loop (Duflo and Banerjee 2011) goes beyond the scope of this chapter, but ascertaining the presence of a poverty trap might be necessary in the design of policies that make significant differences to couriers' lives. Even though the immigrant condition has aided the self-organising of platform couriers through natural networks of self-defence and mutual aid, it has also contributed to the precarity they face, which, in turn, might become a barrier to organising.

Although some level of worker activism and advocacy among platform couriers had begun in 2017 and 2018 in the countries examined in this chapter, the Covid-19 pandemic catapulted platform workers' issues and fights into the public eye, accelerating the organising and policy-making effort (McCallum 2023). The evidence from the experience of New York and Seattle is consistent with previous research; that platform worker organising tends to take place 'on a geographical basis – especially, city-wide – rather than the more familiar workplace model that tends to dominate industrial relations thinking' (Joyce et al. 2023: 36). The organising experience in Argentina, Chile and Mexico also confirms this finding, highlighting that, for platform couriers, the workplace is the city streets, and workers' organising tends to occur spontaneously, emerging from shared vulnerabilities and struggles.

In Argentina, Chile and the US, grassroots organisations have been built by mostly immigrant workers on the basis of national origin and on natural social networks transplanted from couriers' countries and towns of origin (Figueroa et al. 2021). These natural worker networks use social platforms such as WhatsApp, Instagram and Facebook to act as self-defence organisations for workers to protect one another against bike theft and violent crime and to engage in mutual aid to provide economic relief for the families of those who die while working as couriers. However, while the predominance of immigrants in the platform courier workforce facilitates workers' self-organising, it also creates limits to the specific policy solutions sought, particularly in the US. The status of undocumented migrant workers leads to a distrust of government regulations and a preference for 'staying under the radar' due to fear of deportation, hindering worker organisations' pursuit of traditional employment relation formulas, again especially in the US. This was a key factor in unifying workers around the fight for minimum pay standards in New York, as this local-level policy established a pay rate for all platform couriers without dealing with workers' immigration status. Local governments in the US do not have jurisdiction over immigration laws, which are set at the federal (national) level.

The pandemic, the immigrant characteristic of the workforce in all the countries examined (except Mexico) and independent contractor status frame the space and the strategies of worker organisations. In all the countries analysed, couriers seek improvements in working conditions through legal enactment approaches rather than established forms of collective negotiation because they are not recognised as employees entitled to basic rights such as creating a union and collective bargaining. This approach is consistent with existing analyses of platform worker organising (Joyce et al. 2023).

Within the legal frameworks of the countries studied, recognition of the employment relationship is the only path to form a legal labour union and collectively bargain with the platforms. In Latin America, the cases examined are indeed focused on seeking acknowledgement of the presence of an employment relationship at national level. While worker organisations in the US have been seeking state and national policies to classify platform workers as employees, successful legal enactment efforts have been achieved at municipal level in New York and Seattle. Worker organisations in these cities have focused on achieving local rights for platform couriers without dealing with employment classification, mainly by replicating the successful approach of platform ride-hailing drivers in New York and Seattle. The minimum pay standards achieved in these cities would be an effective method of setting wage floors in the platform food delivery industry, thus helping to prevent 'algorithmic wage discrimination' (Dubal 2023) involving unequal pay for the same type of work.

In terms of the role of unions, legally enacted rights in New York and Seattle have been achieved through the efforts of worker centres in alliance with the SEIU, which is becoming the most important union in platform worker advocacy in the US. In New York, the worker centre WJP led the organising and advocacy efforts, with SEIU Local 32BJ playing a supportive role by leveraging its political clout in favour of the new policies. In Seattle, the SEIU played a much more significant role than in New York by founding Working Washington, a worker organisation that has led the organising and policy campaign for platform courier rights. In Latin America, unions have had a much less prominent role. These findings are consistent with the existing analysis that traditional unions have been slow in adapting to the emergence of platform work and that both traditional and alternative unions, like worker centres, have found it difficult to establish collective bargaining agreements with platforms (Bertollini and Dukes 2021; Joyce et al. 2023).

In the Latin American cases examined, there are key factors that limit the role of unions in platform worker organising, including the impact of the informal economy on union density rates and the lack of financial resources for organising and policy campaigns. Unionisation rates around 2020 were 14 per cent in Mexico, 22 per cent in Chile and 27 per cent in Argentina (Gutierrez et al. 2021; Juarez 2022; Parola 2021). Moreover, these rates represent formal employees only, so actual unionisation rates might be lower when accounting for the informal economy, which is of considerable size in Argentina, at 49 per cent; at 27 per cent in Chile (in 2021) and at 57 per cent in Mexico (in 2022) (ILOSTAT 2023a). The financial limitations that unions in these countries face are related to the sources of their income, which depend on membership fees. These incomes are low because of the low pay rates that predominate in all three countries (ILOSTAT 2023b). Another important limiting factor in the role of Latin American unions is the relationship that they have with the new grassroots organisations. For example, in Mexico, Ni un repartidor menos is refusing to become a union because of the negative perception of traditional unions, specifically in relation to union corruption (Alba Vega et al. 2021; Márquez et al. 2022). In Argentina, differences in strategies and goals between ASiMM and delivery workers motivated the emergence of ATR (Bachoer 2022). As a result, platform couriers in these countries have had to undertake their collective struggle without institutional resources or strong trade unions that could support them (Muñoz and Martinez 2022).

CONCLUSIONS

This chapter has discussed how platform couriers have organised and sought the legal enactment of basic rights in Argentina, Chile, Mexico and the US, focusing in the latter case on experiences in New York and Seattle. Confirming the arguments of previous studies, an analysis of these cases shows that platform worker organising is focused on the legal enactment of labour rights via the building and leveraging of associational power. A factor of causation is that, in the analysed countries, platform couriers do not have collective bargaining rights under the existing institutional frameworks.

The experiences of Chile and New York and Seattle show that basic protections can be achieved for platform couriers without tackling independent contractor classification. These cases illustrate how the legal enactment of protections for platform workers, such as the setting of minimum pay standards or wage floors, can gradually reduce the economic advantage that platforms enjoy by adopting independent contractor classification as the centrepiece of their business model. Additionally, evidence from this study reveals the need for policy measures focused on reducing the worker vulnerabilities and precarity which are related to the over-representation of migrant people in the platform courier workforce.[32] A comprehensive policy approach that diminishes the vulnerability of migrant workers would not only promote their full inclusion in the host country but also help to raise standards for all workers in the industry.

Shifting the labour battleground to the policymaking arena has proven to be an effective strategy for courier advocates to codify basic labour rights and set the floor for eventual future negotiations with platform companies in New York and Seattle, as well as in Chile. However, in the absence of strong worker organisations, the implementation and enforcement of the new laws will have to rely on severely under-resourced government agencies. This brings up the need to build worker power not only to achieve legal enactment but also to ensure compliance with the new rights.

According to Trappmann et al. (2020) and Joyce et al. (2023), platform workers lack structural and institutional power, building associational power instead with the use of collective action as a means rather than an aim in seeking the legal enactment of labour rights. However, evidence from this study and previous analyses (Maffie and Gough 2023; Vandaele 2018) indicates that platform couriers might have power resources in two areas: first, in the ability to engage in multi-apping and thus pit platforms against each other (Maffie and Gough 2023);

and second, in the potential ability to disrupt the just-in-time distribution process of the platform food delivery industry (Vandaele 2018). The latter potential source of structural power to disrupt platforms' distribution chains can be enhanced were platform courier organisations to coordinate actions with other worker organisations engaged in campaigns against large platform clients, such as fast-food chains. There is precedent for worker action that leverages platforms' reliance on the delivery of fast-food orders, as the experience of Working Washington against Postmates demonstrates. There might be potential in the US for similar actions in partnership with the SEIU, which has been waging its Fight for $15 campaign to organise fast-food workers since 2012 and has more recently targeted individual chains such as McDonald's and Chipotle (Greenhouse 2019). This type of worker action that connects worker fights along platforms' supply chains would leverage the power resources that lie in the structure of the industry on top of the associational power of platform workers.

The cases examined show that national and subnational legal frameworks, industry structure and the presence of migrant workers all influence worker strategies for achieving improvements in their working conditions. Finally, the cases also shed light on the increasing relevance of external factors, such as the Covid-19 pandemic, which have triggered important waves of organising. Collectivism does not yet, however, extend to collective bargaining, leaving the voice of workers in the platform economy somewhat atonal.

NOTES

1. In May 2023, they began offering the service in Miami and Dallas as pilot cities in the US; see https://theorg.com/iterate/the-5-food-delivery-apps-taking-a-bite-of-the-latin-american-market#cornershop--chile
2. According to the International Organisation for Migration, 'As of March 2023, more than 7 million Venezuelans are outside their country of origin, the second largest displacement in the world.' See https://respuestavenezolanos.iom.int/en/about-regional-venezuela-situation
3. DCWP is the city agency that issues and enforces local regulations to protect consumers and workers in certain industries within the NYC government's jurisdiction.
4. Prior to the passage of these local laws (ordinances), fast-food workers were given short notice of their schedules.
5. For a detailed discussion about each proposal, see Garavaglia (2022).
6. See ILAW's database and news from www.pagina12.com.ar/371749-provincia-de-buenos-aires-ratifican-una-multa-contra-rappi-p
7. For example, SiTraRepA participated in the organisation of the 1st International Congress of Platform Workers in the US.
8. See www.instagram.com/sitrarepa/?hl=en
9. See https://web.facebook.com/jovenestrabajadoresprecarizados?_rdc=1&_rdr
10. See the law www.bcn.cl/leychile/navegar?idNorma=1173544
11. Bulletin 13.496-1 and Bulletin 12.475-13. For a detailed discussion about the origin of the Law, see Arab Verdugo and Frontaura Marzolo (2022).
12. The Fundación Instituto de Estudios Laborales (FIEL) is a non-profit organisation created in 2005 under the mandate of the Board of Directors of Central Unitaria de Trabajadores de Chile (CUT; Workers' United Centre of Chile) in order to provide a space for the strengthening of the trade union movement from an integral perspective of the world of work. See https://fielchile.cl/v2/fundacion

13. An anonymous courier stated that street mobilisations are challenging because, besides the fear of being disconnected/deactivated for being there or close to it (they argued that the apps used geolocation tools to identify who participated), the apps usually offer special economic incentives to work on those days.
14. Regardless of the Court of Appeal of Concepción declaring that Pedidos Ya 'exercised control over the riders and thus established an employment relationship' in the case 'Alvaro Felipe Arredondo Montoya con Pedidos Ya Chile SPA'. See www.ilawnetwork.com/wp-content/uploads/2021/03/https_www.diarioconstitucional.cl_wp-content_uploads_2021_01_6.1.-ICA-DE-CONCEPCION-ROL-N%C2%B0395-2020.pdf
15. Dictamen 1831/39 www.doe.cl/alerta/21102022/202210213004
16. Unionised drivers, Sindicato de Trabajadores Independientes de Conductores de Aplicaciones (Sincapp; Union of Freelance App-Based Drivers) also disagreed with the Dictamen because they claim to be independent workers. Consequently, they also supported and signed the protective appeal introduced by Uber. See https://sindical.cl/trabajadores-apps-contra-nuevo-dictamen
17. They also filed an appeal for reversal. www.diarioconstitucional.cl/wp-content/uploads/2022/11/N%C2%B0145.648-2022.-1.pdf
18. See Sentencia Corte de Santiago 145.648-2022. www.diarioconstitucional.cl/wp-content/uploads/2023/04/N%C2%B0145.648-2022..pdf
19. It is not clear if this association is still active. For more information, see Coddou (2021).
20. The representative interviewed for this research claims that they associate with around 5,000 riders.
21. The representative claims that they did not receive support from the local police, so they organised to get their motorcycles returned so they could keep on working. For more information, see www.t13.cl/etiqueta/defensa-motorizada
22. This union was inherited by Uber when it acquired Cornershop in 2019. See https://dfmas.df.cl/df-mas/por-dentro/el-sindicato-que-tiene-en-aprietos-la-integracion-de-cornershop-con-uber
23. See the implementation calendar 2019-2023 www.maquilasolidarity.org/es/calendario-de-la-implementacion-de-la-reforma-laboral-en-mexico
24. La transformación del modelo de regulación laboral mexicano y sus vínculos con la integración económica en América del Norte www.ilo.org/static/spanish/intserv/working-papers/wp015/index.html#ID0EFGAC
25. See https://ustr.gov/trade-agreements/free-trade-agreements/united-states-mexico-canada-agreement
26. Indeed, a request has been made to Congress for transparency to obtain more information about the proposal that the secretary of labour has been developing (see Appeal for Review RRA 19458/22). https://home.inai.org.mx/wp-content/documentos/AudiosyVersionesEstenograficas/Sesion%20Pleno%2001-02-2023.pdf
27. Public statement to Zoé Robledo, General Director of IMSS, from UNTA, 5 October 2021.
28. See Deudas fantasma y condiciones engañosas detonan protestas de mensajeros del servicio Rappi (10 September 2018). www.periodicocentral.mx/2018/nacional-seccion/item/22929-deudas-fantasma-y-condiciones-enganosas-detonan-protestas-de-mensajeros-del-servicio-rappi
29. See https://niunrepartidormenos.org.mx
30. See https://flexibilidadconderechos.mx/wp-content/uploads/2022/10/Manifiesto-de-piso-mi%CC%81nimo-de-las-trabajadoras-y-trabajadores-de-plataformas-digitales.pdf
31. For more information, see http://pjdgo.gob.mx/que-es-la-reforma-laboral

32. An exception is Mexico, where 78.9 per cent of couriers were born in Mexico. Only 14 of the 1,008 people interviewed declared themselves to be foreign. Of those 14, 12 reported they were Venezuelan (Alba Vega et al. 2021).

REFERENCES

Ahuja K. et al. (2021) Ordering in: the rapid evolution of food delivery, McKinsey and Company, 22 September.

Alba Vega C., Bensusán G. and Vega G. (2021) El trabajo del futuro con derechos laborales: diagnóstico y estrategia de política pública para el reconocimiento de derechos laborales de personas trabajadoras por plataformas digitales, Red de Estudios sobre Desigualdades de El Colegio de México.

Andonova V., Casanova L., Finchelstein D. and Duque J.G. (2023) Invited applied article: the rise of digital entrepreneurship in Latin America, *Internext*, 18 (1), 104–110.

Arab Verdugo F. and Frontaura Marzolo M.F. (2022) Descripción y análisis de la Ley 21.431, que Regula el contrato de trabajadores de empresas de plataformas digitales de servicios, *Revista De Derecho Aplicado* LLM UC, 9. https://doi.org/10.7764/rda.0.9.51169

Arias C.C., Diana Menéndez N. and Haidar J. (2021) ¿Sindicalismo 4.0? La organización de trabajadores de plataformas en Argentina, *Sociología del Trabajo*, 97 (2), 59–69.

Asenjo A. and Coddou A. (2021) Economía de plataformas y transformaciones en el mundo del trabajo: el caso de los repartidores en Santiago de Chile, Informes Técnicos, 17, OIT.

Azuara O., Silva, L. and Rodriguez T.C. (2022) La regulación del trabajo en plataformas en Chile: ¿Nuevo paradigma para la región? Factor Trabajo, 4 October. https://blogs.iadb.org/trabajo/es/la-regulacion-del-trabajo-en-plataformas-en-chile-nuevo-paradigma-para-la-region

Bachoer L. (2022) La conflictividad laboral en las plataformas digitales: un acercamiento al caso de los repartidores en la Ciudad de Buenos Aires (2018–2020), *Revista Controversia*, 218, 267–306.

Benavente F.B. (2022) Uber Eats interpone recurso de protección en contra de la Dirección del Trabajo por considerar que las 18.000 personas que actualmente prestan servicios no pueden ser consideradas como trabajadores dependientes. Diario Constitucional, 23 November. www.diarioconstitucional.cl/2022/11/23/uber-eats-interpone-recurso-de-proteccion-en-contra-de-la-direccion-del-trabajo-por-considerar-que-las-18–000-personas-que-actualmente-prestan-servicios-no-pueden-ser-consideradas-como-trabajadores-de

Bensusán Areous G. (2020) *Ocupaciones emergentes en la economía digital y su regulación en México, Serie Macroeconomía del Desarrollo 203*, Comisión Económica para América Latina y el Caribe (CEPAL).

Bertollini A. and Dukes R. (2021) Trade unions and platform workers in the UK: worker representation in the shadow of the law, *Industrial Law Journal*, 50 (4), 662–688.

Beyer S. (2023) Latin America's food delivery wars, *Catalyst*, 8 May. https://catalyst.independent.org/2023/05/08/latam-delivery

Browning K. and Ley A. (2023) Judge affirms pay raise for food delivery workers in New York, *The New York Times*, 28 September.

Cárdenas, L. (2022) Uber arremete contra Dirección del Trabajo por dictamen: 'Amenaza viabilidad de las plataformas tecnológicas.' *La Tercera*, 22 November. www.latercera.com/nacional/noticia/uber-arremete-contra-direccion-del-trabajo-por-dictamen-amenaza-viabilidad-de-las-plataformas-tecnologicas/7IQV2YV3QRF75N636EO7SAPJW4

City of Seattle (2022) Ordinance 126595, Council Bill 120294, SM 8.37.

City of Seattle (2023a) Ordinance SMC 8.39, App-Based Workers Paid Sick and Safe Time Ordinance. www.seattle.gov/laborstandards/ordinances/app-based-worker-ordinances/app-based-worker-paid-sick-and-safe-time-ordinance

City of Seattle (2023b) An Ordinance relating to app-based worker labor standards; establishing labor standards on deactivation protections for app-based workers working in Seattle; amending Section 3.02.125 of the Seattle Municipal Code; and adding a new Chapter 8.40 to the Seattle Municipal Code. https://seattle.legistar.com/LegislationDetail.aspx?ID=6214973&GUID=20C5F7BD-7898–47C2–9854-E3A42FFCD664

Coddou, Alberto. (2021) El trabajo en plataformas durante la pandemia por COVID-19: Los derechos fundamentales y el caso chileno, Informes Técnicos OIT Cono Sur, No. 19.
Diario Constitucional (2023) Naturaleza jurídica del vínculo de quienes prestan servicios para Uber Eats debe ser determinada en un juicio de lato conocimiento, característica que no exhibe la acción de protección. Diario Constitucional, 7 April. www.diarioconstitucional.cl/2023/04/07/naturaleza-juridica-del-vinculo-de-quienes-prestan-servicios-para-uber-eats-debe-ser-determinada-en-un-juicio-de-lato-conocimiento-caracteristica-que-no-exhibe-la-accion-de-proteccion
Dubal V.B. (2022) Economic security & the regulation of gig work in California: from AB5 to Proposition 22, *European Labour Law Journal*, 13 (1), 51–65.
Dubal V.B. (2023) *Algorithmic wage discrimination requires policy solutions that enforce predictability and U.S. spirit of equal pay for equal work*, Washington Center for Equitable Growth.
Duflo E. and Banerjee A. (2011) Poor economics: a radical rethinking of the way to fight global poverty, *Population and Development Review*, 37 (4), 796–797.
Elbert R. and Negri S. (2021) Delivery platform workers during Covid-19 pandemic in the city of Buenos Aires (Argentina): deepened precarity and workers' response in a context of epidemiological crisis, *Journal of Labor and Society*. https://doi.org/10.1163/24714607-bja10014
El Economista (Ciudad de México & Editorial La República S.A.S.) (2022) Repartidores mexicanos entregan pliego en Secretaria del Trabajo pidiendo derechos. Diario La República, 29 August. www.larepublica.co/globoeconomia/repartidores-entregan-pedido-especial-en-la-stps-exigencia-de-derechos-laborales-3435371
Fairwork (2022) *Labour standards in the platform economy: Chile ratings 2022*. https://fair.work/es/ratings/chile
Fairwork (2023a) *Labour standards in the platform economy: Mexico ratings 2023*. https://fair.work/en/ratings/mexico
Fairwork (2023b) *Labour standards in the platform economy: Argentina ratings 2023*. https://fair.work/en/ratings/argentina
Figueroa M. et al. (2021) *Essential but unprotected: app-based food couriers in New York City*, Cornell ILR Worker Institute.
Flores, Z. (2021) Beat, DiDi, Rappi y Uber inician prueba piloto para dar seguridad social en México. *Bloomberg Línea*, 30 September. www.bloomberglinea.com/2021/09/30/beat-didi-rappi-y-uber-inician-prueba-piloto-en-para-dar-seguridad-social-en-mexico
Garavaglia P. (2022) El avance de las plataformas de trabajo en Argentina, Doctoral disertación, Centro de Implementación de Políticas Públicas para la Equidad y el Crecimiento (CIPPEC).
Greenhouse S. (2019) 'We're organizing to improve lives': New York fast-food workers push to unionize, *The Guardian*, 30 September.
Groover H. (2020) Seattle to require minimum wage for Uber and Lyft drivers, *The Seattle Times*, 29 September.
Gutierrez F. et al. (2021) *Informe de huelgas laborales en Chile*, Observatorio de Huelgas Laborales and UAH/COES.
Hartmann Cortes K. (2021) How did a food-delivery platform's judgement transform freedom of association into a second-class right?, *Comparative Labor Law & Policy Journal*, 2021 (37), 1–9.
Hirschfeld-Kroen J. (2023) The truth about your food delivery: how food delivery apps are trying to kill a worker uprising, Perfectunion.us, 12 May. https://perfectunion.us/doordash-and-grubhub-are-lobbying-to-prevent-a-raise-in-minimum-wage-for-food-delivery-worker-but-los-deliveristas-are-fighting-back
ILAW (2022) Base de datos sobre normas y decisiones sobre el trabajo en plataformas digitales en América Latina https://www.ilawnetwork.com/es/database-on-standards-and-decisions-on-digital-platform-work-in-latin-america/
ILOSTAT (2023a) Statistics on informal economy. https://ilostat.ilo.org/topics/informality
ILOSTAT (2023b) Statistics on wages. https://ilostat.ilo.org/topics/wages
IMARC (2023) *United States online food delivery market report*, IMARC Group.
Irizarry C. (2023) Tips tricks dampen delivery worker celebration of new $18-an-hour wage, *The City*, 6 December.

Irungaray, G. (2023) Apps de delivery: se frenó la ley que busca registrar a los trabajadores. *Perfil*, 19 April. www.perfil.com/noticias/politica/aplicaciones-de-delivery-se-freno-el-debate-de-la-ley-que-busca-registrar-a-los-trabajadores.phtml

Joyce S., Stuart M. and Forde C. (2021) Theorising labour unrest and trade unionism in the platform economy, *New Technology, Work and Employment*, 38 (1), 21–40.

Juarez B. (2022) Sindicalismo en México, una realidad sólo para 14% de las personas trabajadoras, *El Economista*, 2 May. www.eleconomista.com.mx

Leyton García, J.A. and Azócar R. (2022). Análisis crítico de la regulación del trabajo en plataformas en Chile, introducida al Código del Trabajo por la Ley Nro. 21.431. Revista Jurídica del Trabajo, 162–195. http://revistajuridicadeltrabajo.com/index.php/rjt/article/view/126/116

Lisinski C. (2023) Unions back basic benefits bill for Uber, Lyft drivers, WBUR News, National Public Radio, 30 October.

Lutzky L. (2022) Sitrarepa: el joven sindicato que defiende a los repartidores y podría ser la pesadilla de Rappi y Pedidos Ya. *Ámbito Financiero*, 22 September. www.ambito.com/sociedad/sindicato/sitrarepa-el-joven-que-defiende-los-repartidores-y-podria-ser-la-pesadilla-rappi-y-pedidos-ya-n5541263

Madariaga J., Buenadicha C., Molina E. and Ernst C. (2019) ¿Cómo es trabajar para una app en Argentina? Economía de plataformas y empleo, CIPPEC.

Maffie M. and Gough M.D. (2023) Bargaining against the machine: a theory of bargaining power in the gig economy, *Advances in Industrial and Labor Relations*, 27, 83–99.

Márquez C., Escoto A., Gonsales M. and Mariatti A. (2022) Mexico City, Montevideo, and São Paulo: collective action by delivery platform workers in three different scenarios, *Journal of Labor and Society*, 25 (1), 1–32.

Martinez M. (2022) Crece afiliación de empleo independiente en IMSS, *El Economista*, 20 October. www.eleconomista.com.mx/empresas/Afiliacion-de-trabajadores-independientes-en-el-IMSS-suma-a-46923-personas-en-dos-anos-20221020–0066.html

Martinez M. (2023) Hay 'condiciones precarias' para los trabajadores de plataformas, urge la reforma en la materia, *El Economista*, 13 April. www.eleconomista.com.mx/empresas/Hay-condiciones-precarias-para-los-trabajadores-de-plataformas-urge-la-reforma-en-la-materia-20230413–0048.html

Masmoudi I. (2023) News & Commentary, 12 June, OnLabor. https://onlabor.org/june-12–2023

McCallum J.K. (2023) *Essential: how the pandemic transformed the long fight for worker justice*, Basic Books.

Meléndez, M. (2022) Nace el primer sindicato federal para trabajadores de app´s: Unión Nacional de Trabajadores por Aplicación (UNTA) – Intervención y Coyuntura. Intervención Y Coyuntura – Revista De Teoría Y Crítica Política 19 January. https://intervencionycoyuntura.org/nace-el-primer-sindicato-federal-para-trabajadores-de-apps-union-nacional-de-trabajadores-por-aplicacion-unta/

Menendez N. Diana, Haidar J. and Arias C. (2023) Prácticas organizativas de trabajadores de plataformas de reparto: un análisis desde la teoría de los recursos de poder, Papers: *Revista de Sociologia*, 108 (1), e3044-e3044.

Meyer D. and Hicks N. (2021) City Council requires minimum pay, bathroom access for food delivery workers, *New York Post*, 23 September. https://nypost.com/2021/09/23/city-council-oks-bills-boosting-food-delivery-workers-rights

Muñoz K.M. and Martinez A.D. (2022) Self-organization among delivery platforms workers in neoliberal Latin American countries: the cases of Peru and Chile, *Journal of Labor and Society*, 25 (3), 299–328.

NELP National Employment Law Project (2022) Proactive Policy Solutions for Contracted Workers, Policy Brief.

NYC DCWP (2022) *A minimum pay rate for app-based restaurant delivery workers in NYC*, The City of New York, Department of Consumer and Worker Protection. www.nyc.gov/assets/dca/downloads/pdf/workers/Delivery-Worker-Study-November-2022.pdf

NYS Supreme Court (2023) Supreme Court of the State of New York, Appellate Division, First Department, Notice of Motion for Leave to File Brief as Amici Curiae, Case Nos. 2023–04881, 2023–04880.

Parola M. (2021) Sólo uno de cada cuatro trabajadores registrados está sindicalizado en el país, *El Ciudadano*, 16 October. www.elciudadanoweb.com
Pinto M., Smith R. and Tung I. (2019) Rights at risk: gig companies' campaign to upend employment as we know it, National Employment Law Project, 25 March. www.nelp.org/publication/rights-at-risk-gig-companies-campaign-to-upend-employment-as-we-know-it
PR Newswire (2022) America's leading app-based companies launch Flex, a new industry association, PR Newswire, 8 March. www.prnewswire.com/news-releases/americas-leading-app-based-companies-launch-flex-a-new-industry-association-301497791.html
Riquelme, C.S. (2021) Demanda por despido de repartidores de aplicación 'Pedidos Ya', se rechaza. Diario Constitucional 20 December. www.diarioconstitucional.cl/2021/12/20/demanda-por-despido-de-repartidores-de-aplicacion-pedidos-ya-se-rechaza
Rolph A. and Soper T. (2023) Seattle approves first-of-its kind law that protects app-based workers from deactivation, *GeekWire*, 8 August.
Roose K. (2019) After uproar, Instacart backs off controversial tipping policy, *The New York Times*, 6 February.
Ruckstuhl L. (2021) Companies promise new benefits for drivers under mass ballot proposal: labor advocates see attempt to skirt wage laws, WBUR News, National Public Radio, 10 December. www.wbur.org/news/2021/12/10/uber-lyft-instacart-doordash-massachusetts-ballot-q-explainer
Scheiber N. (2021) Uber and Lyft ramp up legislative efforts to shield business model, *The New York Times*, 2 June.
Schwartz L. and Weber N. (2023) Asymmetric by design: how and why labor policy impacts gig workers. https://osf.io/preprints/socarxiv/mh29a
Silverstein A. (2023) Making deliveries: promise and peril for migrants, *The New York Times*, 17 September.
Sumagaysay L. (2022) Uber and Lyft get their first legislative win in campaign to write new labor laws, *MarketWatch*, 2 April.
Stiffler L. (2023) Seattle becomes first U.S. city to permanently require sick leave for delivery and app-based workers, *GeekWire*, 28 March. www.geekwire.com/2023/seattle-is-the-first-u-s-city-to-permanently-require-paid-sick-leave-for-delivery-and-other-app-based-workers
SUSESO (2023) Código del trabajo, artículo 19 (Labor Code, Article 19), Superintendencia de Seguridad Social, Chile. www.suseso.cl/612/w3-propertyvalue-69297.html
Theorg.com (2023) The 5 food delivery apps taking a bite of the Latin American market. https://theorg.com/iterate/the-5-food-delivery-apps-taking-a-bite-of-the-latin-american-market#ifood--brazil
Trappmann V. et al. (2020) *Global labour unrest on platforms: the case of food delivery workers*, Friedrich-Ebert-Stiftung.
UN IOM (2023) About the regional Venezuela situation. https://respuestavenezolanos.iom.int/en/about-regional-venezuela-situation
UNTA (2021) *Trabajadores por aplicación se organizan y demandan a empresa Rappi*. Organización Comunista Revolucionaria, 16 July. https://marxismo.mx/trabajadores-por-aplicacion-se-organizan-y-demandan-a-empresa-rappi
US DOL (2024) Employee or Independent Contractor Classification Under the Fair Labor Standards Act Federal Register, 1 October. www.federalregister.gov
Vandaele K. (2018) Will trade unions survive in the platform economy? Emerging patterns of platform workers' collective voice and representation in Europe, Working Paper 2018.05, ETUI.
Weil D. (2014) The Fissured Workplace. Why work became so bad for so many and what can be done to improve it, Harvard University Press.
Wiessner D. (2023) NYC minimum wage for delivery drivers upheld by appeals court, Reuters, 1 December.
Working Washington (2020) Postmates Workers #GuacOff, #PayUp. https://payup.wtf/guacoff
Working Washington (2022) Seattle's app gap: how gig companies exclude workers from basic protections, and drive pay down below minimum wage. www.workingwa.org/for-media/2022/5/18/new-report-finds-seattle-gig-workers-average-just-958hour-in-net-pay
Yakas B. (2021) Report: NYC food delivery workers face low pay, high risks, *Gothamist*, 15 September. https://gothamist.com/food/report-nyc-food-delivery-workers-face-low-pay-high-risks

Young C.A. (2022) SJC tosses app-based drivers question from ballot, WBUR News, 14 June. www.wbur.org/news/2022/06/14/uber-lyft-massachusetts-ballot-question-thrown-out

Zermeño, L.H.Y.R. (2023) Regulación a Uber, Didi y Rappi, la reforma pendiente, *Reporte Indigo*, 29 June. www.reporteindigo.com/reporte/regulacion-a-uber-didi-y-rappi-la-reforma-pendiente-condiciones-laborales

All links were checked on 5 February 2024.

13. Avenues for social empowerment: the cooperative model for app-based food delivery and beyond

Denise Kasparian

INTRODUCTION

Logistics, meaning the transportation, storage and distribution of goods, has become a key sector in contemporary capitalism (Haidar and Bordarampé 2022). Digital technologies and the restrictions on mobility resulting from the Covid-19 pandemic have boosted one specific activity within this sector: last-mile logistics. This is the final stage of the process required for a good to be delivered to the client, be it the distribution of packages from large warehouses or food delivery. Digital labour platforms have played a major role in organising these activities. In the last decade, their number quintupled: in 2010 there were 142 online web-based and location-based platforms; by 2020 this number had increased to at least 777 (ILO 2021: 19). These platforms are digital infrastructures that organise through the cloud the process of connecting consumers, clients and suppliers with workers. Platform work thus refers to completing a task or providing a service by means of these infrastructures, whose intermediation between supply and demand includes forms of controlling, evaluating and paying workers (López Mourelo 2020). Although it varies depending on geopolitics and countries' regulatory frameworks, platform workers generally lack access to minimum wages and social protection benefits (Berg et al. 2018).

Although food delivery existed as an economic activity prior to digital labour platforms, they have structured food delivery services as a market, sometimes labelled 'foodtech', with defined players, prices and dynamics. Supply is organised through software for fleet management that uses algorithms to determine not only who picks up which order and which route should be taken to the destination but also the price of this service. Demand is managed by providing a centralised offer on a website or an app where customers can choose, order and pay for food and delivery (Haidar and Bordarampé 2022).

Against this backdrop, the cooperative model and principles have inspired projects for platforms that offer alternatives to the precariousness and control that platforms impose. This chapter provides an exploratory analysis of cooperatives in app-based food delivery and beyond, where they have developed alongside other kinds of collective organisation building, such as traditional unionism and new forms of collective representation (Cañada et al. 2023; Grohmann 2022; Vandaele 2021, 2023). Based on a comparative research design, the chapter focuses on six cases in western Europe and North and South America, with the aim of contributing to mapping the pathways to workers' social empowerment in app-based food delivery.

Cooperatives are economic organisations that seek to meet common needs through mutual aid, democratic control and the concept of ownership being shared between the members. 'Platform cooperativism' (Scholz 2023) is the most widely used notion referring to diverse initiatives that aim to transform the internet and digital technologies by introducing solidarity, decent work, democratic practices, transparent data management and the fair distribution of incomes. The argument is made that platform cooperatives differ significantly from mainstream app-based food delivery platforms in respect of various aspects and features that go beyond the organisational form alone. This concerns the contexts and factors that triggered their constitutions, the needs they seek to meet, the actors and alliances involved in their foundation and implementation, their business models and the form and degree to which technology is incorporated.

AN ANALYTICAL FRAMEWORK: PLATFORM PATHWAYS TOWARDS WORKERS' SOCIAL EMPOWERMENT

The cooperative movement emerged in western Europe in the mid-nineteenth century as a worker response to the poor living and working conditions imposed by industrial capitalism and the liberal attempt to establish the 'utopia of the self-regulating market' (Polanyi 1944/2007). There are different types of cooperative in relation to the needs addressed, including public utility cooperatives, consumer cooperatives and worker cooperatives. Since the end of the twentieth century, cooperatives have revitalised, frequently as part of a broader movement towards the advance of social and solidarity economies (Coraggio 2008; Kasparian and Rebón 2022; Vieta 2010; Williams 2014). This new generation of cooperatives gained momentum against a backdrop of rising financial capitalism and neoliberalism, which brought with them the generalisation of job insecurity and the deepening of social inequalities.

The relevance of the cooperative model in the labour sphere became apparent in 2002, when the International Labour Organization promoted it through its Recommendation No. 193 (ILO 2002). According to the International Cooperative Alliance (ICA), at least 12 per cent of the world population is a cooperator in any of the three million cooperatives. One of their main contributions is that they provide jobs or work opportunities to 10 per cent of the employed population.

Collective organisation in the form of cooperatives has thus reappeared as a part of the working-class toolkit. Platform cooperatives are 'businesses that use a website, mobile app, or protocol to sell goods or services. They rely on democratic decision-making and shared ownership of the platform by workers and users' (Scholz et al. 2021: 14). The formation of cooperatives can run into legal and political obstacles in different jurisdictions, and thus the core characteristic of platform cooperatives lies in their identity (Mayo 2019), regardless of the legal form adopted. Moreover, the forms and degree to which digital technology is incorporated vary: there are tech-driven projects, but also tech-enabled and low-tech ventures (Cohen 2018; Cousin 2021). Cooperative platforms promote horizontal relationships by developing a community infrastructure that respects privacy, facilitates user participation in data governance and addresses some of the negative externalities caused by platforms, for example by promoting recycling and the circular economy, as well as choosing to be hosted on servers powered by green energy (Fuster et al. 2021).

Platform cooperatives could potentially stand as a powerful strategy for workers' social empowerment in the digital labour realm, with social power comprehended as 'the capacity to mobilise people for cooperative, voluntary collective actions' (Wright 2019: 131). As Trebor Scholz argues (2023: 19), platform cooperatives offer 'a common reference point' for 'a loosely knit global coalition of cooperatives that operate primarily online'. In other words, social power means the capacity to do things – to produce effects in economic activity through voluntary and collective organisation.

Table 13.1 shows that (platform) cooperatives can contribute to workers' social empowerment along one or more pathways, articulated across four dimensions. Identifying these four dimensions aids the categorisation of the various phenomena encompassed by the umbrella notion of platform cooperatives. Put differently, the relevance of exploring these pathways lies in providing a deeper understanding of the diversity of cooperative experiences in app-based food delivery. This study contributes to a re-signification of the movement of platform cooperativism, oriented around the multiplicity of worker-owned technologies (Grohmann 2023).

Social empowerment through the cooperative model is twofold. On the one hand, cooperatives have the potential to empower workers economically because shared ownership can facilitate better earnings, training opportunities and benefits than conventional ventures. At the same time, cooperatives have the potential to empower workers politically through democratic control, delivering autonomy at work and participation in decision-making processes. Undoubtedly, these potentialities are matched with constraints that challenge cooperatives' ability to increase worker empowerment effectively. The diversity of platform cooperatives also implies different outcomes concerning worker empowerment and the ways of tackling its challenges.

Table 13.1 Four dimensions of social empowerment pathways through platform cooperativism

Dimension	Research question
Context and needs	What is the context in which the platform originated and which needs does it address?
Actors and alliances	Who are the actors involved and what kind of alliances are being built between them?
Features	What does the organisational form and business model look like?
Digital technology	To what extent and in which way is technology incorporated into the platform?

Source: Author's own elaboration.

CASE SELECTION AND METHODS

This chapter focuses on six examples of cooperatives in western Europe and North and South America. Their selection is not bound by any statistical criterion as there is no data available on how many app-based food delivery cooperatives exist. At present, the Platform Cooperativism Consortium registers the existence of 546 projects spread across 50 countries,[1] but it does not offer consistent data on projects' economic sectors. Aimed at furnishing better opportunities for learning (Stake 2013), case selection for this chapter was made on the basis of seeking variety across the four dimensions highlighted in Table 13.1, and includes

CoopCycle (transnational); Central (Argentina); Givit Delivery Coop (Spain); Pídelo en Cleta (Chile); Radish (Canada); and Señoritas Courier (Brazil).

Within the emerging field of platform cooperatives, two models provide much of the foundation: worker cooperatives and multi-stakeholder cooperatives. In worker cooperatives, worker-members[2] share ownership of the means of production they use and are entitled to one vote regardless of the amount of capital invested. They are a viable organisational form to benefit workers and empower them and, although they generally constitute solutions to unemployment rather than alternatives to capitalism (Quijano 2011), they are innovations that expand social power (Kasparian 2022a; Wright 2019) and enlarge economic imaginaries (Gibson-Graham 2006). Four of these six cases are either already worker cooperatives (Central, Givit Delivery Coop and Pídelo en Cleta) or in the process of becoming one (Señoritas Courier).

The original aim of platform cooperatives was to benefit workers, but, given the nature of platform activity (connecting, as it does, different groups of users via digital infrastructure), the multi-stakeholder cooperative model has gained support (Vidal 2022). In general, cooperative members come from a single kind of stakeholder, the group most benefited by the organisation's purpose. For example, in worker cooperatives, the members are the workers of the organisation, whereas, in consumer cooperatives, the consumers are the members. In contrast, multi-stakeholder cooperatives are owned or governed by more than one type of stakeholder, including workers, consumers, volunteers, public administrations or supporters. In this way, they seek to benefit multiple social groups by guaranteeing participation in the cooperative, although not necessarily with the same weights and rights. This has the potential to enable social alliances around platform projects. Radish is a multi-stakeholder cooperative, while CoopCycle is in the process of becoming one.

The techniques used to inform the case studies are semi-structured interviews, participant observation, desk research and literature review. Seven in-person and virtual interviews were conducted with cooperative members and key informants, while participant observation was carried out during virtual and in-person meetings with the Argentine, Brazilian and Chilean teams implementing platform cooperatives and during virtual and in-person panels featuring workers from these cooperatives. Additionally, the author has taken part in the implementation of CoopCycle in Latin America, in particular in Argentina, during the last few years. Throughout this process, participatory dynamics such as debates and workshops took place, providing feedback for both the research and the implementation of the platform. Desk research has provided grey literature, audiovisual materials, brochures, social media communications and news, much of which is readily available public information. Finally, a literature review has been applied to support the empirical studies.

COOPCYCLE: OPEN-SOURCE ACTIVISM IN FRANCE AND TRANSNATIONAL PLATFORM COOPERATIVISM

CoopCycle is a cycle-logistics digital infrastructure and a federation made up of the bike delivery cooperatives using it. This platform cooperative was founded as a non-profit association in 2017 by a group of activists in France, among them an individual who provided software development. Its mission is to foster solidarity between cooperatives, reduce costs by service pooling, and create a common force to advocate couriers' rights. The federation of courier cooperatives is a predecessor organisation to an intended future multi-stakeholder cooperative that will formalise the participation of the different actors involved in its foundation and implementation.

CoopCycle supports three business models: food delivery or foodtech; scheduled courier services for goods; and last-mile services for products purchased online. Although software development was initially directed at supporting foodtech, the technology has recently been redesigned to include new features and developments for scheduled courier and last-mile services. These changes are the result of cooperatives increasingly shifting from food delivery towards scheduled courier services for groceries, goods and packages in the business-to-business sector. This business model is better suited for small worker collectives and for ensuring more regular incomes. Each worker collective is autonomous concerning its working conditions, internal organisation and business model.

Digital technology is one of CoopCycle's main strengths. Its open-source software has a 'Coopyleft' licence, which guarantees its use by cooperatives and worker collectives exclusively. CoopCycle's software was shaped from the outset by the contributions and feedback of courier collectives, even though its founders were not themselves couriers. Exchanges between the founder group and these French collectives arose as delivery platforms went bankrupt or labour conditions deteriorated and as courier collectives wanted to use CoopCycle in their cooperatives (Acosta Alvarado et al. 2021).

Besides being open-source, the software has four notable features: (a) it does not collect data on consumer habits and worker performance; (b) it prioritises the use of open technologies (such as OpenStreetMap for georeferencing); (c) it has a decentralised infrastructure – each cooperative has a server instance that it co-owns and manages autonomously; and (d) there is no algorithmic management of work processes or workers' performance. The software does not assess and rate workers, nor does it deploy gamification strategies. A human dispatcher assigns deliveries to couriers; workers can be geotracked by cooperatives but not by customers; and no features allow customers to evaluate workers. The absence of algorithmic work management allows for the integration of couriers' knowledge into the software (Gnisa 2023). The digital infrastructure, however, is not the only shared asset: CoopCycle provides a well-known brand. Cooperatives in the federation also mutualise communications, commercial offerings, funding and training, among other things. Unlike the venture capital funding of corporate platforms, CoopCycle is supported by the annual fees contributed by member cooperatives, contributions from public subsidies and grants, and volunteer work.

To ensure the democratic participation of couriers, the founders' association established the federation of courier cooperatives. By 2023, CoopCycle's webpage listed roughly 70 courier collectives as members, the vast majority of which are in western Europe. CoopCycle has carried out annual general assemblies in Europe since 2018 and has also experimented with digital democracy tools to channel collective decision-making and facilitate exchanges between worker collectives and project participants. Besides the general assembly, in 2021 courier collectives in Europe chose the first board, according to the principle of 'one co-op, one vote'. The board is made up of ten people from six countries, largely from delivery cooperatives.

Also in 2021, the open-source software triggered implementation outside Europe, resulting in the launch of CoopCycle Latinoamérica, an informal network of initiatives linked to CoopCycle in Argentina, Chile, Mexico and Uruguay. This transnationalisation of CoopCycle was aided by collaboration between cooperatives, as evidenced by the growth of the development team with the onboarding of Argentina (Gigena and Muñoz Cancela 2021; Kasparian

2022b; Muñoz Cancela et al. 2023) and Mexico (Bustillos et al. 2022) and the consequent enhanced capacity to develop new software features.

CENTRAL: SOCIAL MOVEMENT TRADE UNION COOPERATIVISM IN ARGENTINA

Central is a worker cooperative based in the city of Salta and made up of 20 couriers: 15 worker-owners and five who are not members of the cooperative.[3] It was founded in 2017 by two allied organisations, Sindicato Único de Conductores de Motos de la República Argentina (Union of Motorbike Drivers of Argentina) and the Dignity social movement, which assessed that forming cooperatives was a viable strategy to address precarious working conditions for couriers. As in the rest of Latin America, labour informality and precarity are long-standing phenomena, not ones newly introduced by labour platforms. This worker cooperative's main activity is scheduled courier services for goods – thus not necessarily groceries, food or meals – which it now provides to around 300 clients (mostly other companies) with an average of 30 deliveries per day.

This platform cooperative is in a pilot stage and plans to start using the software provided by CoopCycle as a tool for internal logistics and fleet management. During 2022 and 2023, the cooperative was trained in the use of CoopCycle's software by the Federación Argentina de Cooperativas de Trabajo de Tecnología, Innovación y Conocimiento (FACTTIC; Argentinian Federation of Technology Worker Cooperatives), the organisation that localised CoopCycle's software in Argentina. Central's couriers mostly use motorbikes, but the cooperative is committed to incorporating other bikes. FACTTIC has donated a cargo bike and two computers to Central as part of a project financed by the National Ministry of Science to foster social technologies through cooperative-university partnerships, in this case, with the University of Buenos Aires.

Looking at workers' social empowerment, this cooperative faces many economic limitations. Some of the couriers in Central are not members as membership is regarded as a process that not all couriers are ready or willing to undertake, although the cooperative views this as taking place eventually. Furthermore, Central does not currently generate profits; on the contrary, its small structure is substantially supported by voluntary work and the weekly economic contributions of its couriers. Central computes wages based on tasks or orders delivered, meaning there is no minimum guaranteed income if orders are meagre. All workers supplement their income with other sources and do not devote full workdays to the cooperative. Workers at Central also make use of the national social assistance scheme for participating in a social and solidarity venture.[4] This is critical to keeping the collective project going, as it supplements workers' income and provides capital to the cooperative. Regardless of the number of hours worked, if a worker draws the assistance, then a weekly contribution to the cooperative must be made. Finally, being part of Central provides workers with access to training in cooperative management.

A board is elected at an assembly and all worker-members are eligible to stand. Given the small size of the cooperative, informal meetings between all workers are common, in addition to the mandatory general assembly. In this way, information is shared and available to all workers, who participate in decision-making through these meetings. Regarding work management, a couple of worker-members (who occasionally also perform delivery tasks) coordinate and assign tasks to couriers, who can choose whether or not to take them. Orders are received by phone call or WhatsApp and are shared and assigned to couriers through this messaging service.

GIVIT DELIVERY COOP: INTERCOOPERATION IN SPAIN

Givit Delivery Coop is a worker cooperative that provides professional courier services, distribution from large warehouses and food delivery using motorcycles, some of them electric. Givit began to take shape in 2018 in Granada and was launched in April 2020 by 31 members. At the beginning of 2023, the cooperative united 303 courier-members who worked in 37 teams located across six provinces of Andalucía. In 2022, they made more than a million deliveries and registered more than €4.1 million in revenues. This makes Givit the largest delivery cooperative in Europe, and it is a highly successful business, according to actors such as Confederación Española de Cooperativas de Trabajo Asociado (COCETA; Spanish Confederation of Worker Cooperatives) and Federación Andaluza de Empresas Cooperativas de Trabajo (Andalucian Federation of Worker Cooperative Enterprises).

Givit began in 2018 as a project within Gestcoop, a cooperative for business development (cooperativa de impulso empresarial). This type of incubator cooperative is a special regime of worker cooperatives stipulated by Andalucian cooperative law, aiming to channel the entrepreneurial initiative of members through professional guidance, the provision of business skills and common services and mentoring during the first years.[5] Givit members present this initiative as the result of a strategic alliance between Gestcoop and Givit to transform precarious working conditions in the delivery sector. As Maca Motos, Gestcoop's finance coordinator puts it:

> [Gestcoop] was created for the integral accompaniment of social economy entities. We mainly support the digitalisation... necessary to optimise their processes... Givit, the last-mile delivery cooperative, was born in response to this precarious situation in the delivery market... We believed that professionalising the sector was much better, that by collaborating rather than competing we would move further, that things would be better and that conditions would, in an integral way, not just salary, be better for the entire team… We always talk about the fact that there is a group intelligence that we must make the most of because each one contributes and enriches the other.[6]

Within this intercooperation, Gestcoop is in charge of integral management, which includes legal, operational, financial and platform management, while Givit handles the courier activities. With respect to digital technology, the platform software has three strong values: it provides legal certainty to all parties, document trackability and an embedded cooperative identity given its robust development in data access and transparency. For example, the platform registers assemblies and has a repository of voting results. In terms of work management, the platform tracks couriers' routes and measures productivity, resulting in weekly reports that allow for the elaboration of projections and the scheduling of shifts for the next week. Gestcoop does not charge for the service provided to Givit or for the use of the platform.

The software is offered to restaurants to request and track the delivery services provided by the cooperative and also gives access to data, heat maps and consumption trends.[7] This aligns with the goal of having an impact on the delivery market or industry as a whole rather than just on a group of workers from a single cooperative. In this regard, the cooperative seeks out large clients, offering them more than delivery services. Clients include major chains and restaurants, such as Burger King and KFC, while workers' clothing displays not only the logo of the cooperative but also that of the restaurant to which they are providing delivery services. As one cooperative member puts it: 'Let's not fool ourselves; if we want to compete, we have to be able to count on a good portfolio of customers that will allow us to scale our business and be profitable and efficient. We count on Burger King and KFC deliveries.'[8]

Givit is certainly a tool for worker empowerment in economic terms. Worker-members have decent incomes, annual leave, promotion and incentives for positions of responsibility and training. They are also provided with clothes, personal protective equipment and vehicles. Workers also participate in assemblies and have software access to relevant data on the cooperative. However, the division of tasks between Gestcoop and Givit may ultimately crystallise the distinction between intellectual and manual labour. These practices in the division of labour, along with data management concerning consumer habits and worker performance, may thus eventually undermine the potential of this initiative to be a politically empowering tool for workers.

PÍDELO EN CLETA: MUNICIPAL LOCAL DEVELOPMENT POLICIES AND CYCLE ACTIVISM IN CHILE

The Department of Local Economic Development of the municipal government of Renca, a commune located in the north-west of the city of Santiago, launched a public policy of economic revitalisation in the context of the Covid-19 pandemic and isolation measures on the one hand and the rise of e-commerce and delivery on the other. Its goals were to create new jobs and connect Renca neighbours with local entrepreneurs by providing a free, ecologically friendly and sustainable bicycle-powered alternative. This included creating a local online marketplace that initially brought together 50 restaurants and cooperatives to provide delivery services. This service was to be provided at no cost to restaurants or customers during a four-month pilot period, with couriers being compensated by the municipal government.

One of the project's cooperatives was Pídelo en Cleta ('Order by Bike'), presented as 'the first municipal delivery by bike in the country'[9] and formed in mid-2021 by six cyclists who went through a recruitment and training process before registering as a worker cooperative. In addition, the municipal government developed branding for the project and provided clothing and backpacks. Worker-members believe that, despite their lack of familiarity prior to joining the cooperative, the project was viable because they were all passionate about bikes, had experience in bike mechanics or even in designing bike clothing and were interested in developing a cooperative alternative to boost local economies.

When the municipal project concluded, some worker-members decided to stay in the cooperative while others left and new members joined. Pídelo en Cleta currently has six worker-members. As the online marketplace died off and food delivery demand declined with the easing of the pandemic and conclusion of the municipal programme, the worker cooperative introduced a second service. In addition to delivering food, goods and packages, it implemented a bike mechanics workshop for which it received a grant from the Technical Cooperation Service under the Chilean Ministry of Economy to provide training and prepare premises for development.

Furthermore, Pídelo en Cleta began to be in touch with two key players: Centro Internacional de Economía Social y Cooperativa (CIESCOOP; International Centre for the Social and Cooperative Economy) of the University of Santiago, and FACTTIC, which was localising CoopCycle's software for use in Argentina. These alliances enabled Pídelo en Cleta to receive training and assistance in business models and cooperative management from CIESCOOP, as well as to begin exchanges and training with FACTTIC to adopt the CoopCycle software. The couriers considered digital technology adoption a crucial issue as it would better position them with restaurant customers interested in digitalised delivery management. However, the process of technology incorporation was halted because the grant received stipulated that the cooperative improve its mechanical services. Nonetheless, Pídelo en Cleta has recently submitted another grant application to strengthen courier services and consolidate both areas of the cooperative: micro-electromobility and app-based courier services.

The cooperative is currently unable to attain the minimum wage for its workers. As in Central, income is distributed on the basis of task completed, order delivered or bike repaired, and all the workers have other jobs to enhance their income. Out of the cost of each delivery or bike repair, 10 per cent goes to support the cooperative structure, 1 per cent for mechanical maintenance, and the rest to the workers. The cooperative has recently taken on a member who is a CIESCOOP researcher undertaking a project to define the cooperative's business model to secure decent wages for workers.

This small worker collective has one worker designated for dispatch functions and a manager, who is one of the cooperative's founding couriers. Because they have fewer than 20 members, Chilean cooperative frameworks have a simple management structure in which no board is elected. Instead, an assembly of worker-members elects a general manager who also serves as a kind of board chair. General assemblies and informal meetings are used to make decisions and, whereas they were weekly at the start of the cooperative, they are now less frequent. Meetings are combined with groups in instant messaging apps like WhatsApp. It presents as a collective that fully respects the horizontality of the cooperative.

RADISH: RESTAURANTS UNITE IN CANADA

Radish is a solidarity cooperative based in Montreal. Solidarity cooperatives are multi-stakeholder cooperatives legally established as such in 1997 in the Canadian province of Quebec. Radish was founded in 2020 by seven restaurant owners who, 'having worked and owned restaurants… wanted to create the company [they] would have liked to have worked with given the chance' (Radish website). During the pandemic, restaurants had lost control of their client base to app-based food delivery platforms, which had also narrowed their profit margins while providing a service they perceived as low quality. Hence, Radish was originally created to provide local restaurants with an alternative food delivery service based on affordable fees and high quality. This solidarity cooperative charges a commission of up to 20 per cent per transaction to restaurants, and there are no delivery fees for customers.

Later, the cooperative also developed Marché Radish, a weekly delivery of reusable crates containing locally sourced restaurant products, such as ready-to-eat meals and ingredients, alongside goods from bakeries, butchers and florists. As explained in the FAQ section of the Marché Radish website, 'instead of traditional on-demand food delivery, which can be costly…, we offer a weekly delivery service that bundles various products into one crate, lowering the cost… while offering more variety and being better for the environment'. The launch of this service resulted from learning about business models: Radish believes traditional on-demand food delivery is a successful model for restaurants of a certain segment, being unsustainable for local businesses which have been excluded from the digital economy since delivering small orders from local shops apart from one another is not sufficiently profitable.

The cooperative has a marketplace website where both types of delivery service can be requested, paid for and tracked. Moreover, the cooperative is planning to develop an app. The means of transportation used by couriers is primarily cars, but, in 2021, the cooperative incorporated four electric cargo bikes. In contrast to other platform cooperatives, Radish has solved its investment issues by relying on the law of cooperatives applying in Canada. This norm favours investments which are:

> in the form of equity… that can actually grow in value over time just like in a regular company, which has allowed us to get access to a lot of capital that we would normally not have for an early-stage company… We've actually been able to get a lot of investment from the restaurants themselves and the employees themselves. (Mansib Rahman, Radish co-founder)[10]

Radish members are restaurants, workers (both couriers and head office workers) and consumers: the cooperative has 60 restaurant members and 18 worker members (Desautels 2022). Its governance and member participation are clearly structured: the three groups have an equal number of seats on the board: three restaurant owners, three consumers and three workers. The seats representing workers must be occupied by at least one courier and one head office worker (Rafélis de Broves, 2024). Members are entitled to share in the profits, in the case of workers according to performance and hours worked; for restaurants based on sales volume realised through the platform. There is a fourth group also represented on the board: supporting members. These are investors who, according to the federal law of cooperatives, can have a maximum of 20 per cent of the seats on the board, even if they own more in shares, as governance rights are detached from equity. Additionally, all members possess the right to vote in the general assembly on the overall direction of the organisation.

Work management practices ensure a more autonomous setting for couriers. The cooperative does not resort regularly to algorithmic surveillance or gamification and couriers receive fewer follow-up messages or incentives, are not rated by customers and have access to local and available support teams by phone or in person (Rafélis de Broves, 2024). Besides the political empowerment triggered by member participation and the absence of algorithmic control, workers at Radish are incorporated as employees and so enjoy a minimum hourly wage that provides a certain income stability. According to Radish's website, unlike traditional platforms, their couriers receive a higher basic wage and do not depend on tips. As a result, it is clear that a restaurant-led platform cooperative can also serve as a model of worker empowerment.

SEÑORITAS COURIER: CYCLE ACTIVISM WITH AN INTERSECTIONAL GENDER PERSPECTIVE IN BRAZIL

Señoritas Courier is a worker collective of nine cis women and LGBTQI+ people that offers sustainable courier services in the city of São Paulo. Many of the couriers are Black women from the periphery, and some are over 40 years old, above the average age of the typical app-based delivery workforce. Señoritas Courier was founded in 2019 with the objective of challenging labour precarisation, securing decent work and encouraging sustainability (Salvagni et al. 2022). It aims to contest the prevailing notion that women are slower, more fearful and less autonomous in transit, while supporting the empowerment of cis women and trans people. Additionally, it tackles issues of harassment and discrimination regarding these social groups, as well as gender inequality, from a perspective of feminist economics.

Concerning the actors involved, the founder of the project, Aline Os, was a university professor resorting to bike deliveries to supplement her income; then demand surpassed her capacity to respond individually. The idea of Señoritas Courier took initial shape before continuing to develop on a course for businesses based on the use of bicycles:

> There was a lot of demand, and I couldn't meet all the demands. I posted a story on a social network saying I wanted to pass the demand on to other people. Ten women responded and said they would do the work. Then I created a WhatsApp group, and the first ten were the first ones. (Aline Os, Señoritas Courier founder)[11]

Señoritas Courier's business model is based on providing courier services by appointment and by bicycle. It primarily performs deliveries in the cosmetics sector, as well as to the offices of solicitors and, less frequently, food deliveries, given the difficulty of meeting the immediacy required for this task (Grohmann 2022). Demand increased during the Covid-19 pandemic, but afterwards deliveries dropped. Therefore, the couriers added other services to their offerings: training in bicycle mechanics to foster couriers' autonomy and bike tours on culture and history, with a focus on diversity and territory. Nonetheless, some workers have had to leave Señoritas Courier, looking for other sources of income.

Señoritas Courier uses an online form and social media chats (WhatsApp and Instagram) to manage orders (Salvagni et al. 2022). The automated form available to order deliveries highlights the relevant parameters with respect to pricing, working conditions and the financial structure of the collective: prices are calculated not only depending on distance, time, weight and weather conditions, but also include fees if the service is provided during weekends, before or after a typical working day or at night. As a result, the form generates a price and informs the customer which part of it goes to the courier and which to the collective.

The cooperative model is viewed by Señoritas Courier's workers as the best legal figure to secure their ownership and self-organisation. However, Brazil's legal framework and the high costs of establishing cooperatives have slowed this process. The barriers are not only legal but also political and cultural: Señoritas Courier is more connected with social movements, non-profit organisations and cycle delivery collectives than with the traditional Brazilian cooperative movement (Grohmann 2022), which is related much more to agribusiness than to small cooperative and solidarity economy initiatives.

Besides being able to organise the collective according to the cooperative model, there is a second challenge: developing a cooperative platform for delivery work that belongs to the couriers in the context of a highly masculinised logistics sector. At present, the collective has engaged the support of Núcleo de Tecnologia do Movimento dos Trabalhadores Sem Teto (MTST; Technology Centre of the Homeless Workers' Movement) and the University of Campinas to promote digital inclusion. Since 2023, Señoritas Courier workers have been learning programming together with MTST to advance the appropriation of technologies and platforms. Three criteria guide this embryonic development: care, economic inclusion and workers' autonomy. Although the workers have been in touch with the CoopCycle project both in Europe and in South America, they prefer to build a platform of their own from the ground up that could later be used and adapted by other collectives in the country.

Señoritas Courier has one worker dedicated to administrative, financial, communications, dispatch and customer service functions. The worker collective is small and not yet registered as a cooperative, so there are no governance or decision-making structures. The important issue in this regard, however, is the training that workers receive, not just in digital technology and business administration but also, in a more informal sense, in the communications and social skills that empower individuals. For example, at public events where Señoritas Courier participates, different couriers narrate the story and situation of the collective.

DISCUSSION: PATHWAYS, SOCIAL EMPOWERMENT AND CHALLENGES

This section compares the pathways that the selected platforms describe with reference to the four dimensions set out in Table 13.1, and assesses the challenges that these platforms present for social empowerment. The six case studies explored here generally seek to improve couriers' working conditions while some also provide socio-labour inclusion to marginalised groups. Instead of focusing on strengthening small organisations in niche markets, Givit Delivery Coop aims at changing the sector as a whole and, hence, deploys a different business model. There are also cooperatives that address other issues posed by the platform economy, such as Radish, which offers a fairer platform for restaurants looking for alternatives to the major operators in app-based food delivery, while Pídelo en Cleta is a cooperative launched by a municipal programme to boost local development during the pandemic, and Señoritas Courier has the goal of empowering cis women and gender-fluid people. This last case represents an alternative way of organising delivery work enabled by digital technology and is particularly powerful and almost unique in terms of its inclusion of cis women and trans people from an intersectional perspective (see also the case of Las Mercedes in Barcelona, developed by Salvagni et al. 2022).

The initiatives demonstrate different synergies, attesting to the 'multi-stakeholder' spirit of platform cooperativism. Volunteer workers with software development knowledge grouped together in a non-profit organisation in the case of CoopCycle; trade unions in traditional courier services allied with a social movement with the support of tech worker cooperatives in Central; a business development cooperative partnered with Givit; a municipal government incubated and supported Pídelo en Cleta, which later also received the support of tech worker cooperatives and a university; a group of restaurants created the solidarity cooperative Radish; and a university professor supplemented incomes through a project of socio-labour inclusion in collaboration with a social movement and a university to develop a platform exclusively for Señoritas Courier.

CoopCycle, a federation of courier cooperatives, supports various business models, but local cooperatives are increasingly resorting to scheduled deliveries to secure regular incomes. This has an impact on CoopCycle's technology design through democratic decision-making. Central is a worker cooperative mainly devoted to scheduled courier services for goods. Similarly, Señoritas Courier performs this kind of service alongside activities related to sustainable mobility, although it has not yet been able to register as a worker cooperative given the regulatory and other constraints in Brazil. Likewise, Pídelo en Cleta is struggling to consolidate two service areas: micro-electromobility and app-based courier services. In this case, registering as a worker cooperative was easier given the support of the municipal government. Givit is also a worker cooperative, but supported by Gestcoop, another cooperative engaged in business development, which provides software and overall management to assist with the development of a business-to-business model of distribution from large warehouses and food delivery for large clients. The solidarity cooperative Radish focuses on food delivery and the weekly delivery of crates by car.

Finally, the digital technologies used are diverse too. CoopCycle is the only platform cooperative in the sector that has scaled up beyond national and even regional borders owing to its use of open-source technology (which is limited to cooperative use) and being open to transnational intercooperation. CoopCycle is an open-source application, and Givit has developed its own platform; both vary in their features and the ways in which they are designed. CoopCycle tends to develop new features by taking into account the opinions of worker collectives and does not gather data on consumer habits or worker performance, whereas Givit does collect this type of data and makes it available to restaurants, while also providing features such as a repository of voting results that aid the consolidation of workers' democratic practices. Whereas Central and Pídelo en Cleta rely on phones and WhatsApp, and are, or have been, trained in the use of CoopCycle's software, Señoritas Courier also uses also a website and its project is to develop an app of its own with the aid of a social movement and a university. Though probably not falling within the same scaling model as Givit, Señoritas Courier intends to make its software available to more worker collectives in Brazil, while Radish is also following this path and planning to develop an app of its own.

As the platform economy consolidates, cooperatives could be increasingly seen as viable alternatives to the precarisation, discrimination and control stemming from digital labour platforms. Unpacking the variety of outcomes in terms of workers' economic and social empowerment contributes to enhancing our grasp of platform cooperativism while also mapping potentialities and difficulties – see Table 13.2. While several platform cooperatives are on their way towards consolidating, research has been able to focus on their main challenges and emerging issues. When assessing long-term sustainability and, hence, the degree to which cooperatives can effectively deliver social power, two economic challenges arise: funding and competition.

Regarding funding, corporate platforms typically rely on venture capital, whereas the cooperative sector tends to seek support from foundations and governments. In Radish, the legal framework enables equity investment that can grow in value over time, together with participation in decision-making. Through collaborations with universities or cooperative federations, Central, Pídelo en Cleta and Señoritas Courier access state grants or support from the wider cooperative movement. Pídelo en Cleta shows the potential as well as the limitations of public policies aimed at creating cooperatives. Although public support was crucial in the foundation and during the first steps of this cooperative, the end of the programme implied

Table 13.2 *Comparison of the six case studies in terms of workers' social empowerment*

Platform cooperative	Workers' social empowerment – economic	Workers' social empowerment – political
CoopCycle	Federation provides mutualised resources (open-source software)	Annual assembly, digital democracy, board representatives, 'one co-op, one vote'
Central	Income based on tasks plus social assistance scheme; training; all workers supplement income with other jobs	Assemblies/informal meetings, Board representatives through elections
Givit Delivery Coop	Workers have decent incomes, annual leave, promotions, incentives for positions of responsibility and training; they are provided with clothes, personal protective equipment and vehicles	Assemblies; software measures worker productivity; Gestcoop is in charge of integral management
Pídelo en Cleta	Income based on tasks; training; all workers supplement income with other jobs	Assemblies/informal meetings; general manager is elected
Radish	Members share in the profits; minimum hourly wages for couriers; higher base wage than traditional platforms	Members have equal number of seats on the board and the right to vote in the general assembly; no algorithmic surveillance, no ratings
Señoritas Courier	Some members have had to leave to look for other sources of income; training in management and digital technologies	Informal meetings since it is not yet registered as a cooperative

Source: Author's own elaboration.

having to deal alone with the management of the cooperative as well as the redefinition of the business model in changing market conditions. In the case of Givit, intercooperation has been valuable, especially given the legal framework that favours cooperative incubation by other cooperatives, as with the Andalucian cooperative statute. The incubation approach is particularly fruitful because the start-up phase is heavily reliant on funding. Finally, member contribution in CoopCycle stands as fundamental and, at the same time, the availability of open-source software allows for the reduction of costs for worker collectives.

With respect to competition, the platform model relies on network effects to create monopolies. This presents a difficult scenario for cooperative initiatives. However, platform cooperatives do not scale like corporate platforms. Instead of seeking profit maximisation, cooperatives tend to create networks to mutualise infrastructures and resources to guarantee the well-being of their members and communities.

Scaling out cooperatives entails at least two political challenges. First is maintaining cooperative values and principles while expanding (Spicer 2018). In large-scale structures, democratic participation and a sense of belonging may be overlooked. Even without considering the question of scale, members' active participation in platform cooperatives is a challenge (Bunders 2023; Mannan and Pek 2023). Concerning market competition, along with the diversification of services offered (Central, Pídelo en Cleta, Radish, Señoritas Courier), the deployment of a business model aimed at big chain restaurants (Givit) and CoopCycle's scaling out through a federation all seem to be powerful strategies. The long-term sustainability of CoopCycle may reside in strengthening transnational networks of mutual aid that secure not only shared resources but shared identities and collective commitment.

In circumstances where scale means geographic expansion, these quandaries can be exacerbated by contrasts and inequalities between the community of origin and other territories. Hence, second, the scaling-up of cooperatives also rests on being able to expand beyond borders while operating under a rationale of fairness and equity. Technologies can operate in a variety of settings through local processes of functioning construction that act to resignify them (Thomas et al. 2019). This means that processes do not follow a one-way route from a supposedly homogeneous centre to the rest of the world where copies of the original are established (Chakrabarty 2008). Rather than replicating models, the geographical growth of cooperatives should be fuelled by adaptations that take into account reciprocal influences, differences and pre-existing inequalities (Kasparian 2022b).

CoopCycle is the only platform cooperative that has scaled up beyond national and regional borders. In this context, although all the cooperatives within the federation are entitled to one vote, it is worth considering the distribution of informal power. Ensuring an inclusive and egalitarian transnational cooperative platform requires paying attention to the different weights of the cooperatives that make up the federation to influence new developments according to not only the cooperatives' size (Gnisa 2023) but also their location (Kasparian 2022b).

Notwithstanding these challenges, the sustainability of the cooperative platform model should be assessed from a broader perspective. In platform capitalism, the pursuit of profit is heavily reliant on cost reduction, hence compromising the objective of upholding equitable working conditions, a key focus of cooperatives. However, even reducing costs may not be enough. There are concerns over the capacity of corporate platforms, especially labour platforms, to maintain long-term sustainability (Srnicek 2018). On the contrary, specific elements of the cooperative model have the potential to facilitate sustainability (Coca 2017). For instance, worker ownership fosters motivations for the long-term viability and expansion of the business as well as for the establishment of networks within the cooperative ecosystem. The viability of cooperatives is also dependent upon legal and regulatory frameworks that frequently prove to be inadequate or insufficient for cooperatives in comparison to those regulating corporate companies.

In sum, whereas platform cooperativism serves as a powerful 'common reference point', the literature on this subject, as well as the cooperative movement's history, demonstrates that the cooperative model serves different needs, employs a variety of organisational and legal forms and does not tend to take a techno-determinist view of platform labour. This diversity provides some potential for worker organising. However, platform cooperatives do face economic and political challenges in terms of workers' social empowerment. The range of avenues for implementing platform cooperatives also gives rise to different ways in which such challenges might best be addressed.

CONCLUSIONS

This chapter has four main contributions to make to the discussion. First, cooperatives seem to be easily constituted and, except in one case (Señoritas Courier), there is no evidence of great difficulties in establishing them. It should be considered, nevertheless, that this could be a bias inherent in the study's case selection.

Second, some definitions focus on the cooperative identity of these ventures (Mayo 2019). This characterisation could be nuanced because the contexts, needs and actors involved in their foundations and implementation demonstrate values, goals, trajectories and political backgrounds that exceed those of the cooperative movement. In most cases, cooperatives are an adaptive resource for channelling fairer conditions for the players involved.

Third, platform cooperatives differ from mainstream corporate platforms not only in that the former are organised according to fairer ownership and governance conditions. Digital technologies assume a radically different role in platform cooperatives: avoiding techno-determinist perspectives, the platform component of a project is envisioned in many cases as the arrival point of a long process of collective organising to address the social needs and issues that the platform economy entails.

Finally, given that their foundations are strongly linked with Covid-19 isolation measures and the temporary increase in the demand for food delivery, several of these cooperatives have begun redefining their business models, shifting towards scheduled courier services or adding bike-related services. This also testifies to the agility and flexibility of cooperatives, whether out of necessity or otherwise. One of the cooperatives (Givit) has designed a different model through intercooperative collaboration, offering app-based food delivery services to big chains in a business-to-business model.

Among the strengths concerning workers' social empowerment, these various paths collectivise an individualistic job, professionalising it and providing workers with training opportunities. This is frequently accompanied by technological appropriation, workplace freedom and participation in the cooperatives' governance and ownership structures. Democratic decision-making is fostered, legally guaranteed and achievable given the small size of most of them. Furthermore, they address discrimination issues by thematising the deeply established gender inequality in our societies and emphasising care, economic inclusion and autonomy. As for how these cooperatives are addressing the challenges for social empowerment in the platform economy, the cooperatives have identified diverse funding strategies and market competition approaches.

As for the weaknesses, in some cases, access to ownership does not mean better wages given that ventures need to consolidate economically. A potential solution lies in reaching a critical mass that would ensure sufficient income for couriers as many worker cooperatives currently have lower turnover than corporate delivery platforms. For small cooperatives with low capital flow, being able to have positive economic results in the short term is essential. Otherwise, their interest in technological adoption may diminish as they focus on more urgent activities. In this regard, public support and training are key aspects.

The initiatives outlined in these six case studies show that the cooperative model is an effective tool to help create innovative responses to the challenges posed by labour platforms, and that cooperatives' responses are able to surpass the usually considered critiques revolving around precarisation and control, offering pathways towards broader workers' social empowerment.

ACKNOWLEDGEMENTS

I am thankful to Diego Fernández Peychaux, Cecilia Muñoz Cancela, Marco Marrone, Olivier Rafélis de Broves, Patricio Inostroza and the interviewees from Central, CoopCycle, FACTTIC and Pídelo en Cleta for sharing their time and knowledge with me. I am grateful to Julieta Grasas for generously helping me with desk research. I want to acknowledge the funds and intellectual community provided by the Institute for the Study of Employee Ownership and Profit Sharing, the Institute for the Cooperative Digital Economy-Platform Cooperativism Consortium and the Fund for Scientific and Technological Research of the Argentinian National Agency for the Promotion of Research, Technological Development and Innovation. Finally, I am thankful for the comments and feedback from colleagues at the ETUI Workshop and to the editors of this book, Kurt Vandaele and Silvia Rainone, for their insightful comments.

NOTES

1. https://directory.platform.coop/#13.19/-54.7641/20.02763
2. The employment status of workers varies depending on national regulatory frameworks. In some countries, worker cooperatives can include salaried employees as well as worker-members; in others, cooperatives must adhere to the membership link between workers and the organisation and, thus, are not allowed to hire workers on a regular basis. Moreover, cooperative workers have access to different kinds of employment protection. In some countries, worker-members enjoy the same social protection benefits as salaried employees of conventional companies; in others, they have their own social protection regimes; in yet others, they merely access a downgraded regime since they are classified as self-employed. In these situations, it is common to see cooperatives develop ad hoc social protection policies to fill the void.
3. The Argentine Cooperatives Act 20,337 stipulates an associational – non-labour – link between workers and the cooperative. However, Resolution 360/75 of Instituto Nacional de Acción Cooperativa allows worker cooperatives to hire personnel for limited periods and under certain circumstances.
4. Boosting Work (Potenciar trabajo) is a social scheme aimed at promoting the social inclusion of people in vulnerable situations. Programme participants receive a monthly income equivalent to half the minimum wage to pursue their studies or work on socio-productive projects. These projects are often linked to social movements that develop social, solidarity and popular economy initiatives.
5. https://www.juntadeandalucia.es/organismos/empleoempresaytrabajoautonomo/areas/economia-social/cooperativas/conceptos-clases.html
6. https://youtu.be/xbqXDdN54js
7. Givit Dossier, available online at: www.givit.pro
8. https://sputniknews.lat/20201117/vivimos-una-era-de-plataformas-cooperativas-los-nuevos-riders-prometen-un-negocio-mas-justo-y-etico-1093521200.html
9. www.youtube.com/watch?v=7k8T5jFP8Pc&ab_channel=MunicipalidaddeRenca
10. www.youtube.com/watch?v=8ugDaXEMCG0&feature=youtu.be&ab_channel=CommonWealth, the quote being drawn from the virtual panel 'The future of digital co-ops: how policy can help scale the sector'.

11. www.uol.com.br/carros/colunas/pedala/2020/06/30/coletivo-de-mulheres-e-lgbts-ganha-notoriedade-em-entregas-de-bike-por-sp.htm?cmpid=copiaecola

REFERENCES

Acosta Alvarado A.S., Aufrère L. and Srnec C. (2021) CoopCycle, un projet de plateforme socialisée et de régulation de la livraison à vélo. https://hal.science/hal-03364001

Berg J. et al. (2018) *Digital labour platforms and the future of work: towards decent work in the online world*, ILO.

Bunders D.J. (2023) Silicon law of oligarchy: patterns of member participation in the decision-making of platform cooperatives, *Socio-Economic Review*, 22 (3). https://doi.org/10.1093/ser/mwad058

Bustillos D., González E. and Viornery J. (2022) *Rodando Juntas*, TDP/Ideamos/BID/BID Lab.

Cañada E., Izcara C. and Zapata M.J. (2023) Putting fairness into the gig economy: delivery cooperatives as alternatives to corporate platforms, *Societies*, 13 (3), 68–87.

Chakrabarty D. (2008) *Provincializing Europe: postcolonial thought and historical difference*, Princeton University Press.

Coca N. (2017) How innovative funding models could usher in a new era of worker-owned platform cooperatives, Shareable.net, 28 August.

Cohen B. (2018) *Post-capitalist entrepreneurship startups for the 99%*, CRC Press.

Coraggio J.L. (2008) La sostenibilidad de los emprendimientos de la economía social y solidaria, *Revista Otra Economía*, 2 (3), 41–57.

Cousin L. (2021) Towards a digitally-enabled cooperative movement, *Work Together: The Global Newsletter for Cooperatives active in Industry and Services*, September, 12–14.

Desautels K. (2022) Une entreprise de livraison pour restaurants vise la carboneutralité, *Métro*, 22 February.

Fuster Morell M., Espelt R. and Renau Cano M. (2021) Cooperativismo de plataforma: análisis de las cualidades democráticas del cooperativismo como alternativa económica en entornos digitales, CIRIEC-España. *Revista de Economía Pública, Social y Cooperativa,* 102, 5–31.

Gibson-Graham J.K. (2006) *The end of capitalism (as we knew it): a feminist critique of political economy*, University of Minnesota Press.

Gigena H. and Muñoz Cancela C. (2021) Cooperativas de plataformas como estrategias de desarrollo local: la experiencia CoopCycle Argentina, in Altschuler B. et al. (eds.) *Gestión de iniciativas económicas colaborativas y economía social y solidaria*, Universidad Nacional de Quilmes-Universidad Nacional de Moreno, 52–63.

Gnisa F. (2023) Social choices in platform design: technology from a worker's standpoint in digital platform cooperatives. http://dx.doi.org/10.2139/ssrn.4499827

Grohmann R. (2022) Worker-owned platforms: cooperatives and collectives of platform riders, *Matrizes*, 16 (1), 209–233.

Grohmann R. (2023) Not just platform, nor cooperatives: worker-owned technologies from below, *Communication, Culture and Critique*, 16 (4) 274–282.

Haidar J. and Bordarampé G. (2022) La logística de última milla: impactos de la pandemia en las plataformas de reparto en Argentina, in Dalle P. (ed.) *Estructura social de Argentina en tiempos de pandemia, Vol. 2: Respuestas estatales, experiencias de trabajadoras/es y estrategias colectivas de resistencia en tres sectores estratégicos*, Ediciones Imago Mundi, 299–315.

ILO (2021) *World employment and social outlook 2021: the role of digital labour platforms in transforming the world of work*, ILO.

ILO (2002) *Recommendation 193: recommendation concerning the promotion of cooperatives*, ILO.

Kasparian D. (2022a) *Co-operative struggles: work conflicts in Argentina's new worker co-operatives*, Brill.

Kasparian D. (2022b) *The local implementation of platform co-ops in Argentina*, Institute for the Cooperative Digital Economy.

Kasparian D. and Rebón J. (2022) The production of change: the social power in recuperated enterprises, *Journal of Co-operative Studies*, 55 (3), 25–36.

López Mourelo E. (2020) *El trabajo en las plataformas digitales de reparto en Argentina: análisis y recomendaciones de política*, ILO Country Office for Argentina.
Mannan M. and Pek S. (2023) Platform cooperatives and the dilemmas of platform worker-member participation, *New Technology, Work and Employment*, 39 (2). https://doi.org/10.1111/ntwe.12273
Mayo E. (2019) *Digital democracy? Options for the International Cooperative Alliance to advance platform coops*, ICA.
Muñoz Cancela C., Kasparian D. and Grasas J. (2023) Análisis socio-técnico de la implementación argentina de la plataforma cooperativa CoopCycle, *Otra Economía*, 16 (29), 41–59.
Polanyi K. (1944/2007) *La gran transformación: crítica del liberalismo económico*, Fondo de Cultura Económica.
Quijano A. (2011) ¿Sistemas alternativos de producción?, in de Sousa Santos B. (ed.) *Producir para vivir: los caminos de la producción no capitalista*, Fondo de Cultura Económica, 369–389.
Rafélis de Broves, O. (2024). David contre Goliath? Les plateformes coopératives à l'assaut d'Uber. In L'Esprit Libre (Eds.), Interstices - Esquisses sur les utopies réelles au Québec. Éditions L'Esprit Libre.
Salvagni J., Grohmann R. and Matos É. (2022) Gendering platform co-operativism: the rise of women-owned rider co-operatives in Brazil and Spain, *Gender & Development*, 30 (3), 707–724.
Scholz T. (2023) *Own this! How platform cooperatives liberate workers and democratize the internet*, Verso.
Scholz T., Mannan M., Pentzien J. and Plotkin H. (2021) Policy recommendations to support cooperative ownership in the digital economy, Policy Paper, Platform Cooperativism Consortium and Berggruen Institute.
Spicer, J. S. (2018). Exceptionally Un-American? Why Co-operative EnterprisesStruggle in the United States, But Scale Elsewhere. Ph.D. thesis in Philosophyin Political Economy. Department of Urban Studies and Planning. MassachusettsInstitute of Technology.
Srnicek N. (2018) *Capitalismo de plataformas*, Caja Negra.
Stake R.E. (2013) Estudios de casos cualitativos, in Denzin N.K. and Lincoln Y.S. (eds.) *Manual de investigación cualitativa, Vol. 3: Las estrategias de investigación cualitativa*, Gedisa, 154–197.
Thomas H., Becerra L. and Bidinost A. (2019) ¿Cómo funcionan las tecnologías? Alianzas socio-técnicas y procesos de construcción de funcionamiento en el análisis histórico, *Pasado Abierto*, 10, 127–158.
Vandaele K. (2021) Collective resistance and organizational creativity amongst Europe's platform workers: a new power in the labour movement?, in Haidar J. and Keune M. (eds.) *Work and labour relations in global platform capitalism*, Edward Elgar Publishing, 206–235.
Vandaele K. (2023) Vulnerable food delivery platforms under pressure: protesting couriers seeking 'algorithmic justice' and alternatives, in Ness I. (ed.) *Routledge handbook of the gig economy*, Routledge, 205–219.
Vidal V. (2022) *Turning Fairbnb Coop into a multi-stakeholder cooperative*, Institute for the Cooperative Digital Economy.
Vieta M. (2010) The new cooperativism, *Affinities: A Journal of Radical Theory, Culture, and Action*, 4, 1–11.
Williams M. (2014) The solidarity economy and social transformation, in Satgar V. (ed.) *The solidarity economy alternative: emerging theory and practice*, University of KwaZulu-Natal Press, 37–63.
Wright E.O. (2019) *How to be an anticapitalist in the twenty-first century*, Verso.
All links were checked on 29 January 2024.

14. The spillover effect of algorithmic management and how (not) to tame it

Nastazja Potocka-Sionek and Antonio Aloisi

INTRODUCTION: EVERYTHING COMES FROM SOMEWHERE

Digital tools represent a constitutive element of today's work environments. Indeed, large portions of the workforce are now steered by systems that process granular data collected from various sources through technological infrastructure or the involvement of customers and colleagues. Workers can receive instructions from (semi-)automated decision-making systems, be constantly tracked by wearable devices or digital log stamps, and even be dismissed for not achieving algorithmically set goals. These processes can be observed in manufacturing, warehousing, trade, hospitality and office-based occupations, to offer just a few examples. Still, a lingering question remains: where do such processes come from?

In his gloomily far-sighted book, *Spillover: Animal Infections and the Next Human Pandemic*, David Quammen (2012: 33) popularised the notion of spillover, the process whereby 'a pathogen passes from members of one species, as host, into members of another'. While his work focuses on the relationship between humans, animals and the ecosystem, much can be learned by considering situations that allow a particular 'bug' to infect a new host species, thrive within it and then spread among (and beyond) its members. This chapter borrows Quammen's potent terminology to reveal how the set of practices that fall within the umbrella definition of algorithmic management (AM), which first appeared in the context of the platform economy, is increasingly affecting jobs in other areas of the labour market. While metaphors are, by definition, imperfect, this is a compelling parallel to describe how some features of AM have lost their context-specificity and become 'viral', spilling across a panoply of industries.

Given the novelty of the phenomenon, there is no commonly agreed definition of AM (Baiocco et al. 2022; Heinrich et al. 2022). However, to capture its scope in full, it must be acknowledged that any role within the set of managerial prerogatives can be offloaded to software. Thus, the present chapter applies a broad, generic understanding of the term without engaging with definitional nuances. Drawing from the current literature, AM is defined here as the use of software to automate organisational functions traditionally carried out by human managers (Mateescu and Nguyen 2019; Wood 2021).

Preliminary studies on AM, which date back to 2015, almost exclusively focused on the platform economy (Lee et al. 2015; Rosenblat and Stark 2016; Ivanova et al. 2018). In fact, only recently have researchers begun to isolate distinct AM practices from the platform economy and discuss them in a broader context (Stark and Pais 2020). Still, what is intended as AM often overlaps with the organisational model of digital labour platforms, or else tends to be conflated with it. Thus, the link between platform work and AM seems ineluctably indissoluble, which poses the risk of the part being confused with the whole. This risk must be diligently averted in light of the increasing recognition of the impact of AM on society.

Against this background, the goal of this chapter is to track the process of these 'infectious' AM systems as they move from a relatively small subsegment to the broader labour market. Reverting to key tenets of the platformisation trend, without narrowly considering the dominant question of workers' employment classification, can help to unpack the tools and practices that have been adopted to engage, dispatch, manage, control and assess people who perform platform work. This tendency is tracked across three dimensions: factual, jurisprudential and legislative. After providing evidence of the unfolding AM spillover, the chapter discusses the case law on AM and the regulatory instruments that address it. The prevalence of platform work continues to be strongly visible across the three dimensions, even though AM systems are gradually gaining independent prominence for both litigation and legislation. Judicial and legislative spillover is occurring, albeit only to a limited extent.

On closer inspection, the vast majority of cases on AM have been decided by courts or administrative bodies in the context of platform companies, generally focusing on the issue of employment classification. In particular, AM is strictly related to the notion of control, which has been key to the reclassification of platform workers as employees (Kellogg et al. 2020). However, the case law on platform workers' employment classification has, slowly yet consistently, paved the way for a mature and holistic understanding of AM. More recently, some cases have examined AM systems deployed by platforms and/or in more conventional workplaces in isolation from the employment classification issue, thereby shifting the focus to data protection, non-discrimination and working conditions issues for larger swathes of workers.

In the policymaking realm, much effort has been directed towards regulating AM in the platform economy at both domestic and European Union levels. As the AM spillover is becoming increasingly noticeable, a crucial dilemma concerns whether consideration of AM as a context-specific issue, to be addressed through targeted interventions in certain specific realms, suffices as a solution. The chapter argues that narrow regulatory interventions risk missing their target. AM should be perceived as a universal trend, while broader regulation encompassing the entire labour market should be designed to respond effectively to related challenges. Even though some broader instruments are emerging that intend to regulate AM beyond the platform economy, this trend is still in its early days. Both enforcement and regulatory action are needed to address the identified spillover effect, moving beyond the important but insufficient initiatives focusing on platform work and artificial intelligence (AI).

Two caveats concerning the scope of this chapter should be noted. First, the analysis is predominantly focused on food delivery companies. This is not to say that AM systems are unique to food delivery platforms; rather, many of the AM mechanisms used in this sector are shared with other types of platform, including those in transport and care as well as in crowdwork (Fieseler et al. 2019; Jarrahi et al. 2020). However, platforms in no other sector have attracted as much attention as those providing food delivery services. Despite the increasing interest in these other types, the food delivery sector remains the most prevalent in the scholarly, judicial and policy debate, which means that it has strongly shaped the discourse on AM (Franke and Pulignano 2023; Lord et al. 2023; Potocka-Sionek 2023). Second, the focus is on the cases and regulations of current EU member states.

IN THE BEGINNING WAS THE APP: DOCUMENTING THE SPILLOVER

Digital labour platforms started to emerge at the turn of the twenty-first century. In 1995, a US platform called World Wide Waiter (now Waiter.com) began offering food delivery from about 60 Silicon Valley restaurants to clients, thus serving as a precursor to modern food delivery apps. In Europe, most digital labour platforms were established after 2010 (Fabo et al. 2017). Among the most prominent examples in the food delivery sector, Takeaway (now Just Eat Takeaway) was launched as far back as 2001; Deliveroo was set up in 2013 and both Foodora and Glovo were founded a year later (Cant 2019).

The advent of platform work in Europe was experienced as a transformative force, catching commentators and regulators alike off guard. The initial tremors of this shift were felt through grassroots protests staged by workers (Tassinari and Maccarrone 2020), giving rise to the first jolt of awareness among those interested in the dynamics of the platform economy. As workers gained increasing associational power, food delivery apps emerged as a primer for discussions not only on issues such as pay or employment status but also on the functioning of the AM systems fuelling the business models (Bessa et al. 2022; Stuart et al. 2023).

Digital platforms have undeniably served as a laboratory for experimentation with tools and practices such as automated shift allocation, geolocation, nudges, dynamic pricing, rewards and penalties, which represent the 'core' of the notion of AM (Moore and Joyce 2020). Within the multifaceted realm of platform work, these digitalised organisational practices act as quintessential pillars epitomising the entire model (Aloisi 2020; Vallas and Schor 2020). Issues such as rating systems, account deactivation protocols and constant monitoring have become focal points of both discussion and concern. As experts delved deeper into the operational intricacies of platform companies, they recognised the profound implications of the partial delegation of the full life cycle of decision-making functions, ranging from online applications to scheduling and pay determination to dismissal (Ivanova et al. 2018; Levy and Barocas 2018). From a legal perspective, these new managerial practices have prompted fundamental questions concerning the need to reassess existing labour legislation, fuelled by a vast amount of varied and conflicting court proceedings.

Moreover, as the dust settled, attention started to shift to AM beyond platform work. Observers soon realised that workers who once operated within more traditional labour structures were now subject to algorithmic evaluations and data-driven decision-making processes. At this point, AM had already been implemented in various sectors, with warehouses, fulfilment centres, logistic hubs, fast food and dark kitchen chains, and cleaning and maintenance services serving as expansive arenas for experimentation (Ajunwa 2018; Cattero and D'Onofrio 2018). These environments, characterised by physically demanding working conditions and the confluence of poorly remunerated positions with tight managerial regimes, were witnessing the amalgamation of long-standing despotism with game-changing technologies (Wood 2020). Even before the digital age, these industries were already bearing witness to management practices that prioritised control over workers (Baiocco et al. 2022).

However, the evolution of such practices has taken a distinctive turn following the emergence of digital labour platforms. In the quest for greater operational efficiency, related organisational strategies have become entrenched in this labour market segment, along with other arrangements such as bogus self-employment, task-based payments and gamification tactics. In addition, both employees and genuinely self-employed workers, the latter not falling within the scope of the labour law measures that rationalise managerial prerogatives, are becoming exposed to algorithmic monitoring and decision-making (De Stefano 2020). This change stems partly from the attribution of decisional functions to machines and partly from the assignment of semi-decisional roles (Vallas and Schor 2020) to co-workers and/or final clients who can 'influence the nature of control' (Duggan et al. 2023). To this must be added the internalisation of metrics and rules by workers themselves.

Today, associating AM with platform work remains a natural inclination, considering that the aspects used to document the novelty and contentious nature of gig work are now integral components of the core definition of AM. Still, these practices are by no means limited to what can be observed in the platform economy. Over a period of only a few years, AM systems have become ubiquitous (Fumagalli et al. 2022), partially reshaping the notion of control from physical to intangible instantiations (Fana and Villani 2023).

Evidence concerning the extent of the use of AM systems in ordinary workplaces remains scant, not least due to the lack of a commonly agreed definition and the difficulty of capturing such data from a statistical perspective. Regarding the use of AI in the workplace as a proxy (Lane et al. 2023), based on a study by the Organisation for Economic Co-operation and Development (OECD), around 21 per cent of companies now use AI for human resources (HR) management. According to a study by the Joint Research Centre (JRC) of the European Commission (Fernández-Macías et al. 2023), a significant proportion of workers, such as clerks and operators in high-technology industries, knowledge-intensive services and public administration, now apply digital devices at work on a daily basis and are subject to some form of digital monitoring or, less often, AM. Similar trends have been detected in the case of those working outside their employer's premises, for example at home or in public spaces.

The widespread adoption of digital infrastructure is having a spillover effect. Software such as teleconferencing tools, cloud spaces, web repositories, document sharing/collaboration packages and other digital equipment operate as 'superspreaders' for the dissemination of AM functions. In all sectors and economic activities, online applications are essential infrastructure for AM because they enable electronic monitoring and the collection and processing of data, these being the entry points for any cycle of automated decision-making. The JRC study regarding the platform economy noted the automated allocation of work shifts or working time to be the most widespread form of AM, with more than 10 per cent of German workers and almost 20 per cent of Spanish ones being subject to such practices (Fernández-Macías et al. 2023). More broadly, assuming a technology-agnostic perspective, it must be acknowledged that any digital tool, such as smartphones, laptops, swipe cards and wearables, can facilitate, at least to some extent, the transmissibility of managerial tasks encompassed by the notion of AM.

The Covid-19 pandemic also acted as a superspreader, with the enhanced adoption of remote work arrangements for white-collar workers resulting in the mass application of technological infrastructure for executing relevant working duties (Aloisi and De Stefano 2022a). The same happened to those workers whose activities were not 'remotable': a deep digital acceleration reshaped their working conditions too, enabling more pervasive surveillance. According to European Agency for Safety and Health at Work (EU-OSHA) findings from 2023, 78 per cent of interviewed workers declared themselves to be subject to some form of digital data-driven management and surveillance organisational models. They reported having digital technologies determining their speed of work, monitoring them, assigning tasks or shifts, evaluating them or even checking their vital signs (Pesole 2023).

As per a 2023 OECD survey (Lane et al. 2023), it is the cost of the associated technology that is the major barrier to the adoption of AI by employers. Thus, it is likely that the more widespread availability of such technology and the corresponding reduction in costs could expand its adoption. In the case of viruses, 'ecological circumstance provides opportunity for spillover' (Quammen 2012: 432), while economic convenience could afford the conditions necessary for the wider adoption of AM tools. Moreover, a higher digitalisation rate is associated with the deeper penetration of AM into more conventional work settings. Constant evaluation and little, if any, possibility of objection to automated decisions are potentially the most acute problems here, along with a lack of transparency, procedural fairness and accountability, heightened occupational safety and health risks and the erosion of self-determination (Salvi del Pero et al. 2022). This set of problems is cross-cutting and spans all economic activities, albeit to varying degrees.

The similarities to epidemics do not end there. AM practices are often undetectable or subtle precisely because they rely on mundane tools that are not explicitly designed to pursue such goals or are not marketed as such (Moore 2018). These aspects can have chilling effects on individual awareness and workers' collective resistance. Like viruses, AM functions 'compete', 'evade' and 'evolve' (Quammen 2012: 217). Difficult though it may be, exploring the role of AM in conventional work environments offers a compelling opportunity to examine the (new) dynamics of the control exerted over workers and their working conditions (Aloisi and De Stefano 2022b). A key issue lies in discerning how AM in traditional settings differs, if at all, from its usage and conceptualisation within the platform economy. More research is required to unravel these distinctions and elucidate the nuanced ways in which AI is shaping working practices across diverse sectors.

The factual spillover is rapidly unfolding. Hence, the crucial questions on which this chapter is focused are as follows. Are the existing judicial and regulatory responses keeping pace with developments? What are the lessons to be learned from the first wave of litigation concerning AM in the food delivery sector and the first generation of laws targeting AM in the platform economy? Finally, what is the way forward when it comes to addressing the AM spillover most effectively?

SEQUENCING THE CONCEPT AND RELEVANCE OF AM IN THE CASE LAW ON FOOD DELIVERY PLATFORMS

Courts and administrative bodies (such as labour inspectorates) have extensively engaged with AM since the early days of litigation concerning food delivery platforms. Employment classification cases revolved around certain aspects of what is now known as AM even before the term became widespread. Here, the reference has often been implicit, without a single mention of an algorithm or an automated decision-making system. Instead, the courts have descriptively analysed the digitalised management systems deployed by food delivery platforms with the aim being to establish whether couriers are genuinely independent or should be reclassified as employees of a particular platform. Thus, various facets of AM have come to the fore in this regard.

In February 2018, in one of the first decisions that reclassified a Deliveroo courier as an employee, the Commission Administrative de règlement de la relation de travail / Administratieve Commissie ter regeling van de arbeidsrelatie (CRT/CAR; Belgian

Administrative Commission for the Regulation of Labour Relations)[1] noted that freedom to choose the time slots during which couriers would be required to work was 'quite relative' as they were obliged to reserve working periods in advance, according to the availability offered by the platform and subject to the platform's approval. The booking possibilities depended on statistics related to performance, and couriers risked losing priority if they reserved time slots that did not correspond to the periods most favourable to the platform's activity. The CRT/CAR also recognised that the platform 'reserves for itself exorbitant possibilities of control' by using global positioning systems (GPS) and that maintaining a good ranking was essential for having access to effective working possibilities. All these AM-related features were considered indicative of the existence of an employment relationship between couriers and Deliveroo.

Subsequent cases in other EU member states have analysed the more advanced and 'intrusive' management systems deployed by food delivery platforms. For example, in the Foodora judgment in Italy, the Corte di Cassazione concluded that couriers lacked autonomy during the 'functional phase' of the agreement – during the execution of the relationship – as the modalities of performance were substantially determined by the platform.[2] More specifically, Foodora rewarded couriers' commitment to making deliveries strictly within 30 minutes from the time indicated for the collection of the food, and would issue sanctions. The Chambre sociale (Labour Chamber) of the French Cour de Cassation emphasised further AM aspects in its decision to reclassify Take Eat Easy couriers as employees.[3] It viewed the geotracking system that enabled the real-time monitoring of each courier's position and the system of bonuses and penalties applied to couriers to be indices of the power of direction and control exercised by the platform. The court did not, however, perceive the management system as a limitation of couriers' freedom to organise their work schedule. Rather, it held that couriers were free to choose their time slots, although this factor was irrelevant in light of others hinting at the existence of an employment relationship.

Furthermore, some judgments have perceived AM as a sign of integration into the platforms' organisation and, relatedly, of the inability of workers to operate as independent economic entities. For example, the Tribunale di Torino (Turin Civil Court) stated that deliveries were algorithmically assigned by Uber Eats 'on the basis of criteria completely unrelated to the preferences and general interest of the couriers themselves'.[4] This implied that the couriers had no organisational independence and were unable to offer their services on the market directly to other users. This represents yet another facet of AM analysed in some prior judgments concerning the employment classification of couriers.

The Tribunal Supremo in Spain expressed arguably the most holistic view of AM in relation to digital labour platforms in its Glovo judgment of September 2020.[5] More specifically it drew attention to three facets of platforms' control of work performance. First, Glovo assigned services according to the rating of each courier, which decisively restrained their freedom to choose their schedules and refuse orders. Second, it had the power to issue sanctions to couriers based on their behaviours. Third, the platform carried out real-time monitoring of the provision of its service. The court's detailed reasoning here is illustrative of how various functions are performed by algorithms in a range of managerial practices: the organisation of services, rating, sanctions and monitoring. This case shows that such functions are strictly intertwined and mutually reinforcing, substantially limiting couriers' freedom and endowing platforms with vast managerial powers.

Case law on the employment classification of couriers in EU member states shows that AM has gradually been recognised as a sign of the major involvement of platforms in the way work is executed. Referring to the spillover terminology, the case law provides ample examples of the 'sequencing (e.g., reading out the genetic spelling)' (Quammen 2012: 128) of some fragments of managerial systems, which has been pivotal to the recognition of couriers' subordination to platforms and, ultimately, their employee status. Adjudication bodies have recognised the impact of AM throughout the work cycle, from the beginning (selection and matching) to the very end (including deactivation as a sanction for non-compliance with algorithmically determined rules). Various facets of AM have been subsumed into different forms of managerial control. For example, ratings were sometimes seen as a form of control and sometimes as a limitation of the freedom to organise work performance. Likewise, bonuses were perceived as a means of steering the behaviour of couriers[6] or as part of their performance evaluation.[7] Thus, there is a certain fluidity in terms of how AM features are linked to typical managerial prerogatives.

These nuances notwithstanding, a broad conceptualisation of AM emerges from the case law. It can be referred to as 'algorithmic management *sensu largo*', as it not only relates to the management of the organisation of work ('algorithmic management *sensu stricto*') but, more broadly, also to real-time control, *ex ante* evaluation, and unorthodox sanctions such as account deactivation. It is apparent that, although the use of AM does not necessarily lead to automatic employment reclassification,[8] the recognition of its role in shaping work dynamics has been pivotal to the reclassification of food delivery couriers as employees.

MOBILISING DATA PROTECTION LAWS AS AN ALTERNATIVE LITIGATION STRATEGY

More recently, courts and data protection authorities (DPAs) have started to scrutinise in even more detail the operation of AM by digital labour platforms, beyond the employment classification context (Hiessl 2023). The main question in this emerging body of cases is not whether platform workers should be reclassified as employees but whether AM systems are compliant with existing national and/or EU legislation, mostly in the field of data protection and non-discrimination. This section tracks these developments in the food delivery sector, encompassing data up to December 2023.

In a decision from June 2021,[9] the Garante per la protezione dei dati personali (Garante; the Italian DPA) fined Glovo's subsidiary, Foodinho, €2.6 million and mandated that it amend the way it processed couriers' data. Among the identified infringements, the platform was found to have violated couriers' right to information on the functioning of the system and to have failed to safeguard the accuracy and fairness of the algorithmic results used to rate performance. Multiple provisions of the General Data Protection Regulation (GDPR), including the principles of transparency, data minimisation and lawfulness, as well as prohibiting the use of automated processing, were invoked, along with national labour provisions (Agosti et al. 2023). Very similar reasoning was applied in the 'twin' decision on Deliveroo issued just a month later.[10]

In addition to the decision of the Garante, AM practices have been challenged vis-à-vis both transparency and predictability. In a judgment issued by the Tribunale di Palermo in March 2023,[11] Uber Eats was found to have violated national legislation[12] by failing to provide sufficient information on algorithmic data processing and decision-making concerning its couriers to the most representative Italian trade union (Filcams CGIL). Among the issues that were challenged, the algorithm's dataset was unspecified, as were the criteria for the 'minimum average evaluation' and the 'other factors' leading to internal decisions. Moreover, the mitigation measures regarding automated decisions, such as the promotion or deactivation of a courier's account, their level of accuracy and the metrics used to measure their parameters, were unknown. The court obliged Uber Eats to be more specific concerning the overly generic and vague information it provided.

In June 2023, Tribunale di Palermo again ruled on the AM mechanisms used by a food delivery platform.[13] This time, the case concerned Glovo's algorithm for distributing deliveries to workers. The violation of workers' information rights, as exercised both individually and collectively with regard to the use of 'automated decision-making or monitoring systems' under Legislative Decree 104/2022, was found to represent anti-union conduct (Veruggio 2023). The court mandated that Glovo disclose the algorithm's logic and selection mechanisms.

In line with these cases regarding access to data issues, one prior ruling has addressed algorithmic discrimination – the order issued by Tribunale Ordinario di Bologna in the Deliveroo case in December 2020.[14] This case concerned the 'self-service booking system' that couriers used to book their time slots. Those couriers with the highest score based on data concerning their performance (the highest 'reliability' and 'participation' ratings) could book a time slot of their preference, whereas those with a lower score had to accept the remaining shifts. The score was automatically reduced when a courier failed to participate in a previously booked shift without having cancelled it at least 24 hours in advance, regardless of the reason for the absence. Thus, couriers had to suffer the negative consequences of a lower score even if there was a salient and legitimate reason for the late cancellation. The court considered this algorithm to have an indirectly discriminatory effect on those couriers who were exercising their right to engage in strike action (Purificato 2021).

Taken together, these decisions represent important progress, reflecting the shift in attention from employment classification to data transparency and access to information as a proxy for improving understanding of the organisational model and curbing the expansion of employers' discretion. Of course, the understanding of an algorithm implemented by a digital labour platform cannot be fully separated from the issue of the classificationof food delivery couriers. Algorithmic transparency and fairness can also serve to establish the existence of an employment relationship. Put plainly, the more information provided on AM, the more likely it is to elucidate the true nature of the relationship between workers and digital platforms (Wray 2023). Thus, even though the subject matter of these two streams of litigation concerning food delivery platforms differs, they should not be seen as separate silos.

Despite the spillover effect of AM on the traditional labour market, there is limited jurisprudence on algorithmic transparency, or on AM more broadly, beyond the platform economy. While platform workers have been highly successful in claiming their data rights, the same was not true for Amazon warehouse workers in a case decided by Verwaltungsgericht Hannover (Hanover Administrative Court) in February 2023 on the use of hand-held scanners to gather real-time data on workers' performance.[15] These data were then evaluated using performance management software and considered in relation to task allocation and for training purposes and personnel decisions. Landesbeauftragte für den Datenschutz Niedersachsen (the Lower Saxony DPA) had already prohibited the use of such systems,[16] reasoning that the practices violated Section 26 of the Bundesdatenschutzgesetz (BDSG; German Federal

Data Protection Act) because they were not necessary for the achievement of Amazon's interests, such as control of the logistics process, monitoring of employees' qualifications and objective evaluation of workers (Hiessl 2023). Following Amazon's appeal against this order, Verwaltungsgericht Hannover held that Amazon had a substantial legitimate interest in the collection of the relevant data and that such collection was suitable and necessary to protect that interest.[17] It found no violation of the BDSG and so overruled the DPA's order. This ruling is currently under appeal,[18] and has been heavily criticised in the literature for taking Amazon's argument 'almost at face value' (Abraha 2023: 14) and underestimating the negative effect of constant surveillance on workers.

Beyond the context of data protection, a noteworthy case concerning the AM system applied to Amazon warehouse workers was decided by Sąd Okręgowy w Poznaniu (District Court of Poznań) in Poland, in June 2020. Here, the main problem was not the lack of transparency regarding Amazon's algorithm, even though the court did recognise its variability and lack of predictability (it was pointed out that performance standards shifted over time based on the performance of other workers, leaving workers uncertain as to their ability to meet these benchmarks); rather, the case concerned the dismissal of a worker from the Amazon fulfilment centre for having failed to achieve minimum performance outcomes, as established on the basis of data gathered from peers considering productivity, outcome quality and attendance rates.[19] The minimum threshold corresponded to the results achieved by 90 per cent of employees. The core issue was the systemic feature whereby the algorithm ignited a 'race' of workers against their peers and that the attainment of acceptable results was always, by default, impossible for the 10 per cent lowest-performing workers even if they exercised the utmost due diligence in the execution of their tasks. The court held that this system violated Polish labour law, and thus determined that the dismissal was unsubstantiated and ineffective.

It is impossible to draw firm conclusions from the scarce judgments on AM beyond the platform economy. GDPR and national data protection regulations have been invoked with mixed results, and little is currently known about the efficacy of traditional labour laws in the AM context. However, there have been instances where the courts have demonstrated a receptiveness to the influence of AM, not just in terms of reclassification but also as a contributing factor to the risk of infringement of a broader set of labour law provisions.

CONTAINING THE SPREAD OF AM IN PLATFORM WORK: INITIAL REGULATORY EFFORTS AT EU AND DOMESTIC LEVELS

As with case law, the regulation of (certain aspects of) AM has so far predominantly targeted platform work. 'Digital rights' – the set of rights connected to AM, data protection, disconnection and others intended to protect platform workers from the negative impacts of AM – have been embedded in a number of legislative and policy initiatives, whether at EU, state or regional level, as well as in bottom-up initiatives led by social partners (trade unions and employer associations).

At EU level, the first set of regulations targeting AM has been introduced in the Platform Work Directive (PWD), adopted by the European Parliament and the Council in October2024.[20] Chapter III of the Directive bans platforms from processing personal data in certain cases where AM systems are involved (Art. 7(1)), obliges platforms to perform a data-protection impact assessment (Art. 8) and mandates crucial transparency duties concerning automated monitoring and decision-making (Art. 9). Moreover, it provides for a right to human oversight (Art. 10) and human review (Art. 11) of AM decisions, introduces important consultation rights for the representatives of platform workers (Art. 13–15) and imposes certain obligations concerning safety and health on platforms (Art. 12). Most of these provisions, apart from the consultation rights and the obligations related to health and safety, also cover people performing platform work as self-employed. In this way, the Directive recognises the link between AM and working conditions, as well as its impact on employees and the self-employed (Bronowicka 2023). This framework strengthens the 'classical' data protection model enshrined in GDPR,[21] which is only somewhat suited to addressing the challenges posed by AM (Abraha 2022). Notably, Chapter III of the PWD encountered much less political opposition than the employment presumption (Aloisi et al. 2023) which was the main cause of the Directive being on the verge of rejection. In fact, the finally agreed version of the Directive strengthened some of the AM-related provisions originally proposed in the European Commission's draft from December 2021 by, inter alia, expanding the catalogue of prohibited usages of AM systems, mandating data protection impact assessment, ensuring the right to data portability and fortifying information and consultation rights. Overall, the provisions on AM in the PWD are a much-welcomed and crucial step forward in protecting people performing platform work against some of the greatest risks stemming from algorithmic opacity.

Looking at the bigger picture, however, the introduction of these rules in an instrument limited to the domain of platforms reveals, by default, an overly simplistic and already outdated understanding of the phenomenon. Those who are not organised by platforms, be they workers or the self-employed in traditional sectors, cannot rely on this additional layer of data rights. Such a policy option had been chosen by the drafters of the PWD as a more 'focused' solution that accounts for the 'business specificities' of the platform business model (European Commission 2021, Annex A11.2: 25), despite widespread recognition of the already occurring spillover effect of AM and the advocacy of trade unions and academics for broadening the scope of this instrument. Still, the PWD is commonly perceived as a stepping stone towards the further regulation of this aspect beyond the platform ecosystem (Bronowicka 2023).

Along with the PWD, there are multiple national and regional laws addressing only platform workers, often limited to a specific sector. Some of these platform-specific regulations merely reiterate and reinforce the 'digital rights' established by other instruments. For example, in Italy, the Capo V-bis of Legislative Decree 81/2015, which addresses only self-employed couriers, reaffirms the protection of privacy in accordance with the provisions of EU Regulation 2016/679 and Legislative Decree 196/2003 (the privacy law). Some policy initiatives go beyond the existing *acquis* and guarantee new rights, although these are still tailored solely for (some categories of) platform workers. Examples of such specific rights include the right to data portability (including the portability of ratings); the right to refuse assignments as introduced by, for example, regulations in the Italian region of Lazio;[22] and the right to disconnect, as provided for in the French 'El Khomri' law'.[23]

More recently, revised labour law in Croatia has introduced a set of detailed provisions on the AM mechanisms used by digital platforms. In essence, it obliges the platforms (or 'aggregators' – the intermediaries who employ workers) to inform workers about the logic of decision-making within the automated management system and to ensure the availability and transparency of information on platform work. Moreover, platforms are required to appoint an authorised person to supervise workers' safety and workload, in addition to one whose task is to review automated decisions. The possibility of establishing professional communication with other workers and participants in the business process must also be ensured. These regulations have been effective from 1 January 2024.[24]

Aside from these statutory interventions, several collective agreements in the field of platform-based delivery have addressed 'digital rights' (Lamannis 2023).[25] Perhaps the most progressive provisions were included in the Spanish Just Eat agreement from December 2021. Apart from addressing the right to disconnect and the right to privacy from digital surveillance (Wray 2021), it created an 'algorithmic committee' tasked with ensuring that transparency obligations and human oversight requirements are complied with.

Undoubtedly, platform work has been an area of much-needed experimentation on regulations addressing AM, and it has evidenced the regulatory need in this regard. At the same time, consensus is growing that regulating AM for the narrow category of couriers alone or, more broadly, even for all platform workers, only scratches the surface of the problems at hand. It can be said that such a legislative technique simply reproduces the bias according to which AM is considered a platform-specific issue, and that this may result in a further polarisation of the labour market in terms of protection schemes.

THE SECOND WAVE OF AM REGULATION WITHIN AND BEYOND THE CONFINES OF PLATFORM WORK

A growing body of regulatory initiatives has sought to respond to AM-related risks more systematically. Spain was the first country in Europe to adopt an AM-specific regulation that covers more than the platform economy. Law 12/2021 ('Riders' Law')[26] introduces algorithmic transparency rights that encompass all employers, not only digital labour platforms. Moreover, Article 64(4)(d) of the Estatuto de los Trabajadores (ET; Workers' Statute) provides works councils with the right to be informed about the parameters, rules and instructions upon which algorithms or AI systems are based, provided they are used for decision-making practices that may affect working conditions and/or access to and maintenance of employment. This text expands on the GDPR provisions that already regulate companies' obligations to inform the worker when automated processing and profiling systems are in place, addressing the individualised dimension of such a right (Todolí-Signes 2021b). The lack of a collective dimension to transparency and information rights in data protection law is also partially addressed in the 'Riders' Law'. However, besides allowing workers to learn more about the parameters, rules and instructions of algorithms or AI systems, the law does not introduce additional rights regarding co-determination or systems of redress (Aranguiz 2021; Aloisi 2022). Furthermore, its practical application is limited.

Another example of a national regulation addressing AM beyond platform work – that is, also in conventional workplaces – is the Italian Legislative Decree transposing the EU Directive on Transparent and Predictable Working Conditions,[27] which has been effective since August 2022. As per Section 4(8), the employer is required to inform workers of 'fully automated' decision-making and monitoring systems[28] that are used to provide information for hiring, managing or terminating the employment relationship or assigning tasks. In addition, information must be disclosed on the purposes, logic and functioning of automated systems; the categories of data and the main parameters used to program or train such systems; the control measures adopted for the decision processes; their level of accuracy, robustness and cybersecurity; the metrics used; and their potentially discriminatory impacts.

Portuguese Law 13/2023 (the 'Decent Work Agenda'), in force since May 2023, represents the most recent initiative at the time of writing. This law specifies that collective bargaining agreements can regulate the use of algorithms, AI and associated technologies solely in a way that is advantageous for employees (Art. 3(3)). It also expressly clarifies that equality and non-discrimination provisions apply to decision-making based on algorithms or other AI systems (Art. 24(3)). Moreover, it obliges employers to inform new employees when they are hired of the parameters, rules and instructions on which algorithmic or AI systems are based (Art. 106(3)(iv)).

At EU level, the AI Act applies to those AM systems fuelled by AI and used at work.[29] As specified in Annex III, , AI systems adopted in the context of 'employment, workers' management and access to self-employment' qualify as 'high-risk' systems. More precisely, reference is made to AI systems intended to be used for recruitment purposes, for deciding about promotion and the termination of work contracts and for task allocation, monitoring and evaluating the performance and behaviour of people in work-related relationships. Even though this catalogue captures some of the most common uses of AM in the work context, not all relevant systems are included (Cefaliello and Kullmann 2022). The AI Act is also technology-specific – it focuses solely on AI systems. Another crucial limitation is that the classification depends on the provider's intended purpose, which may differ from the use to which such systems are put. In other words, a system might not be intended to monitor or evaluate workers, although it may be suitable for such purposes and eventually used in that way by the employer (Klengel and Wenckebach 2021).[30]

AI systems that are classified as high-risk need to comply with a set of requirements. A risk management system must be put in place, consisting of 'a continuous iterative process planned and run throughout the entire lifecycle of a high-risk AI system' (Art. 9(2)). Providers must identify and mitigate the known and foreseeable risks, estimate and assess those that may emerge when a high-risk AI system is deployed 'in accordance with its intended purpose and under conditions of reasonably foreseeable misuse' (Art. 9(2)(b)) and adopt risk management measures (Art. 9(2)(d)).

Even though it constitutes an important piece in the growing legislative puzzle of AM beyond platform work, the AI Act has been widely criticised in the literature for not paying enough attention to workers' rights (Klengel and Wenckebach 2021; Todolí-Signes 2021a). This lack of employment specificity largely stems from the internal market legal basis and the Act's main objectives. Its efficacy in the employment context may also be hindered by some broader, structural limitations, such as the threat that it will reinvigorate the 'constitutionally disruptive' clash between social and economic rights (Garben, 2017; De Stefano and Taes 2023). Since the AI Act has only recently entered into force, it is too early to make firm predictions regarding the role that it will play in the governance of AM tools at work.

The adequacy of the current EU *acquis* and of 'traditional' (not AM-specific) domestic instruments to overcome the challenges related to AM in the employment context remains to be tested. As discussed, while data protection regulations are beginning to be mobilised in courts in the context of the platform economy and, to a lesser extent, other sectors, the same cannot be said of laws regulating working conditions, occupational health and safety, and collective rights, among others. As for GDPR, the inherent limitations due to the open-textured nature of some of the provisions are becoming increasingly evident. Moreover, the inclusion of carve-outs in the provisions means that GDPR is imperfectly suited to effective regulation of the intricate dynamics of AM in the workplace.

The 'competition' between the first and the second wave of legal instruments highlights their limited effectiveness as well as the need for more active enforcement and reinforcement. Hence, some scholars advocate a 'universalistic' approach to addressing the broader spectrum of employment (Kelly-Lyth and Adams-Prassl 2021). The growing calls for a comprehensive, and employment-specific, approach are firmly grounded, as current data underscore the spillover of AM beyond the confines of the platform economy. With the influence of AM systems beginning to permeate diverse domains, it might be an opportune time to consider extending regulatory interventions to all categories of worker, thereby overcoming the limitations of existing frameworks. Recognising the urgent need for a broader response, the escalating cross-sectoral prevalence of AM underscores the need to address the entire phenomenon rather than confining regulatory efforts to its manifestation in a small segment of the labour market or through specific technologies that may soon be supplanted by new advances, such as so-called foundation models and generative AI.

Yet, even if there is growing agreement on the need for an AM-specific regulatory intervention, there is no consensus on how, specifically, this might be achieved. Should a comprehensive instrument governing various aspects of the use of technologies in hiring, monitoring, decision-making and disciplinary activities within professional ecosystems be introduced (for example an 'AM at work directive')? Or should narrower instruments targeting specific aspects of AM (such as an individual health and safety directive on the AM of work) be developed instead? The issue is all the more complex because many AM-related challenges (such as the potentially negative impact on mental health and well-being) also exist in the broader context and thus require more comprehensive regulatory intervention.

Be that as it may, the shaping of regulations in this domain will need to reflect not only the technical considerations but also a broader commitment to safeguarding and advancing fundamental rights at work. There is increasing recognition of the need for the implementation of comprehensive measures. In addition, there are growing calls for collaborative efforts, suggesting the need for joint regulation by unions and employer associations, not only at company level but also within the broader industrial framework.

CONCLUSIONS

This chapter has sought to elucidate the implications of the AM spillover effect: the spread of AM systems and practices from the platform economy to the broader labour market. By examining comprehensive insights from existing literature, case law and regulatory initiatives, this chapter captures these spillover effects in three dimensions: the prevalence of new management methods in conventional settings; the jurisprudence on AM in platform work and beyond; and the regulatory initiatives targeting AM, whether in platform work or more broadly. These dimensions are all interconnected, making it imperative to consider all related aspects when formulating comprehensive and 'future-proof' responses. Furthermore, this chapter provides a normative critique of the emerging fragmented regulatory approach, contending that a holistic perspective should guide future regulatory efforts. A comprehensive solution requires both the effective implementation of the existing legal framework and the design of AM-specific legislation to close the regulatory gaps in the EU and national *acquis*.

AM systems have predominantly been brought before the courts with the aim of reclassifying platform workers; such cases thereby serve as a proxy for the existence of traditional managerial prerogative rather than an attempt to secure the improvement of working conditions. As well as demonstrating the existence of an employment relationship, they have been key to understanding the algorithmic control exercised by platforms. Platform workers' litigation strategy has been shaped by a two-pronged approach: claiming employment reclassification and mobilising national and/or EU data protection and non-discrimination provisions. Similarly, regulation has expanded from the primary goal of clarifying platform workers' employment status to guaranteeing information and transparency rights in technology-based work contexts. This approach should advance an understanding of working conditions in the platform economy and the broader implications for society.

Given the growing body of evidence concerning AM in conventional settings, there is increasing consensus that the regulation of AM systems should transcend the boundaries of platform work rather than being tethered to it. While it is undeniable that the lack of a digital labour platform does not exclude the presence of AM practices, what is truly definitive is reference to the algorithmic or automated nature of the business model, meaning that such tools and functions are partly or fully offloaded to digital infrastructure, leaving limited space for human intervention. So, while couriers are largely assessed using customer reviews and feedback, a similar model can be found in other sectors where the same goal is pursued using different tools, for example peer assessments or management by objectives.

Still, most regulatory efforts continue to focus on platform workers or target exclusively one of several underlying technologies that can be used to fuel AM systems; that is, AI or personal data. Unquestionably, recent initiatives could serve as a stepping stone towards broader AM regulation in the workplace. The vicissitudes of the PWD could also redirect attention to the spillover effects. The challenges posed by AM cannot be addressed with a narrow regulatory instrument such as the AI Act, which devotes most of its provisions to systems that are classified as high-risk AI systems, nor with sector-specific instruments. Such laser-sharp interventions risk becoming obsolete or ineffectual once adopted and transposed, given the profound challenges presented by AM. Thus, AM should be addressed with comprehensive measures that extend beyond limited, remedial and individualised perspectives. Such measures should focus on the relevant practices (hiring, monitoring, organising, remunerating, dismissing and so on) rather than the underlying technologies that enable their execution.

By and large, a phenomenon as multifaceted as AM demands a nuanced, holistic and evolving approach. Taming its spillover effect necessitates action on two fronts: first, enforcing the existing instruments and rectifying the gaps in horizontal legislation through the contribution of administrative bodies and social partners; and second, adopting a modern framework for regulating data protection and automated decision-making in workplaces. Such a dual approach will mitigate the risk of regulatory measures merely reacting to changes rather than actively steering them, thereby ensuring a more proactive and adaptive stance in the face of rapidly evolving workplace dynamics. It is now also in the hands of MS to regulate AM practices at work. To date, only partially and in very few EU countries (Spain, Italy and Portugal) have broader AM-specific responses been deployed; therefore, a more comprehensive regulatory approach is still in its early stages. To avoid further fragmentation, challenging though it may be, action at the supranational level is required.

To conclude by returning to the spillover metaphor, implementing localised infection-control efforts exclusively to address (certain groups of) platform workers or specific technologies, such as AI, risks missing the target. Indeed, doing so in a haphazard manner may not yield the desired results. The challenge is to mobilise existing legal instruments to reinforce a general immunisation response to AM. A combination of data protection, non-discrimination and information and consultation provisions will effectively avoid the harm stemming from the misguided use of AM tools. Antibodies like these could limit the infection or prevent its most severe consequences. Moreover, as the big data at the heart of AM requires large and dense aggregations of data subjects to operate efficiently, the collective implementation of the existing guardrails is essential. Hence, containment measures in the case of data-borne transmission need to be adopted at the level of populations and communities, not single individuals.

ACKNOWLEDGEMENTS

We are very grateful to Despoina Georgiou, Silvia Rainone and Kurt Vandaele for their generous comments on an earlier draft of this chapter. We would also like to thank the participants in the workshop held by the ETUI in June 2023 for the stimulating discussion and feedback on our presentation.

NOTES

1. Administrative Commission for the Regulation of Labour Relations, decision of 23 February 2018, 116 – FR – 20180209.
2. Judgment of 24 January 2020, RG 11629/2019, para. 33.
3. Judgment of 28 November 2018, 17-20.079.
4. Judgment of 18 November 2021, RG 4991/2020.
5. Judgment of 23 September 2020, 4746/2019.
6. Judgment of the Dutch Supreme Court, 24 March 2023, ECLI:NL:HR:2023:443.
7. Judgment of the French Supreme Court, 28 November 2018, 17-20.079.
8. See, for example, the judgment of the Cour du travail de Bruxelles / Arbeidshof Brussel (Brussels labour tribunal), 8 December 2021, JT 08/12/2021.
9. Injunction against Foodinho srl – 10 June 2021 [9675440].
10. See the injunction order against Deliveroo Italy srl – 22 July 2021 [9685994].
11. Judgment of 31 March 2023, RG 645/2023.
12. Legislative Decree 152/1997, as amended by Legislative Decree 104 of 27 June 2022, transposing Directive (EU) 2019/1152 of the European Parliament and of the Council of 20 June 2019 on transparent and predictable working conditions in the European Union.
13. Tribunale di Palermo, 20 June 2023.
14. Order 2949/2019.
15. Ref: 10 A 6199/20.
16. Decision of 28 October 2020 (unpublished).
17. The three essential purposes pursued by Amazon were ‘the control of logistics processes, the control of the individual qualification of employees, and the creation of objective assessment bases for individual feedback and personnel decisions’. See para. 62 of the judgment. For detailed reasoning on why the use of FCLM and ADAPT was suitable and necessary, see paras. 66–91.
18. Appeal pending before Oberverwaltungsgericht (higher administrative court) Lüneburg, under case 11 LC 105/23.
19. VIII Pa 135/19, Sąd Okręgowy w Poznaniu, 10 June 2020 (unpublished).

20. Directive (EU) 2024/2831 of the European Parliament and of the Council of 23 October 2024 on improving working conditions in platform work
21. Regulation (EU) 2016/679 of the European Parliament and of the Council of 27 April 2016 on the protection of natural persons with regard to the processing of personal data and on the free movement of such data, and repealing Directive 95/46/EC (General Data Protection Regulation).
22. 'Provisions for the protection and safety of digital workers' (Art. 5).
23. Law 2016-1088 of 8 August 2016 on labour, the modernisation of social dialogue and the securing of professional careers.
24. An unofficial English translation of this regulation is available at https://uznr.mrms.hr/wp-content/uploads/labour-act.pdf.
25. For example, the LaConsegna agreement, Montegrappa agreement, Tadan agreement and agreement on riders' rights concluded in Italy by Regione Toscana (the Region of Tuscany) and CGIL, CISL and UIL.
26. Law 12/2021 of 28 September, modifying the Workers' Statute approved by Royal Legislative Decree 2/2015 of October 23, to guarantee the labour rights of people dedicated to delivery in the field of digital platforms.
27. Legislative Decree 104 of 27 June 2022, transposing Directive (EU) 2019/1152 of the European Parliament and of the Council of 20 June 2019 on transparent and predictable working conditions in the European Union.
28. Legislative Decree 48 of 4 May 2023 (labour law). Another intervention in the same Decree rewrote para. 8 to the effect that these information obligations 'do not apply to systems protected by industrial and commercial secrecy'.
29. Regulation (EU) 2024/1689 of the European Parliament and of the Council of 13 June 2024 laying down harmonised rules on artificial intelligence and amending Regulations (EC) No 300/2008, (EU) No 167/2013, (EU) No 168/2013, (EU) 2018/858, (EU) 2018/1139 and (EU) 2019/2144 and Directives 2014/90/EU, (EU) 2016/797 and (EU) 2020/1828 (Artificial Intelligence Act)
30. Note that if the user substantially modifies the intended purpose of a high-risk AI system that has already been introduced, this will lead to them being considered a provider for the purposes of the AI Act instead of the initial provider (Art. 28(1)(b) AI Act).

REFERENCES

Abraha H.H. (2022) A pragmatic compromise? The role of Article 88 GDPR in upholding privacy in the workplace, *International Data Privacy Law*, 12 (4), 276–296.

Abraha H.H. (2023) Automated monitoring in the workplace and the search for a new legal framework: lessons from Germany and beyond. https://ssrn.com/abstract=4595760

Agosti C., Bronowicka J., Polidoro A. and Prior G. (2023) *Exercising workers' rights in algorithmic management systems: lessons learned from the Glovo-Foodinho digital labour platform case*, Report 2023.11, ETUI.

Ajunwa I. (2018) Algorithms at work: productivity monitoring applications and wearable technology as the new data-centric research agenda for employment and labor law, *St. Louis University Law Journal*, 63 (1), 21–53.

Aloisi A. (2020) Hierarchies without firms? Vertical disintegration, outsourcing and the nature of the platform. *Quaderni del Premio Giorgio Rota* 8, 11-32.

Aloisi A. (2022) Platform work in Europe: lessons learned, legal developments and challenges ahead, *European Labour Law Journal*, 13 (1), 4–29.

Aloisi A. and De Stefano V. (2022a) Essential jobs, remote work and digital surveillance: addressing the Covid-19 pandemic panopticon, *International Labour Review*, 161 (2), 289–314.

Aloisi A. and De Stefano V. (2022b) *Your boss is an algorithm: artificial intelligence, platform work and labour*, Bloomsbury Publishing.
Aloisi A., Rainone S. and Countouris N. (2023) An unfinished task? Matching the proposed Platform Work Directive with the EU and international 'social acquis', Working Paper 101, ILO.
Aranguiz A. (2021) Spain's platform workers win algorithm transparency, *Social Europe*, 18 March.
Baiocco S., Fernández-Macías E., Rani U. and Pesole A. (2022) The algorithmic management of work and its implications in different contexts, JRC Working Paper 2022/02, European Commission.
Bessa I., Joyce S., Neumann D., Stuart M., Trappmann V. and Umney C. (2022) A global analysis of worker protest in digital labour platforms, Working Paper 70, ILO.
Bronowicka J. (2023) How the Platform Work Directive protects workers' data, Verfassungsblog, 19 July. https://verfassungsblog.de/how-the-platform-work-directive-protects-workers-data
Cant C. (2019) *Riding for Deliveroo: resistance in the new economy*, Polity Press.
Cattero B. and D'Onofrio M. (2018) Organizing and collective bargaining in the digitized 'tertiary factories' of Amazon: a comparison between Germany and Italy, in Ales E. et al. (eds.) *Working in digital and smart organizations: legal, economic and organizational perspectives on the digitalization of labour relations*, Palgrave Macmillan, 141–164.
Cefaliello A. and Kullmann M. (2022) Offering false security: how the draft Artificial Intelligence Act undermines fundamental workers rights, *European Labour Law Journal*, 13 (4), 542–562.
De Stefano V. (2020) 'Masters and servers': collective labour rights and private government in the contemporary world of work, *International Journal of Comparative Labour Law and Industrial Relations*, 36 (4), 424–444.
De Stefano V. and Taes S. (2023) Algorithmic management and collective bargaining, *Transfer*, 29 (1), 21–36.
Duggan J., Carbery R., McDonnell A. and Sherman U. (2023) Algorithmic HRM control in the gig economy: the app-worker perspective, *Human Resource Management*, 62 (6), 883–899.
European Commission (2021) Commission staff working document: impact assessment report accompanying the document Proposal for a Directive of the European Parliament and of the Council on improving working conditions in platform work, SWD(2021) 396 final, Publications Office of the European Union.
Fabo B., Beblavý M., Kilhoffer Z. and Lenaerts K. (2017) *An overview of European platforms: scope and business models*, Publications Office of the European Union.
Fana M. and Villani D. (2023) Is it all the same? Types of innovation and their relationship with direct control, technical control and algorithmic management, *European Journal of Industrial Relations*, 29 (4), 367–391.
Fernández-Macías E., Urzì Brancati M.C., Wright S. and Pesole A. (2023) *The platformisation of work: evidence from the JRC Algorithmic Management and Platform Work Survey (AMPWork), JRC Science for Policy Report*, Publications Office of the European Union.
Fieseler C., Bucher E. and Hoffmann C.P. (2019) Unfairness by design? The perceived fairness of digital labor on crowdworking platforms, *Journal of Business Ethics*, 156 (4), 987–1005.
Franke M. and Pulignano V. (2023) Connecting at the edge: cycles of commodification and labour control within food delivery platform work in Belgium, *New Technology, Work and Employment*, 38 (2), 371–390.
Fumagalli E., Rezaei S. and Salomons A. (2022) OK computer: worker perceptions of algorithmic recruitment, *Research Policy*, 51 (2), 104420.
Heinrich K., Vu M.A. and Vysochyna A. (2022) Algorithms as a manager: a critical literature review of algorithm management, *ICIS 2022 Proceedings*, 9.
Hiessl C. (2023) *Jurisprudence of national courts in Europe on algorithmic management at the workplace*, European Centre of Expertise in the Field of Labour Law, Employment and Labour Market Policies (ECE).
Garben S. (2017) The constitutional (im)balance between 'the market' and 'the social' in the European Union, *European Constitutional Law Review*, 1 (1), 23–61.
Ivanova M., Bronowicka J., Kocher E. and Degner A. (2018) Foodora and Deliveroo: the app as a boss? Control and autonomy in app-based management: the case of food delivery riders, Working Paper Forschungsförderung 107, Hans-Böckler-Stiftung.

Jarrahi M.H., Sutherland W., Nelson S.B. and Sawyer S. (2020) Platformic management, boundary resources for gig work, and worker autonomy, *Computer Supported Cooperative Work*, 29 (1), 153–189.

Kellogg K.C., Valentine M.A. and Christin A. (2020) Algorithms at work: the new contested terrain of control, *Academy of Management Annals*, 14 (1), 366–410.

Kelly-Lyth A. and Adams-Prassl J. (2021) The EU's proposed Platform Work Directive: a promising step, VerfBlog, 14 December. https://verfassungsblog.de/work-directive

Klengel E. and Wenckebach J. (2021) Artificial intelligence, work, power imbalance and democracy: why co-determination is essential, *Italian Labour Law e-Journal*, 14 (2), 157–171.

Lamannis M. (2023) *Collective bargaining in the platform economy: a mapping exercise of existing initiatives*, Report 2023.02, ETUI.

Lane M., Williams M. and Broecke S. (2023) The impact of AI on the workplace: main findings from the OECD AI surveys of employers and workers, OECD Social, Employment and Migration Working Paper 288, OECD Publishing.

Lee M.K., Kusbit D., Metsky E. and Dabbish L. (2015) Working with machines: the impact of algorithmic and data-driven management on human workers, *CHI '15: Proceedings of the 33rd Annual ACM Conference on Human Factors in Computing Systems*, 1603–1612.

Levy K. and Barocas S. (2018) Refractive surveillance: monitoring customers to manage workers, International *Journal of Communication*, 12, 1166–1188.

Lord C, Bates O., Friday A., McLeod F., Cherrett T., Martinez-Sykora A. and Oakey A. (2023) The sustainability of the gig economy food delivery system (Deliveroo, UberEATS and Just-Eat): histories and futures of rebound, lock-in and path dependency, *International Journal of Sustainable Transportation*, 17 (5), 490–502.

Mateescu A. and Nguyen A. (2019) *Explainer: algorithmic management in the workplace*, Data & Society Research Institute.

Moore P.V. (2018) OSH and the future of work: benefits and risks of artificial intelligence tools in workplaces, Discussion Paper, European Agency for Safety and Health at Work.

Moore P.V. and Joyce S. (2020) Black box or hidden abode? The expansion and exposure of platform work managerialism, *Review of International Political Economy*, 27 (4), 926–948.

Pesole A. (2023) *Surveillance and monitoring of remote workers: implications for occupational safety and health, EU OSHA Report*, European Agency for Safety and Health at Work.

Potocka-Sionek N. (2023) Easier done than said? An empirical analysis of case law on platform work in the EU, *Hungarian Labour Law e-Journal*, 1, 46–65.

Purificato I. (2021) Behind the scenes of Deliveroo's algorithm: the discriminatory effect of Frank's blindness, *Italian Labour Law e-Journal*, 14 (1), 169–194.

Quammen D. (2012) *Spillover: animal infections and the next human pandemic*, W.W. Norton & Company.

Rosenblat A. and Stark L. (2016) Algorithmic labor and information asymmetries: a case study of Uber's drivers, *International Journal of Communication*, 10 (2016), 3758–3784.

Salvi del Pero A., Wyckoff P. and Vourc'h A. (2022) Using artificial intelligence in the workplace: what are the main ethical risks?, OECD Social, Employment and Migration Working Paper 273, OECD Publishing.

Stark D. and Pais I. (2020) Algorithmic management in the platform economy, *Sociologica*, 14 (3), 47–72.

Stuart M. et al. (2023) Labor unrest and the future of work: global struggles against food delivery platforms, *Labor Studies Journal*, 48 (3), 287–297.

Tassinari A. and Maccarrone V. (2020) Riders on the storm: workplace solidarity among gig economy couriers in Italy and the UK, *Work, Employment and Society*, 34 (1), 35–54.

Todolí-Signes A. (2021a) Making algorithms safe for workers: occupational risks associated with work managed by artificial intelligence, *Transfer*, 27 (4), 433–452.

Todolí-Signes A. (2021b) Cambios normativos en la digitalización del trabajo: comentario a la 'Ley Rider' y los derechos de información sobre los algoritmos, *IUSLabor*, 2, 28–65.

Vallas S. and Schor J.B. (2020) What do platforms do? Understanding the gig economy, *Annual Review of Sociology*, 46, 273–294.

Veruggio M. (2023) Il giudice: 'Glovo riveli i segreti del suo algoritmo', *Gli Stati Generali*, 7 July. www.glistatigenerali.com/sindacati/il-giudice-glovo-riveli-i-segreti-del-suo-algoritmo

Wood A.J. (2020) *Despotism on demand: how power operates in the flexible workplace*, Cornell University Press.

Wood A.J. (2021) Algorithmic management consequences for work organisation and working conditions, JRC Working Papers Series on Labour, Education and Technology 2021/07, European Commission.

Wray B. (2021) Gig Economy Project – Just Eat signs 'pioneer' labour agreement with Spanish unions, *Brave New Europe*, 17 December. https://braveneweurope.com/gig-economy-project-just-eat-signs-pioneer-labour-agreement-with-spanish-unions

Wray B. (2023) Gig Economy Project – Accessing the algorithm to build union power: the case of Palermo, *Brave New Europe*, 7 July. https://braveneweurope.com/accessing-the-algorithm-to-build-union-power-the-case-of-palermo

All links were checked on 19 February 2024.

15. The limits of fissurisation in platform work: the case of food delivery services

Anke Hassel

INTRODUCTION

Over the last decade, the food delivery sector in the European Union has seen significant growth and transformation, driven by technological advances and changing consumer behaviour.[1] In the early phase, the market saw rapid expansion with services like Delivery Hero, Just Eat Takeaway and Uber Eats scaling-up operations across various European countries. These platforms began integrating advanced technologies to improve service efficiency and the customer experience. In particular, the adoption of platform technologies and online payment systems and the development of sophisticated logistics algorithms helped these platforms increase their reach and efficiency. There was a notable shift towards app-based ordering, making food delivery more accessible and convenient.

As the market grew, food delivery companies faced increasing regulatory scrutiny over labour practices, particularly concerning the status of delivery workers as independent contractors rather than employees. Various European countries started examining and, in some cases, redefining the legal frameworks governing gig economy workers. The sector also experienced consolidation, with larger companies acquiring smaller or regional players to expand their market share. This period saw significant mergers and acquisitions, reshaping the competitive landscape.

During the Covid-19 pandemic, unprecedented demand for food delivery services due to lockdowns and restaurant closures boosted the industry and accelerated the adoption of online food ordering among consumers, forcing many traditional restaurants to pivot to delivery and takeaway offerings. This also led to the diversification of food delivery platforms' services beyond restaurant meals, including groceries, alcohol and even non-food items. This expansion opened new revenue streams and partnerships. Technological innovation also continued, with trials for drone deliveries and the use of AI to optimise delivery routes and operations.

From the rise of delivery service platform work over the last decade, two issues have emerged. First, how do we regulate platform work in a way that protects platform workers from exploitation but does not decimate an industry that serves consumers, facilitates digital tools and provides income? Second, what is the role of platform work in the wider process of the transformation of work? Is platform work a strategy to experiment with new forms of work that are less based on dependent employment relationships and include more elements of self-employed work? Are there spillover effects for other types of work in the service economy? This volume tackles these questions from different perspectives using app-based food delivery services as an industry case study.

At first glance, the EU has little to worry about regarding platform work. The number of workers using labour platforms ranges between 7 and 15 per cent (Pesole et al. 2018). The European Council estimates that, in 2022, about 28 million people worked for platform firms, with more than 90 per cent of them self-employed. This number is expected to increase to 43 million workers by 2025 (European Council 2024).

About 14 per cent of the workforce in the EU is self-employed. This figure has been declining recently, to 13.2 per cent in 2023 (Cedefop 2022). While platform work is expected to increase further, there is little evidence that it will have significant effects on the diffusion of badly paid solo self-employment. In general, highly developed countries have lower self-employment levels than poorer ones. In the United States, where platform work began, registered self-employment reaches only 6.6 per cent of the workforce. Similarly, northern Europe has less than 10 per cent of its workforce as self-employed. Less affluent economies tend to have higher levels of self-employment, often connected to informal employment. Here, many job seekers who cannot find jobs turn to setting up small businesses to earn an income. There is no indication that the growth of platform work has increased precarious self-employment overall. On the contrary, the positive development of labour markets in the EU – despite Covid-19 and the energy shock – has led to more employment and fewer self-employed.

Nevertheless, platform work must be taken seriously as a new emerging labour pattern that has far-reaching implications for work. Platform firms are experimenting not only with crossing the border between employment and self-employment but also with new forms of algorithmic management, automated assessments, hiring and firing and the intrusive collection of personal data. As platform work is facilitated by online software systems, it creates data and algorithms for optimising new services and understanding both the customers and the workers who use platforms. Moreover, the hiring of marginalised groups of workers for tasks that are both highly routinised and non-routine is also part of the transformation of work. Therefore, platform-mediated services are part of a wider process of the ongoing fissuring of work. Fissuring is a term first used by US labour lawyer David Weil to describe employers' tendencies to rid themselves of responsibilities as employers through subcontracting, temp agencies and new types of employment relationship (Weil 2014).

Food delivery is a testing ground for a service that combines algorithm-driven logistics and new regulatory challenges of defining dependent and independent work relationships. It attracts migrant workers – often irregular – and operates in areas that are not (yet) regulated through either legislative initiatives or collective agreements. It acts as a microcosm of various strands in the transformation of work that can indicate broader developments.

Even though the research literature on platform work has grown substantially in recent years, there are still many open questions about the characterisation of the sector, its regulation, working conditions and wages. This final chapter pulls together some of the themes of the other chapters and formulates some overall conclusions from the volume.

THE BUSINESS AND EMPLOYMENT MODEL OF FOOD DELIVERY FIRMS

Food delivery firms are organised as platforms that match customers buying food and meals with suppliers (restaurants and supermarkets). Platform firms are digital intermediaries in two- or multi-sided markets, providing the infrastructure and enabling transactions between voluntarily participating independent parties – mainly customers on the one hand and vendors or service providers on the other. Apart from being digital intermediaries, platforms also act as market participants and offer services as organisations (Kenney and Zysman 2020). More than traditional businesses, as Heiner Heiland demonstrates in Chapter 2, platforms reshape urban infrastructures and influence labour dynamics, while being simultaneously shaped by specific characteristics of the urban environment. Food delivery platforms drive changes such as the rise of ghost kitchens and alterations in traffic patterns, impacting local economies.

Moreover, platform firms aim to forge alliances with consumers by emphasising service orientation and convenience (Culpepper and Thelen 2020; Rahman and Thelen 2019). This puts pressure on their employment model, characterised as it is by a low level of security for couriers and intensive lobbying against further regulation (see also Chapter 3). The specific nature of platform-based work has struggled with the status of self-employed versus employed.

While food delivery firms do not compete with established industries (such as ride-hailing platforms competing with taxis), their business model is restricted by price pressures in the restaurant and food market, which are symbolised by low mark-ups and tight competition. As the business model of food delivery platforms shapes their employment regime, it is worth delineating some of its features to gain a better understanding of the implications.

Overall, investors in food delivery platforms have different expectations regarding profitability. As Kurt Vandaele points out in Chapter 3, international operating platforms can earn rents based on matching customers and restaurants, and from practices of 'regulatory arbitrage'. They aim to build exclusive and long-standing relations with restaurants. If platforms expect to become profitable, they aim to do so by dominating the market and hoping for market concentration or even monopolies.

While food delivery services gained business during the pandemic, when restaurants were shut, the period since 2022 has been rather sluggish. Some industry insiders argue that the delivery model will not succeed. For instance, in Germany, many smaller delivery services folded in the years immediately after the pandemic (2022 and 2023). Gorillas has reduced its presence in German cities drastically; Getir has been reducing staff; and smaller firms have disappeared from the scene (Klotz 2024).

Some delivery platforms have managed to attract supermarkets as investors for their operations, but find it difficult to break even. The supermarket delivery company Flink, a German platform, which is the market leader in France, has supermarket giants Rewe and Carrefour as investors and exclusive partners. While the firm promised profitability by the end of 2024, investors are sceptical about these forecasts and reluctant to increase their funding (Handke 2024). This indicates that the market for food delivery service platforms is in turmoil, and there are questions about the sustainability of the business model.

The opportunities for food delivery firms to become profitable are restricted by the price pressures in the market. While investors do not expect quick profitability but hope for higher returns through market dominance and more insights into last-mile delivery logistics, delivery services only generate returns if customers accept the mark-ups. Refusal means that courier services are price sensitive and operations must be kept at low cost. Cost pressures lead to comparatively low wages, flexible work arrangements and a push towards self-employment, which excludes social security contributions, sick pay and other employment-related spending. The platform employment model allows food delivery firms to hire workers as self-employed (at least initially), which makes it fragmented and fissured (Weil 2014), with firms shying away from their responsibilities towards their workers. Moreover, platform firms usually combine their flexible employment relationships with a high degree of hierarchical control organised via algorithmic management tools.

An alternative to the commercial platform firms is the cooperative model for app-based food delivery, as Denise Kasparian discusses in Chapter 13. These foodtech outlets offer different business approaches to workers' social empowerment. In particular, cooperatives can accommodate several different organisational and legal forms which are less deterministic and less focused on platform technology. Platform cooperatives differ from corporate platforms regarding ownership and governance and regarding their technologies.

The technologies of food cooperatives are developed for collective organising, not for managerial control. They aim to address the needs of the community. Cooperatives are often funded by regional governments and universities and do not aim to become profitable. Their strengths lie in the status of workers, collective organisation and trends towards professionalism and training, while their technologies allow for workplace freedom and participation in the governance of the cooperative. This includes democratic decision-making and attempts to ensure inclusion and to push back against discrimination. However, as Kasparian shows, cooperatives offer neither good wages nor stable jobs; furthermore, scaling-up to a critical size is difficult and economic results are low. It is unlikely that they will survive without public support.

A comparison between commercial and cooperative types of food delivery shows that cost pressures and subsequent poor employment conditions are inherent in the business rather than a feature of platform work itself. Delivery services are difficult to make more productive, particularly if investment in technology is low.

CHANGING LABOUR MARKET DEMOGRAPHICS AND THE ROLE OF MIGRANT WORKERS

At first glance, the food delivery industry seems to be primarily composed of young, male, migrant workers. This impression is fuelled by ethnographic studies in big cities but also by everyday observation. In this context, it is argued that food delivery platform work developed over the last decade initially by using students on temporary or self-employed contracts but then increasingly moved towards (irregular) migrant workers. This led to deteriorated working conditions and a lower propensity to mobilise.

Chapter 5, by Cosmin Popan and Kristin Jesnes, paints a picture of the transformation of the sector in three phases. The first was a mixture of local students and migrants working in delivery services. In the second (before the Covid-19 pandemic), students were gradually replaced by male migrants on motorcycles, working excessive hours as self-employed couriers. Finally, in phase three, there has been an influx of irregular migrants. Media reports and academic studies show an increasing number of irregular migrants renting accounts to work as food couriers, particularly in western Europe.

While it seems clear that the concentration of migrant workers in food delivery services is higher than in other sectors, it is much harder to show the dominance of migrant workers in official statistics. Chapter 9, by Carl Fredrik Söderqvist, illustrates the issue. According to official statistics, the share of non-Swedish workers in the category of couriers declined from 96 to 84 per cent between 2014 and 2020. While this is a substantial decline, it does not support the view that the sector is completely or even overwhelmingly dominated by increasingly irregular migrant workers. Similarly, Chapter 7, by Agnieszka Piasna and Wouter Zwysen, shows that 75 per cent of all delivery platform workers have their place of birth in the country in which they work. Again, this is a lower share than in other industries, but does not confirm an overall impression of the dominant role of migrant workers.

The reason why we should be cautious to extrapolate from ethnographic studies in inner cities to a more general assessment of the phenomenon is that it might lead to the wrong conclusions regarding working conditions, worker representation and mobilisation. These findings fit well with research by Juliet Schor on the heterogeneity of the work arrangements of platform workers regarding working hours and attachment. She argues (Schor 2021: 2) that the:

> combination of the technological structure of gig work (nearly automatic, open-access employment, algorithm-driven work process) plus workers' ability to choose schedules and hours yields an unusually heterogeneous labour force on a range of dimensions, especially patterns of work in other jobs and portfolios of household incomes.

It is likely, therefore, that worker experiences are also more heterogeneous than in conventional workplaces.

In Schor's view, the implication is that management control cannot be reduced to algorithmic control but it is enshrined by these workers' labour market position. In other words, workers who are highly dependent on platform work have higher fears of losing their jobs. This is an additional disciplinary force that strengthens algorithmic control. Other workers who have other jobs or other income, or know that this job is only transitory, have less fear of being deactivated. They are potentially more autonomous in their jobs and more satisfied. The distinction is important in understanding the nature of the work and the ability to mobilise workers. A tight labour market that also offers alternatives to migrant workers will change the vulnerable status of delivery workers and might additionally contribute to their willingness to organise or protest (see Piasna and Drahokoupil 2021).

To assess the full range of delivery workers, it is important to avoid drawing conclusions from extreme cases. For refugees and migrants without recognised skills and language abilities, delivery service platforms are highly attractive employers as the barriers to entry are extremely low. Similarly, platforms might find these workers attractive because of their vulnerable status in society and the labour market. They might thus form only one small part of the phenomenon but still be easily stereotyped as a new employment pattern, as in the case of Uber, the largest and most visible transport platform which has dominated the research literature and led to the term 'Uberization' (Davis 2016). Uber is a leader in experimentation with algorithmic management and power relations, and the workforce has also become more immigrant, less white, and poorer, at least in the United States (Parrott and Reich 2018; Wells et al. 2019). However, even in the field of transport platforms, Uber is only one player among others and has not generally set the industry's standards (see Schor 2021).

WORKING CONDITIONS

Working conditions for platform delivery workers are precarious. As Piasna and Zwysen highlight in Chapter 7, using data from a survey of delivery and transport workers, platform delivery workers stand out because they have comparatively lengthy working hours for comparatively low pay. This has to do with long periods of unpaid work when delivery workers are waiting for assignments. They also run substantial risks given that they usually pay for their own work equipment and are not insured against accidents at work. Moreover, they are relatively more dependent on platform work and have higher shares of their income deriving from platforms. Compared to other types of platform worker, they often use several platform apps simultaneously (multi-apping). Multi-apping reflects the high level of income insecurity and unpredictability of platform delivery work.

Piasna and Zwysen apply a framework that maps the different dimensions of work, combining and contrasting flexibility, fragmentation, economic security and cost-shifting to characterise the nature of platform work. The intersectionality of these factors highlights the power imbalance between workers and platforms and helps in understanding the challenges when regulating platform work. While introducing employee status may cover some of the insecurities and social risks, it only partially addresses the power imbalance and vulnerability of workers.

In a similar vein, Valeria Pulignano and Damian Grimshaw point out in Chapter 8 that working conditions can vary with different regime types. In 'open' regimes, self-employed workers enter and exit the platform freely and can remain inactive without sanctions. They have a degree of discretion over tasks and can refuse some. In comparison, 'closed' regimes restrict the autonomy of workers regarding access and control. The authors use the cases of Takeaway (a closed regime) and Deliveroo (an open one) to show that closed regimes are better at mitigating unpaid waiting time. For workers, it makes a difference that they tend to be employees in closed regimes and self-employed in open ones. But, even in closed regimes, there are instances of unpaid breaks and unpaid time due to fewer shifts being assigned to workers where performance ratings are low.

Both these chapters highlight that the employment status of delivery workers is only a partial answer to addressing precarious and fissured working conditions. While employment entails a set of labour and employment rights, particularly regarding social security and working hours, these rights are of limited value in the context of a lack of job security. Only in a broader context of better regulation, social protections and employment rights will the employment relationship be beneficial for platform workers.

THE MOBILISATION OF WORKERS AND ITS OUTCOMES

Food delivery platforms are a new phenomenon dating back no more than a decade. Firms are start-ups with no established trajectory of industrial relations or formalised labour standards. Moreover, as just mentioned, they are cost-sensitive and recruit among vulnerable groups in labour markets, including increasingly among migrants. In other words, platforms appear difficult to organise, and resistance to collective bargaining and workers' representation is strong. This is even more so because of the 'super-exploitation' that some workers face due to their vulnerable status (particularly as irregular migrants and refugees) and the opportunities for algorithmic control. The contribution of migrant workers to collective mobilisation and organising efforts emerges from the analysis of the US and South American context. In Chapter 12, María Figueroa and María Eugenia Rodriguez show that, while migrant workers have been pivotal in advocating for better working conditions, they are often undocumented and rely heavily on platform work, thus facing heightened vulnerability and precariousness. This situation discourages many from participating in collective actions due to fear of losing their jobs or facing deportation.

As Popan and Jesnes report in Chapter 5, there are examples in Europe too, specifically in Germany, Portugal, Spain, Belgium and Italy of the hiring of irregular migrants as delivery couriers. They mention the case of shell companies in Italy hiring irregular workers to work for Uber Eats at a fraction of normal earnings and that Spain similarly reports the use of unprotected irregular migrants. While it is problematic for trade unions to work with irregular workers, they have started to provide legal support.

Nevertheless, and despite adverse circumstances, there is a strong movement among food delivery workers and their unions towards representation and the establishment of standards, particularly in Europe. Food delivery workers have been at the forefront of platform worker mobilisation when it comes to organising strikes, electing works councils and either joining or setting up trade union representation. There is less evidence from other parts of the platform economy (transport or online gig work) regarding workers' mobilisation.

Chapter 4, by Vincenzo Maccarone and colleagues, analyses the waves of mobilisation by platform workers and their different degrees of success in formalising labour relations. Focusing on instances of protest in different countries, they aim to establish the connection between workers' mobilisation and different industrial regimes. Different industrial relations contexts help to better understand different workers' potential for agency.

While there was much self-organisation in the early days, the authors paint a more complex picture and highlight that there are many different forms of organising. Mainstream unions tended to remain on the sidelines initially, although there was convergence between grass-roots organising and institutional opportunities in Italy and Germany. The role of German works councils and national collective bargaining in Italy facilitated workers' voice and the involvement of established trade unions in both cases. Informal groups and communications networks were used to sustain workers' self-organisation.

Chapter 6, by Mark Stuart and colleagues, also looks at workers' mobilisation across Europe. Drawing on the 430 instances of protest between 2017 and 2023 contained in the Leeds Index of Platform Labour Protest, they map patterns of protest against different industrial relations regimes. Union involvement and type of protest correlate with regime type: patterns of protest are different in liberal pluralist and social partnership regimes, for example, with unions more involved in the latter but less engaged in the former. In liberal pluralist and state-centred regimes (in southern Europe), more strikes are found taking place without union involvement. More institutionalised forms of organising and collective bargaining take place in countries featuring social partnership and organised corporatism, and legal action is reported mostly in fragmented state-centred regimes. The authors conclude that industrial relations regime type is important in understanding both the nature and the essential characteristics of platform labour protests.

It is not too surprising that forms of labour protest in platform firms are shaped by the industrial relations institutions of the country in which they take place. In state-centred industrial relations countries, regulation is usually strong, and legal action offers a promising route. Similarly, in more pluralist countries, direct action and strikes are necessary to gain recognition. In countries with stronger institutionalised forms of workplace representation, these tools have the most leverage.

Establishing workers' voice in contexts of high vulnerability and weak institutions remains a challenge. Theories of segmented labour markets (Piore 1979) point to labour markets being divided into a primary labour market, largely reserved for natives and characterised by stable employment relationships, employment protection and social security, and a secondary labour market that contains jobs at the bottom of the hierarchy and that are insecure. The secondary labour market serves to buffer the business cycle and acts as a reserve pool for the primary labour market. Primary and secondary labour markets interact and complement each other, and are mediated by industrial relations and labour market institutions. In pluralist countries, the secondary labour market is not as distinct from the primary labour market, whereas in countries with strong industrial relations institutions, they are separated and create more dualistic labour markets (King and Rueda 2008). This interaction can be seen in other industries with poor working conditions and vulnerable workers (such as the meat preparation industry), where similar effects can be found (Wagner and Hassel 2016).

This explains the interests of trade unions in social partnership and corporatist countries in regulating platform work and including platform workers in formal industrial relations structures. If the secondary market becomes too cheap, it will start to expand into the primary market and undermine job security and job quality. Governments and mainstream unions in highly regulated systems will therefore take an interest in these sectors to protect not just vulnerable workers but all workers, with trade unions organising in the primary labour market having an interest in establishing minimum standards in the secondary market to protect their own members.

As a result, mainstream unions and other forms of workers' collective representation coexist in the organisation of food delivery workers. Depending on the institutional context, some forms of new organising will be absorbed by existing institutions while others may disappear or form new trade unions. An added complexity is that the vulnerability of irregular migrant workers will make their participation in organised action rather difficult as they have to earn a living in contexts where employment protection is non-existent. At the same time, unions in the primary labour market will target employment practices among highly vulnerable workers to shore up the terms and conditions of their own members. Even so, the interaction between labour protests, informal and formal collective action and the investment by unions in pursuing a cause does have the power to bring about effective regulation which counters labour abuses. The example of German meat processing industries has shown how these different factors can effectively lead to regulation that protects highly vulnerable workers who, by themselves, have very weak bargaining power (Ban et al. 2022; Wagner and Hassel 2016).

ALGORITHMIC MANAGEMENT

How transformative is algorithmic management (AM) in the context of platform work? Are app-based food delivery services and other firms in the platform economy the vanguard of a movement in human resources that will spill over to mainstream work? Chapter 14, by Nastazja Potocka-Sionek and Antonio Aloisi, takes us directly to this question by discussing the different aspects of AM regarding platform work in EU member states. First, AM can be a signifier for an assessment as to whether platform work is self-employment or not. Second, the use of AM data might violate data protection regulations and can be used to force greater transparency in AM and better human resource practices. Third, the use of AM is important in establishing limits to the expansion of employers' discretion and the use of non-discrimination provisions.

AM replaces classic managerial functions with rules that are enforced in an automated fashion without human interaction. Instead of workplace supervisors ordering employees to perform certain tasks at a certain time, the platform's app distributes tasks to those who have logged on and are available for work. Those who are logged on are usually required to perform the task and follow the particular protocol, and they are not normally free to decline at short notice – at least, not without facing consequences. To exercise AM, the app not only allocates tasks but also monitors their execution. This relies on surveillance of behaviour, including the logging off and on process, locational data and customer feedback. Surveillance and monitoring are also part of traditional employment relationships in which most workers are under control in offices and workplaces and are assessed on a continuous basis, and this connection has been used in court cases to show that AM is equivalent to managerial prerogative by giving management a way to control and direct platform workers. The understanding of the employment relationship, however, which is traditionally composed of the employer's right to manage and the complementary duty of care, is seriously challenged by software that decouples management from an interpersonal relationship and instead installs a set of rules that it can monitor and execute automatically.

In court cases based on misclassification, the responses vary from one EU member state to another although, generally, they have helped in better understanding the potential and limits of AM. AM has been used to argue in favour of the existence of an employment relationship based on its role in enforcing the obligation to work during certain time periods, its use of GPS and its deployment of ranking systems in allowing access to tasks. Moreover, the way platforms use AM to predetermine how the service is executed and to operate their systems of bonuses and penalties has been seen as a sign of managerial control. Finally, couriers being unable to function outside the system (as independent contractors) or insist on their own preferences shows how dependent delivery workers are on the platform. The Glovo judgment by the Spanish Tribunal Supremo summarised three aspects of platform control: the rating of couriers, the sanctions system and the real-time monitoring of service delivery. These features of AM are key aspects of the decision to classify delivery workers as employees.

It is the aspect of control, however, not the algorithms, that turns delivery workers into employees; algorithms are, rather, a deflection from seeing these relationships as part of active management. By pointing to the presence of AI and AM, platforms argue that they are not commanding the platform workers (and that they are, therefore, not employers). However, since AM systems are designed to perform supervision and monitoring tasks, they are part of a relationship that can be classified as one based on employment. Control and command can take place in automatic and non-personal settings. This is likely to be the most important implication of labour courts' rulings on platform workers: whether rankings and ratings are made anonymously online does not make them less valuable in terms of their management potential.

Data protection is the second critical issue regarding AM. To manage a platform effectively, data must be collected on the behaviour of delivery workers as well as on customers, orders and levels of satisfaction. Some behavioural data is highly sensitive, such as movements, breaks, speed of driving and interaction with others. To the extent that this data then becomes part of AI-driven management tools, it is covered by the EU's AI Act. However, the AI Act is rather narrow in its approach and might become obsolete given the broader challenge presented by AM. There is, therefore, a regulatory gap in which AM needs to be treated more comprehensively so that it encompasses practices such as hiring, organising, dismissing and remuneration.

So, the challenge of AM concerns more than delivery platform workers. It must be set into a broader framework that includes data protection, discrimination and consultation in general, and which must be developed with social partners. It remains to be seen to what extent automated decision-making is more or less discriminatory compared to human discretion. The more complex the work tasks are and the more autonomy they require, the more difficult it will be to apply AM to other work environments.

SETTING LIMITS ON FISSURISATION: THE PLATFORM WORK DIRECTIVE

The European Parliament adopted the Platform Work Directive in April 2024. The Directive makes three provisions to improve working conditions for platform workers: first, it contains the presumption of an employment relationship, unless the platform proves otherwise, and provides criteria for that assessment; second, it bans certain types of AM, such as automated hiring and firing; and third, it restricts the collection of sensitive data that can indicate someone's emotional state or religious beliefs (European Parliament 2024).

It is important to note, however, that, while the Directive increases pressure on companies to prove that workers are self-employed, it does not prohibit the self-employment of affected workers. Moreover, national courts will retain significant discretion in their decisions on what counts as sufficient proof for self-employment as this is not specified in the Directive.

Member states have already taken various approaches to regulating platform work. These include, among others, the easing of processes to mount legal challenges to the employment status of platform workers (as seen in Portugal and Spain); improving the oversight of digital job markets through labour market institutions (Finland); strengthening taxation and the customs control of platforms (Estonia); and granting collective bargaining rights to platform workers through agreements between the social partners (Denmark) (OECD 2020).

The central issue across countries is that platform workers are typically not considered employees but self-employed workers. The lack of employee status means that platform workers are denied basic social protection and workers' rights, do not benefit from minimum wages and do not pay into, or are insufficiently covered by, social security systems such as unemployment insurance, workplace accidents and pensions – see Table 15.1. Moreover, platform work, including app-based food delivery, often undermines national labour law by circumventing and contradicting its norms (see Chapter 10).

Some countries, such as France, have therefore introduced legislation that aims to provide more social protections specifically to platform workers. The 'El Khomri' law (Law 2016–1088) obliges platforms to protect platform workers in the case of occupational accidents and pay towards their vocational training. It also specifically includes platform workers within laws on the right to strike and join a union. Furthermore, the French parliament has introduced additional legislation on platforms just for transport and delivery workers (see Chapter 11). A similar, and stricter, approach has been taken by Italy.

The specific regulation of platform workers sometimes refers to them as occupying a 'third' status (between employment and self-employment) (Daugareilh et al. 2019). Third status has been discussed extensively, not least in the context of its potential to undermine existing

Table 15.1 *Social protections of self-employed workers in selected European countries*

Country	Pensions	Unemployment benefits	Healthcare	Work accident benefits	Parental benefits
Austria	Full	None	Full	Full	Full
Denmark	Full	Partial to full	Full	None	Full
Finland	Full	Partial to full	Full	Partial to none	Full
France	Full	None	Full	Partial to none	Partial to full
Germany	Partial to none	None	Full	None	Partial to full
Italy	Full	None	Full	Full	Full
Netherlands	Partial to full	None	Full	None	Partial to full
Norway	Full	None	Full	None	Full
Sweden	Full	Partial to full	Full	Full	Full
United Kingdom	Full	None	Full	None	Partial to none

Source: Based on Sieker (2022).

employment rights and create ‘inexpensive alternatives to employment’ (Aloisi 2022). It also sets off new waves of court cases to prove which employment category is appropriate, and, perhaps with this in mind, Belgium, Greece, Spain and Portugal have already legislated that platform workers should be presumed to be employees.

In essence, the Directive does not resolve the critical tension in classifying platform workers as employed or self-employed. Whether national courts consider platform work, in the light of algorithmic management, to be a form of employment or self-employment, or leave further room for discretion on a case-by-case basis depends on national labour law contexts, social protections and legal traditions. Here, national judges will once more keep their significant discretion in interpreting what constitutes subordination after the Directive is implemented (see Chapter 10). The Directive is unlikely to change the complex structures and chains of subcontracting, which are central to app-based food delivery and critical for the current situation of platform workers.

It remains to be seen how each EU member state will incorporate the Directive and whether the subsequent regulation of platform work will be properly enforced. Compliance with labour laws and regulations has been an issue for platforms across member states thus far and is likely to remain an issue once the Directive comes into force. In this regard, it is interesting to note the different reactions by platforms to the adoption of the Directive: an Uber spokesperson declared that the EU has confirmed the status quo, a view that Wolt and Free Now have supported (Kafsack and Sachse 2024). Lieferando instead welcomed the regulation, saying that it will help address bogus self-employment (in contrast to Uber Eats and Wolt, Lieferando tends to employ its delivery workers directly).

Moreover, as we have pointed out, another foreseeable problem is that some platform workers lack work, or even residence, permits. In the case of (irregular) migrant workers, for example, the risk remains that, despite the Directive, employers and authorities will pay no heed to breaches. To improve the national regulation of platform work, it is essential to strengthen national labour inspectorates and ease the legal processes involved in cases of breaches (OECD 2020).

CONCLUSIONS

The chapters in this volume give a precious overview of the characteristics of platform work in app-based food delivery. Taking different aspects together, it emerges that this sector is a specific niche market that combines tech firms' experimentation with market creation, on the backs of marginalised workers with little social capital, to offer low-value-added online-governed services. It is also a unique case in the sense that the characteristics of the workers and the business model itself are quite specific.

Regarding workers, food delivery platforms offer easy entry for all types of worker into a highly flexible segment of the labour market. There are no formal skills required to become a food delivery worker, not even a driver's licence. Time arrangements can be extremely flexible as long as workers do not attempt to earn a full income. At the same time, the use of apps also replaces any local knowledge of the neighbourhood. It is exceptionally accessible for anyone who is fit enough to ride a bike. This makes food delivery an easy entry point for students, but also for migrant workers, including irregular migrants.

Regarding the business model, profit margins in most platform work, particularly in food delivery, are still low or negative. The value of the industry does not lie in the overall profitability of the service but in its use case for tech applications in the service economy, which attracts investors and allows for market experimentation and development. Moreover, it is part of the further understanding of last-mile logistics that might be expanded to other parts of the retail sector. It is also a source of data on consumer habits regarding takeaway food.

The easy entry for workers and the fluid nature of the business make mobilisation and self-regulation difficult. Nevertheless, there has been a wave of mobilisation and protest within the sector. Mobilisation stems from the easy interaction of workers who meet each other on the street and their concentration in big cities. Unlike Uber (taxi) drivers, who are tucked away in cars, delivery couriers are usually accessible and recognisable in urban areas. For unions and activists, it is not so difficult to address delivery workers. They have therefore become a rallying point for organising platforms in general and attempts to enforce labour standards and workers' representation.

The mobilisation of platform workers will only be sustained if appropriate and effective standards of labour regulation are developed and then enforced. There is a danger that workers might not be able to defend the labour rights they have.

The European Platform Work Directive aims to push the industry towards better working conditions by assuming that platform work often more closely resembles an employment relationship than one featuring independent contractors. It also provides important rights on AM and data protection, which can offer a blueprint for future policymaking initiatives covering all workers, beyond the platform economy. The Directive will not, however, be a panacea for poor working conditions in the sector. This will depend on the mobilisation of workers, union representation and effective enforcement to ensure that delivery workers receive the social rights at work they deserve. Moreover, the European landscape for the social regulation of platform work will remain patchy and continue to reflect different social models of employment relations and social protection in the EU.

Ultimately, delivery platform work is likely to remain an occupation with low economic value added, little social mobility and low levels of social protection. In the context of fast demographic change and labour shortages in many sectors, the question remains whether food delivery services are the best use of non-routine low-skilled work. Investors' subsidisation of the sector is distorting labour markets and is potentially wasteful given the attempts of governments to provide training and facilitate skilled migration. In a broader context, this should be a discussion point beyond the fight to improve labour conditions and wages for food delivery workers.

NOTE

1. I would like to thank Pit Lee and Anna Kubaszewska for their superb research assistance when preparing the material for this chapter.

REFERENCES

Aloisi A. (2022) Platform work in Europe: lessons learned, legal developments and challenges ahead, *European Labour Law Journal*, 13 (1), 4–29.
Ban C., Bohle D. and Naczyk M. (2022) A perfect storm: COVID-19 and the reorganisation of the German meat industry, *Transfer*, 28 (1), 101–118.
Cedefop (2022) Self-employment. www.cedefop.europa.eu/en/tools/skills-intelligence/self-employment?year=2022&country=EU#5
Culpepper P.D. and Thelen K. (2020) Are we all Amazon primed? Consumers and the politics of platform power, *Comparative Political Studies*, 53 (2), 288–318. https://doi.org/10.1177/0010414019852687
Daugareilh I., Degryse C. and Pochet P. (2019) The platform economy and social law: key issues in comparative perspective, Working Paper 2019.10, ETUI.
Davis G.F. (2016) *The vanishing American corporation: navigating the hazards of a new economy*, Berrett-Koehler Publishers.
European Council (2024) *EU rules on platform work*. www.consilium.europa.eu/en/policies/platform-work-eu
European Parliament (2024) Parliament adopts Platform Work Directive, Press Release, 24 April. www.europarl.europa.eu/news/en/press-room/20240419IPR20584/parliament-adopts-platform-work-directive
Handke K. (2024) Kooperation zwischen Flink und Rewe vor dem Aus? Das sagt der Lieferdienst dazu, *Business Insider*, 15 February. https://de.finance.yahoo.com/nachrichten/kooperation-zwischen-flink-rewe-sagt-180339295.html
Kafsack H. and Sachse M. (2024) Was die neue EU-Regulierung für Uber, Lieferando und Co. Bedeutet, *Frankfurter Allgemeine Zeitung*, 24 April. www.faz.net/aktuell/wirtschaft/unternehmen/was-die-neuen-eu-regeln-fuer-uber-lieferando-und-co-bedeuten-19676023.html
Kenney M. and Zysman J. (2020) The platform economy: restructuring the space of capitalist accumulation, *Cambridge Journal of Regions, Economy and Society*, 13 (1), 55–76. https://doi.org/10.1093/cjres/rsaa001

King D. and Rueda D. (2008) Cheap labor: the new politics of 'Bread and Roses' in industrial democracies, *Perspectives on Politics*, 6 (2), 279–297.
Klotz N. (2024) Lebensmittel-Lieferdienste: 'Die Rechnung geht einfach nicht auf', *Business Insider*, 26 February.
OECD (2020) Regulating platform work in the digital age, Going Digital Toolkit Policy Note 1. https://goingdigital.oecd.org/toolkitnotes/regulating-platform-work-in-the-digital-age.pdf
Parrott J. and Reich M. (2018) *An earnings standard for New York City's app-based drivers: economic analysis and policy assessment*, UC Berkeley Center on Wage and Employment Dynamics.
Pesole A. et al. (2018) *Platform workers in Europe: evidence from the COLLEEM survey*, Publications Office of the European Union. https://doi.org/10.2760/742789
Piasna A. and Drahokoupil J. (2021) Flexibility unbound: understanding the heterogeneity of preferences among food delivery platform workers, *Socio-Economic Review*, 19 (4), 1397–1419.
Piore M. (1979) *Birds of passage: migrant labour and industrial societies*, Cambridge University Press.
Rahman K.S. and Thelen K. (2019) The rise of the platform business model and the transformation of twenty-first-century capitalism, *Politics & Society*, 47 (2), 177–204.
Schor J.B. (2021) Dependence and heterogeneity in the platform labor force, Policy Brief, Hertie School. www.denkfabrik-bmas.de/fileadmin/Downloads/Publikationen/Brief-3_Schor_final_FINAL-ua.pdf
Sieker F. (2022) Platform work and access to social protection across major European countries, *Journal of International and Comparative Social Policy*, 38 (3), 193–207.
Wagner B. and Hassel A. (2016) Posting, subcontracting and low-wage employment in the German meat industry, *Transfer*, 22 (2), 163–178.
Weil D. (2014) *The fissured workplace: why work became so bad for so many and what can be done to improve it*, Harvard University Press.
Wells K.J., Attoh K. and Cullen D. (2019) *The Uber workplace in D.C.*, Georgetown University.
All links were checked on 18 June 2024.

Index